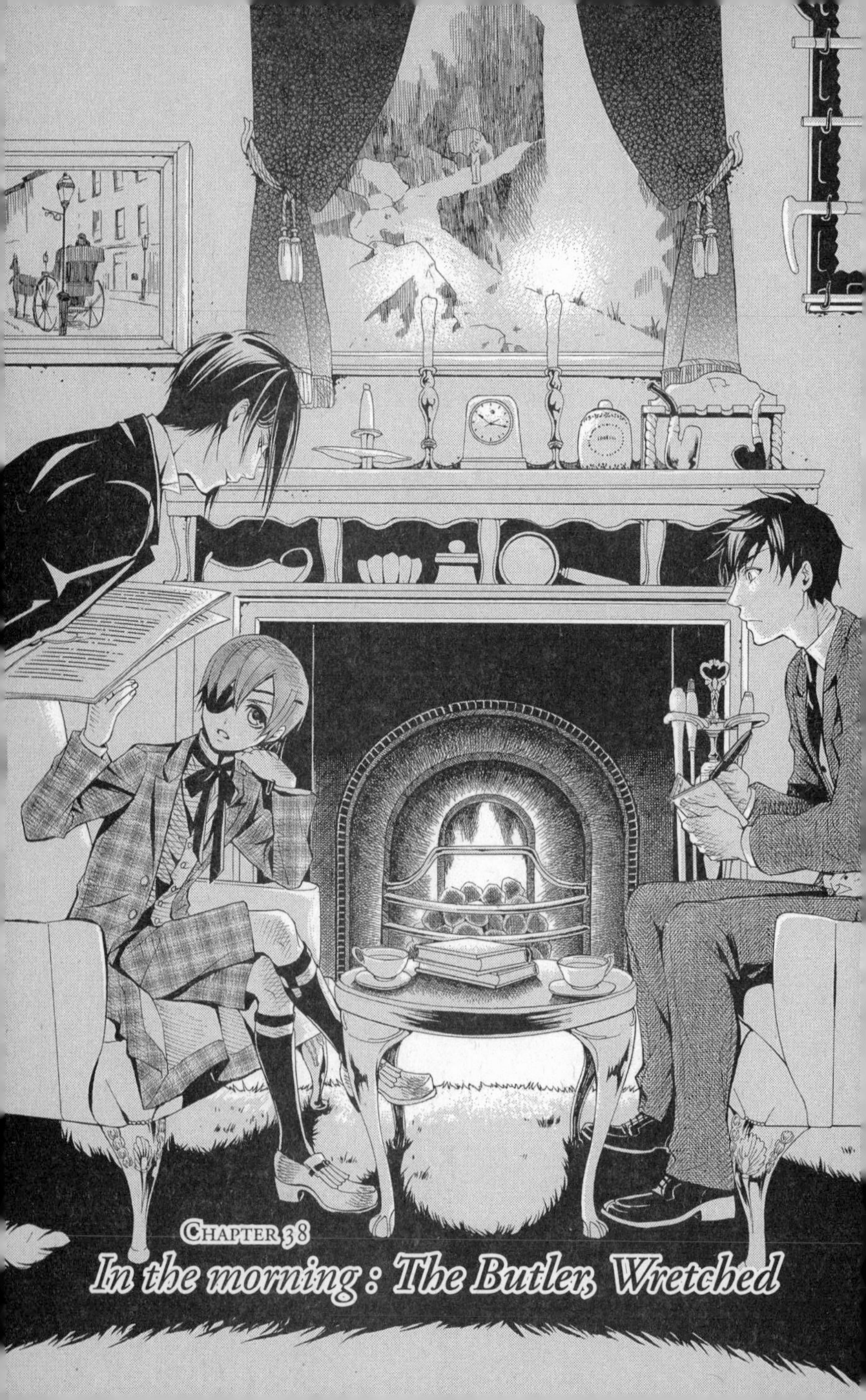
CHAPTER 38
In the morning : The Butler, Wretched

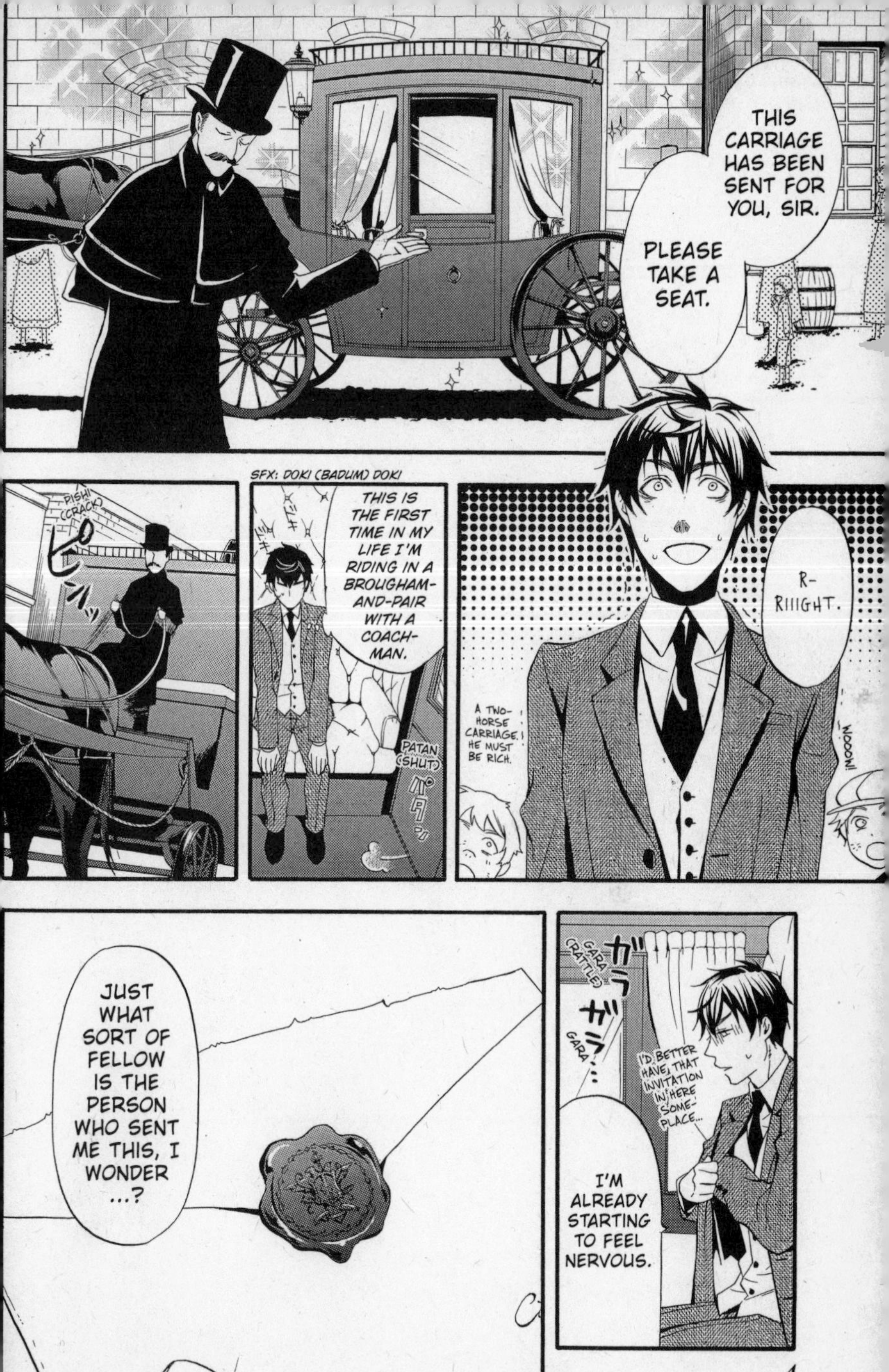
THIS CARRIAGE HAS BEEN SENT FOR YOU, SIR.
PLEASE TAKE A SEAT.
R-RIIIGHT.
WOOOW!
A TWO-HORSE CARRIAGE. HE MUST BE RICH.
SFX: DOKI (BADUM) DOKI
THIS IS THE FIRST TIME IN MY LIFE I'M RIDING IN A BROUGHAM-AND-PAIR WITH A COACHMAN.
PATAN (SHUT)
PISHI (CRACK)
GARA (RATTLE) GARA
I'D BETTER HAVE THAT INVITATION IN HERE SOMEPLACE...
I'M ALREADY STARTING TO FEEL NERVOUS.
JUST WHAT SORT OF FELLOW IS THE PERSON WHO SENT ME THIS, I WONDER ...?

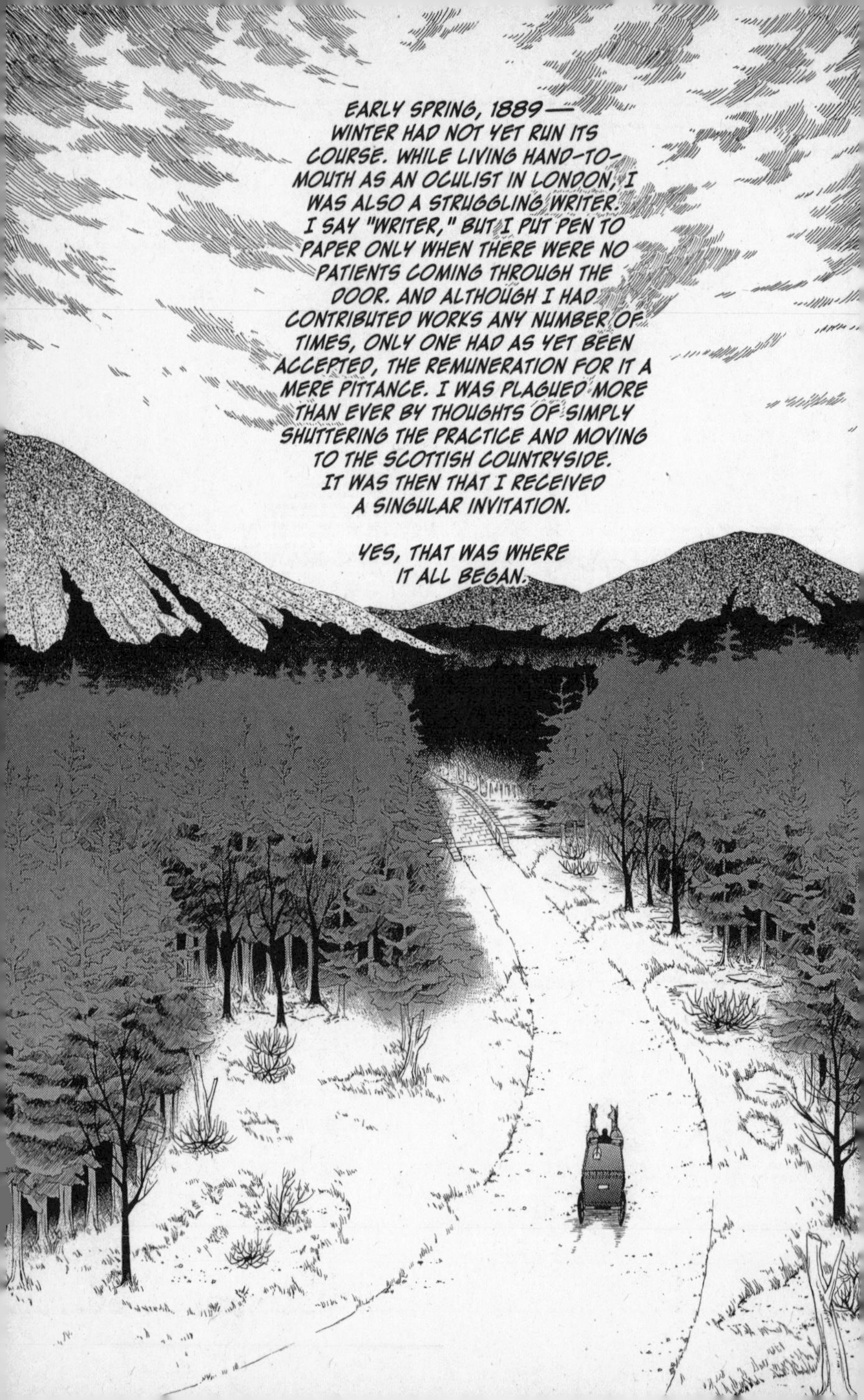
EARLY SPRING, 1889— WINTER HAD NOT YET RUN ITS COURSE. WHILE LIVING HAND-TO-MOUTH AS AN OCULIST IN LONDON, I WAS ALSO A STRUGGLING WRITER. I SAY "WRITER," BUT I PUT PEN TO PAPER ONLY WHEN THERE WERE NO PATIENTS COMING THROUGH THE DOOR. AND ALTHOUGH I HAD CONTRIBUTED WORKS ANY NUMBER OF TIMES, ONLY ONE HAD AS YET BEEN ACCEPTED, THE REMUNERATION FOR IT A MERE PITTANCE. I WAS PLAGUED MORE THAN EVER BY THOUGHTS OF SIMPLY SHUTTERING THE PRACTICE AND MOVING TO THE SCOTTISH COUNTRYSIDE. IT WAS THEN THAT I RECEIVED A SINGULAR INVITATION.
YES, THAT WAS WHERE IT ALL BEGAN.

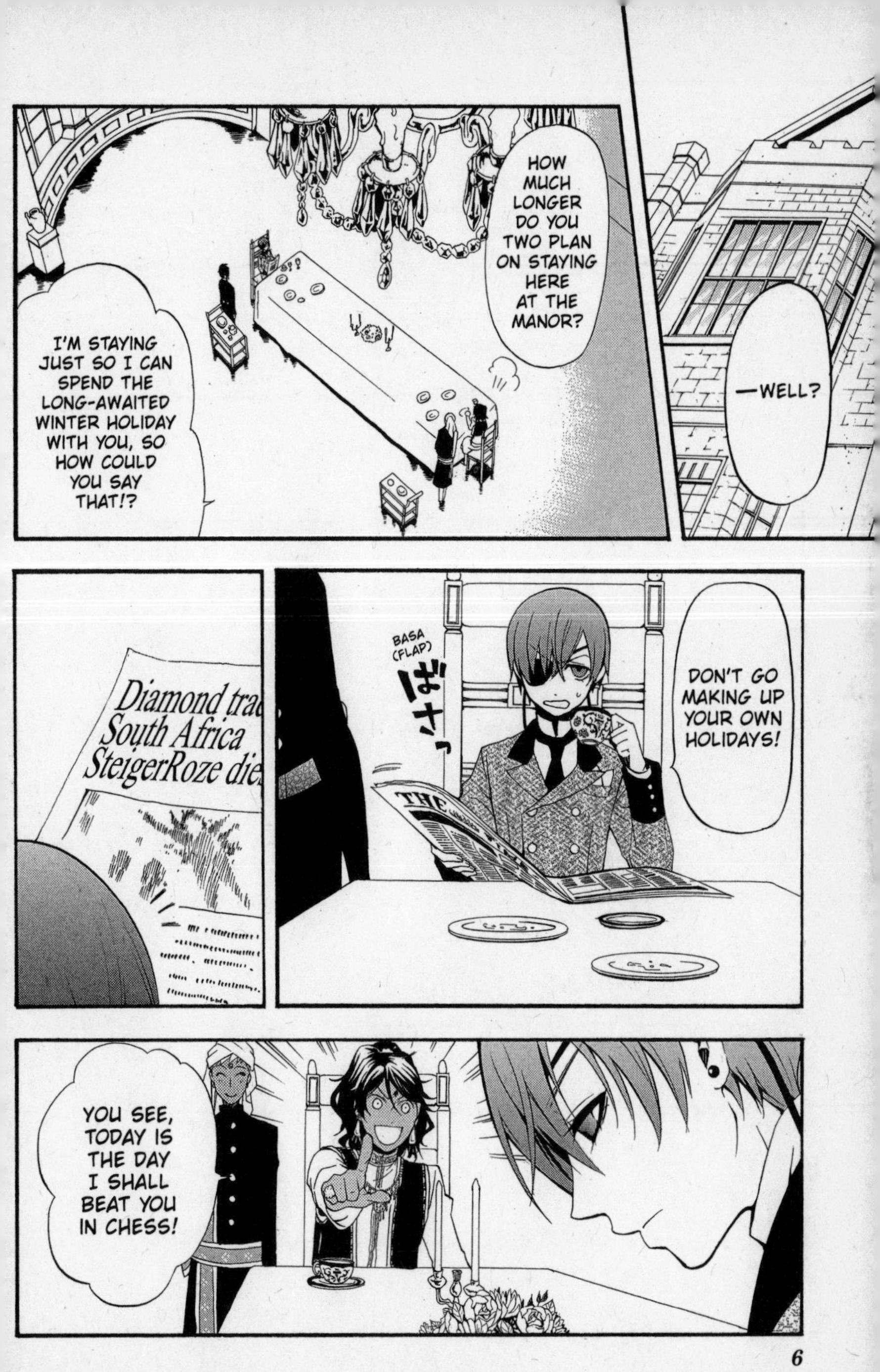
—WELL?
HOW MUCH LONGER DO YOU TWO PLAN ON STAYING HERE AT THE MANOR?
I'M STAYING JUST SO I CAN SPEND THE LONG-AWAITED WINTER HOLIDAY WITH YOU, SO HOW COULD YOU SAY THAT!?
DON'T GO MAKING UP YOUR OWN HOLIDAYS!
BASA (FLAP)
ばさっ
THE
South Africa
YOU SEE, TODAY IS THE DAY I SHALL BEAT YOU IN CHESS!

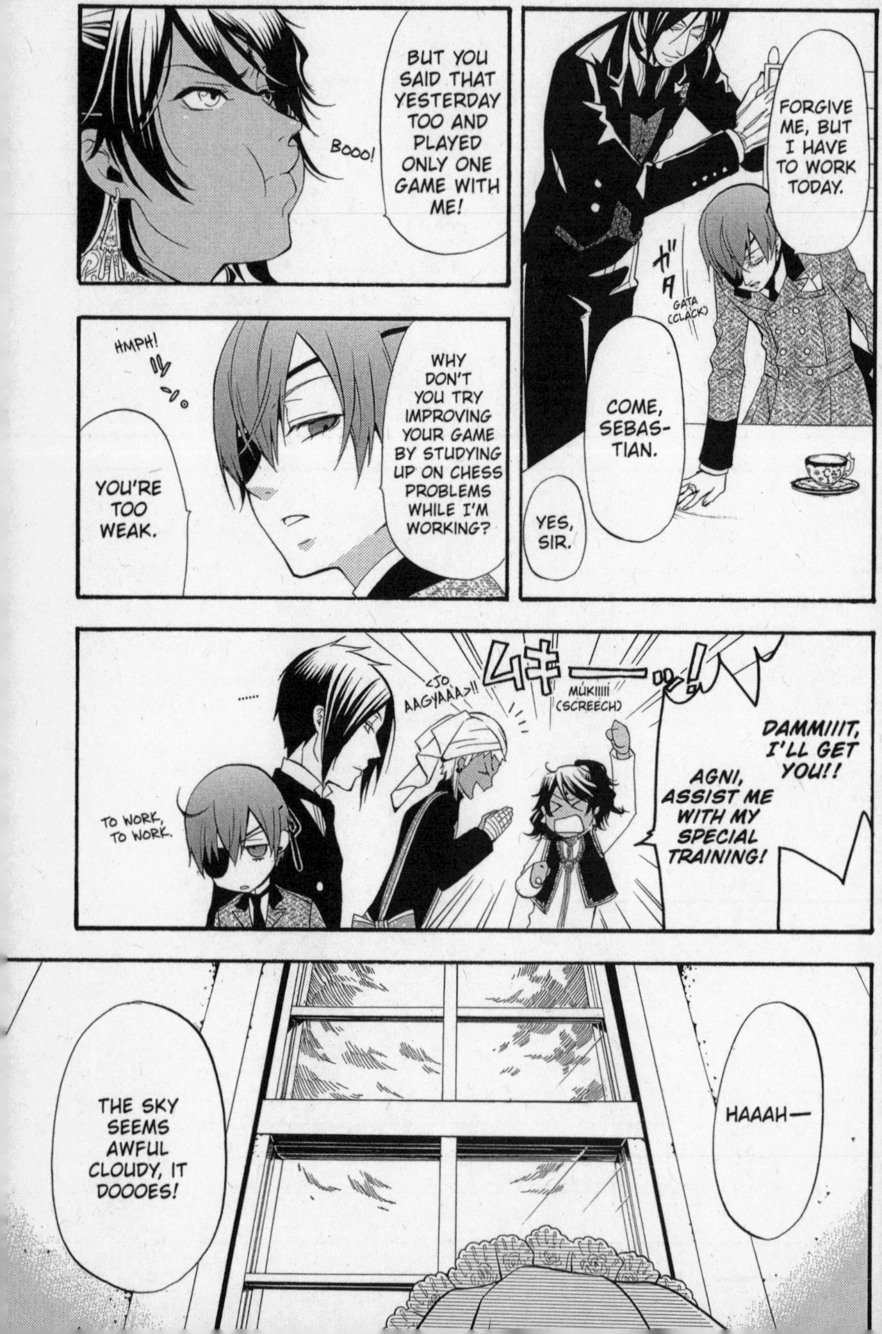
FORGIVE ME, BUT I HAVE TO WORK TODAY.
ガタ
GATA (CLACK)
COME, SEBASTIAN.
YES, SIR.
BUT YOU SAID THAT YESTERDAY TOO AND PLAYED ONLY ONE GAME WITH ME!
BOOO!
WHY DON'T YOU TRY IMPROVING YOUR GAME BY STUDYING UP ON CHESS PROBLEMS WHILE I'M WORKING?
HMPH!
YOU'RE TOO WEAK.
DAMMIIIT, I'LL GET YOU!!
AGNI, ASSIST ME WITH MY SPECIAL TRAINING!
ムキーッ!
MUKIIIII (SCREECH)
<JO AAGYAAA>!!
......
TO WORK, TO WORK.
HAAAH—
THE SKY SEEMS AWFUL CLOUDY, IT DOOOES!

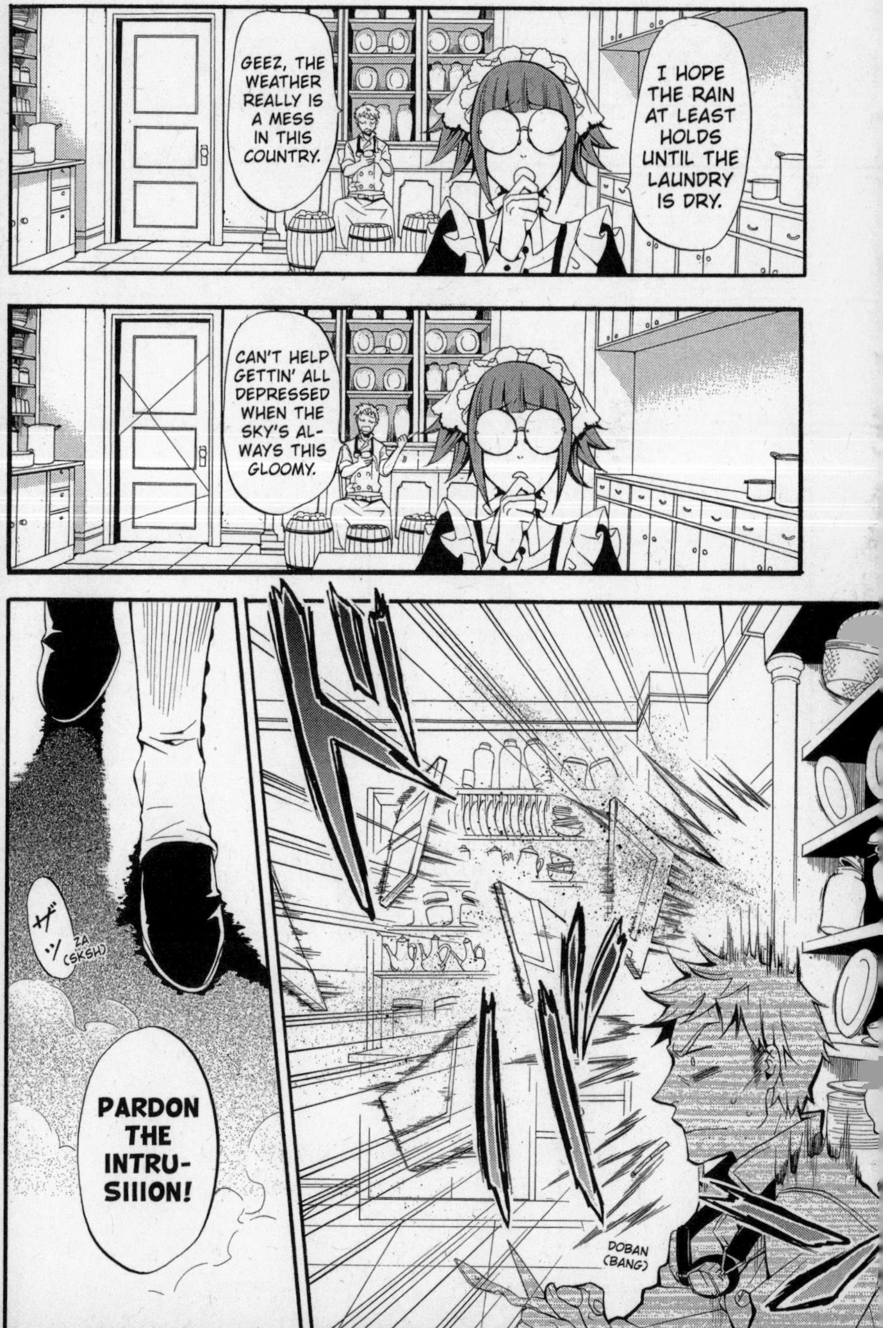
I HOPE THE RAIN AT LEAST HOLDS UNTIL THE LAUNDRY IS DRY.
GEEZ, THE WEATHER REALLY IS A MESS IN THIS COUNTRY.
CAN'T HELP GETTIN' ALL DEPRESSED WHEN THE SKY'S AL-WAYS THIS GLOOMY.
DOBAN (BANG)
ザッ
ZA (SKSH)
PARDON THE INTRU-SIIION!

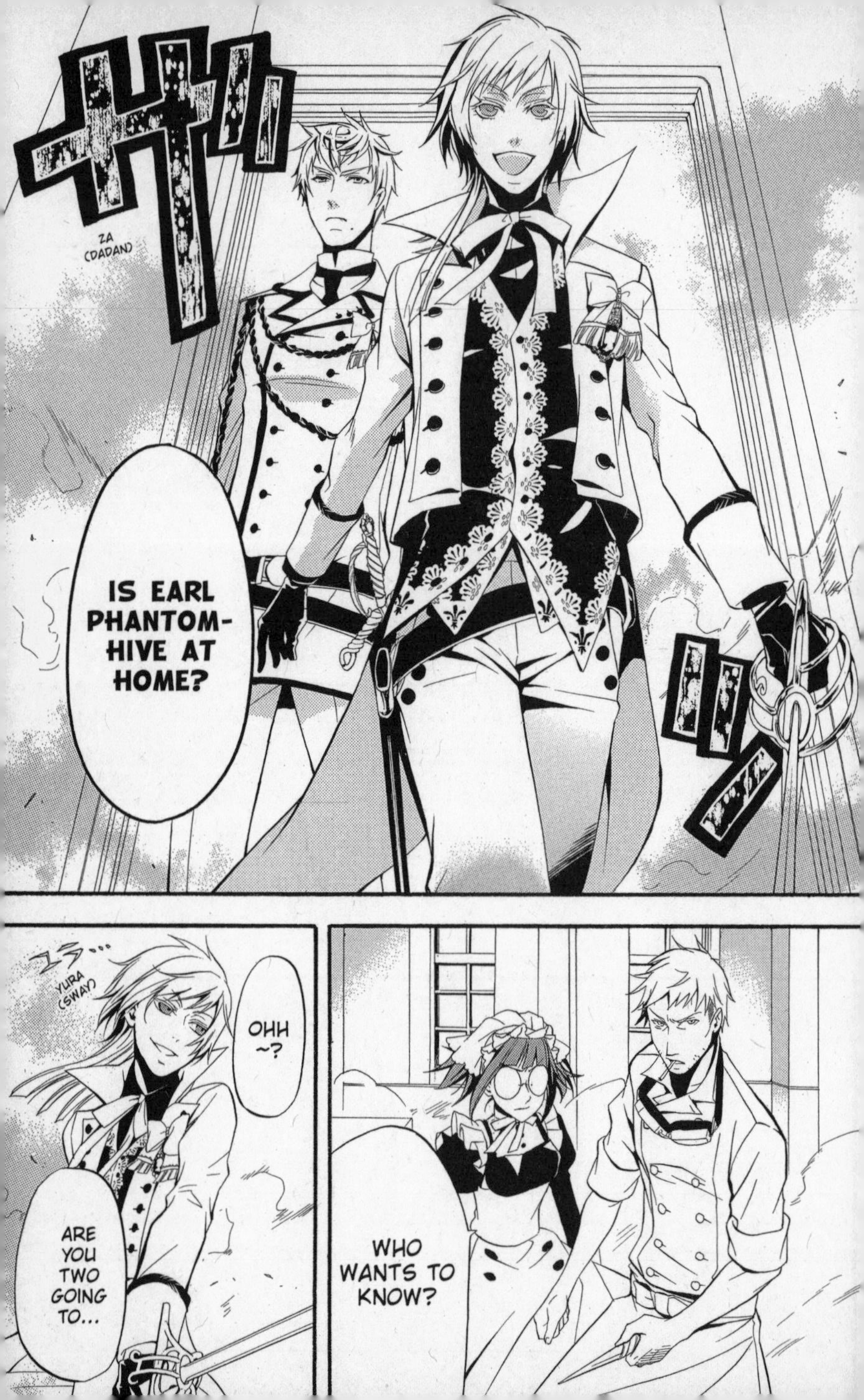
ZA (DADAN)
IS EARL PHANTOMHIVE AT HOME?
WHO WANTS TO KNOW?
ユラ…
YURA (SWAY)
OHH ~?
ARE YOU TWO GOING TO...

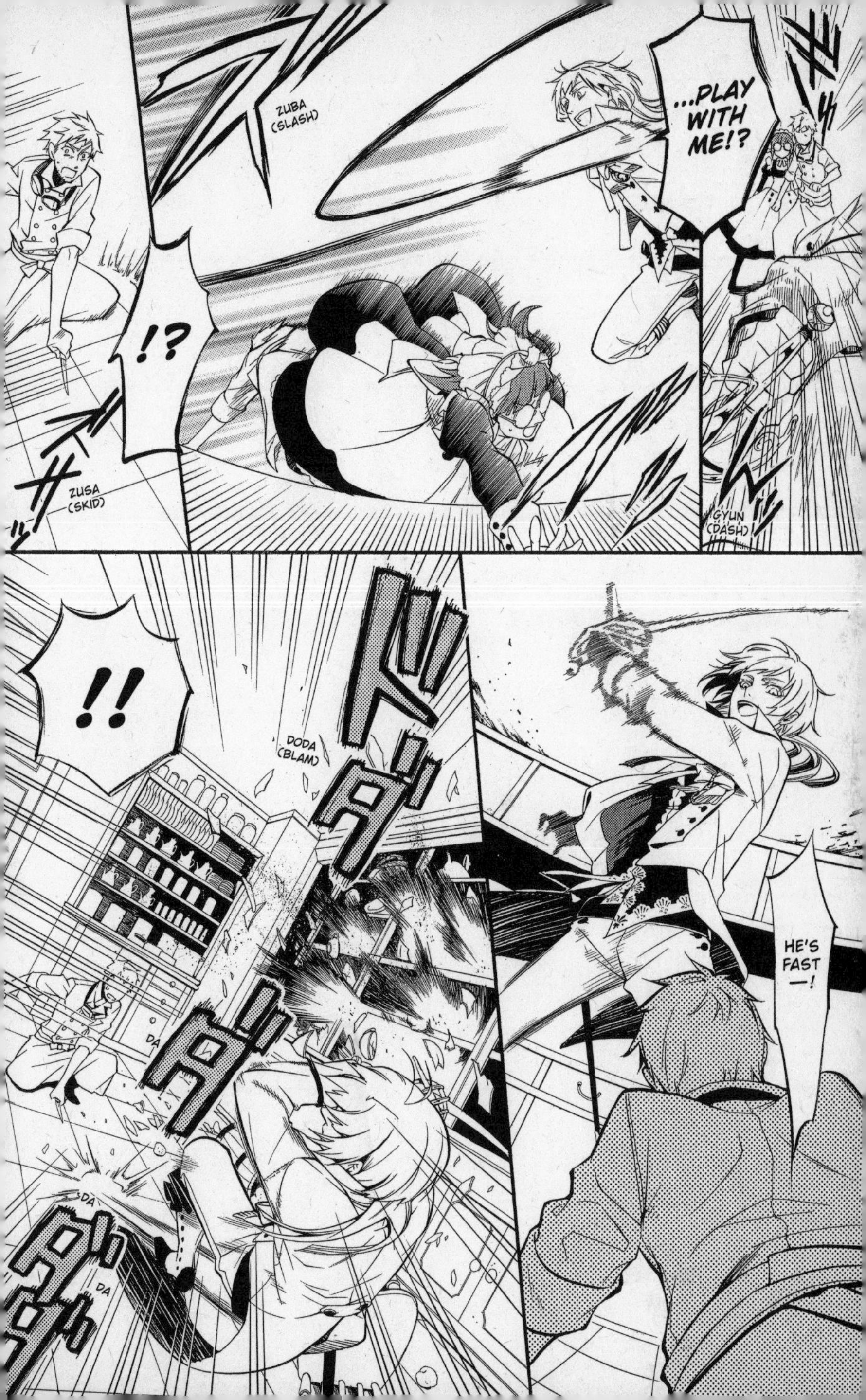

...PLAY WITH ME!?
GYUN (DASH)
ZUBA (SLASH)
!?
ZUSA (SKID)
HE'S FAST—!
!!
DODA (BLAM)
DA
DA
DA

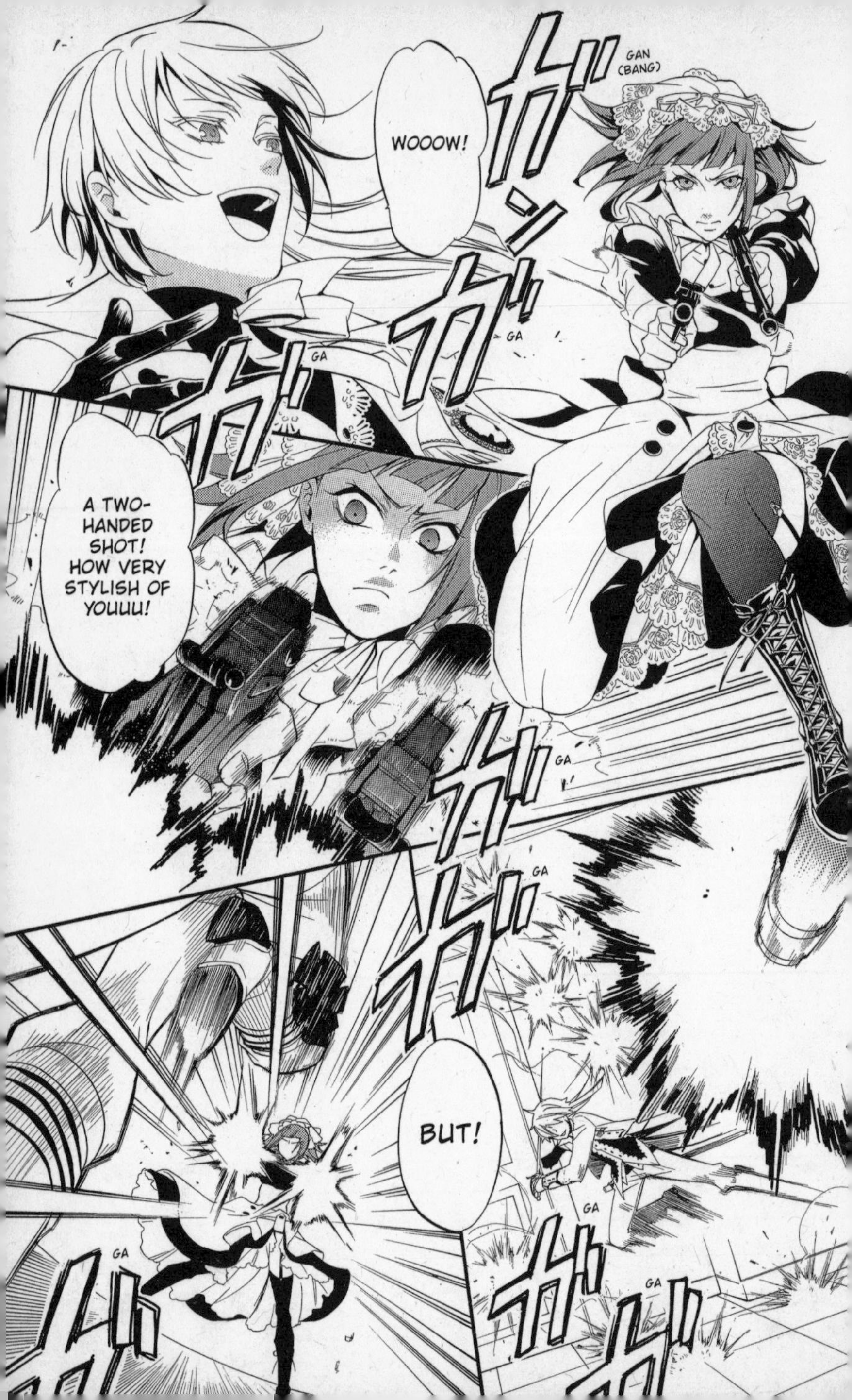
GAN (BANG)
GA
WOOOW!
GA
A TWO-HANDED SHOT! HOW VERY STYLISH OF YOUUU!
GA
GA
BUT!
GA
GA
GA

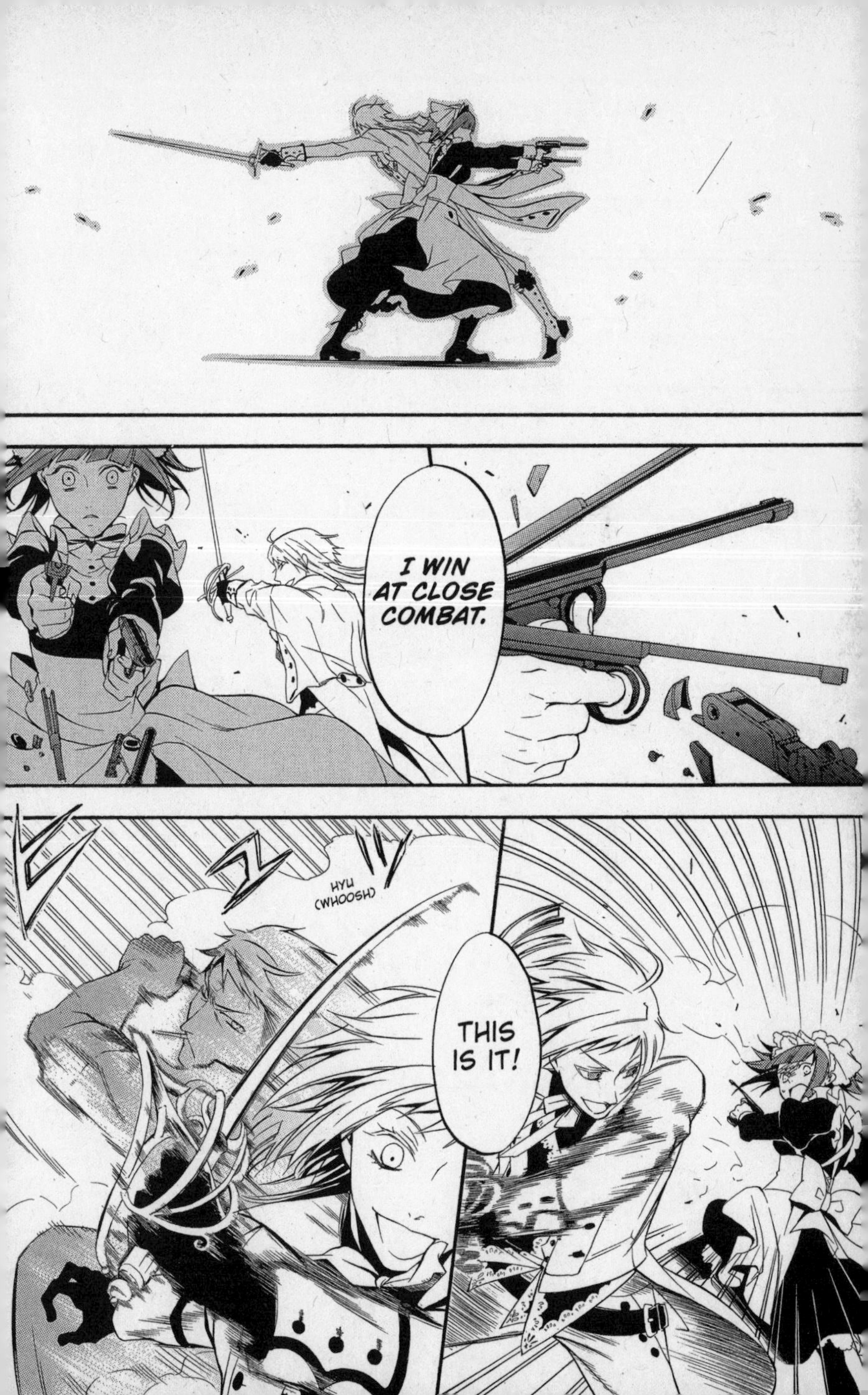
I WIN AT CLOSE COMBAT.
HYU (WHOOSH)
THIS IS IT!

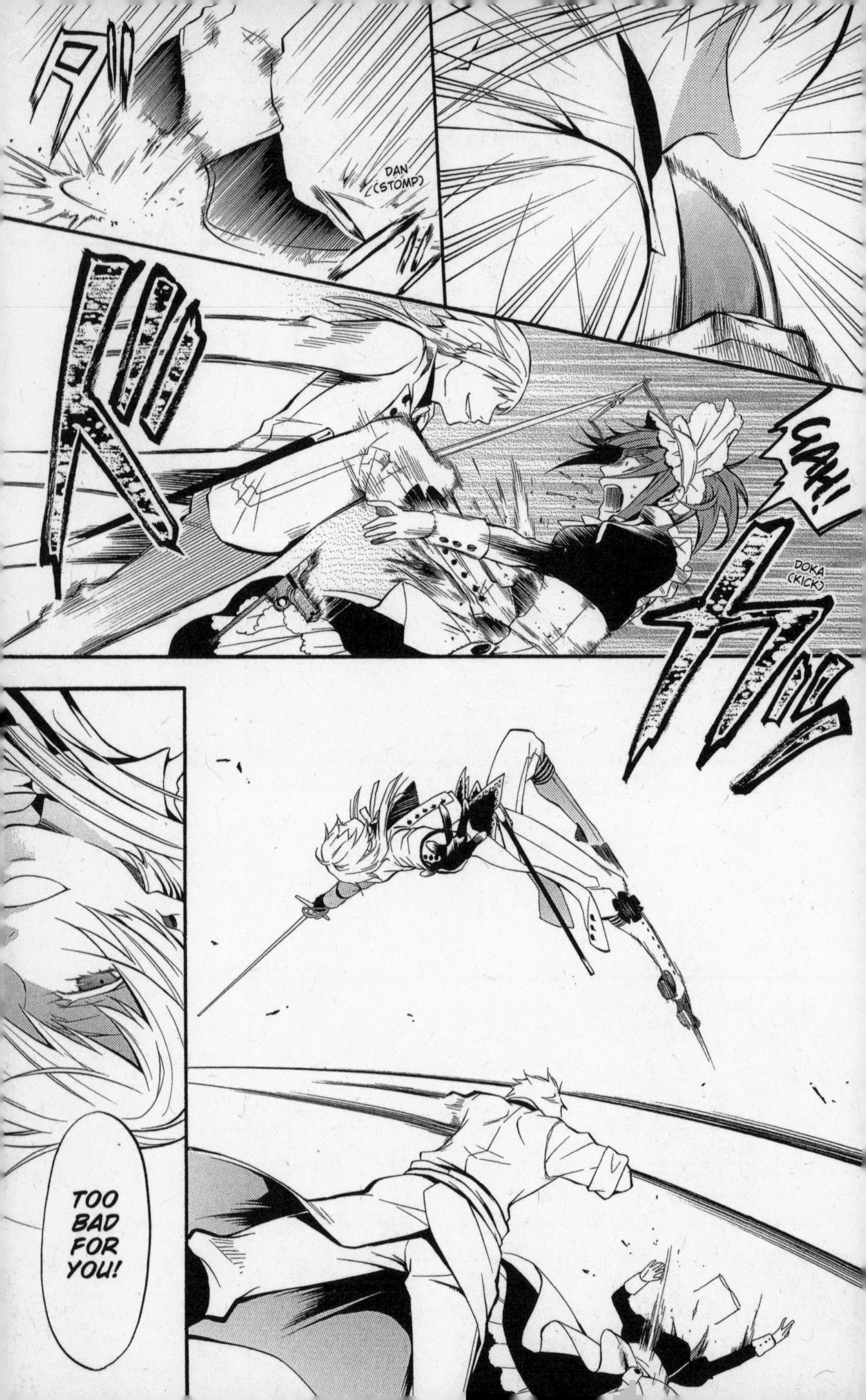
DAN (STOMP)
GAAH!
DOKA (KICK)
TOO BAD FOR YOU!

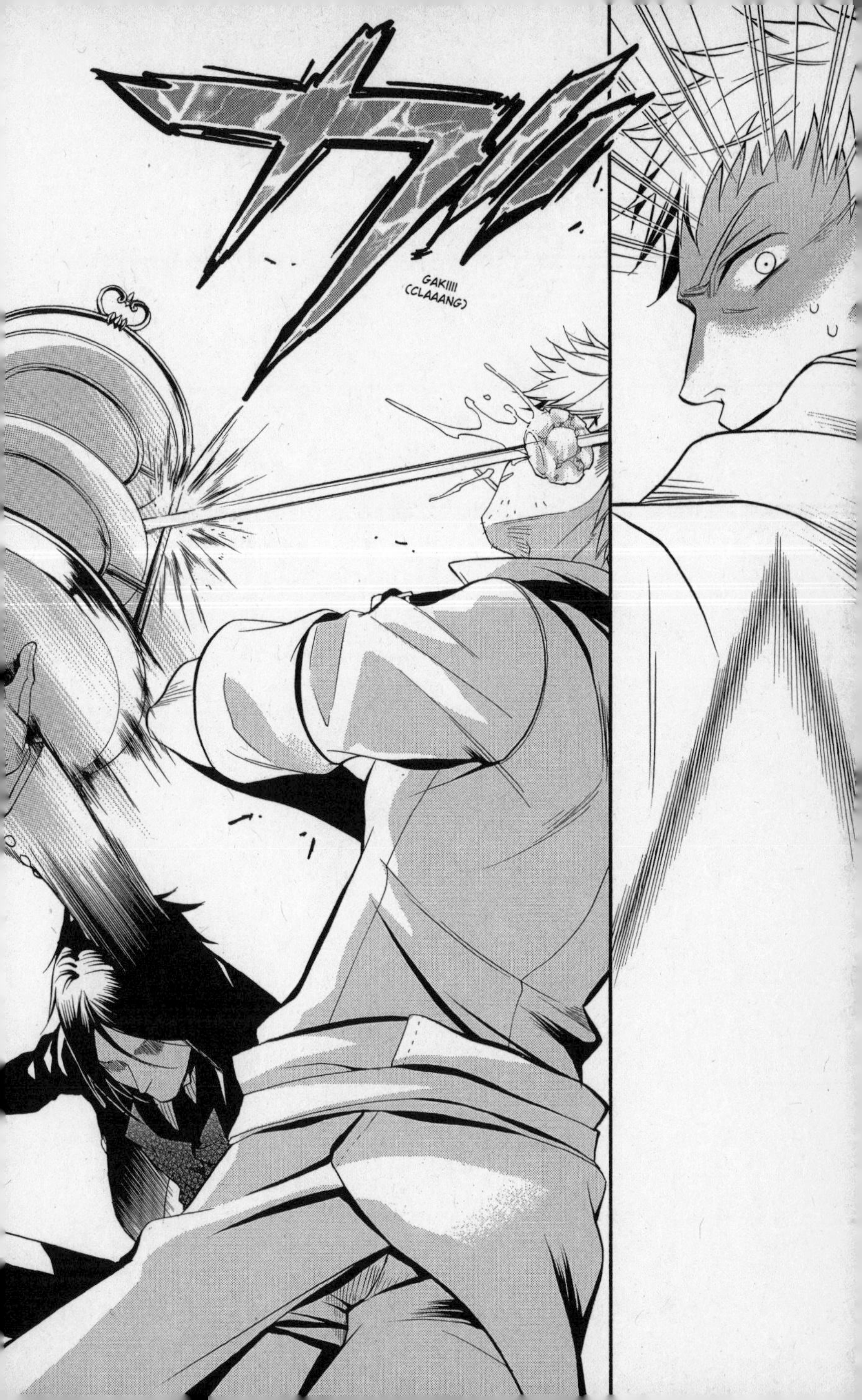
GAKIIII
(CLAAANG)

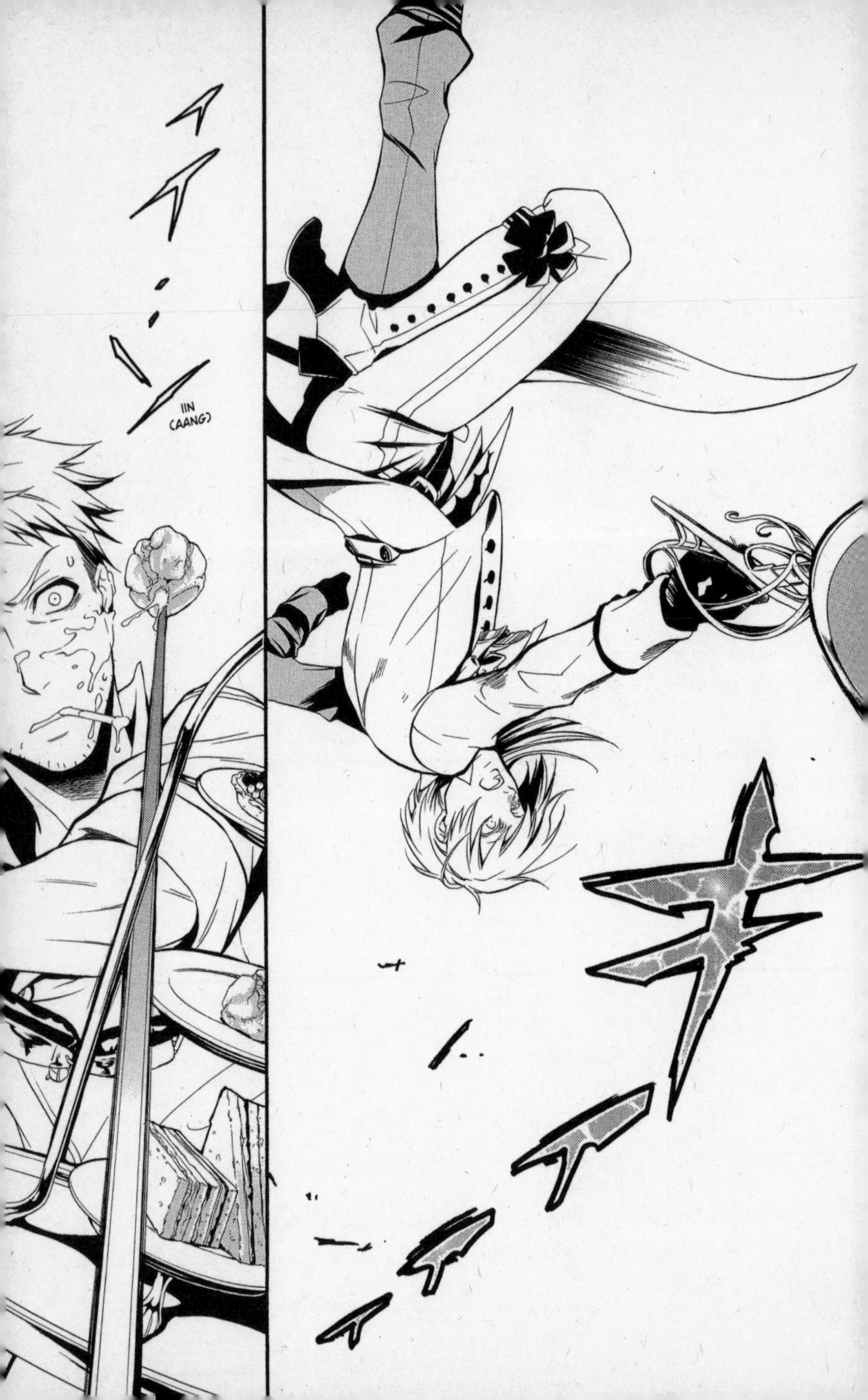
IIN
(AANG)

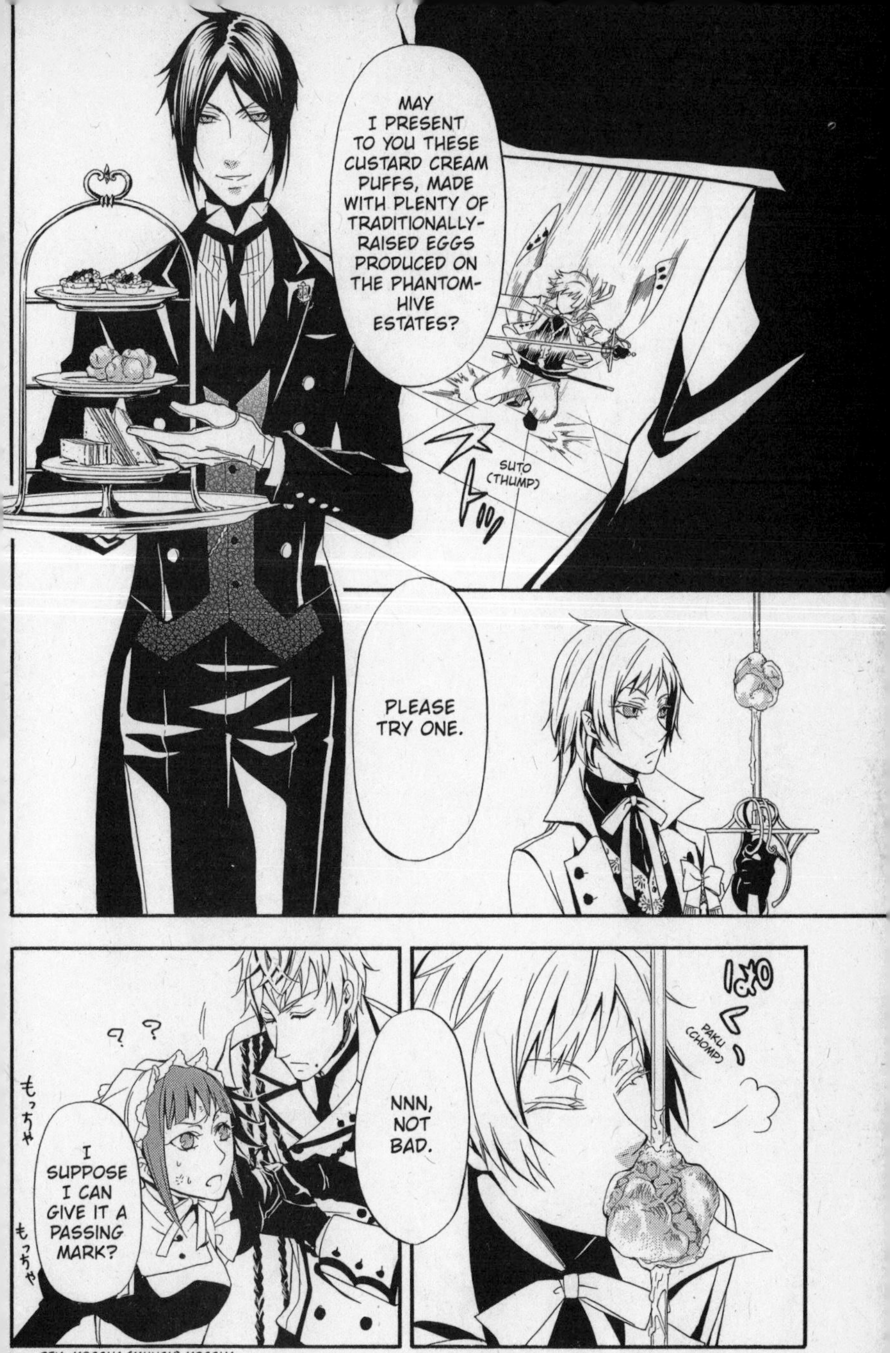
SUTO (THUMP)
MAY I PRESENT TO YOU THESE CUSTARD CREAM PUFFS, MADE WITH PLENTY OF TRADITIONALLY-RAISED EGGS PRODUCED ON THE PHANTOM-HIVE ESTATES?
PLEASE TRY ONE.
PAKU (CHOMP)
NNN, NOT BAD.
I SUPPOSE I CAN GIVE IT A PASSING MARK?
もっちゃ
もっちゃ

SFX: MOCCHA (MUNCH) MOCCHA

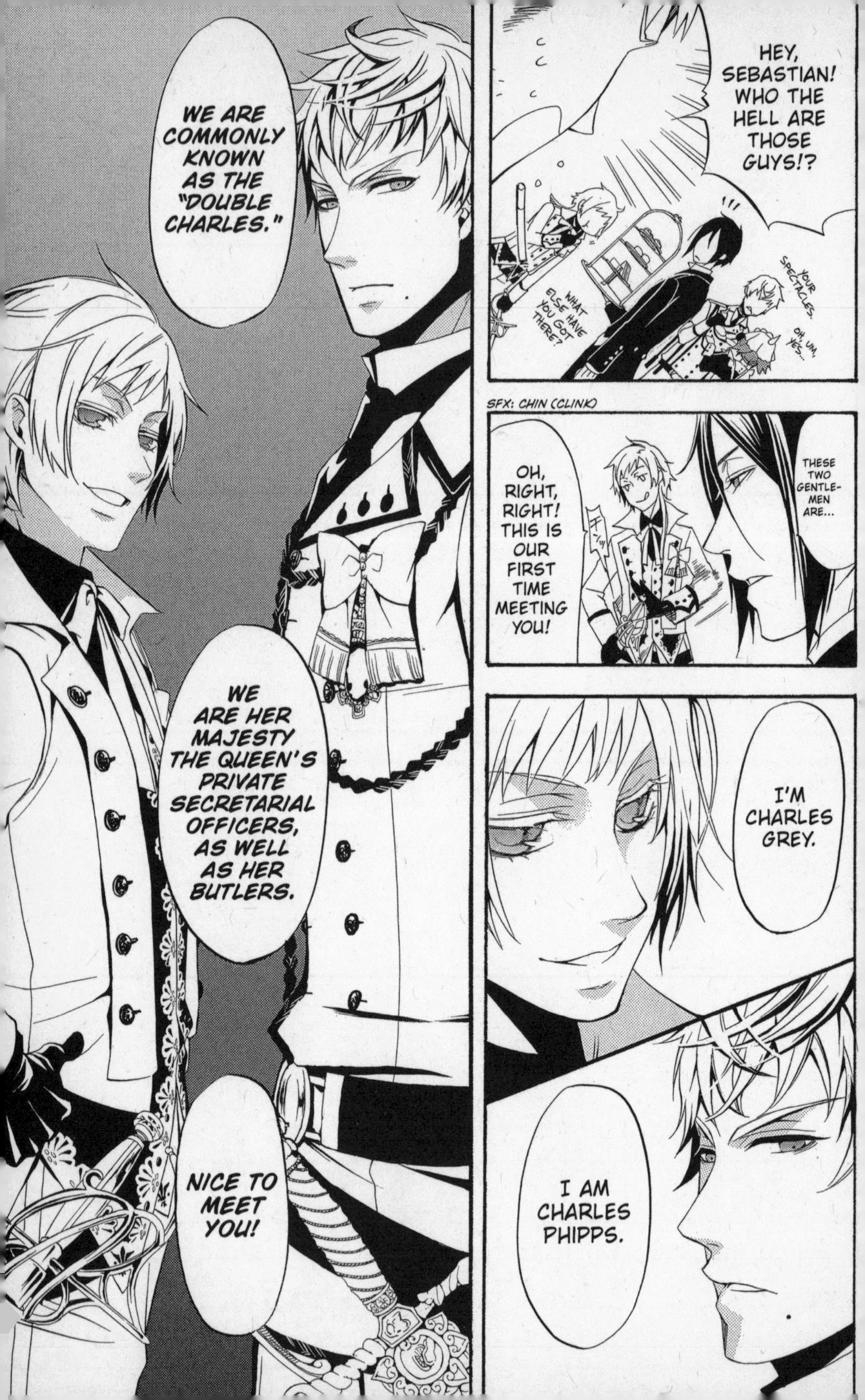
HEY, SEBASTIAN! WHO THE HELL ARE THOSE GUYS!?
YOUR SPECTACLES.
OH, UM, YES...
WHAT ELSE HAVE YOU GOT THERE?
SFX: CHIN (CLINK)
THESE TWO GENTLEMEN ARE...
OH, RIGHT, RIGHT! THIS IS OUR FIRST TIME MEETING YOU!
I'M CHARLES GREY.
I AM CHARLES PHIPPS.
WE ARE COMMONLY KNOWN AS THE "DOUBLE CHARLES."
WE ARE HER MAJESTY THE QUEEN'S PRIVATE SECRETARIAL OFFICERS, AS WELL AS HER BUTLERS.
NICE TO MEET YOU!

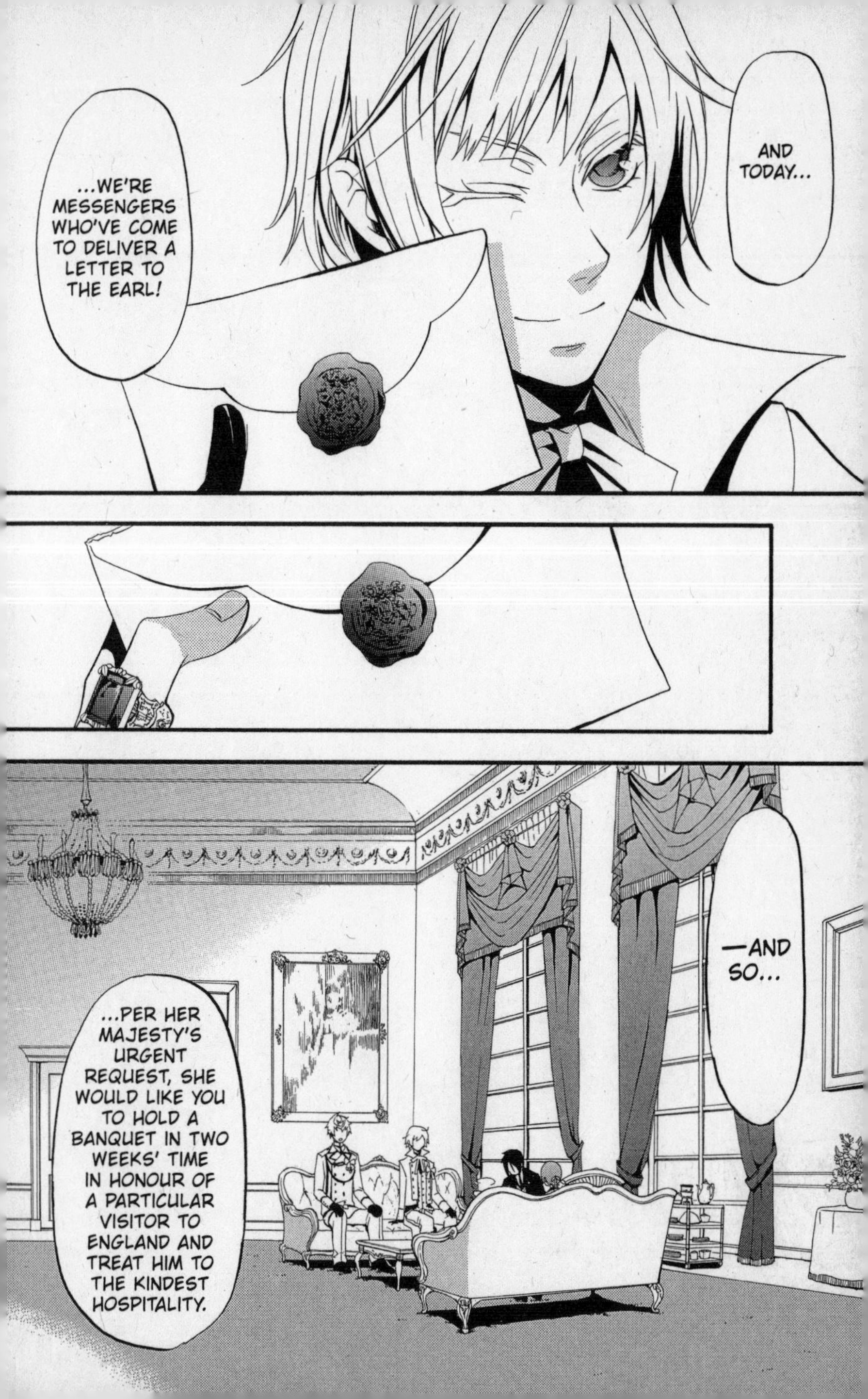
AND TODAY...
...WE'RE MESSENGERS WHO'VE COME TO DELIVER A LETTER TO THE EARL!
—AND SO...
...PER HER MAJESTY'S URGENT REQUEST, SHE WOULD LIKE YOU TO HOLD A BANQUET IN TWO WEEKS' TIME IN HONOUR OF A PARTICULAR VISITOR TO ENGLAND AND TREAT HIM TO THE KINDEST HOSPITALITY.

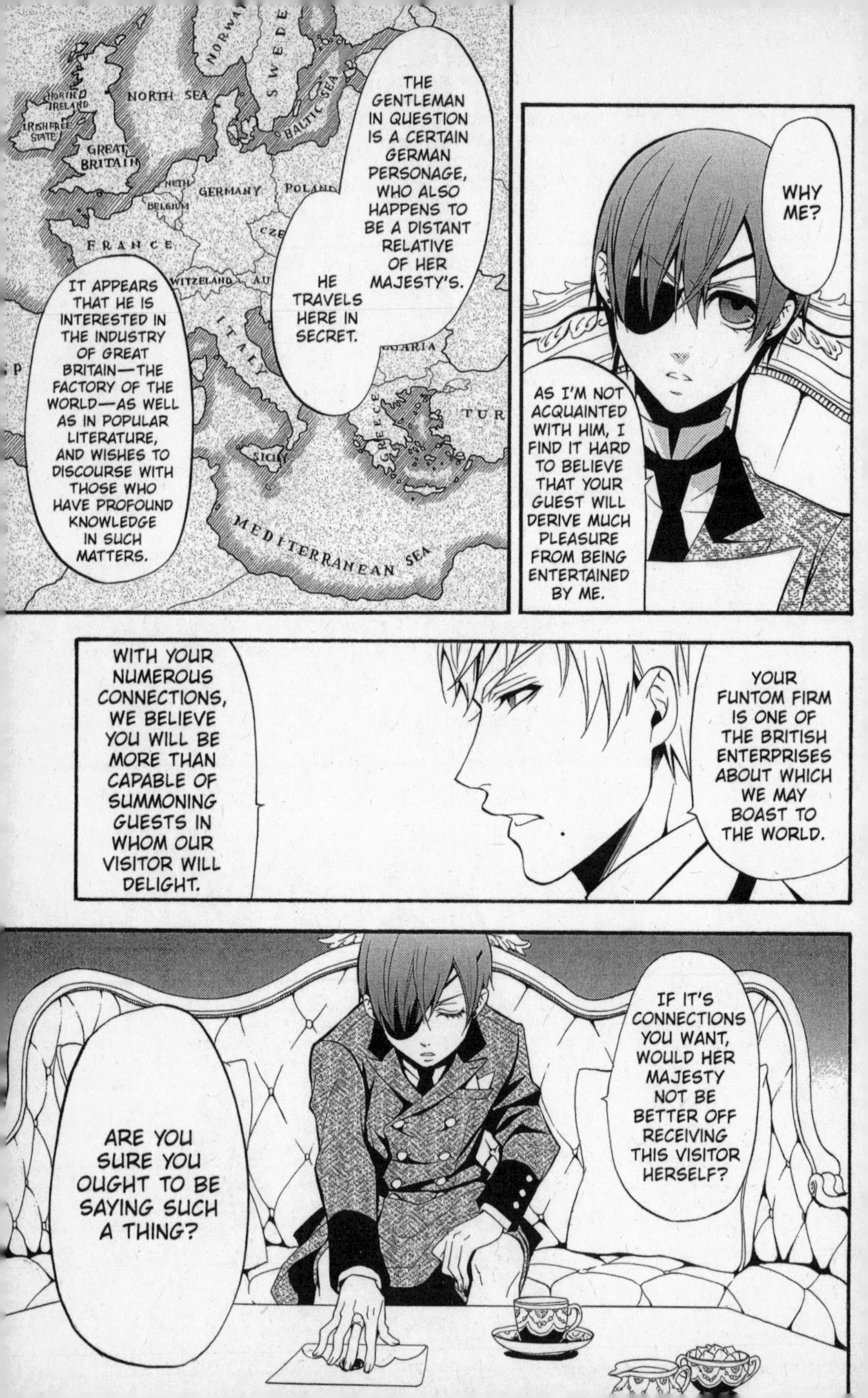

WHY ME?
AS I'M NOT ACQUAINTED WITH HIM, I FIND IT HARD TO BELIEVE THAT YOUR GUEST WILL DERIVE MUCH PLEASURE FROM BEING ENTERTAINED BY ME.
THE GENTLEMAN IN QUESTION IS A CERTAIN GERMAN PERSONAGE, WHO ALSO HAPPENS TO BE A DISTANT RELATIVE OF HER MAJESTY'S.
HE TRAVELS HERE IN SECRET.
IT APPEARS THAT HE IS INTERESTED IN THE INDUSTRY OF GREAT BRITAIN—THE FACTORY OF THE WORLD—AS WELL AS IN POPULAR LITERATURE, AND WISHES TO DISCOURSE WITH THOSE WHO HAVE PROFOUND KNOWLEDGE IN SUCH MATTERS.
NORTH SEA
BALTIC SEA
NORTH IRELAND
IRISH FREE STATE
GREAT BRITAIN
NETH
BELGIUM
GERMANY
FRANCE
ITALY
SICILY
GREECE
MEDITERRANEAN SEA
YOUR FUNTOM FIRM IS ONE OF THE BRITISH ENTERPRISES ABOUT WHICH WE MAY BOAST TO THE WORLD.
WITH YOUR NUMEROUS CONNECTIONS, WE BELIEVE YOU WILL BE MORE THAN CAPABLE OF SUMMONING GUESTS IN WHOM OUR VISITOR WILL DELIGHT.
IF IT'S CONNECTIONS YOU WANT, WOULD HER MAJESTY NOT BE BETTER OFF RECEIVING THIS VISITOR HERSELF?
ARE YOU SURE YOU OUGHT TO BE SAYING SUCH A THING?

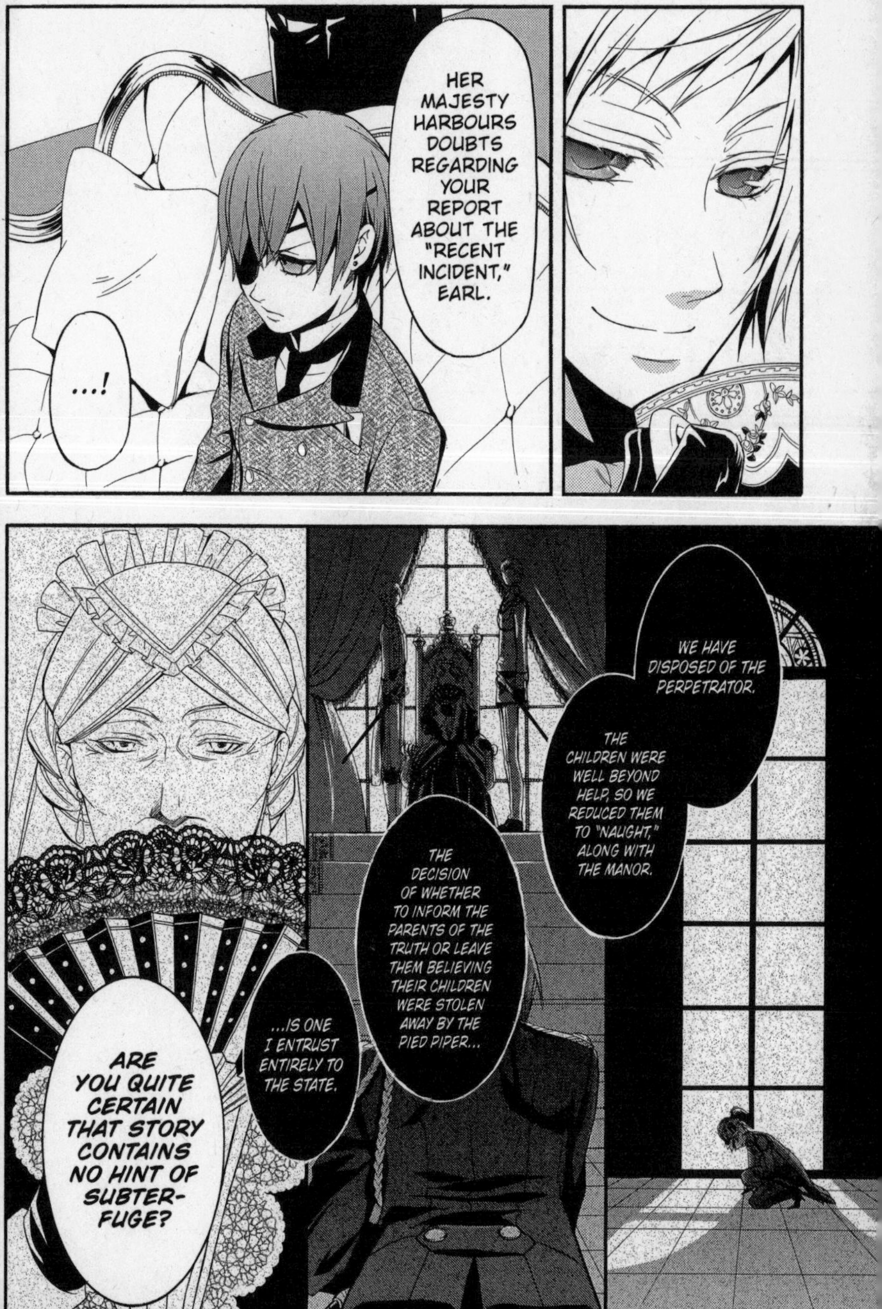
HER MAJESTY HARBOURS DOUBTS REGARDING YOUR REPORT ABOUT THE "RECENT INCIDENT," EARL.
...!
WE HAVE DISPOSED OF THE PERPETRATOR.
THE CHILDREN WERE WELL BEYOND HELP, SO WE REDUCED THEM TO "NAUGHT," ALONG WITH THE MANOR.
THE DECISION OF WHETHER TO INFORM THE PARENTS OF THE TRUTH OR LEAVE THEM BELIEVING THEIR CHILDREN WERE STOLEN AWAY BY THE PIED PIPER...
...IS ONE I ENTRUST ENTIRELY TO THE STATE.
ARE YOU QUITE CERTAIN THAT STORY CONTAINS NO HINT OF SUBTER-FUGE?

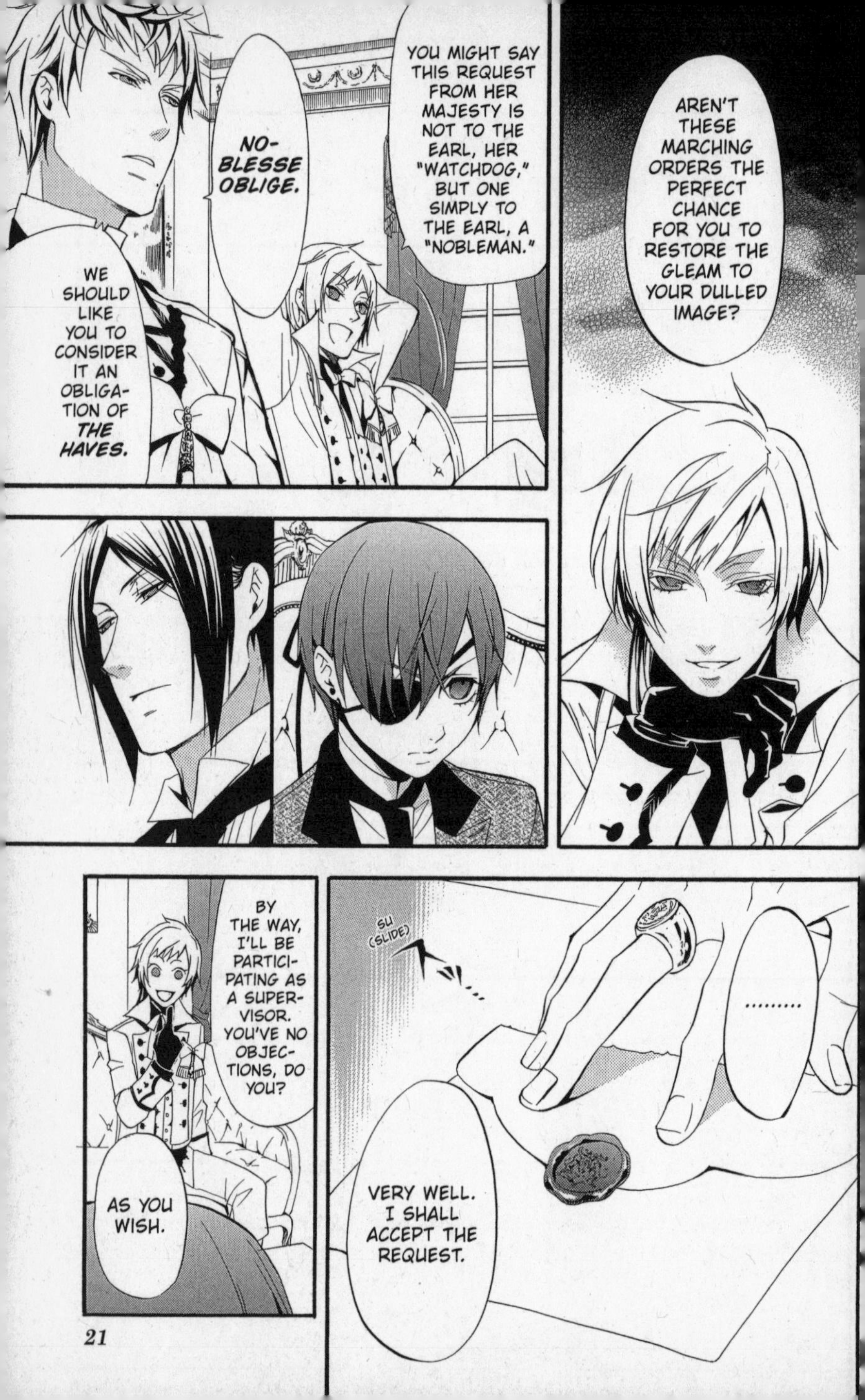
AREN'T THESE MARCHING ORDERS THE PERFECT CHANCE FOR YOU TO RESTORE THE GLEAM TO YOUR DULLED IMAGE?
YOU MIGHT SAY THIS REQUEST FROM HER MAJESTY IS NOT TO THE EARL, HER "WATCHDOG," BUT ONE SIMPLY TO THE EARL, A "NOBLEMAN."
NO-BLESSE OBLIGE.
WE SHOULD LIKE YOU TO CONSIDER IT AN OBLIGA-TION OF THE HAVES.
SU (SLIDE)
....
VERY WELL. I SHALL ACCEPT THE REQUEST.
BY THE WAY, I'LL BE PARTICI-PATING AS A SUPER-VISOR. YOU'VE NO OBJEC-TIONS, DO YOU?
AS YOU WISH.

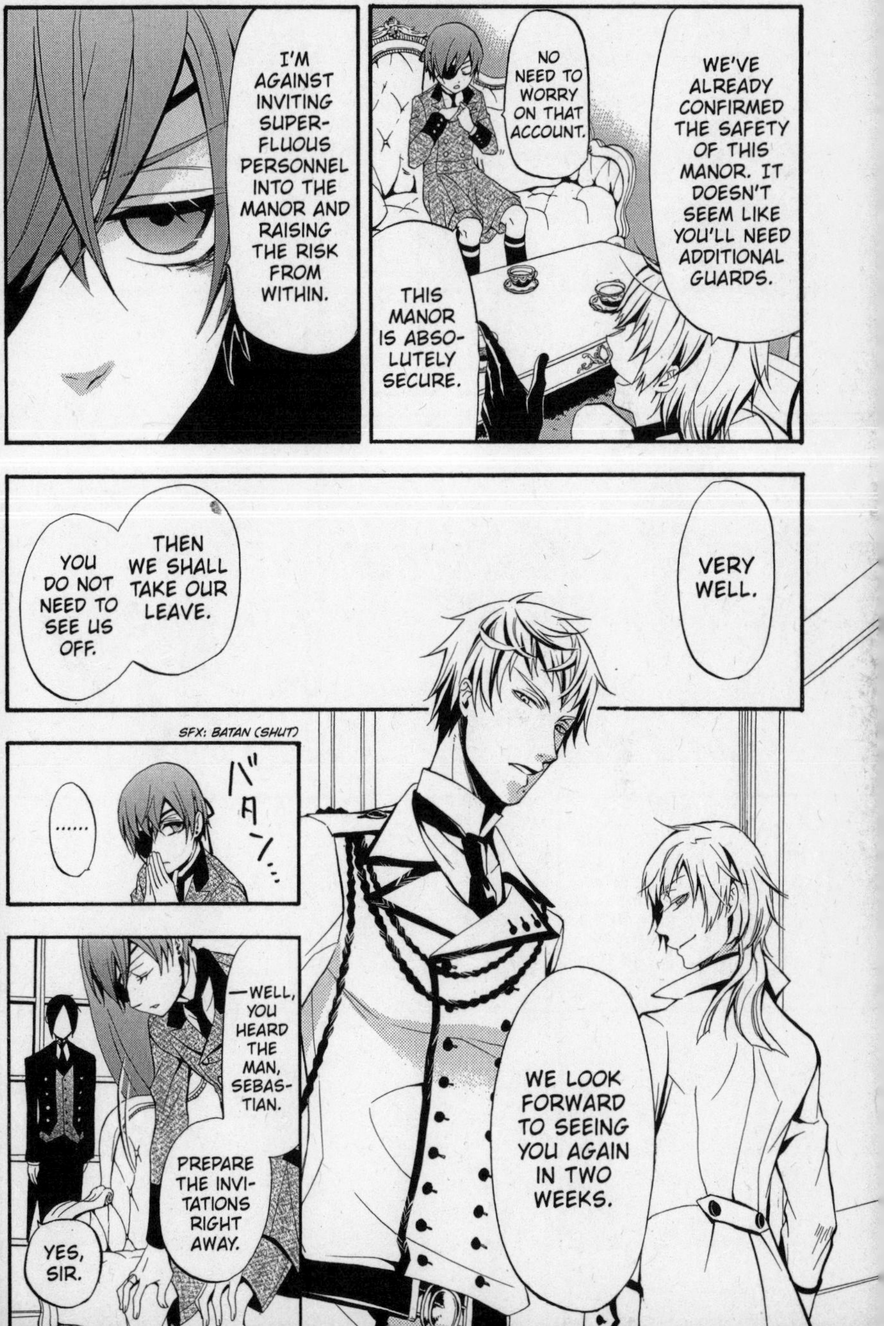
WE'VE ALREADY CONFIRMED THE SAFETY OF THIS MANOR. IT DOESN'T SEEM LIKE YOU'LL NEED ADDITIONAL GUARDS.
NO NEED TO WORRY ON THAT ACCOUNT.
THIS MANOR IS ABSOLUTELY SECURE.
I'M AGAINST INVITING SUPERFLUOUS PERSONNEL INTO THE MANOR AND RAISING THE RISK FROM WITHIN.
VERY WELL.
THEN WE SHALL TAKE OUR LEAVE.
YOU DO NOT NEED TO SEE US OFF.
WE LOOK FORWARD TO SEEING YOU AGAIN IN TWO WEEKS.
SFX: BATAN (SHUT)
バタン…
……
—WELL, YOU HEARD THE MAN, SEBASTIAN.
PREPARE THE INVITATIONS RIGHT AWAY.
YES, SIR.

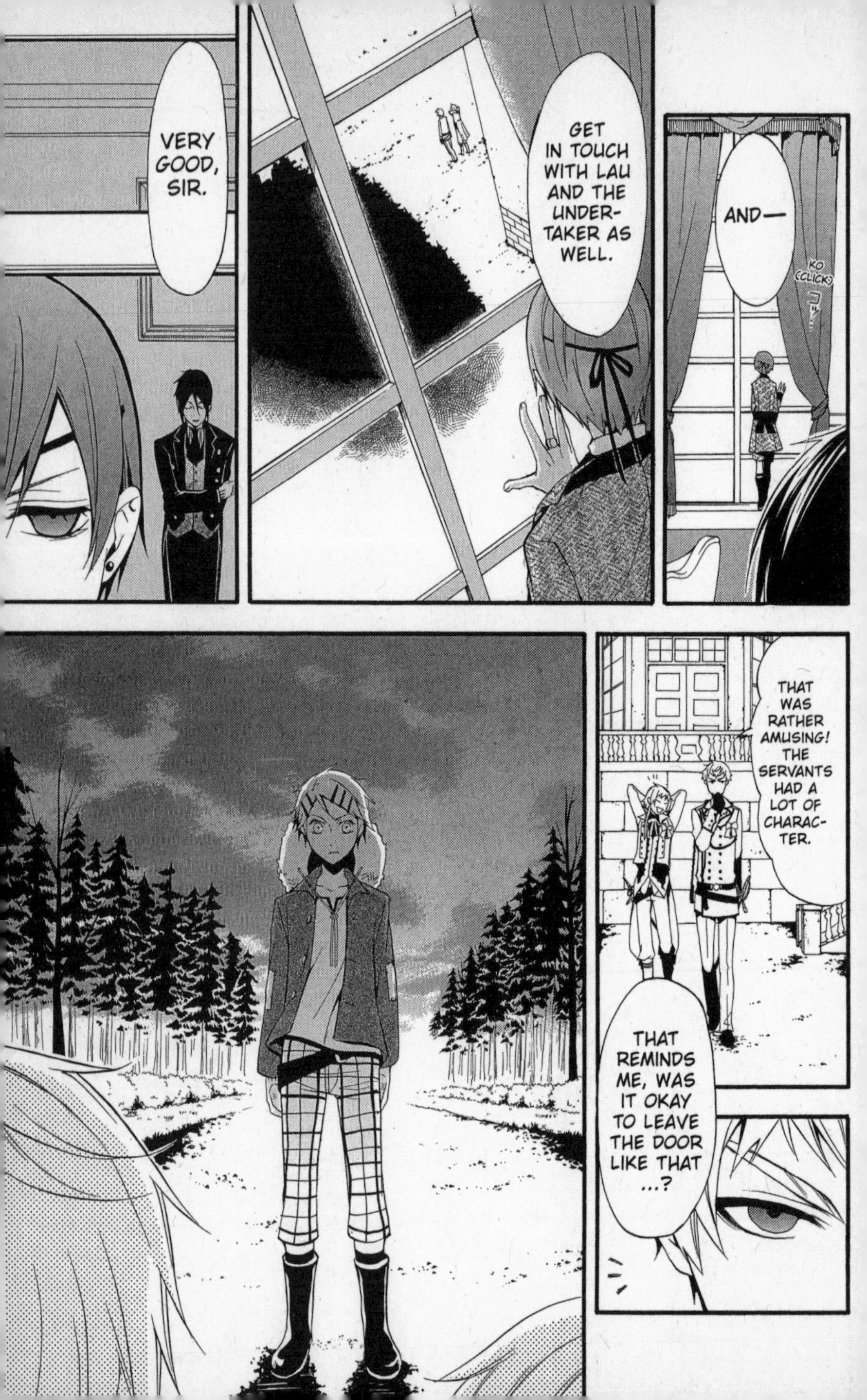
AND—
KO (CLICK)
GET IN TOUCH WITH LAU AND THE UNDER-TAKER AS WELL.
VERY GOOD, SIR.
THAT WAS RATHER AMUSING! THE SERVANTS HAD A LOT OF CHARAC-TER.
THAT REMINDS ME, WAS IT OKAY TO LEAVE THE DOOR LIKE THAT ...?

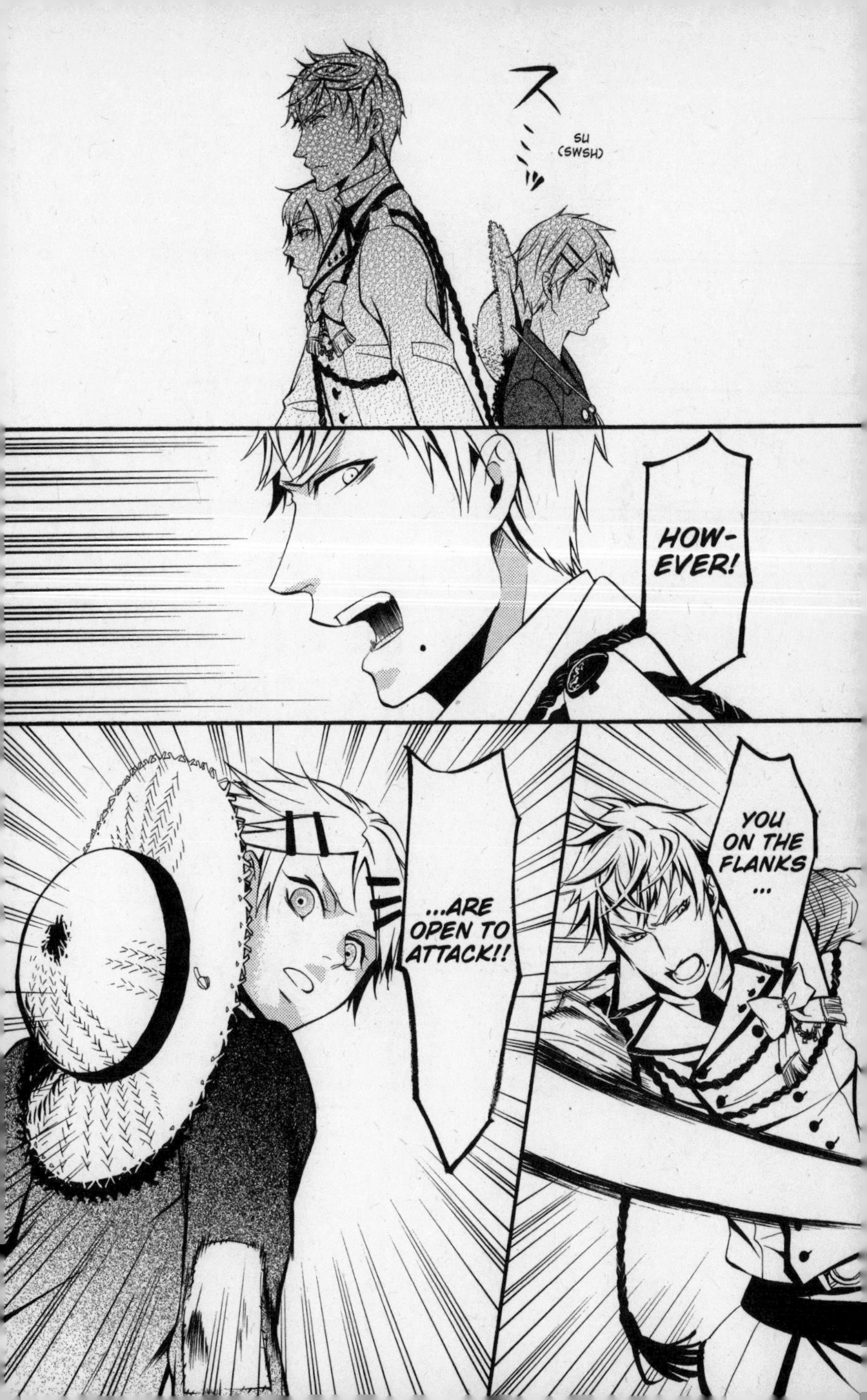
ス
SU (SWSH)
HOW-EVER!
YOU ON THE FLANKS ...
...ARE OPEN TO ATTACK!!

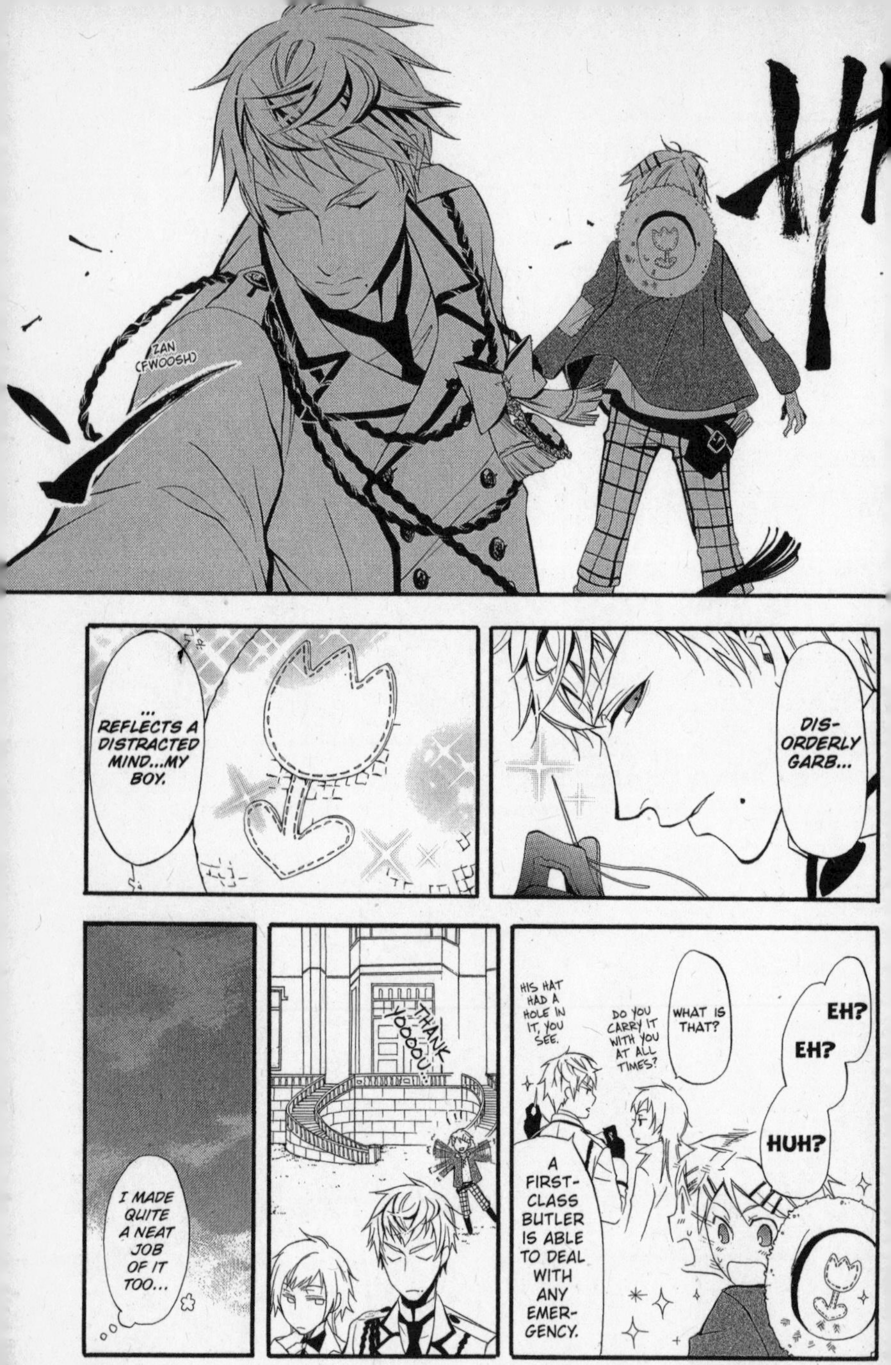
ZAN (FWOOSH)
DIS-ORDERLY GARB...
...REFLECTS A DISTRACTED MIND...MY BOY.
EH? EH? HUH?
WHAT IS THAT?
DO YOU CARRY IT WITH YOU AT ALL TIMES?
HIS HAT HAD A HOLE IN IT, YOU SEE.
A FIRST-CLASS BUTLER IS ABLE TO DEAL WITH ANY EMERGENCY.
THANK YOOOOU...
I MADE QUITE A NEAT JOB OF IT TOO...

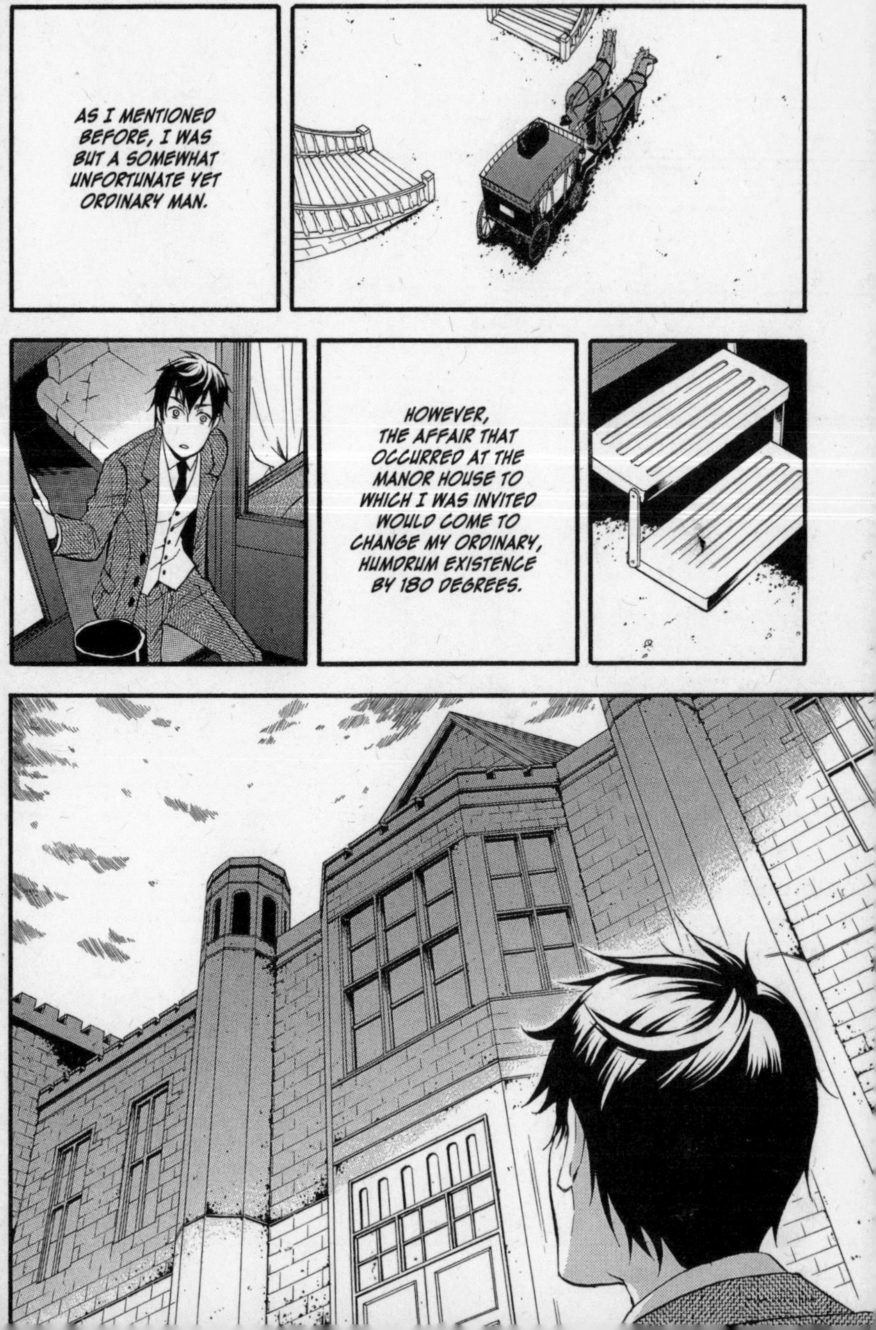
AS I MENTIONED BEFORE, I WAS BUT A SOMEWHAT UNFORTUNATE YET ORDINARY MAN.
HOWEVER, THE AFFAIR THAT OCCURRED AT THE MANOR HOUSE TO WHICH I WAS INVITED WOULD COME TO CHANGE MY ORDINARY, HUMDRUM EXISTENCE BY 180 DEGREES.

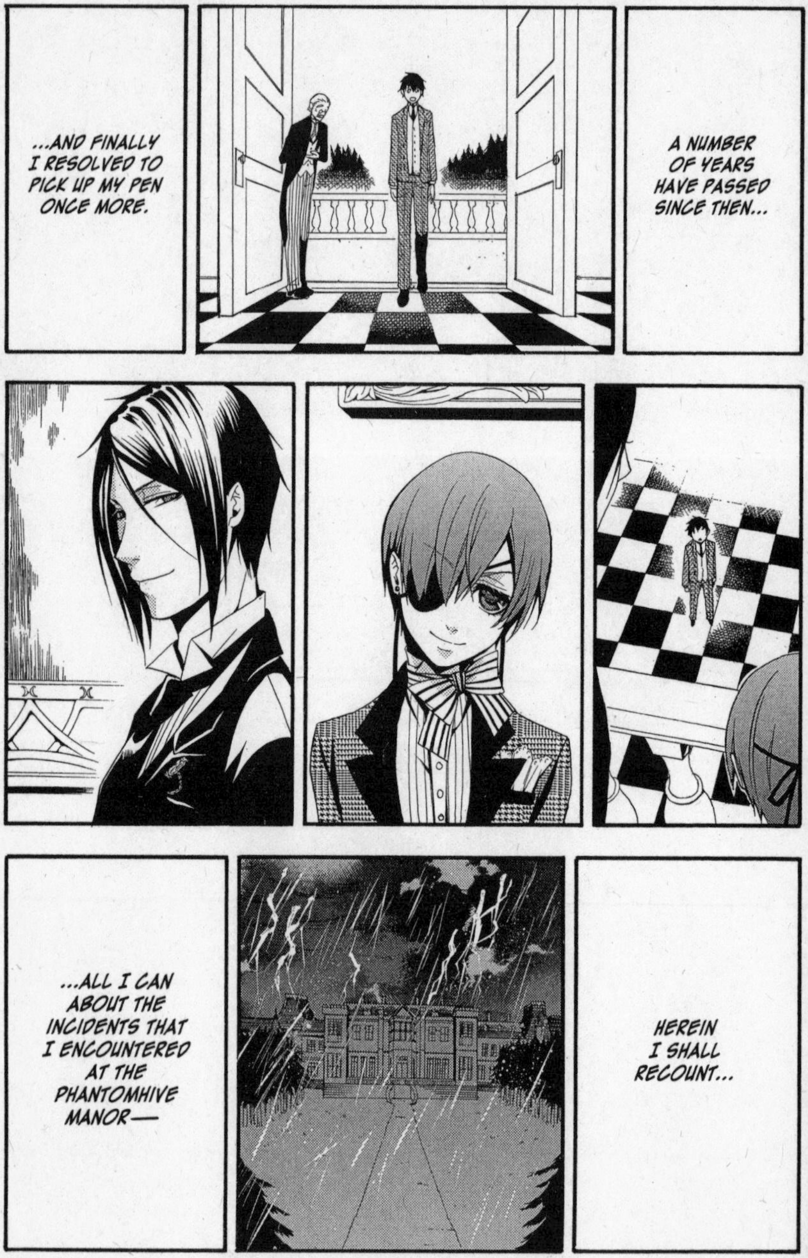
A NUMBER OF YEARS HAVE PASSED SINCE THEN...
...AND FINALLY I RESOLVED TO PICK UP MY PEN ONCE MORE.
HEREIN I SHALL RECOUNT...
...ALL I CAN ABOUT THE INCIDENTS THAT I ENCOUNTERED AT THE PHANTOMHIVE MANOR—

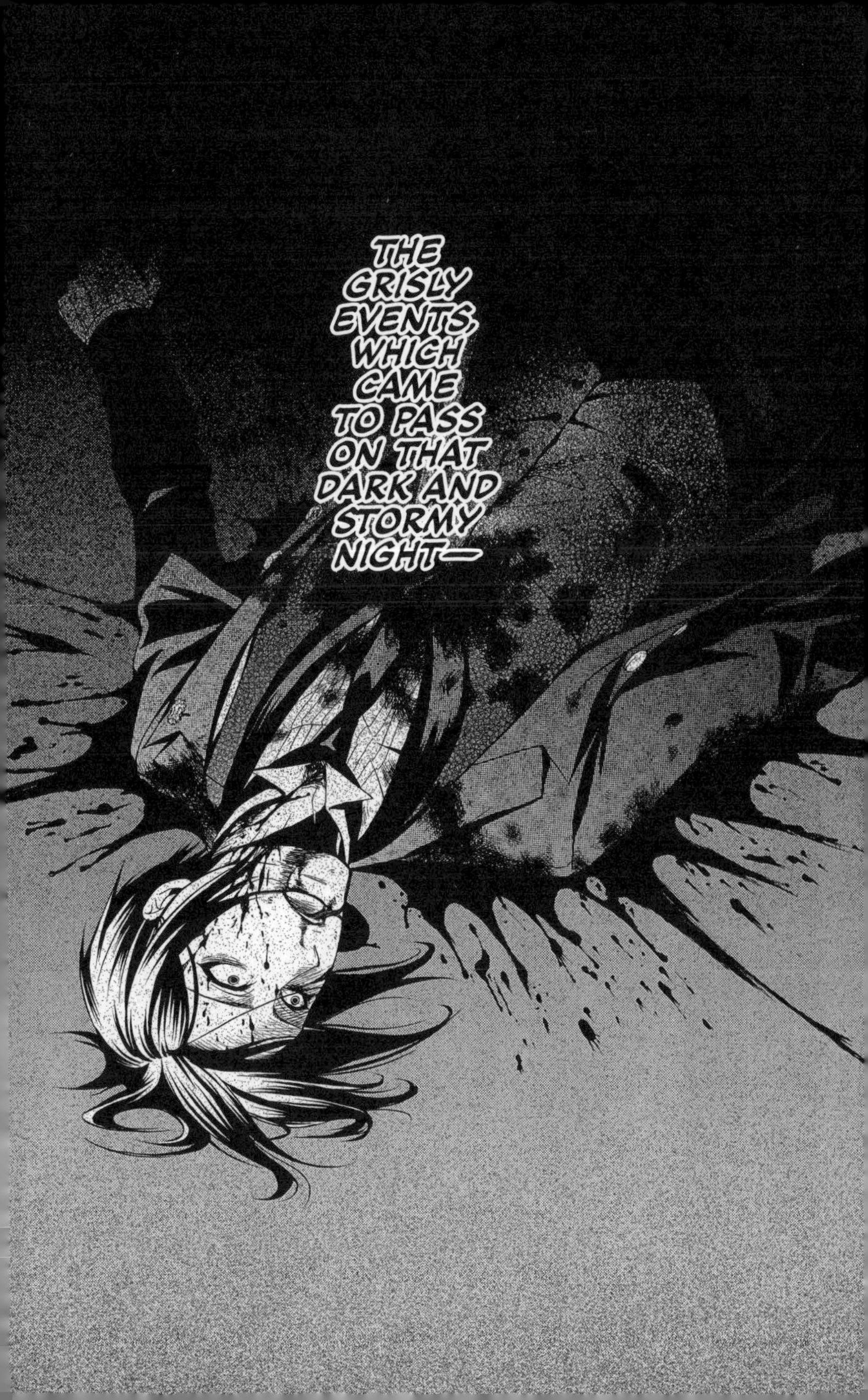
THE GRISLY EVENTS, WHICH CAME TO PASS ON THAT DARK AND STORMY NIGHT—

Black Butler

Chapter 39
At noon : The Butler, Startled

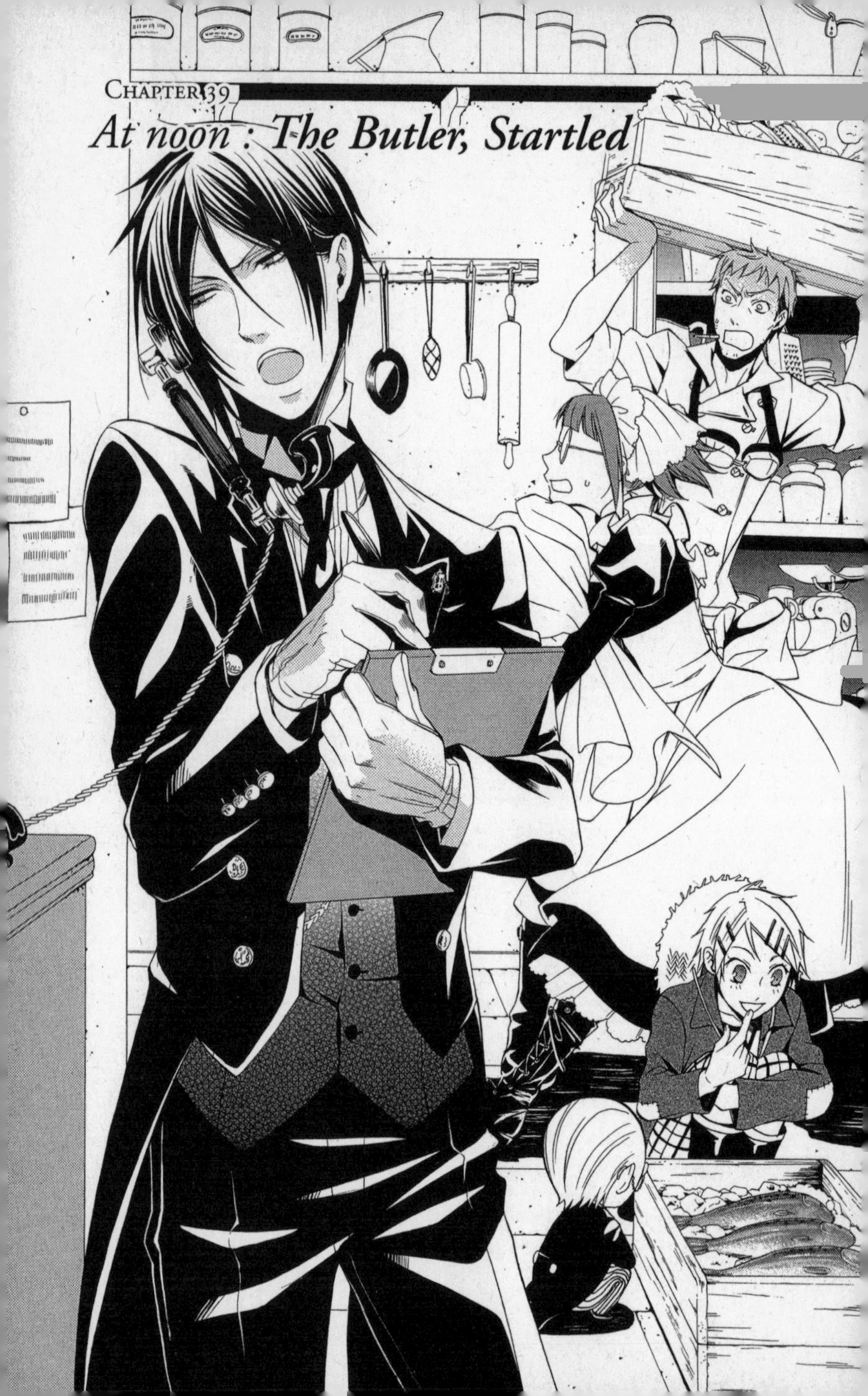

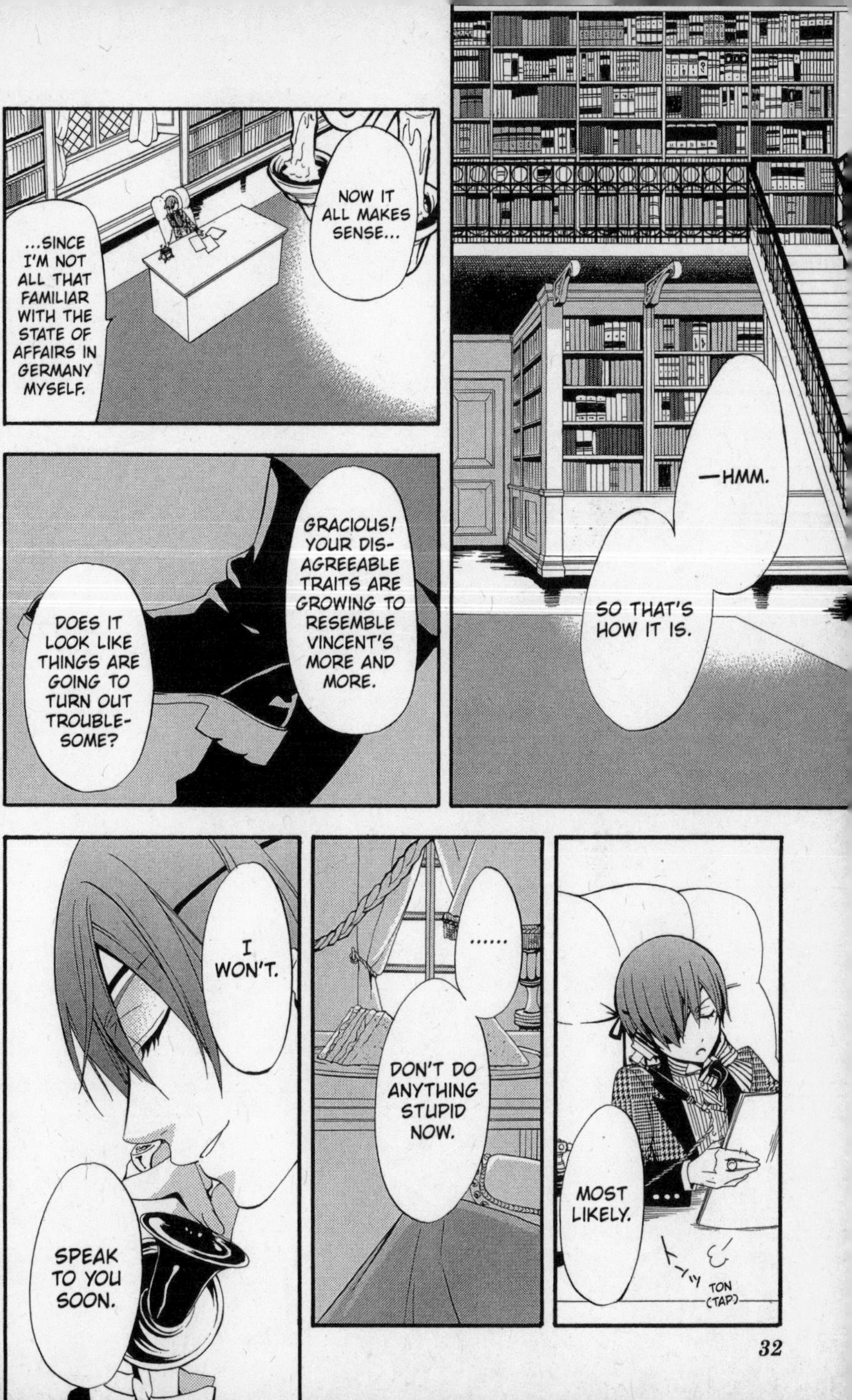
—HMM.
SO THAT'S HOW IT IS.
NOW IT ALL MAKES SENSE...
...SINCE I'M NOT ALL THAT FAMILIAR WITH THE STATE OF AFFAIRS IN GERMANY MYSELF.
GRACIOUS! YOUR DIS-AGREEABLE TRAITS ARE GROWING TO RESEMBLE VINCENT'S MORE AND MORE.
DOES IT LOOK LIKE THINGS ARE GOING TO TURN OUT TROUBLE-SOME?
MOST LIKELY.
TON (TAP)
......
DON'T DO ANYTHING STUPID NOW.
I WON'T.
SPEAK TO YOU SOON.

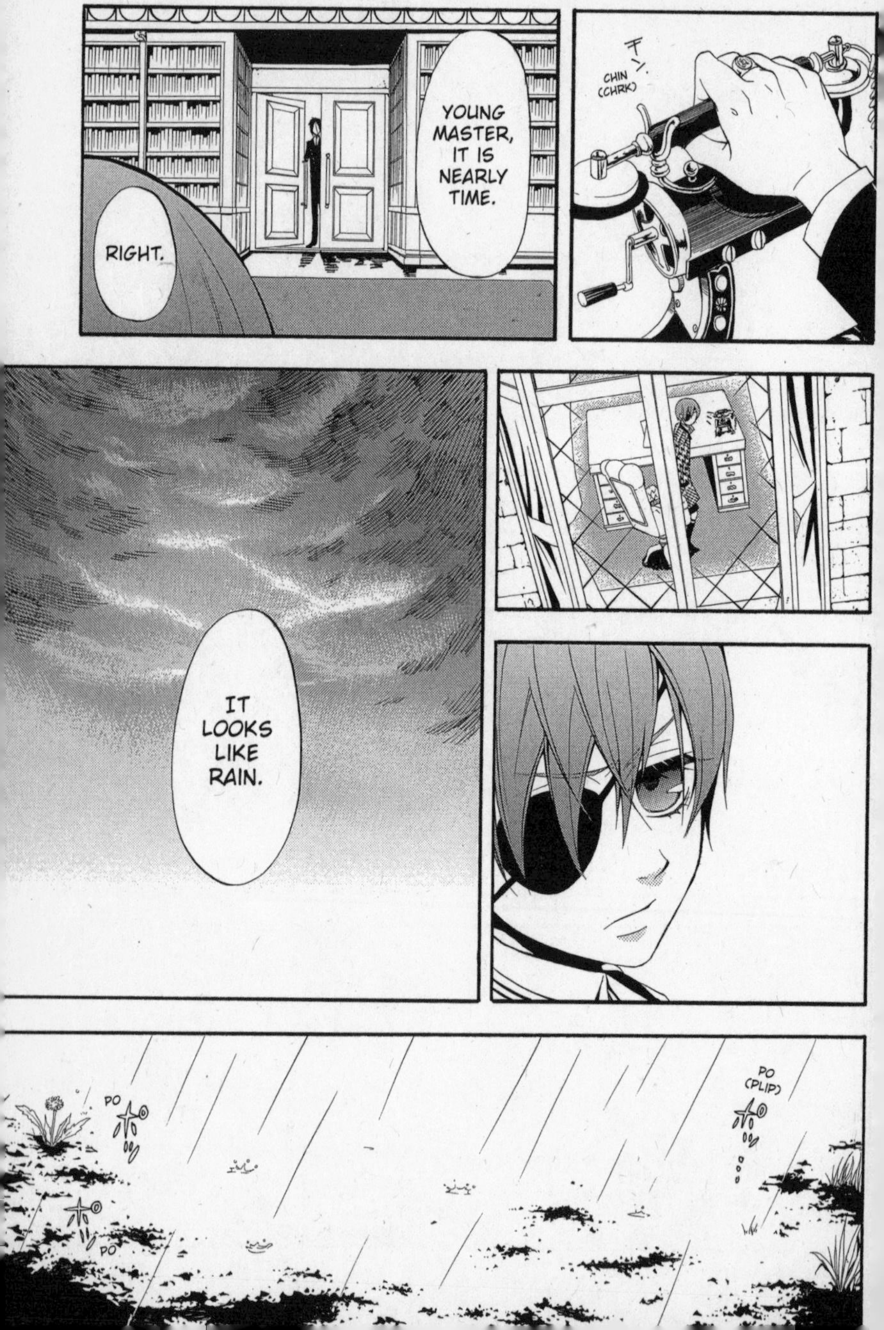
CHIN (CHRK)
YOUNG MASTER, IT IS NEARLY TIME.
RIGHT.
IT LOOKS LIKE RAIN.
PO (PLIP)
PO
PO

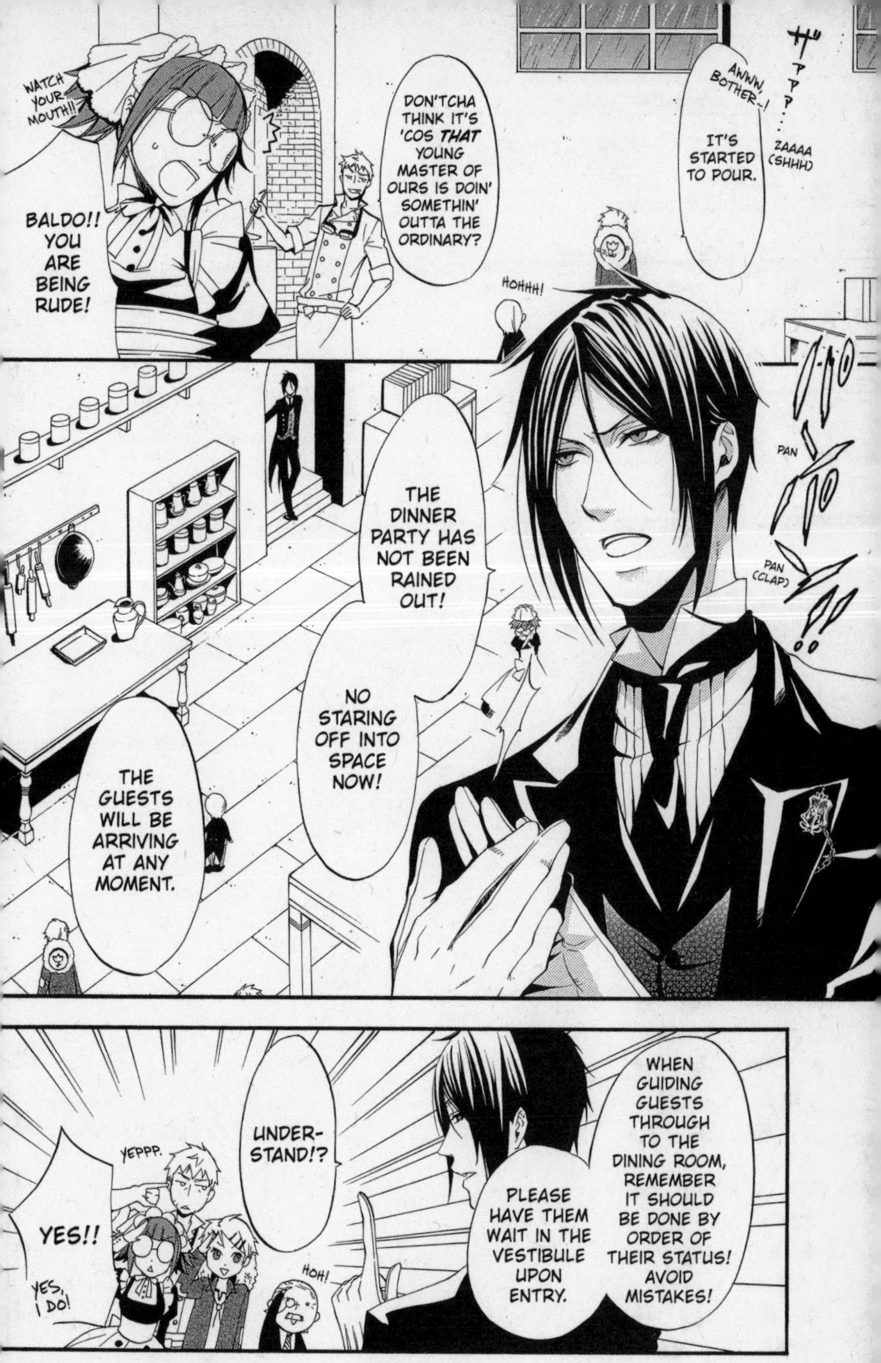

ZAAAA (SHHH)
AWWW, BOTHER~!
IT'S STARTED TO POUR.
HOHHH!
DON'TCHA THINK IT'S 'COS *THAT* YOUNG MASTER OF OURS IS DOIN' SOMETHIN' OUTTA THE ORDINARY?
WATCH YOUR MOUTH!!
BALDO!! YOU ARE BEING RUDE!
PAN
PAN (CLAP)
THE DINNER PARTY HAS NOT BEEN RAINED OUT!
NO STARING OFF INTO SPACE NOW!
THE GUESTS WILL BE ARRIVING AT ANY MOMENT.
WHEN GUIDING GUESTS THROUGH TO THE DINING ROOM, REMEMBER IT SHOULD BE DONE BY ORDER OF THEIR STATUS! AVOID MISTAKES!
PLEASE HAVE THEM WAIT IN THE VESTIBULE UPON ENTRY.
UNDER-STAND!?
HOH!
YEPPP.
YES!!
YES, I DO!

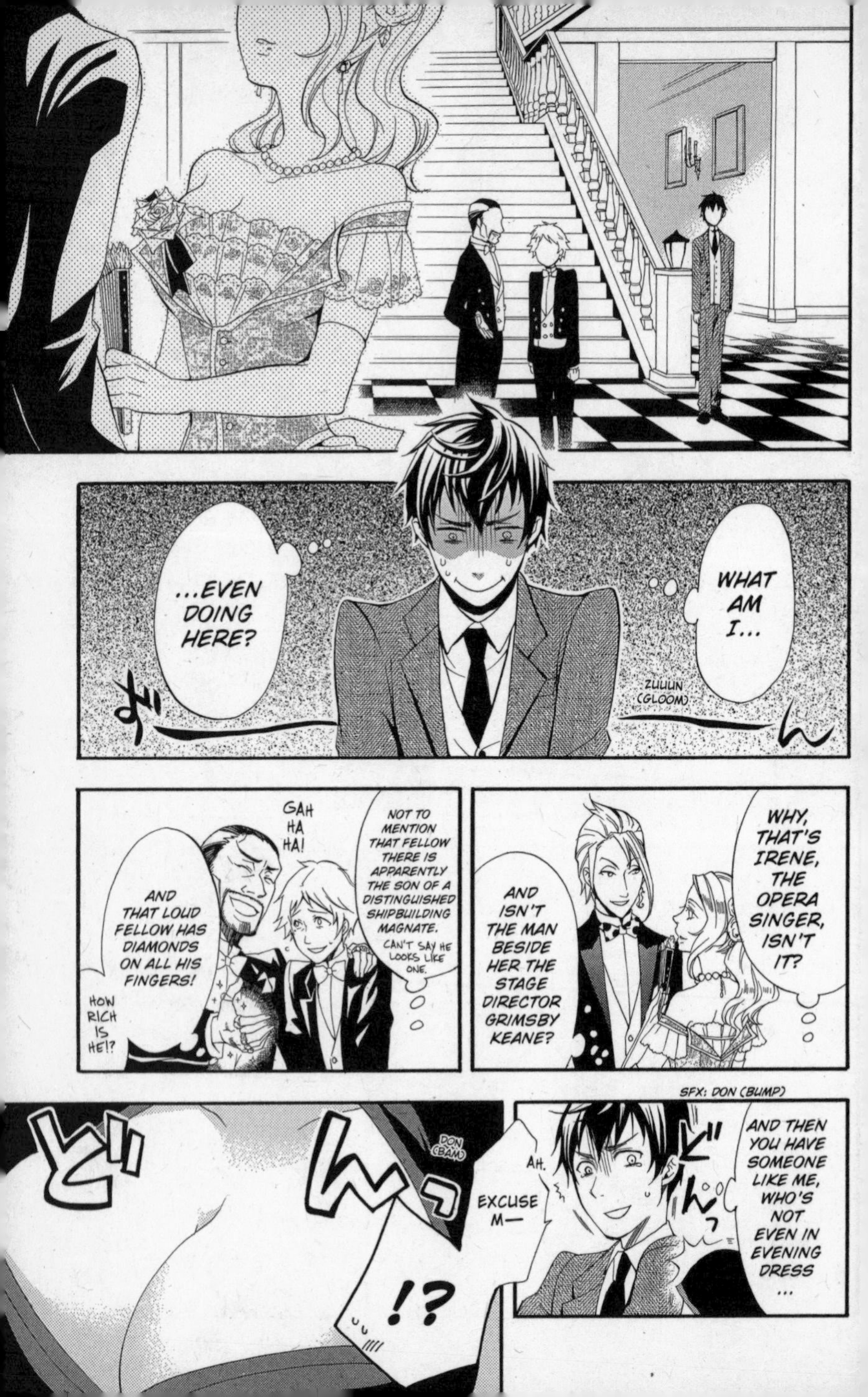
WHAT AM I...
...EVEN DOING HERE?
ZUUUN (GLOOM)
WHY, THAT'S IRENE, THE OPERA SINGER, ISN'T IT?
AND ISN'T THE MAN BESIDE HER THE STAGE DIRECTOR GRIMSBY KEANE?
NOT TO MENTION THAT FELLOW THERE IS APPARENTLY THE SON OF A DISTINGUISHED SHIPBUILDING MAGNATE.
CAN'T SAY HE LOOKS LIKE ONE.
GAH HA HA!
AND THAT LOUD FELLOW HAS DIAMONDS ON ALL HIS FINGERS!
HOW RICH IS HE!?
SFX: DON (BUMP)
AND THEN YOU HAVE SOMEONE LIKE ME, WHO'S NOT EVEN IN EVENING DRESS...
AH.
EXCUSE M—
DON (BAM)
!?

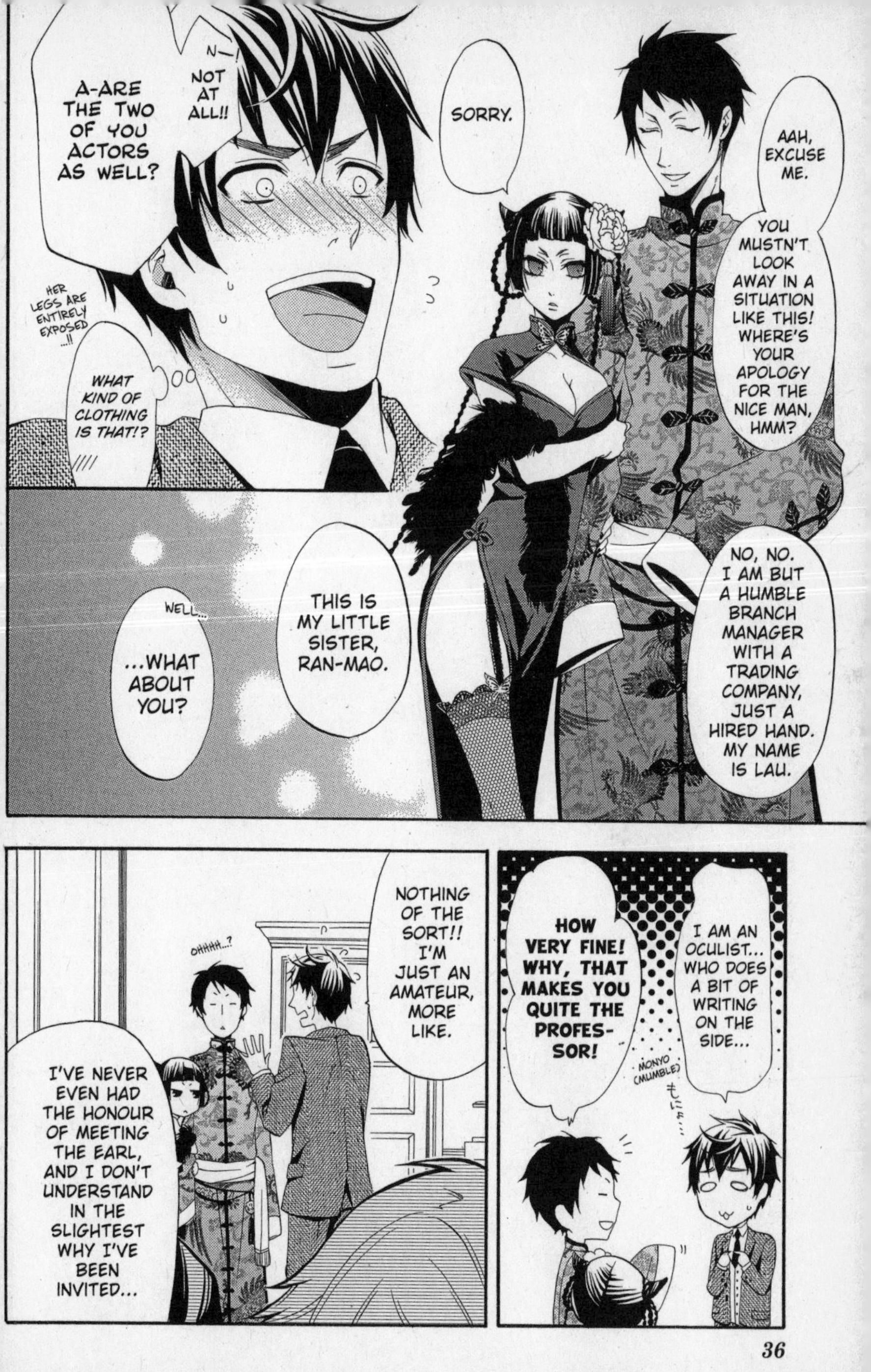
AAH, EXCUSE ME.
YOU MUSTN'T LOOK AWAY IN A SITUATION LIKE THIS! WHERE'S YOUR APOLOGY FOR THE NICE MAN, HMM?
SORRY.
N—! NOT AT ALL!!
A-ARE THE TWO OF YOU ACTORS AS WELL?
HER LEGS ARE ENTIRELY EXPOSED...!!
WHAT KIND OF CLOTHING IS THAT!?
NO, NO. I AM BUT A HUMBLE BRANCH MANAGER WITH A TRADING COMPANY, JUST A HIRED HAND. MY NAME IS LAU.
THIS IS MY LITTLE SISTER, RAN-MAO.
WELL...
...WHAT ABOUT YOU?
I AM AN OCULIST... WHO DOES A BIT OF WRITING ON THE SIDE...
MONYO (MUMBLE)
HOW VERY FINE! WHY, THAT MAKES YOU QUITE THE PROFES-SOR!
NOTHING OF THE SORT!! I'M JUST AN AMATEUR, MORE LIKE.
OHHHH...?
I'VE NEVER EVEN HAD THE HONOUR OF MEETING THE EARL, AND I DON'T UNDERSTAND IN THE SLIGHTEST WHY I'VE BEEN INVITED...

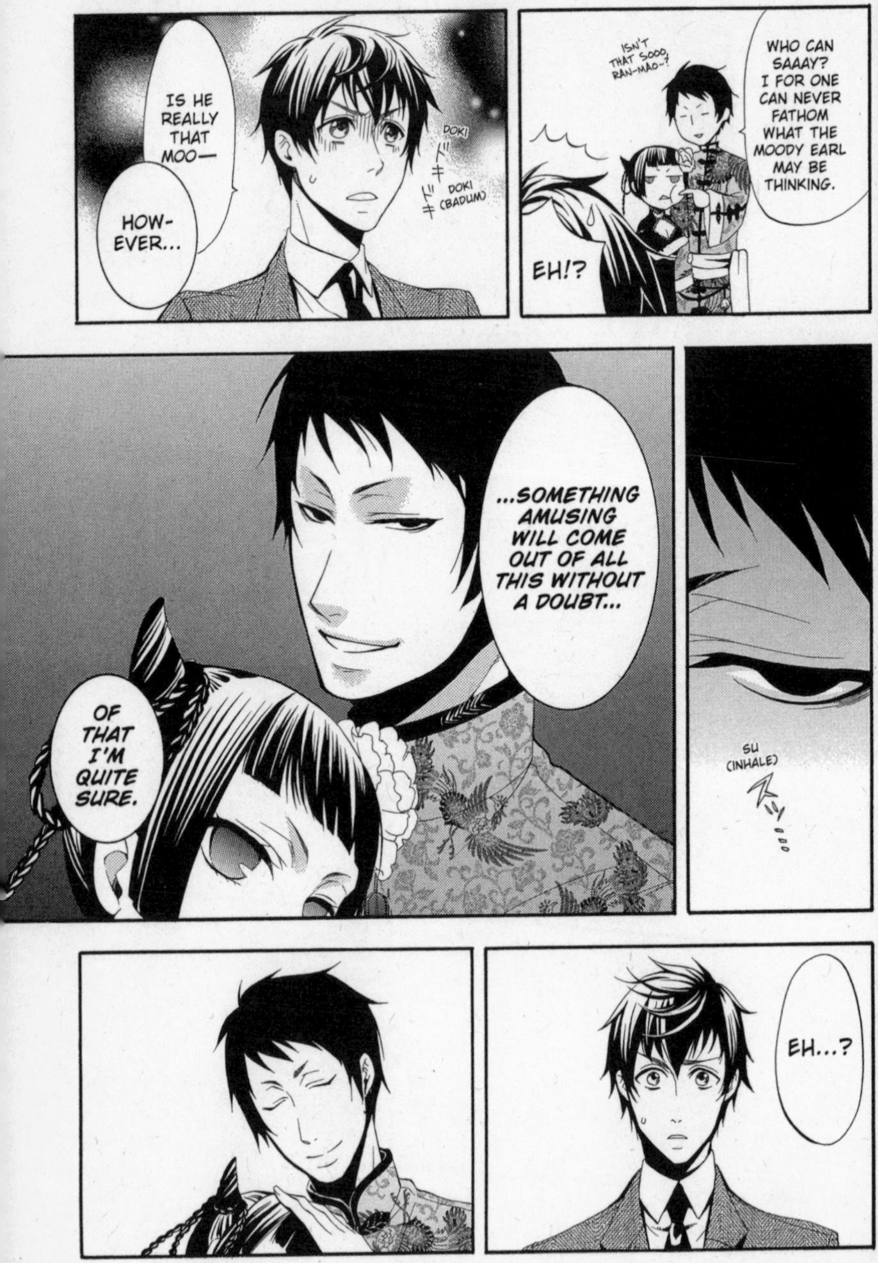
WHO CAN SAAAY? I FOR ONE CAN NEVER FATHOM WHAT THE MOODY EARL MAY BE THINKING.
ISN'T THAT SOOO, RAN-MAO~?
EH!?
IS HE REALLY THAT MOO—
HOW-EVER...
ドキ DOKI
ドキ DOKI (BADUM)
SU (INHALE)
...SOMETHING AMUSING WILL COME OUT OF ALL THIS WITHOUT A DOUBT...
OF THAT I'M QUITE SURE.
EH...?

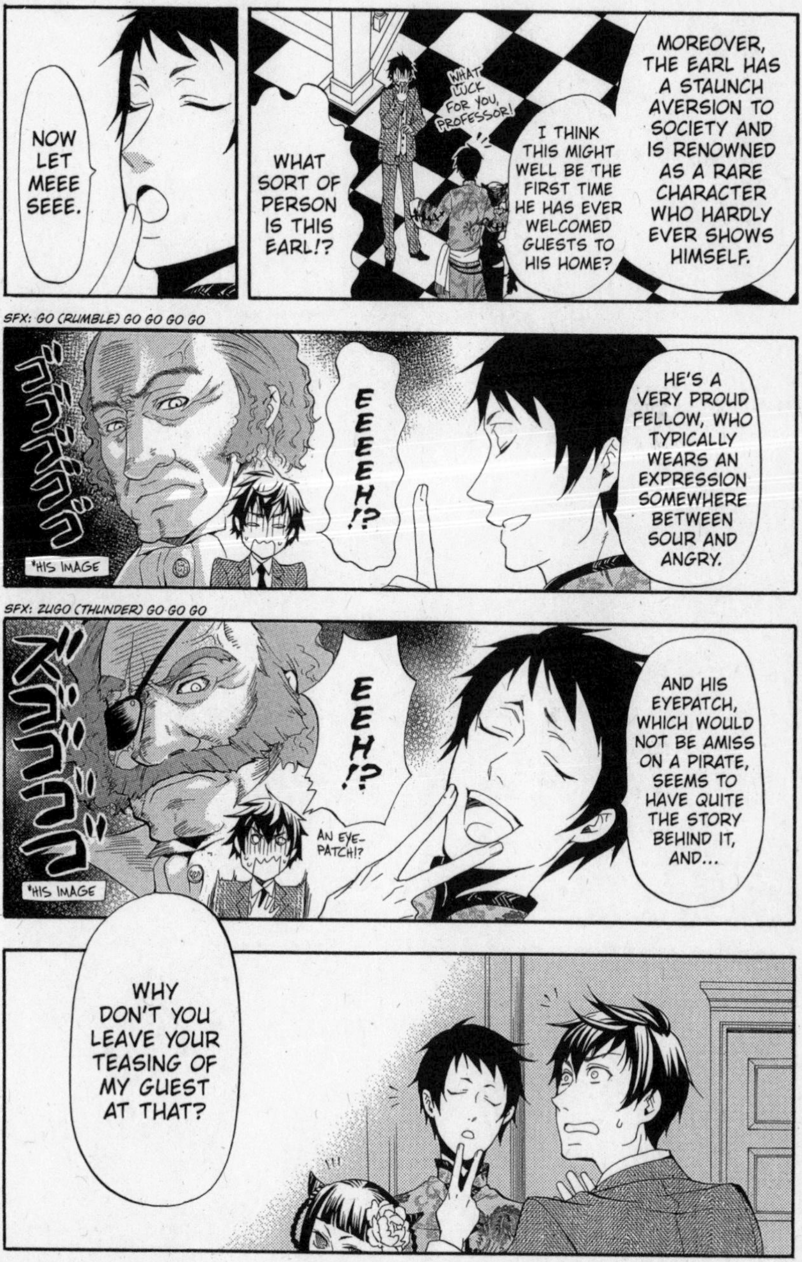
MOREOVER, THE EARL HAS A STAUNCH AVERSION TO SOCIETY AND IS RENOWNED AS A RARE CHARACTER WHO HARDLY EVER SHOWS HIMSELF.
I THINK THIS MIGHT WELL BE THE FIRST TIME HE HAS EVER WELCOMED GUESTS TO HIS HOME?
WHAT LUCK FOR YOU, PROFESSOR!
WHAT SORT OF PERSON IS THIS EARL!?
NOW LET MEEE SEEE.
SFX: GO (RUMBLE) GO GO GO GO
HE'S A VERY PROUD FELLOW, WHO TYPICALLY WEARS AN EXPRESSION SOMEWHERE BETWEEN SOUR AND ANGRY.
EEEEEH!?
*HIS IMAGE
SFX: ZUGO (THUNDER) GO GO GO
AND HIS EYEPATCH, WHICH WOULD NOT BE AMISS ON A PIRATE, SEEMS TO HAVE QUITE THE STORY BEHIND IT, AND...
EEEH!?
AN EYE-PATCH!?
*HIS IMAGE
WHY DON'T YOU LEAVE YOUR TEASING OF MY GUEST AT THAT?

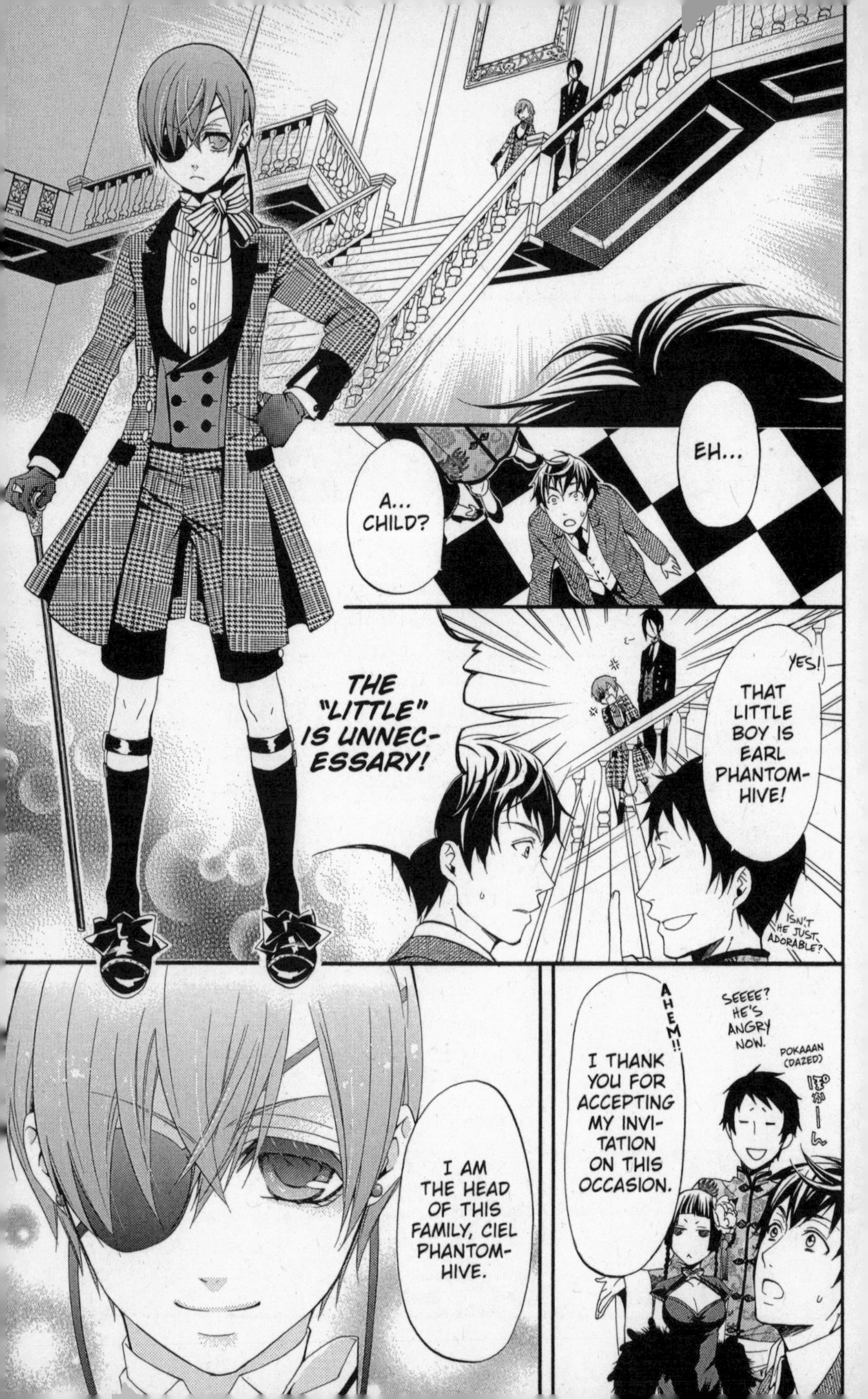
EH...
A... CHILD?
YES!
THAT LITTLE BOY IS EARL PHANTOMHIVE!
ISN'T HE JUST ADORABLE?
THE "LITTLE" IS UNNECESSARY!
POKAAAN (DAZED)
ぽかーん
SEEEE? HE'S ANGRY NOW.
AHEM!!
I THANK YOU FOR ACCEPTING MY INVITATION ON THIS OCCASION.
I AM THE HEAD OF THIS FAMILY, CIEL PHANTOMHIVE.

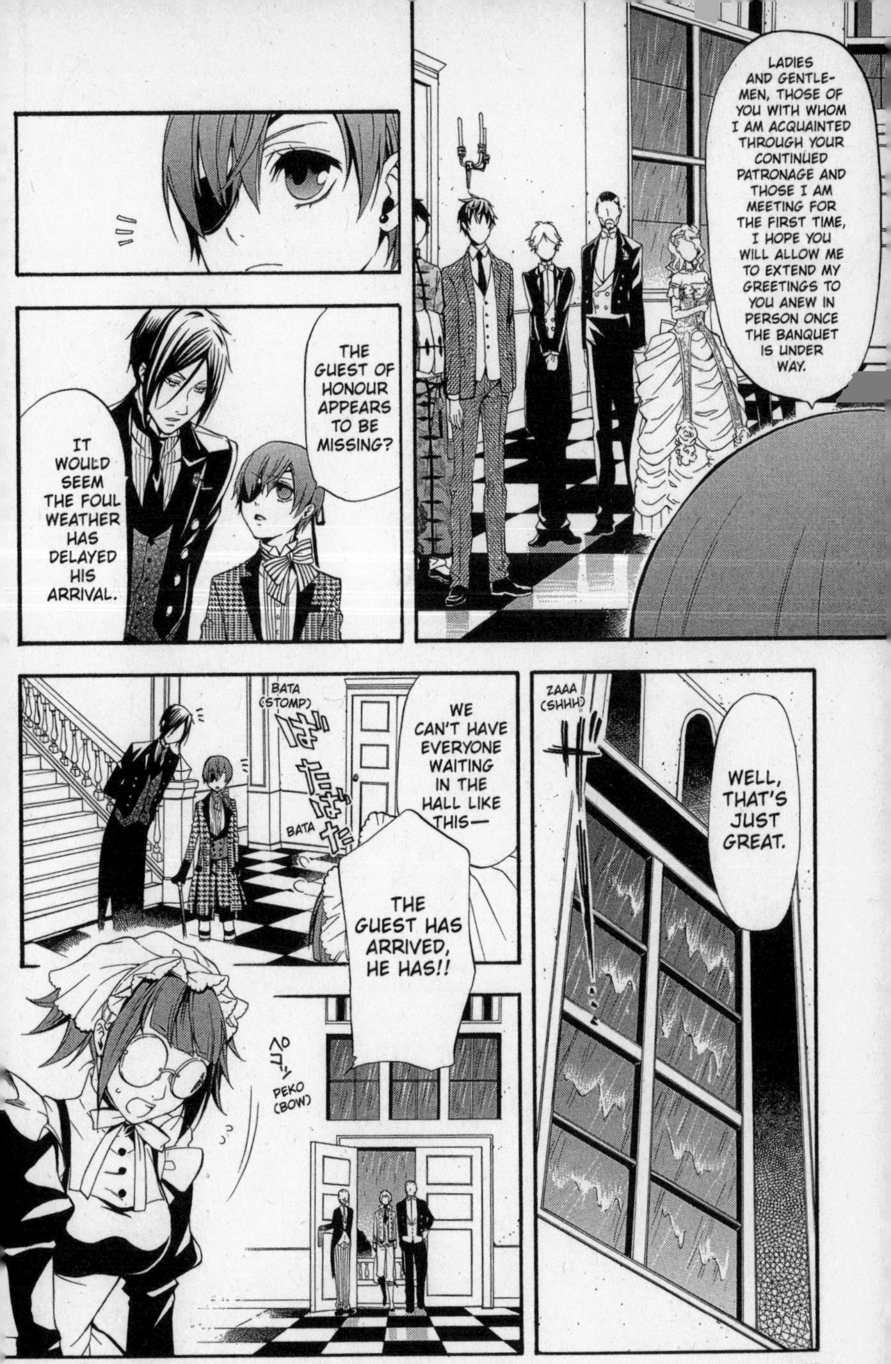

LADIES AND GENTLE-MEN, THOSE OF YOU WITH WHOM I AM ACQUAINTED THROUGH YOUR CONTINUED PATRONAGE AND THOSE I AM MEETING FOR THE FIRST TIME, I HOPE YOU WILL ALLOW ME TO EXTEND MY GREETINGS TO YOU ANEW IN PERSON ONCE THE BANQUET IS UNDER WAY.
THE GUEST OF HONOUR APPEARS TO BE MISSING?
IT WOULD SEEM THE FOUL WEATHER HAS DELAYED HIS ARRIVAL.
ZAAA (SHHH)
WELL, THAT'S JUST GREAT.
BATA (STOMP)
WE CAN'T HAVE EVERYONE WAITING IN THE HALL LIKE THIS—
BATA
THE GUEST HAS ARRIVED, HE HAS!!
PEKO (BOW)

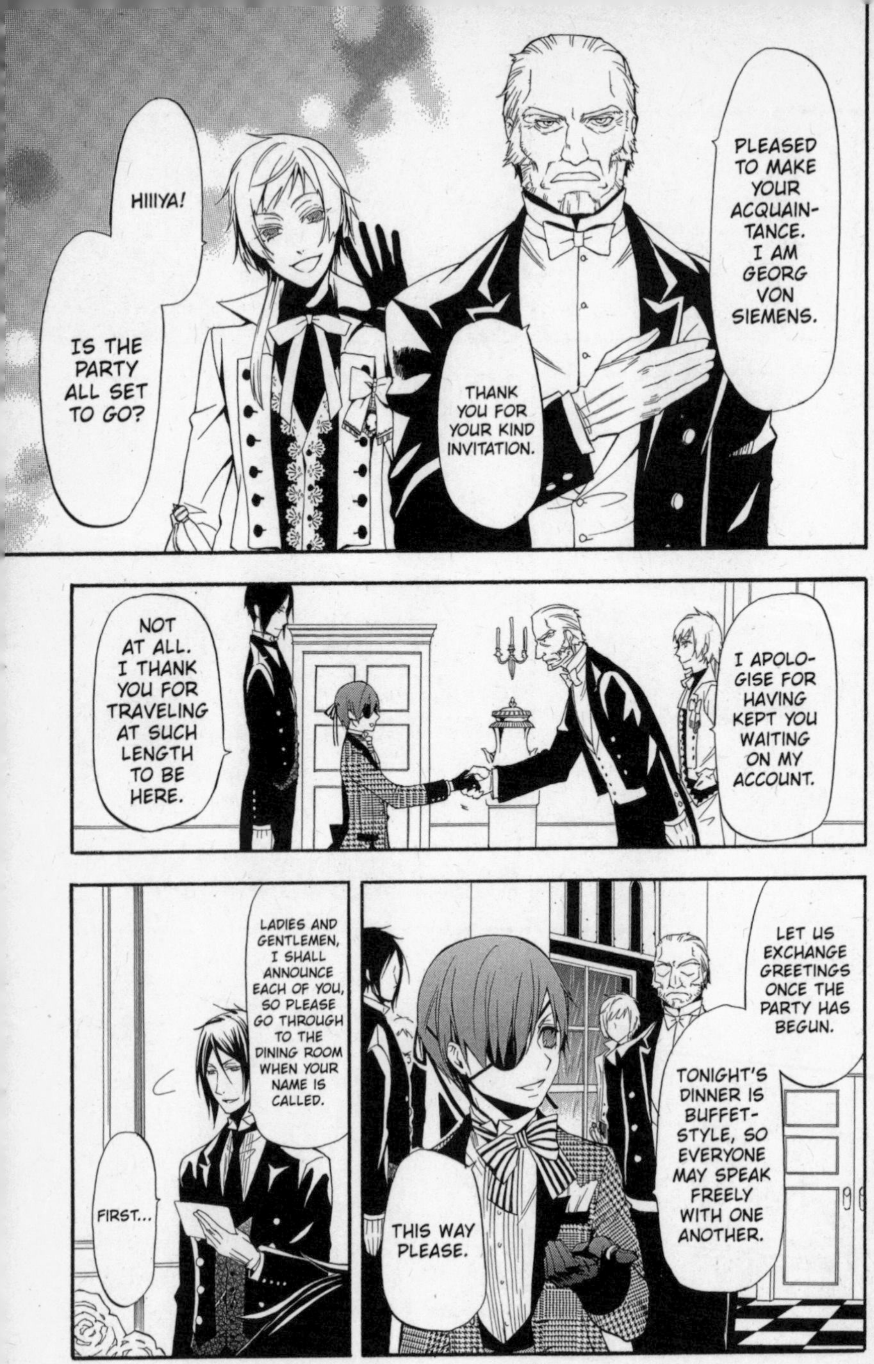
PLEASED TO MAKE YOUR ACQUAIN-TANCE. I AM GEORG VON SIEMENS.
THANK YOU FOR YOUR KIND INVITATION.
HIIIYA! IS THE PARTY ALL SET TO GO?
I APOLO-GISE FOR HAVING KEPT YOU WAITING ON MY ACCOUNT.
NOT AT ALL. I THANK YOU FOR TRAVELING AT SUCH LENGTH TO BE HERE.
LET US EXCHANGE GREETINGS ONCE THE PARTY HAS BEGUN.
TONIGHT'S DINNER IS BUFFET-STYLE, SO EVERYONE MAY SPEAK FREELY WITH ONE ANOTHER.
THIS WAY PLEASE.
LADIES AND GENTLEMEN, I SHALL ANNOUNCE EACH OF YOU, SO PLEASE GO THROUGH TO THE DINING ROOM WHEN YOUR NAME IS CALLED.
FIRST...

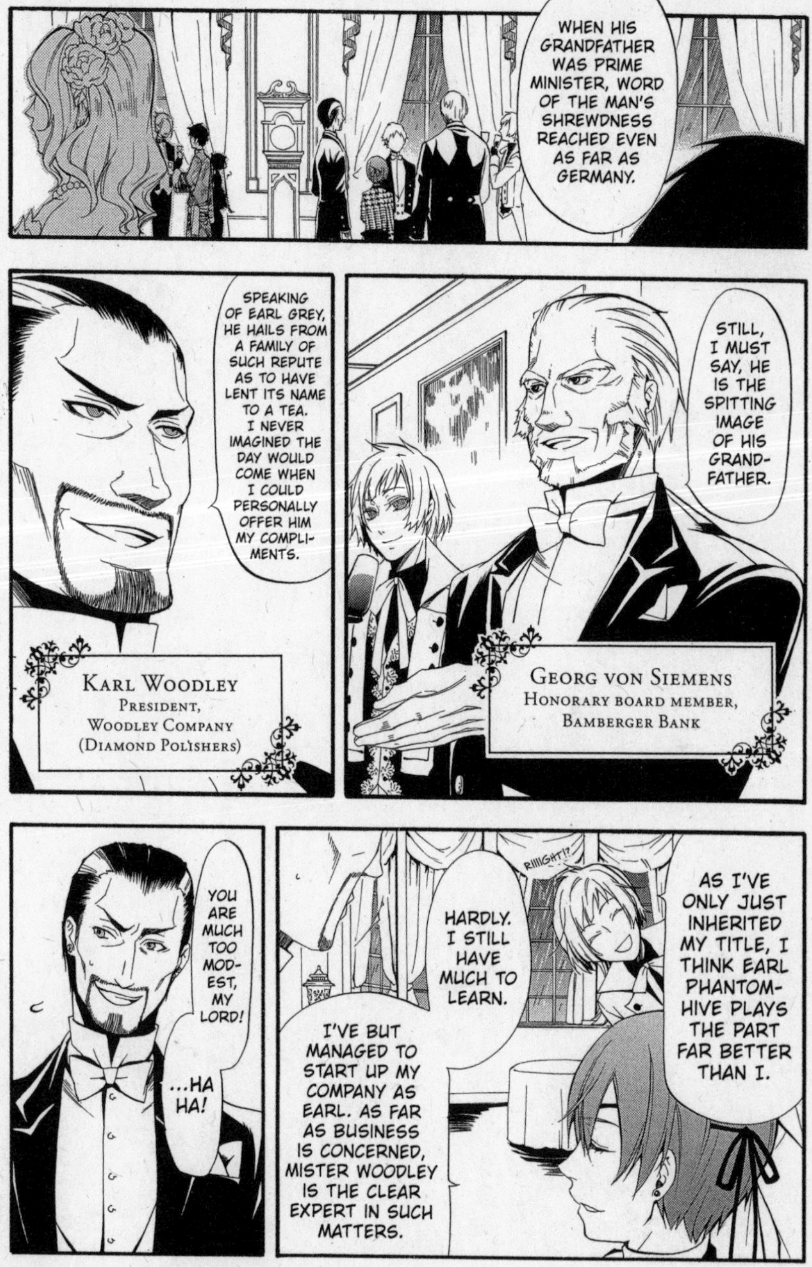
WHEN HIS GRANDFATHER WAS PRIME MINISTER, WORD OF THE MAN'S SHREWDNESS REACHED EVEN AS FAR AS GERMANY.
STILL, I MUST SAY, HE IS THE SPITTING IMAGE OF HIS GRAND-FATHER.
GEORG VON SIEMENS
HONORARY BOARD MEMBER, BAMBERGER BANK
SPEAKING OF EARL GREY, HE HAILS FROM A FAMILY OF SUCH REPUTE AS TO HAVE LENT ITS NAME TO A TEA. I NEVER IMAGINED THE DAY WOULD COME WHEN I COULD PERSONALLY OFFER HIM MY COMPLI-MENTS.
KARL WOODLEY
PRESIDENT, WOODLEY COMPANY (DIAMOND POLISHERS)
AS I'VE ONLY JUST INHERITED MY TITLE, I THINK EARL PHANTOM-HIVE PLAYS THE PART FAR BETTER THAN I.
RIIIGHT!?
HARDLY. I STILL HAVE MUCH TO LEARN.
I'VE BUT MANAGED TO START UP MY COMPANY AS EARL. AS FAR AS BUSINESS IS CONCERNED, MISTER WOODLEY IS THE CLEAR EXPERT IN SUCH MATTERS.
YOU ARE MUCH TOO MOD-EST, MY LORD!
...HA HA!

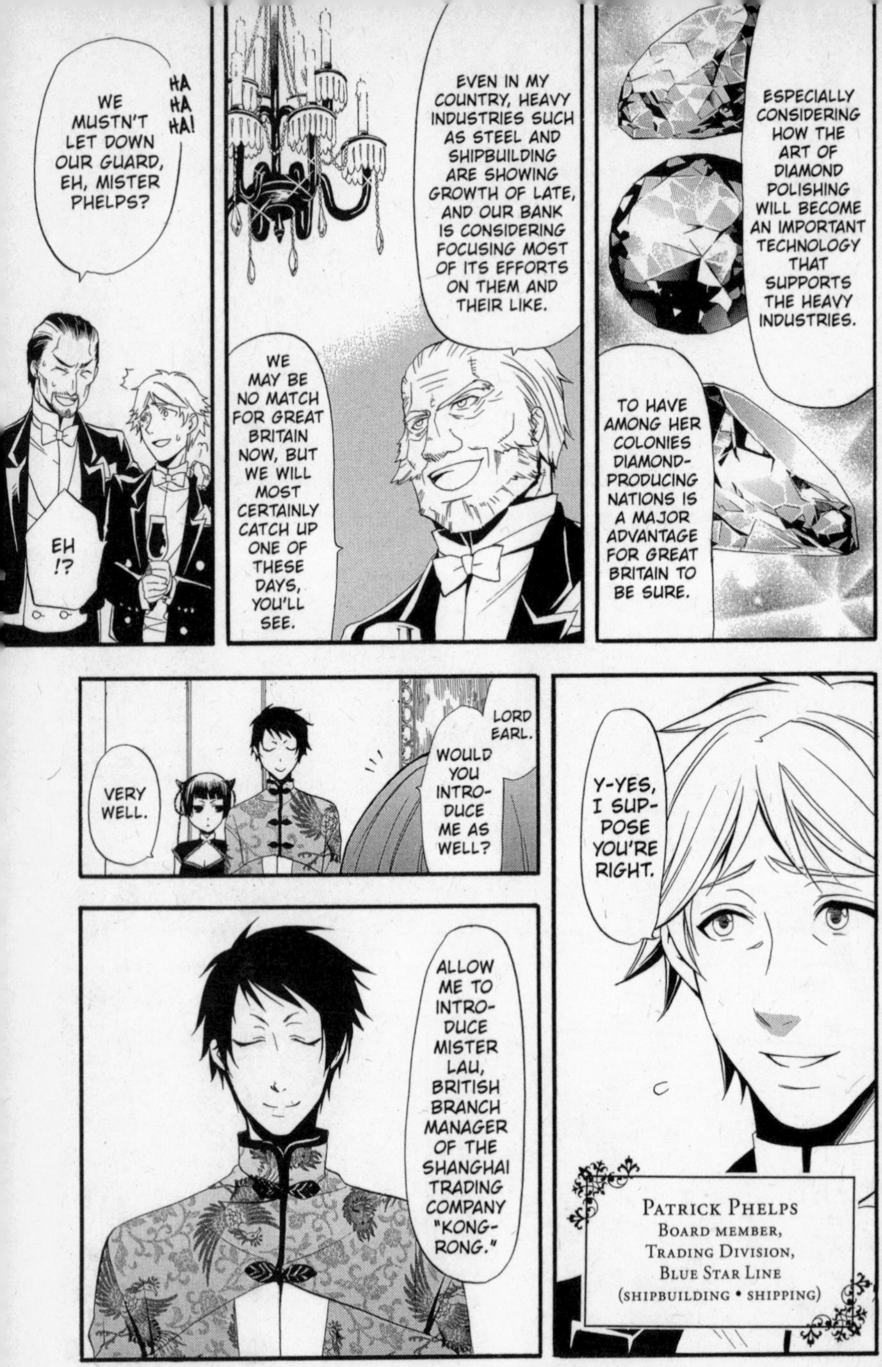
ESPECIALLY CONSIDERING HOW THE ART OF DIAMOND POLISHING WILL BECOME AN IMPORTANT TECHNOLOGY THAT SUPPORTS THE HEAVY INDUSTRIES.
TO HAVE AMONG HER COLONIES DIAMOND-PRODUCING NATIONS IS A MAJOR ADVANTAGE FOR GREAT BRITAIN TO BE SURE.
EVEN IN MY COUNTRY, HEAVY INDUSTRIES SUCH AS STEEL AND SHIPBUILDING ARE SHOWING GROWTH OF LATE, AND OUR BANK IS CONSIDERING FOCUSING MOST OF ITS EFFORTS ON THEM AND THEIR LIKE.
WE MAY BE NO MATCH FOR GREAT BRITAIN NOW, BUT WE WILL MOST CERTAINLY CATCH UP ONE OF THESE DAYS, YOU'LL SEE.
HA HA HA!
WE MUSTN'T LET DOWN OUR GUARD, EH, MISTER PHELPS?
EH!?
Y-YES, I SUPPOSE YOU'RE RIGHT.
PATRICK PHELPS
BOARD MEMBER, TRADING DIVISION, BLUE STAR LINE
(SHIPBUILDING • SHIPPING)
LORD EARL.
WOULD YOU INTRODUCE ME AS WELL?
VERY WELL.
ALLOW ME TO INTRODUCE MISTER LAU, BRITISH BRANCH MANAGER OF THE SHANGHAI TRADING COMPANY "KONG-RONG."

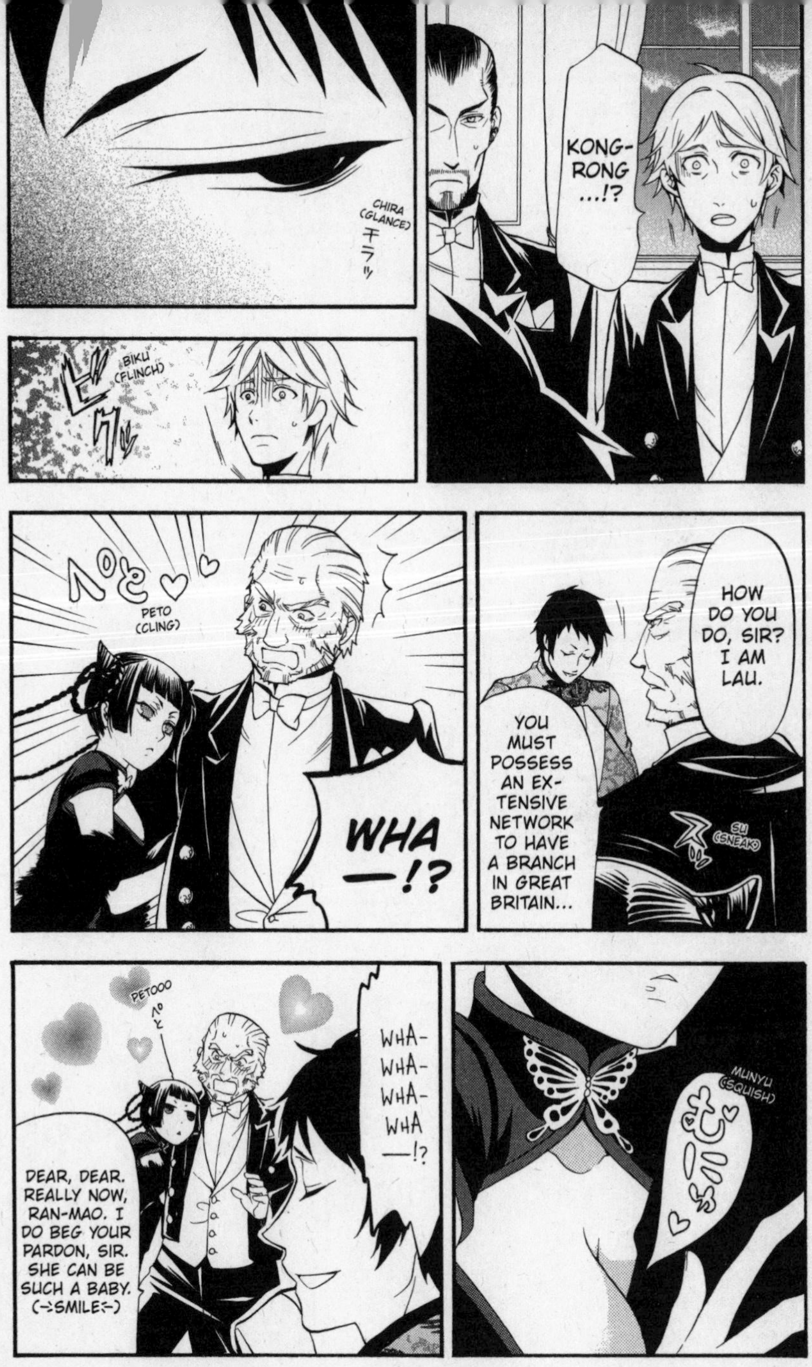

KONG-RONG ...!?
CHIRA (GLANCE)
チラッ
BIKU (FLINCH)
ビクッ
HOW DO YOU DO, SIR? I AM LAU.
YOU MUST POSSESS AN EXTENSIVE NETWORK TO HAVE A BRANCH IN GREAT BRITAIN...
SU (SNEAK)
PETO (CLING)
WHA—!?
MUNYU (SQUISH)
WHA-WHA-WHA-WHA—!?
PETOOO
DEAR, DEAR. REALLY NOW, RAN-MAO. I DO BEG YOUR PARDON, SIR. SHE CAN BE SUCH A BABY. (→SMILE←)

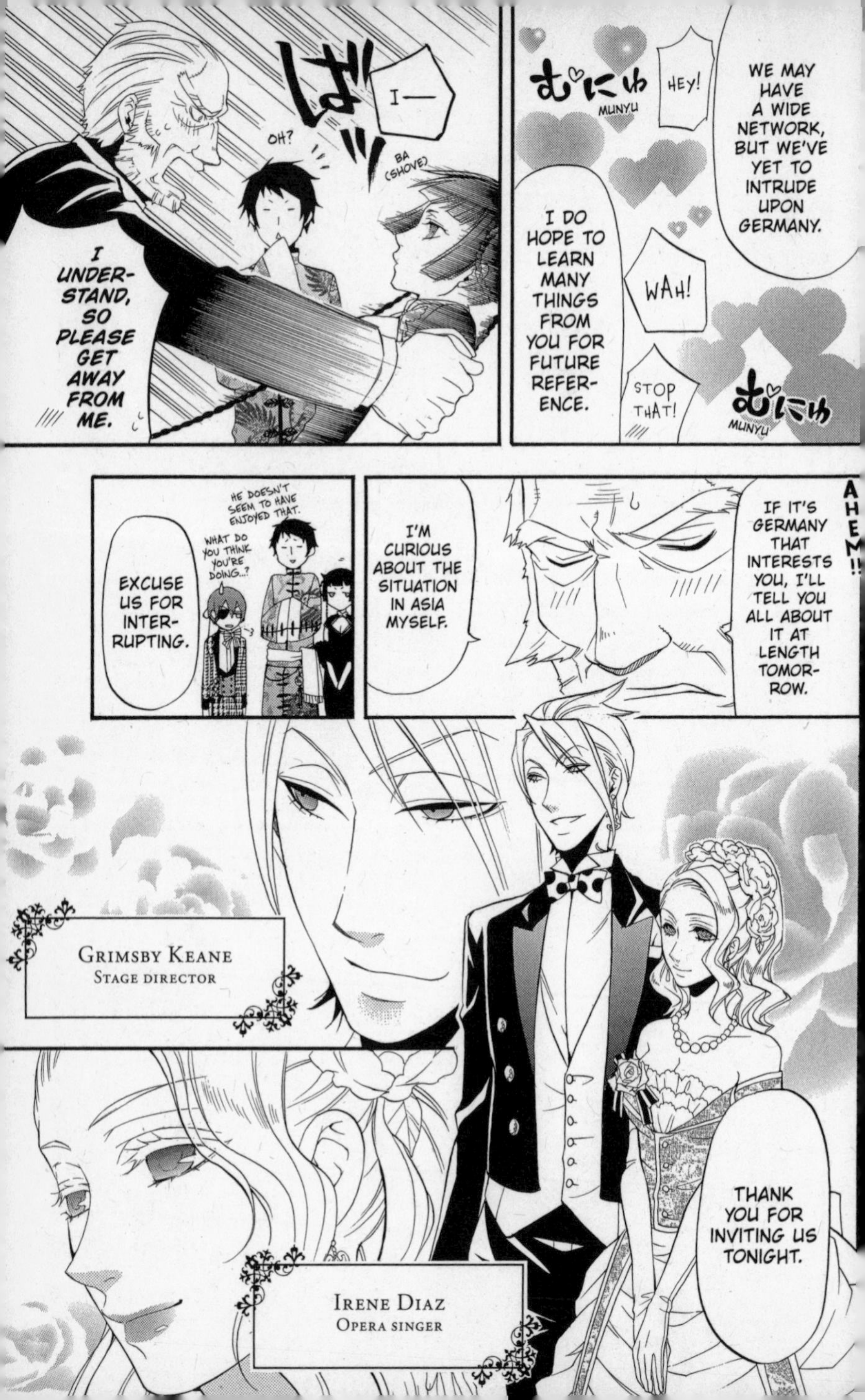
WE MAY HAVE A WIDE NETWORK, BUT WE'VE YET TO INTRUDE UPON GERMANY.
HEY!
むにゅ MUNYU
WAH!
むにゅ MUNYU
STOP THAT!
I DO HOPE TO LEARN MANY THINGS FROM YOU FOR FUTURE REFERENCE.
I—
ばッ BA (SHOVE)
OH?
I UNDERSTAND, SO PLEASE GET AWAY FROM ME.
AHEM!!
IF IT'S GERMANY THAT INTERESTS YOU, I'LL TELL YOU ALL ABOUT IT AT LENGTH TOMORROW.
I'M CURIOUS ABOUT THE SITUATION IN ASIA MYSELF.
HE DOESN'T SEEM TO HAVE ENJOYED THAT.
WHAT DO YOU THINK YOU'RE DOING...?
EXCUSE US FOR INTERRUPTING.
THANK YOU FOR INVITING US TONIGHT.
GRIMSBY KEANE
STAGE DIRECTOR
IRENE DIAZ
OPERA SINGER

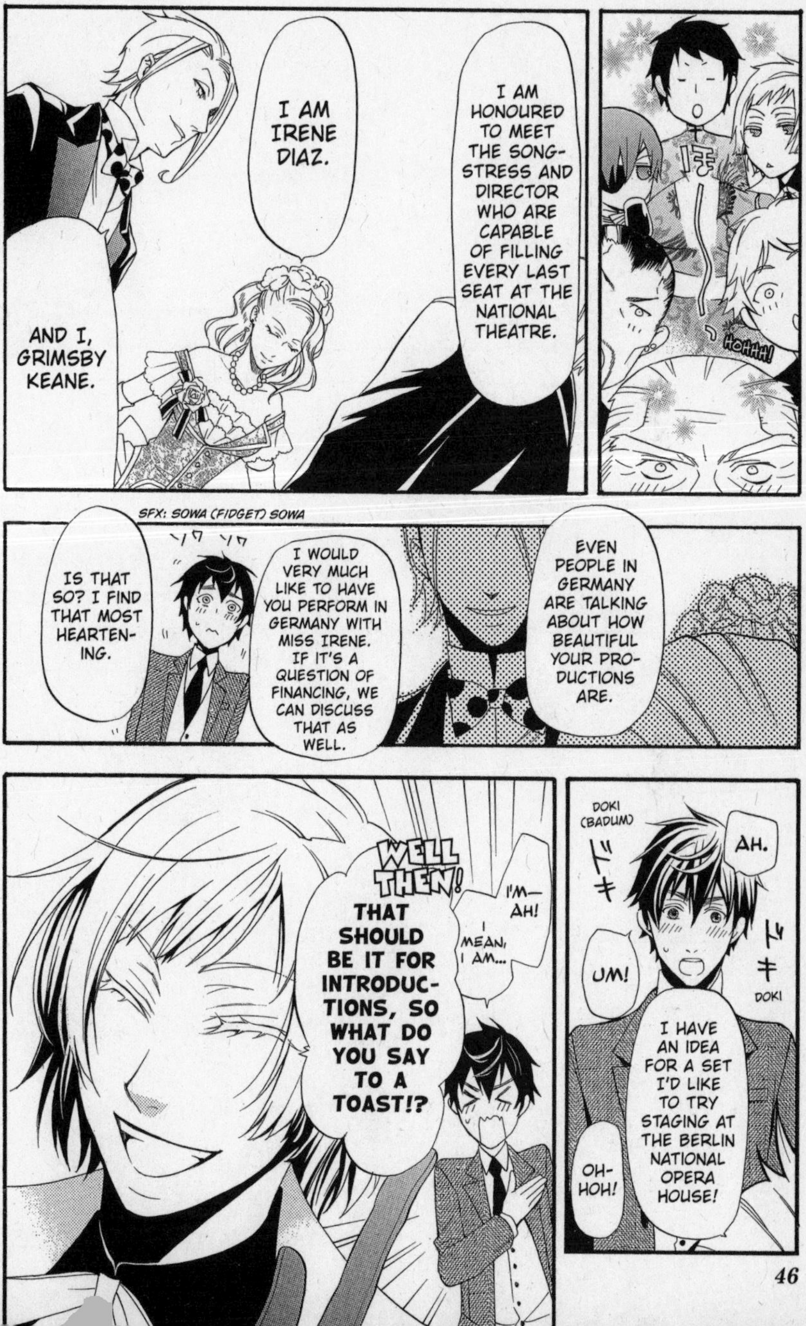
HOHHH!
I AM HONOURED TO MEET THE SONG-STRESS AND DIRECTOR WHO ARE CAPABLE OF FILLING EVERY LAST SEAT AT THE NATIONAL THEATRE.
I AM IRENE DIAZ.
AND I, GRIMSBY KEANE.
EVEN PEOPLE IN GERMANY ARE TALKING ABOUT HOW BEAUTIFUL YOUR PRO-DUCTIONS ARE.
I WOULD VERY MUCH LIKE TO HAVE YOU PERFORM IN GERMANY WITH MISS IRENE. IF IT'S A QUESTION OF FINANCING, WE CAN DISCUSS THAT AS WELL.
SFX: SOWA (FIDGET) SOWA
IS THAT SO? I FIND THAT MOST HEARTEN-ING.
DOKI (BADUM)
AH.
UM!
DOKI
I HAVE AN IDEA FOR A SET I'D LIKE TO TRY STAGING AT THE BERLIN NATIONAL OPERA HOUSE!
OH-HOH!
I'M—AH!
I MEAN, I AM...
WELL THEN! THAT SHOULD BE IT FOR INTRODUC-TIONS, SO WHAT DO YOU SAY TO A TOAST!?

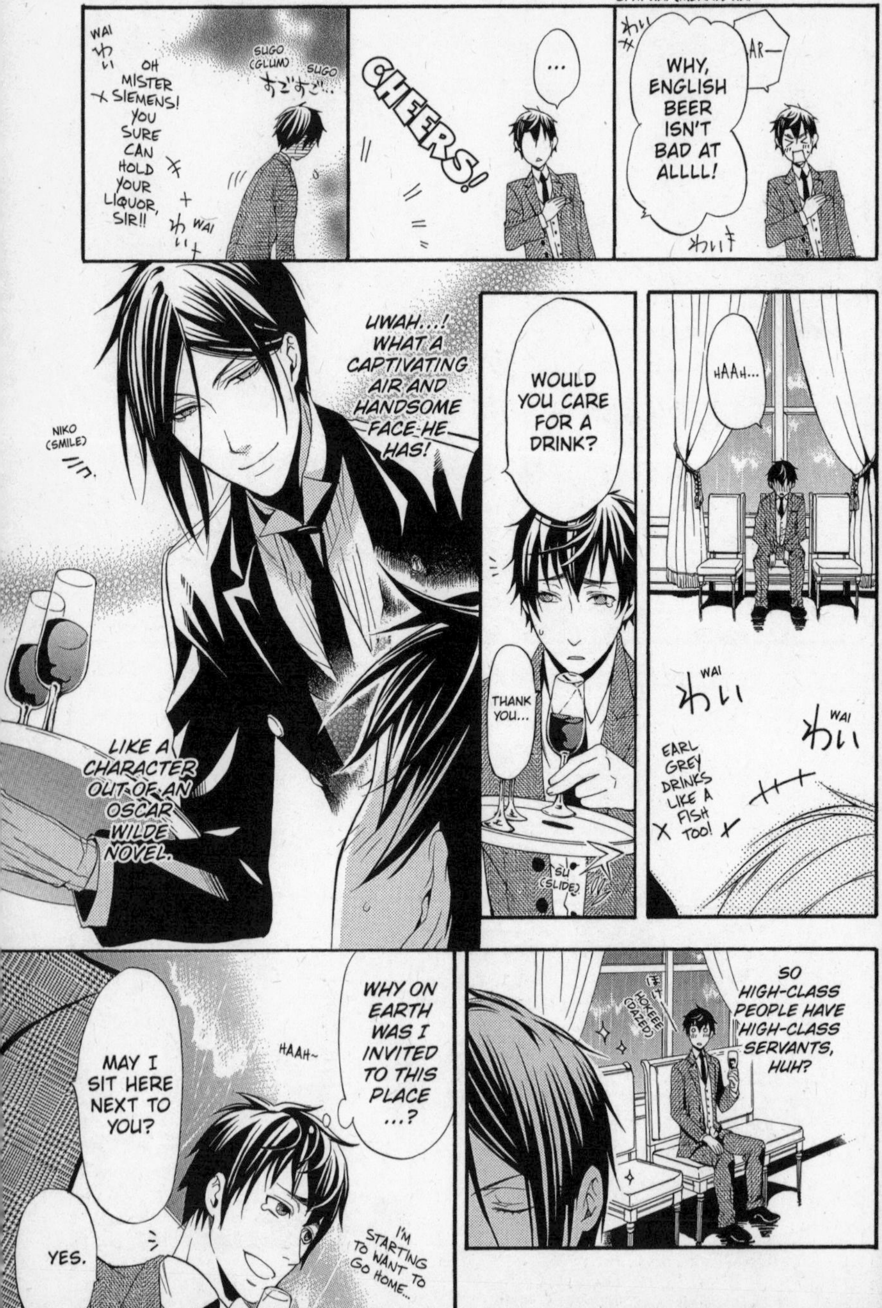
SFX: WAI (MERRY) WAI
AR—
WHY, ENGLISH BEER ISN'T BAD AT ALLLL!
...
CHEERS!
SUGO (GLUM) SUGO
WAI
OH MISTER SIEMENS! YOU SURE CAN HOLD YOUR LIQUOR, SIR!!
WAI
HAAH...
WAI
WAI
EARL GREY DRINKS LIKE A FISH TOO!
WOULD YOU CARE FOR A DRINK?
THANK YOU...
SU (SLIDE)
UWAH...! WHAT A CAPTIVATING AIR AND HANDSOME FACE HE HAS!
NIKO (SMILE)
LIKE A CHARACTER OUT OF AN OSCAR WILDE NOVEL.
SO HIGH-CLASS PEOPLE HAVE HIGH-CLASS SERVANTS, HUH?
HOKEEE (DAZED)
WHY ON EARTH WAS I INVITED TO THIS PLACE ...?
HAAH~
MAY I SIT HERE NEXT TO YOU?
YES.
I'M STARTING TO WANT TO GO HOME...

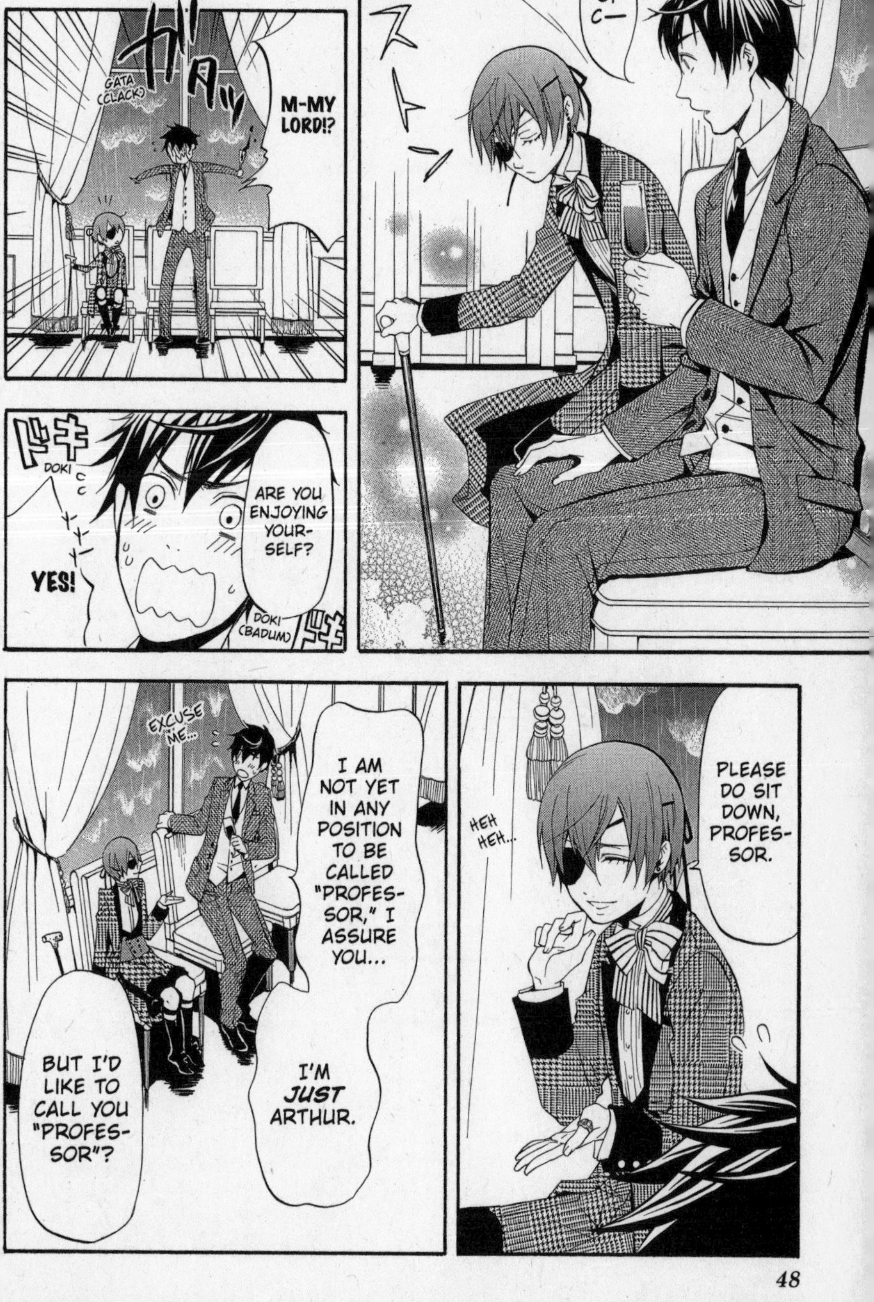

OF C—
SUTON (TUMP)
M-MY LORD!?
GATA (CLACK)
ARE YOU ENJOYING YOURSELF?
DOKI
YES!
DOKI (BADUM)
PLEASE DO SIT DOWN, PROFESSOR.
HEH HEH...
EXCUSE ME...
I AM NOT YET IN ANY POSITION TO BE CALLED "PROFESSOR," I ASSURE YOU...
I'M *JUST* ARTHUR.
BUT I'D LIKE TO CALL YOU "PROFESSOR"?

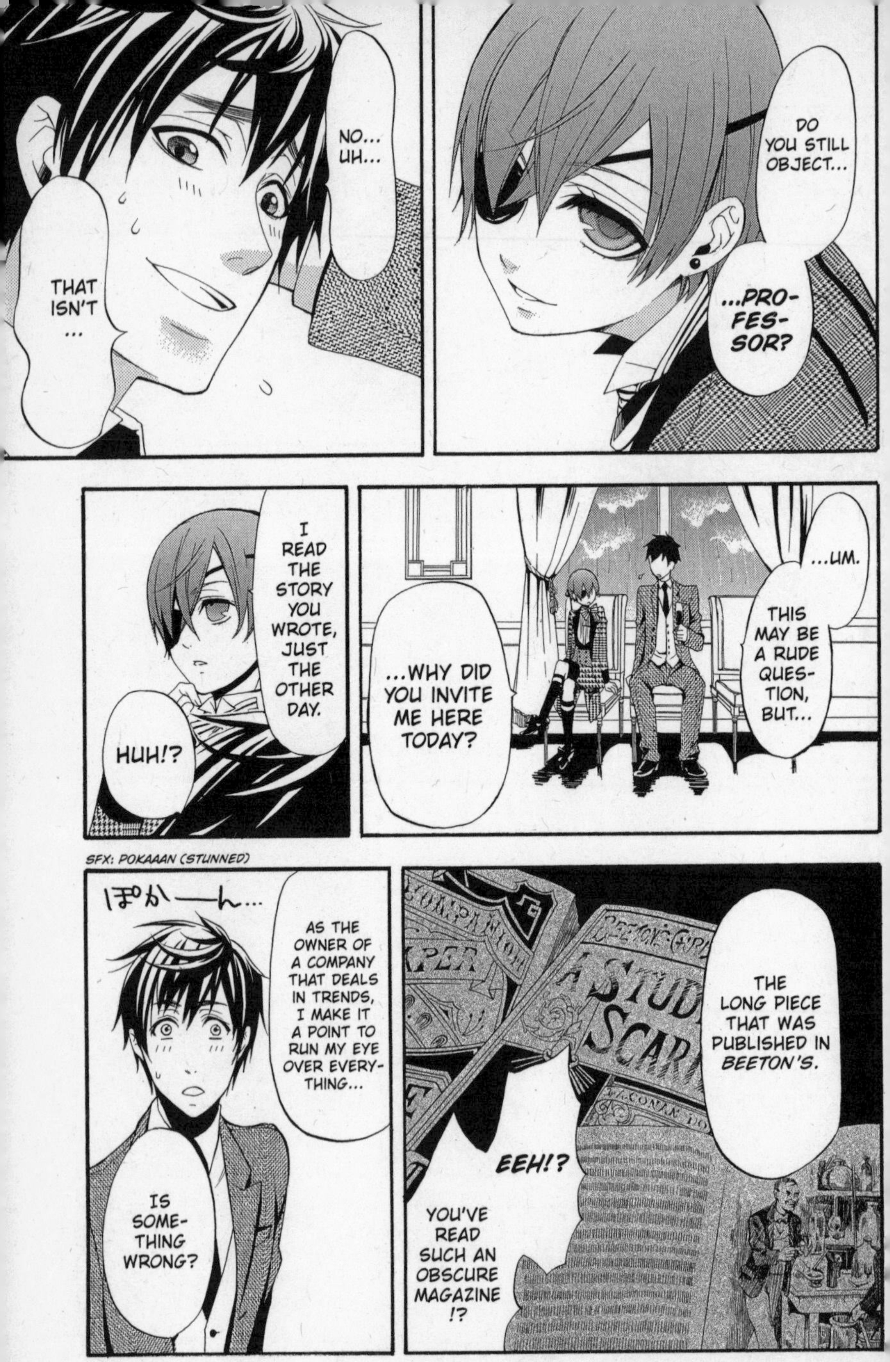
DO YOU STILL OBJECT...
...PRO-FES-SOR?
NO... UH...
THAT ISN'T ...
...UM.
THIS MAY BE A RUDE QUES-TION, BUT...
...WHY DID YOU INVITE ME HERE TODAY?
I READ THE STORY YOU WROTE, JUST THE OTHER DAY.
HUH!?
SFX: POKAAAN (STUNNED)
THE LONG PIECE THAT WAS PUBLISHED IN *BEETON'S.*
EEH!?
YOU'VE READ SUCH AN OBSCURE MAGAZINE !?
ぽかーん…
AS THE OWNER OF A COMPANY THAT DEALS IN TRENDS, I MAKE IT A POINT TO RUN MY EYE OVER EVERY-THING...
IS SOME-THING WRONG?

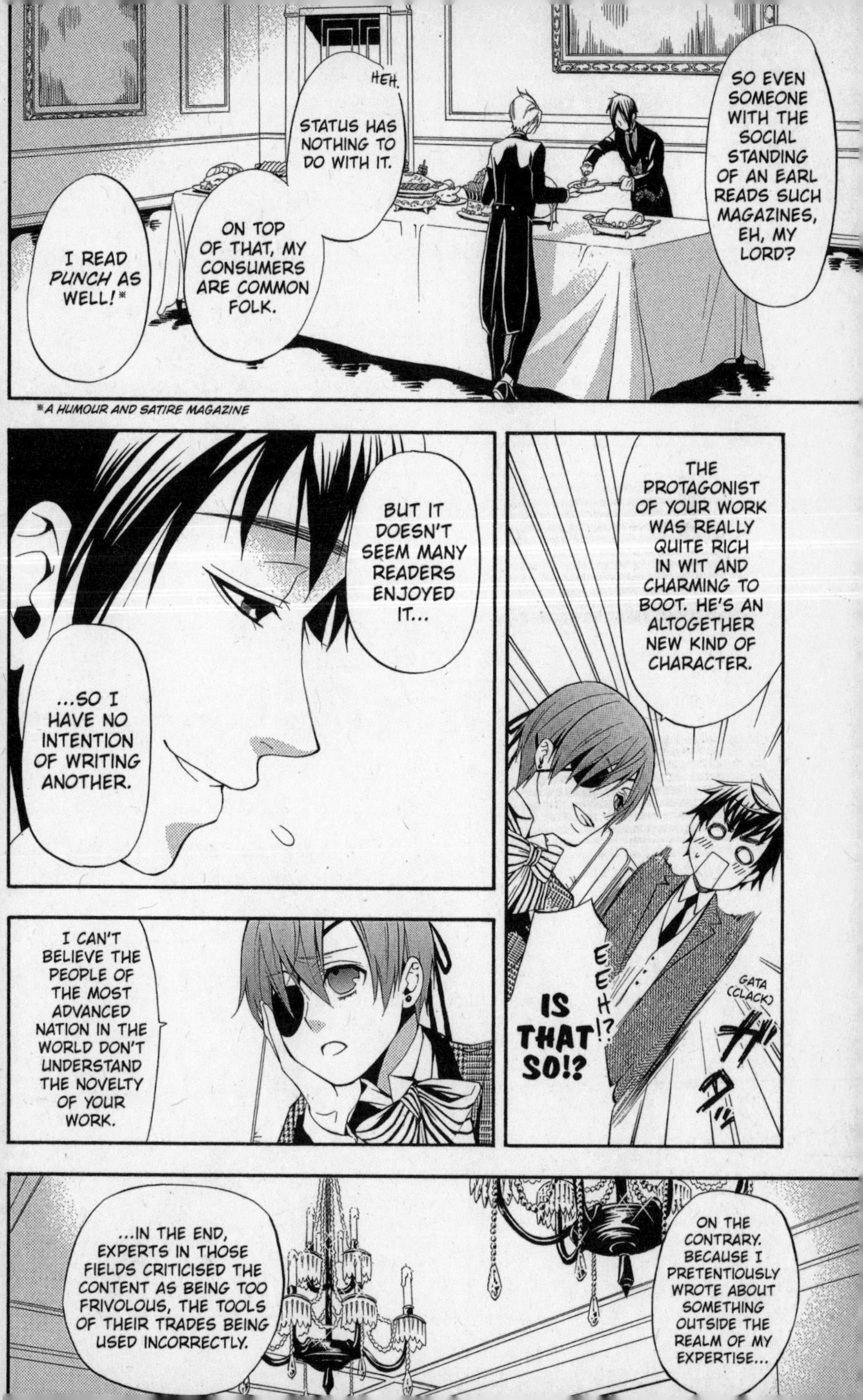
SO EVEN SOMEONE WITH THE SOCIAL STANDING OF AN EARL READS SUCH MAGAZINES, EH, MY LORD?
HEH.
STATUS HAS NOTHING TO DO WITH IT.
ON TOP OF THAT, MY CONSUMERS ARE COMMON FOLK.
I READ *PUNCH* AS WELL!*
*A HUMOUR AND SATIRE MAGAZINE
THE PROTAGONIST OF YOUR WORK WAS REALLY QUITE RICH IN WIT AND CHARMING TO BOOT. HE'S AN ALTOGETHER NEW KIND OF CHARACTER.
EEH!?
IS THAT SO!?
GATA (CLACK)
BUT IT DOESN'T SEEM MANY READERS ENJOYED IT...
...SO I HAVE NO INTENTION OF WRITING ANOTHER.
I CAN'T BELIEVE THE PEOPLE OF THE MOST ADVANCED NATION IN THE WORLD DON'T UNDERSTAND THE NOVELTY OF YOUR WORK.
ON THE CONTRARY. BECAUSE I PRETENTIOUSLY WROTE ABOUT SOMETHING OUTSIDE THE REALM OF MY EXPERTISE...
...IN THE END, EXPERTS IN THOSE FIELDS CRITICISED THE CONTENT AS BEING TOO FRIVOLOUS, THE TOOLS OF THEIR TRADES BEING USED INCORRECTLY.

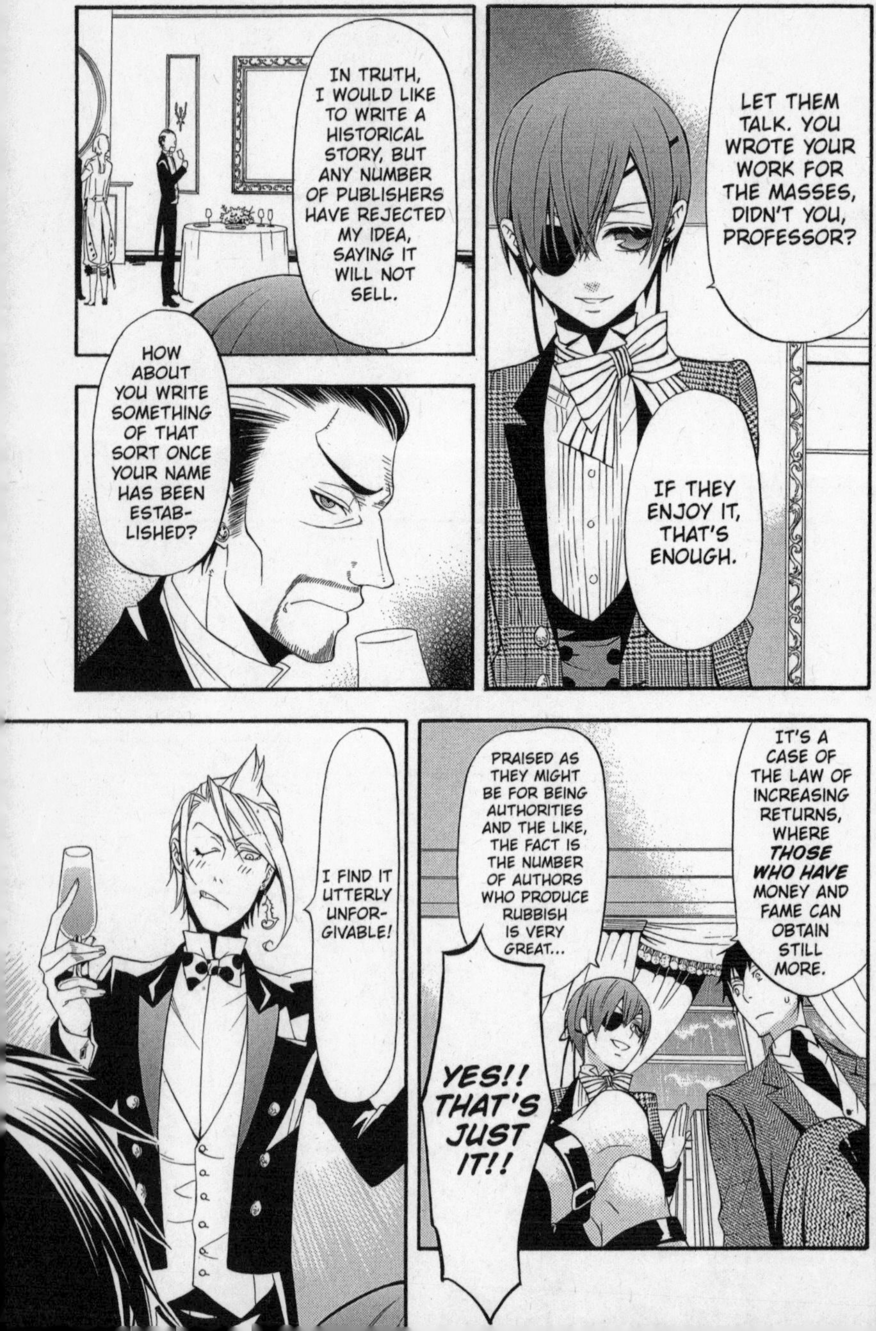
LET THEM TALK. YOU WROTE YOUR WORK FOR THE MASSES, DIDN'T YOU, PROFESSOR?
IF THEY ENJOY IT, THAT'S ENOUGH.
IN TRUTH, I WOULD LIKE TO WRITE A HISTORICAL STORY, BUT ANY NUMBER OF PUBLISHERS HAVE REJECTED MY IDEA, SAYING IT WILL NOT SELL.
HOW ABOUT YOU WRITE SOMETHING OF THAT SORT ONCE YOUR NAME HAS BEEN ESTAB-LISHED?
IT'S A CASE OF THE LAW OF INCREASING RETURNS, WHERE ***THOSE WHO HAVE*** MONEY AND FAME CAN OBTAIN STILL MORE.
PRAISED AS THEY MIGHT BE FOR BEING AUTHORITIES AND THE LIKE, THE FACT IS THE NUMBER OF AUTHORS WHO PRODUCE RUBBISH IS VERY GREAT...
YES!! THAT'S JUST IT!!
I FIND IT UTTERLY UNFOR-GIVABLE!

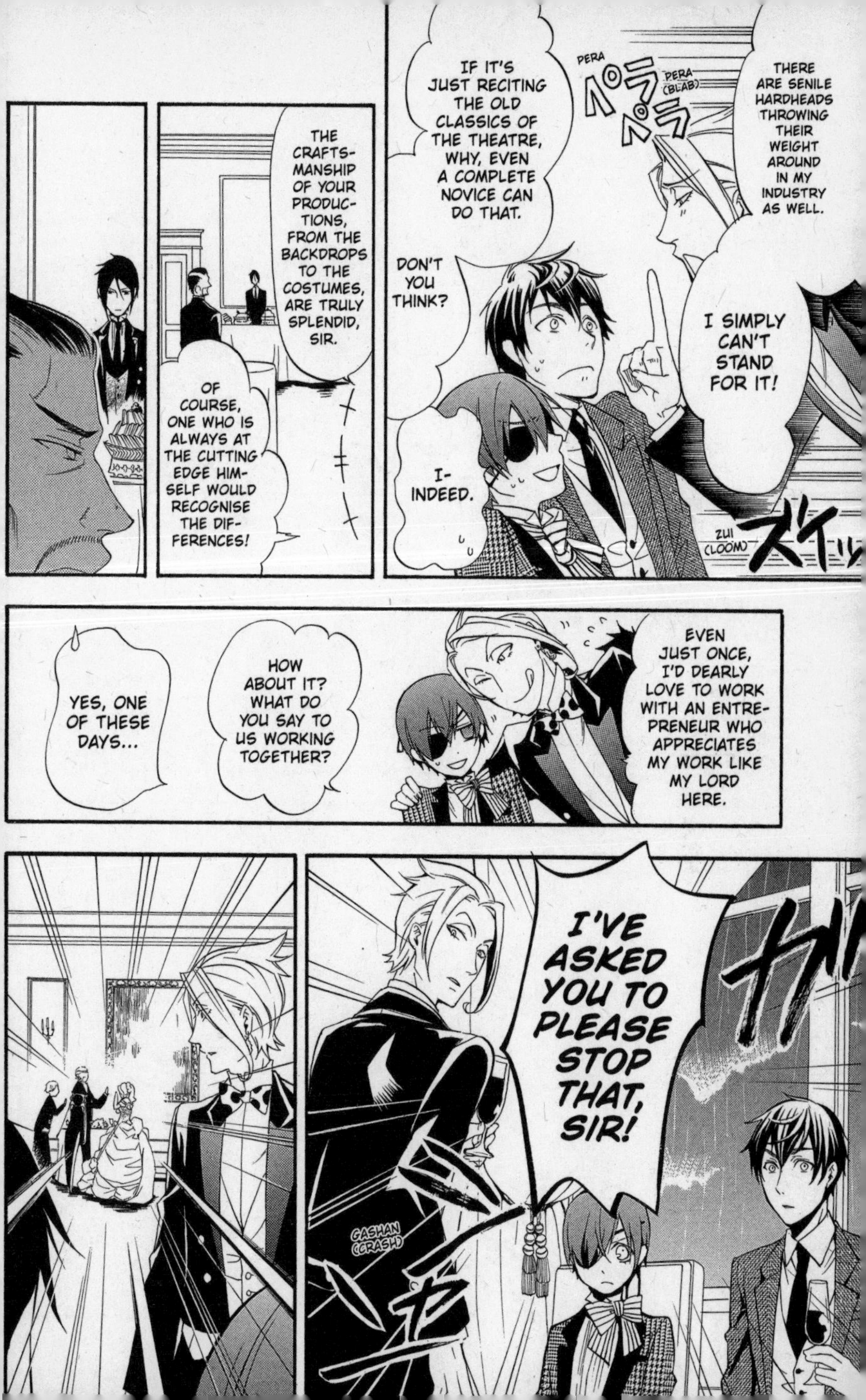
THERE ARE SENILE HARDHEADS THROWING THEIR WEIGHT AROUND IN MY INDUSTRY AS WELL.
PERA PERA (BLAB)
IF IT'S JUST RECITING THE OLD CLASSICS OF THE THEATRE, WHY, EVEN A COMPLETE NOVICE CAN DO THAT.
I SIMPLY CAN'T STAND FOR IT!
DON'T YOU THINK?
I- INDEED.
ZUI (LOOM)
THE CRAFTSMANSHIP OF YOUR PRODUCTIONS, FROM THE BACKDROPS TO THE COSTUMES, ARE TRULY SPLENDID, SIR.
OF COURSE, ONE WHO IS ALWAYS AT THE CUTTING EDGE HIMSELF WOULD RECOGNISE THE DIFFERENCES!
EVEN JUST ONCE, I'D DEARLY LOVE TO WORK WITH AN ENTREPRENEUR WHO APPRECIATES MY WORK LIKE MY LORD HERE.
HOW ABOUT IT? WHAT DO YOU SAY TO US WORKING TOGETHER?
YES, ONE OF THESE DAYS...
I'VE ASKED YOU TO PLEASE STOP THAT, SIR!
GASHAN (CRASH)

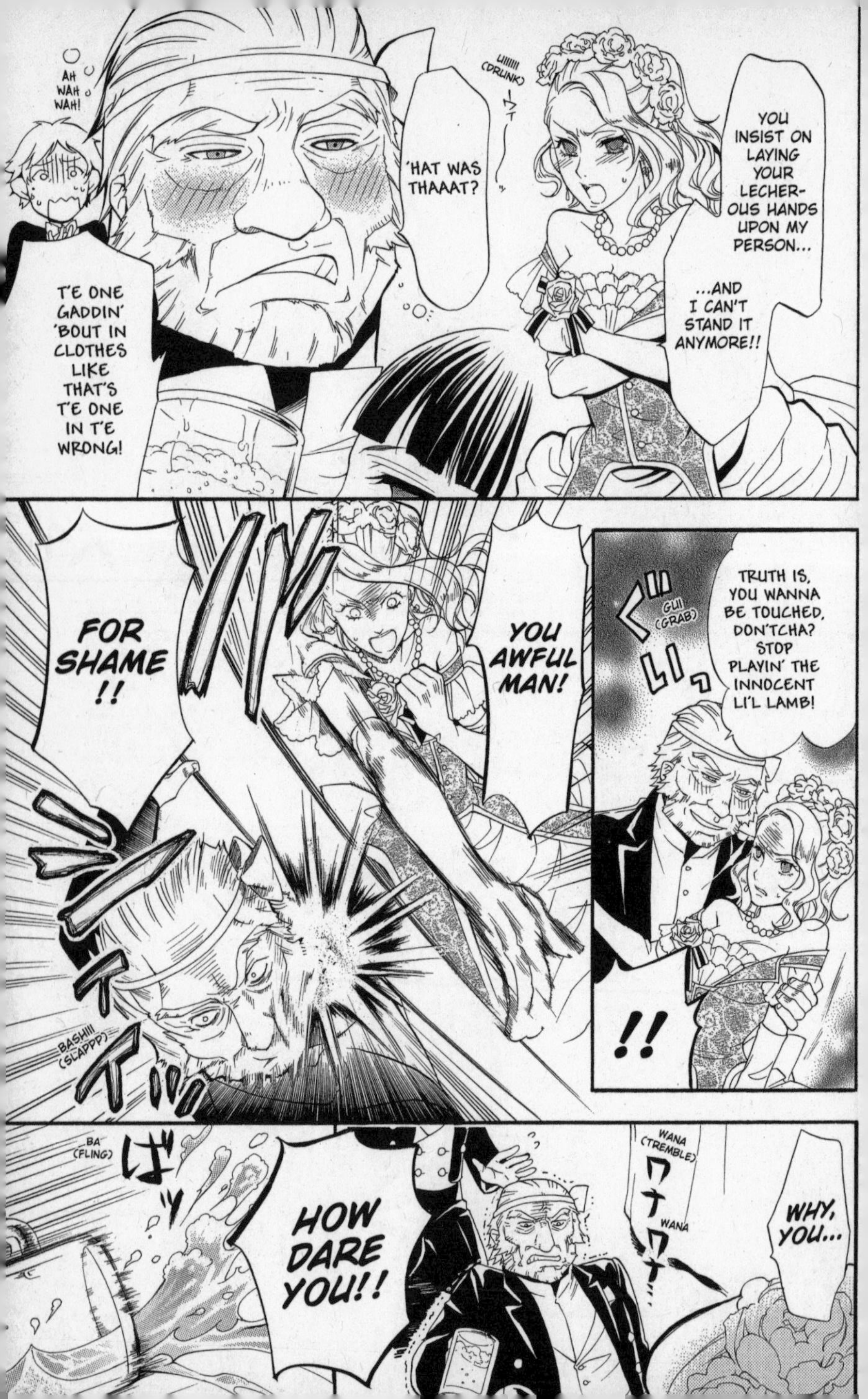
YOU INSIST ON LAYING YOUR LECHER-OUS HANDS UPON MY PERSON...
...AND I CAN'T STAND IT ANYMORE!!
UI!!!!! (DRUNK)
'HAT WAS THAAAT?
AH WAH WAH!
T'E ONE GADDIN' 'BOUT IN CLOTHES LIKE THAT'S T'E ONE IN T'E WRONG!
TRUTH IS, YOU WANNA BE TOUCHED, DON'TCHA? STOP PLAYIN' THE INNOCENT LI'L LAMB!
GUI (GRAB)
!!
YOU AWFUL MAN!
FOR SHAME!!
BASHIII (SLAPPP)
WHY, YOU...
WANA (TREMBLE)
WANA
HOW DARE YOU!!
BA (FLING)

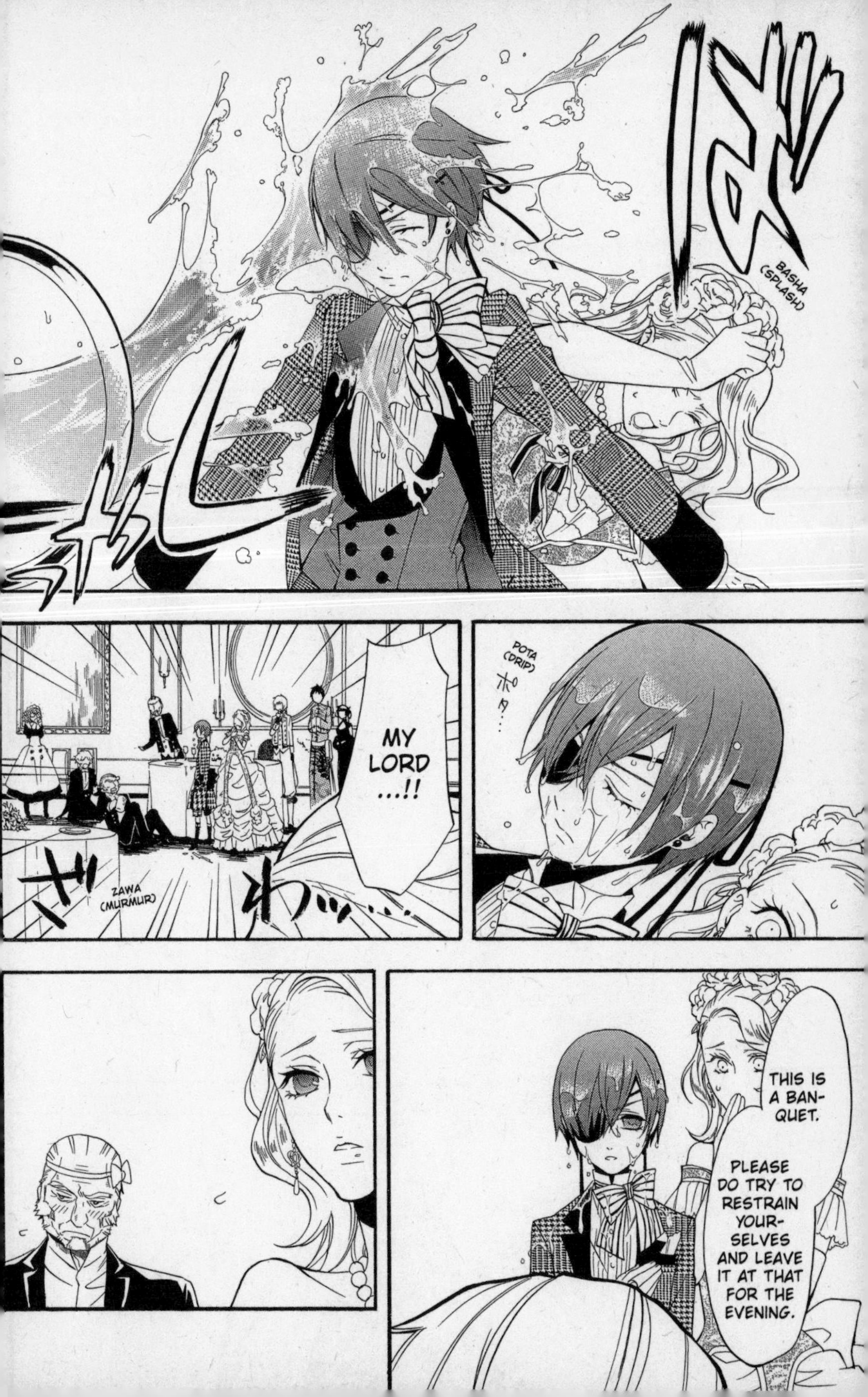
BASHA (SPLASH)
POTA (DRIP)
MY LORD ...!!
ZAWA (MURMUR)
THIS IS A BAN-QUET.
PLEASE DO TRY TO RESTRAIN YOUR-SELVES AND LEAVE IT AT THAT FOR THE EVENING.

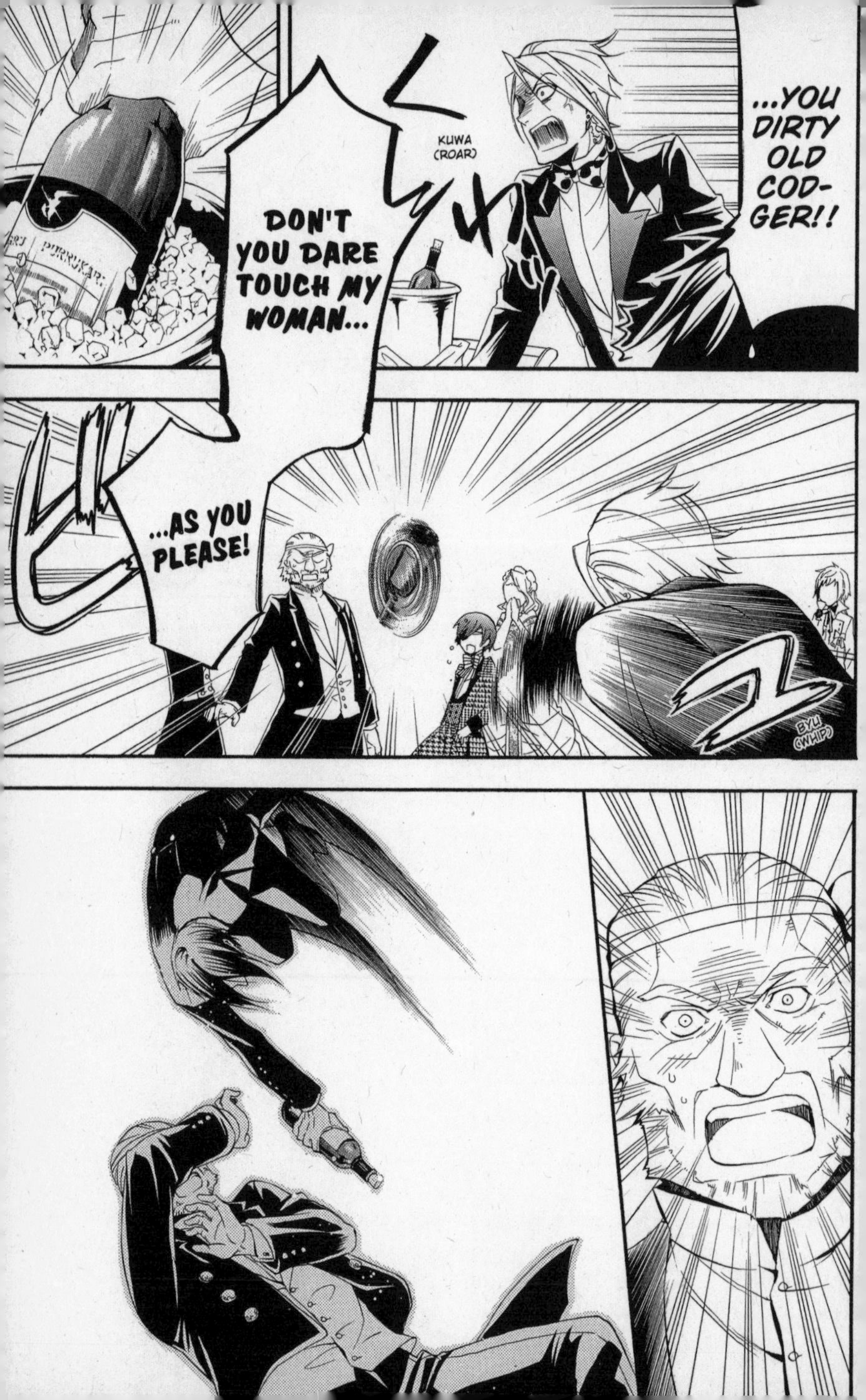
...YOU DIRTY OLD CODGER!!
KUWA (ROAR)
DON'T YOU DARE TOUCH MY WOMAN...
BYU (WHIP)
...AS YOU PLEASE!

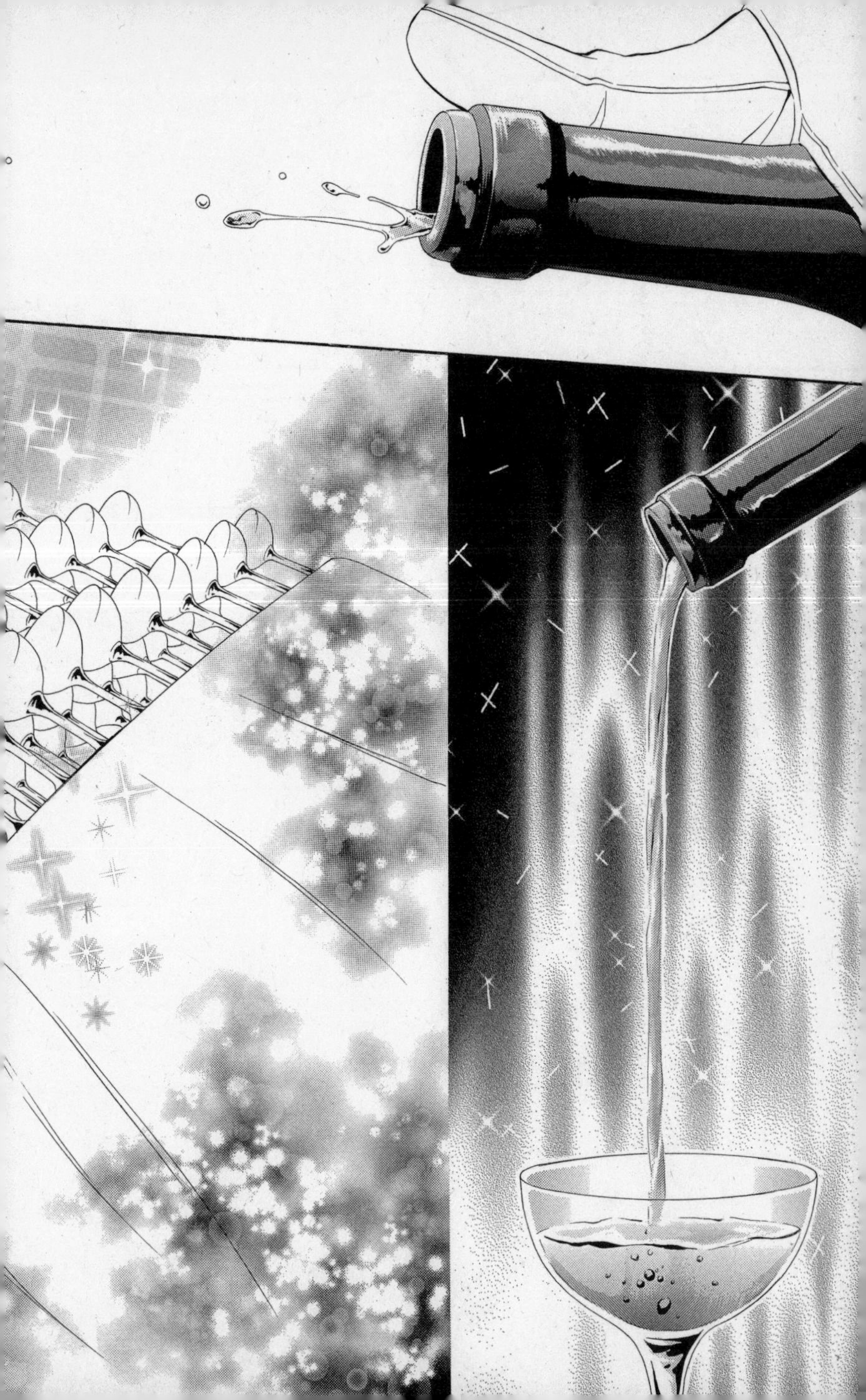

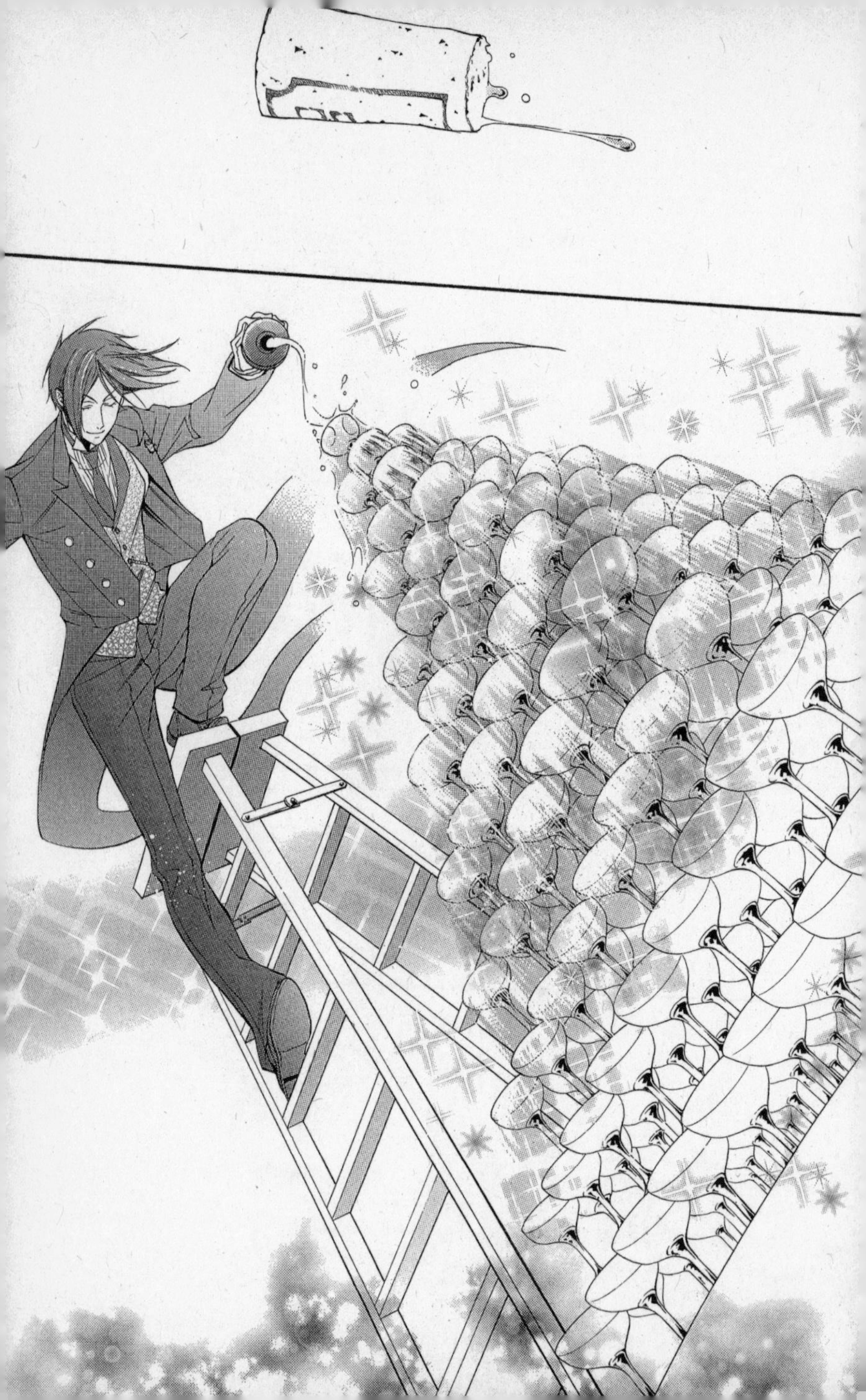

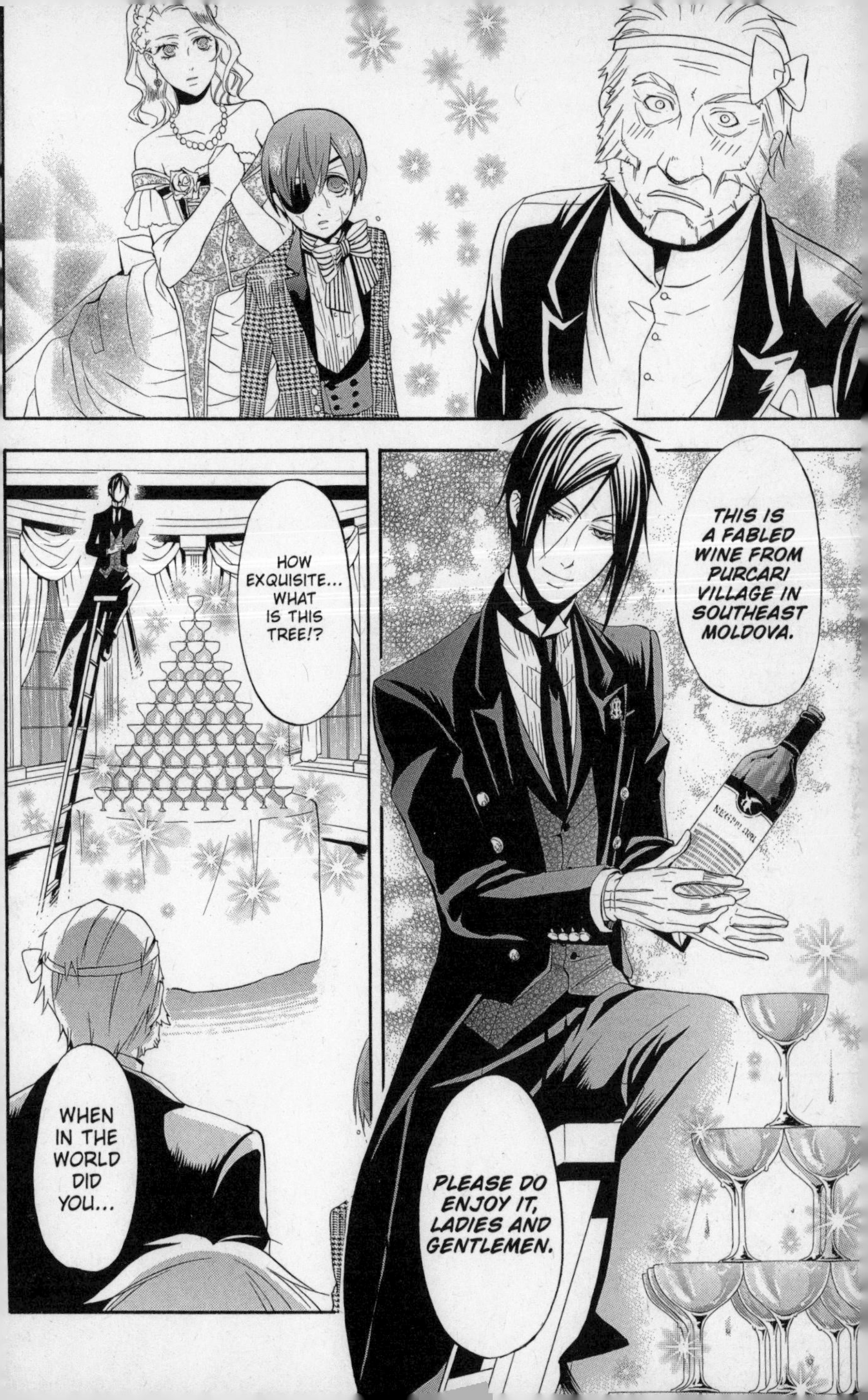
THIS IS A FABLED WINE FROM PURCARI VILLAGE IN SOUTHEAST MOLDOVA.
PLEASE DO ENJOY IT, LADIES AND GENTLEMEN.
HOW EXQUISITE... WHAT IS THIS TREE!?
WHEN IN THE WORLD DID YOU...

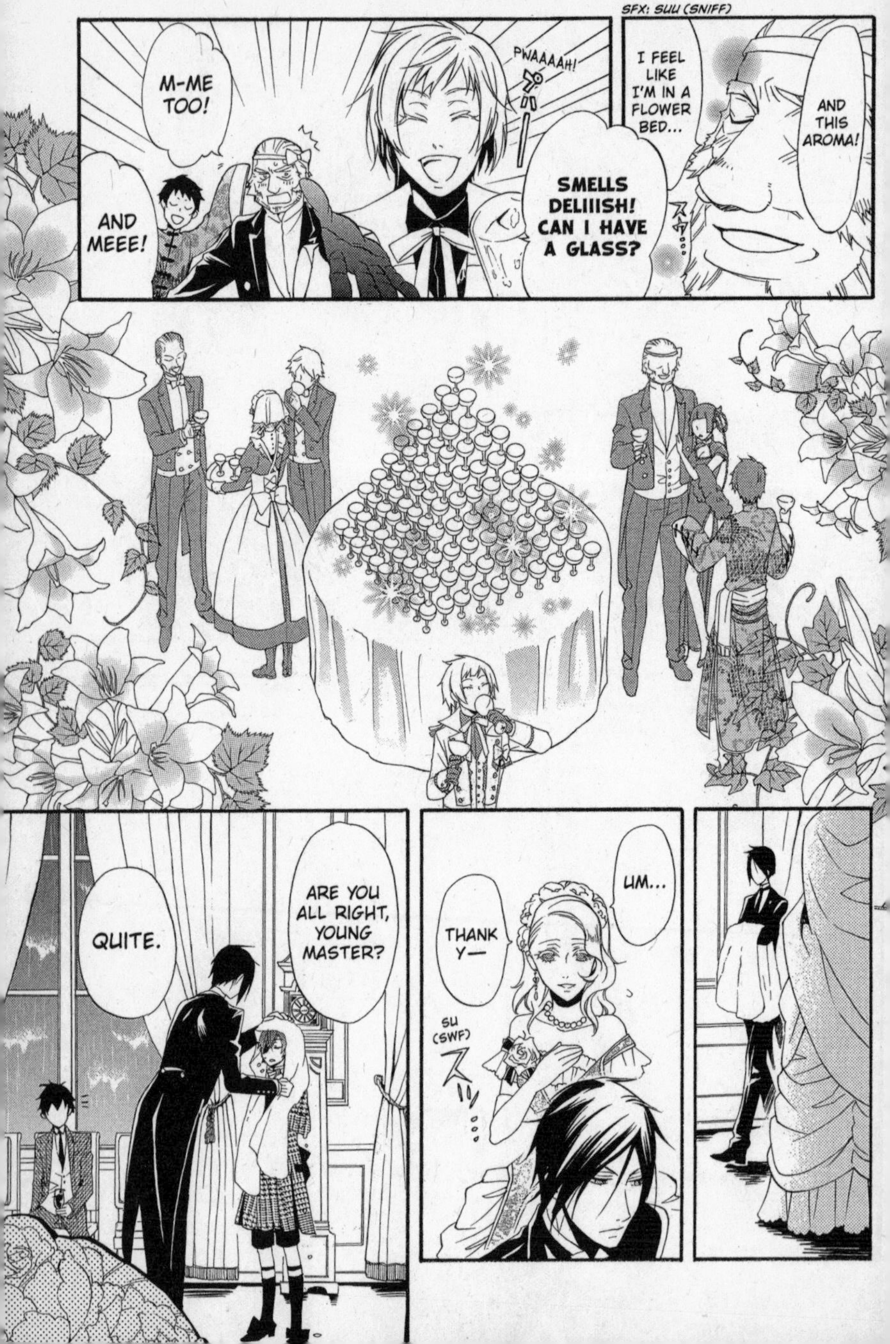
SFX: SUU (SNIFF)
AND THIS AROMA!
I FEEL LIKE I'M IN A FLOWER BED...
PWAAAAH!
SMELLS DELIIISH! CAN I HAVE A GLASS?
M-ME TOO!
AND MEEE!
UM...
THANK Y—
SU (SWF)
ARE YOU ALL RIGHT, YOUNG MASTER?
QUITE.

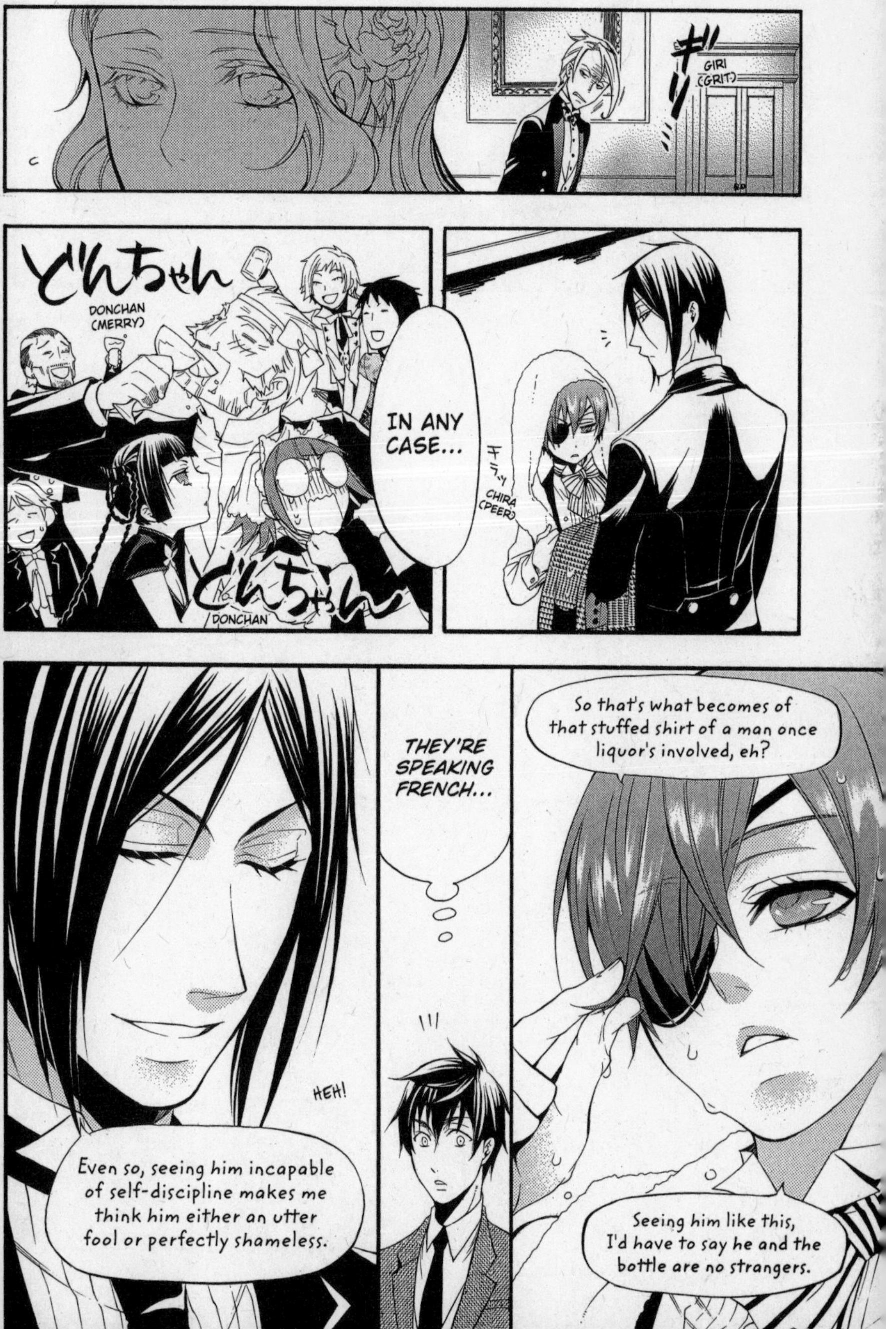
ギリ
GIRI (GRIT)
チラッ
CHIRA (PEER)
どんちゃん
DONCHAN (MERRY)
IN ANY CASE...
どんちゃん
DONCHAN
So that's what becomes of that stuffed shirt of a man once liquor's involved, eh?
Seeing him like this, I'd have to say he and the bottle are no strangers.
THEY'RE SPEAKING FRENCH...
HEH!
Even so, seeing him incapable of self-discipline makes me think him either an utter fool or perfectly shameless.

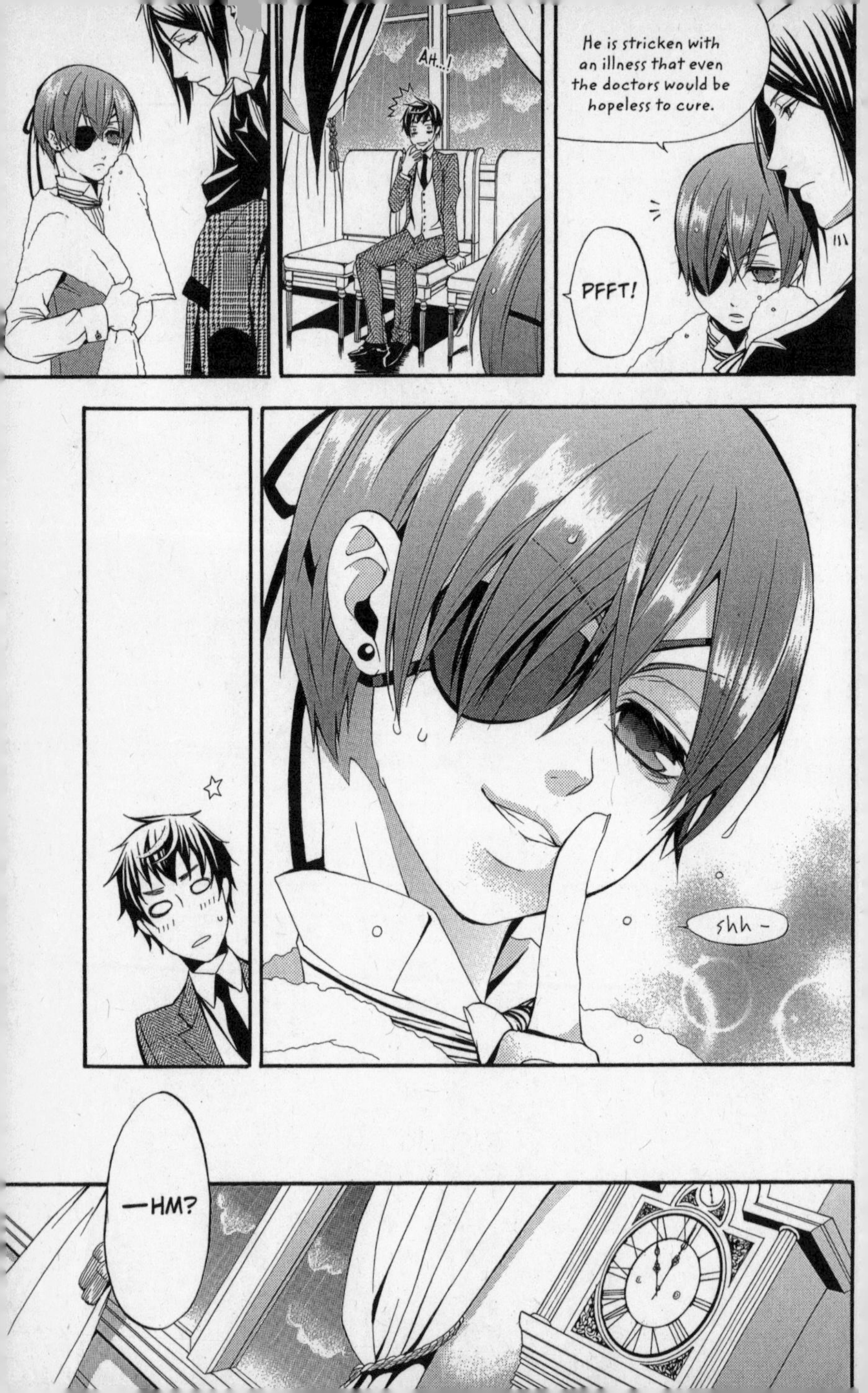
He is stricken with an illness that even the doctors would be hopeless to cure.
PFFT!
AH...!
shh –
—HM?

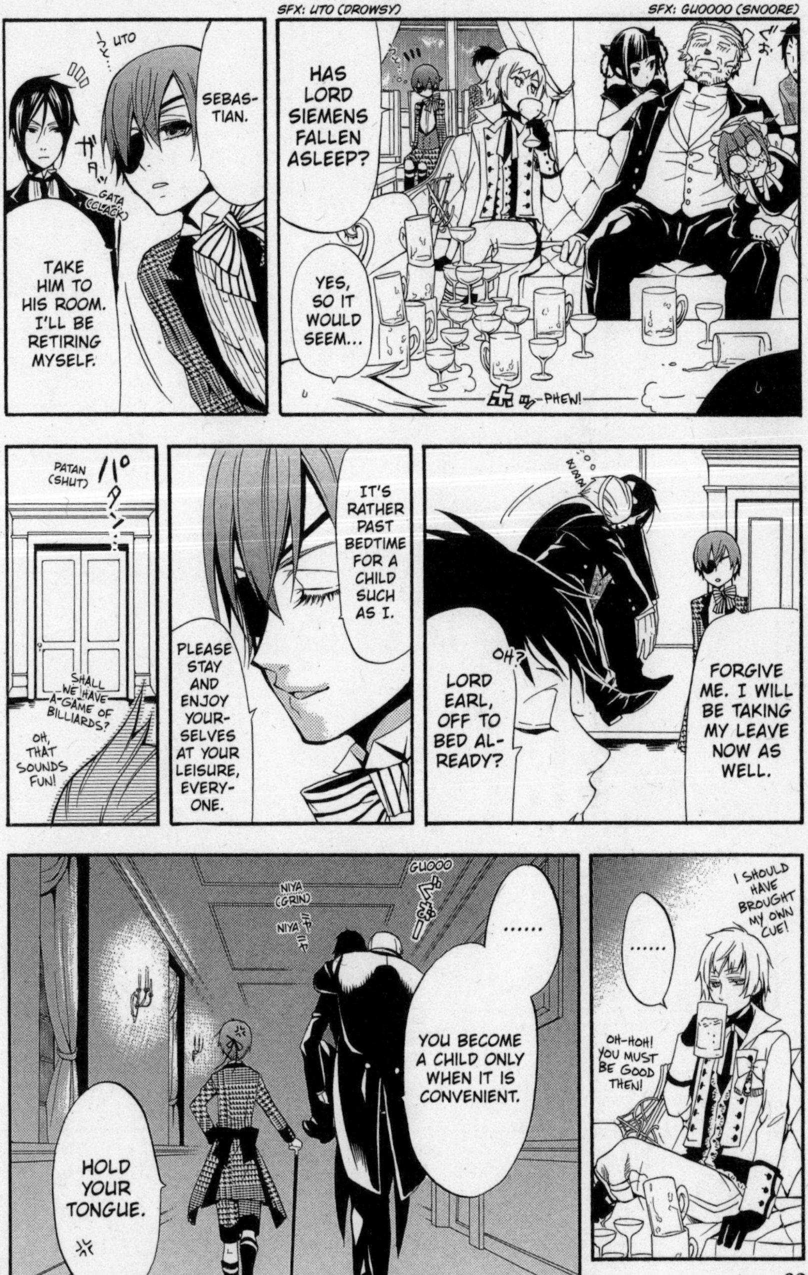
SFX: GUOOOO (SNOORE)
HAS LORD SIEMENS FALLEN ASLEEP?
YES, SO IT WOULD SEEM...
PHEW!
SFX: UTO (DROWSY)
UTO
SEBAS-TIAN.
GATA (CLACK)
TAKE HIM TO HIS ROOM. I'LL BE RETIRING MYSELF.
FORGIVE ME. I WILL BE TAKING MY LEAVE NOW AS WELL.
OH?
LORD EARL, OFF TO BED AL-READY?
IT'S RATHER PAST BEDTIME FOR A CHILD SUCH AS I.
PLEASE STAY AND ENJOY YOUR-SELVES AT YOUR LEISURE, EVERY-ONE.
PATAN (SHUT)
SHALL WE HAVE A GAME OF BILLIARDS?
OH, THAT SOUNDS FUN!
......
I SHOULD HAVE BROUGHT MY OWN CUE!
OH-HOH! YOU MUST BE GOOD THEN!
GUOOO
NIYA (GRIN)
NIYA
......
YOU BECOME A CHILD ONLY WHEN IT IS CONVENIENT.
HOLD YOUR TONGUE.

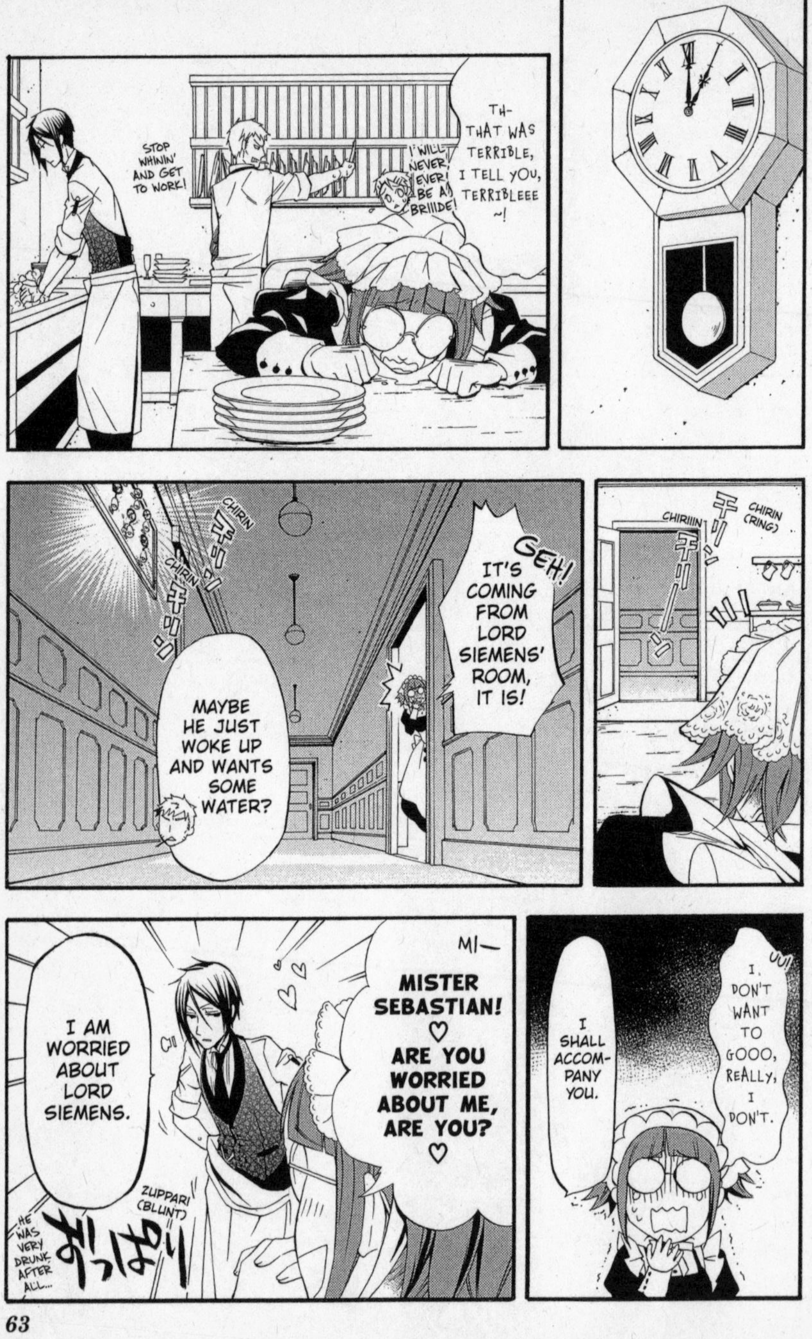
TH-THAT WAS TERRIBLE, I TELL YOU, TERRIBLEEE~!
I WILL NEVER, EVER BE A BRIIIDE!
STOP WHININ' AND GET TO WORK!
CHIRIN (RING)
CHIRIIIN
CHIRIN
GEH!
IT'S COMING FROM LORD SIEMENS' ROOM, IT IS!
CHIRIN
MAYBE HE JUST WOKE UP AND WANTS SOME WATER?
UU!
I, DON'T WANT TO GOOO, REALLY, I DON'T.
I SHALL ACCOMPANY YOU.
MI—
MISTER SEBASTIAN! ♡ ARE YOU WORRIED ABOUT ME, ARE YOU? ♡
I AM WORRIED ABOUT LORD SIEMENS.
ZUPPARI (BLUNT)
HE WAS VERY DRUNK AFTER ALL...

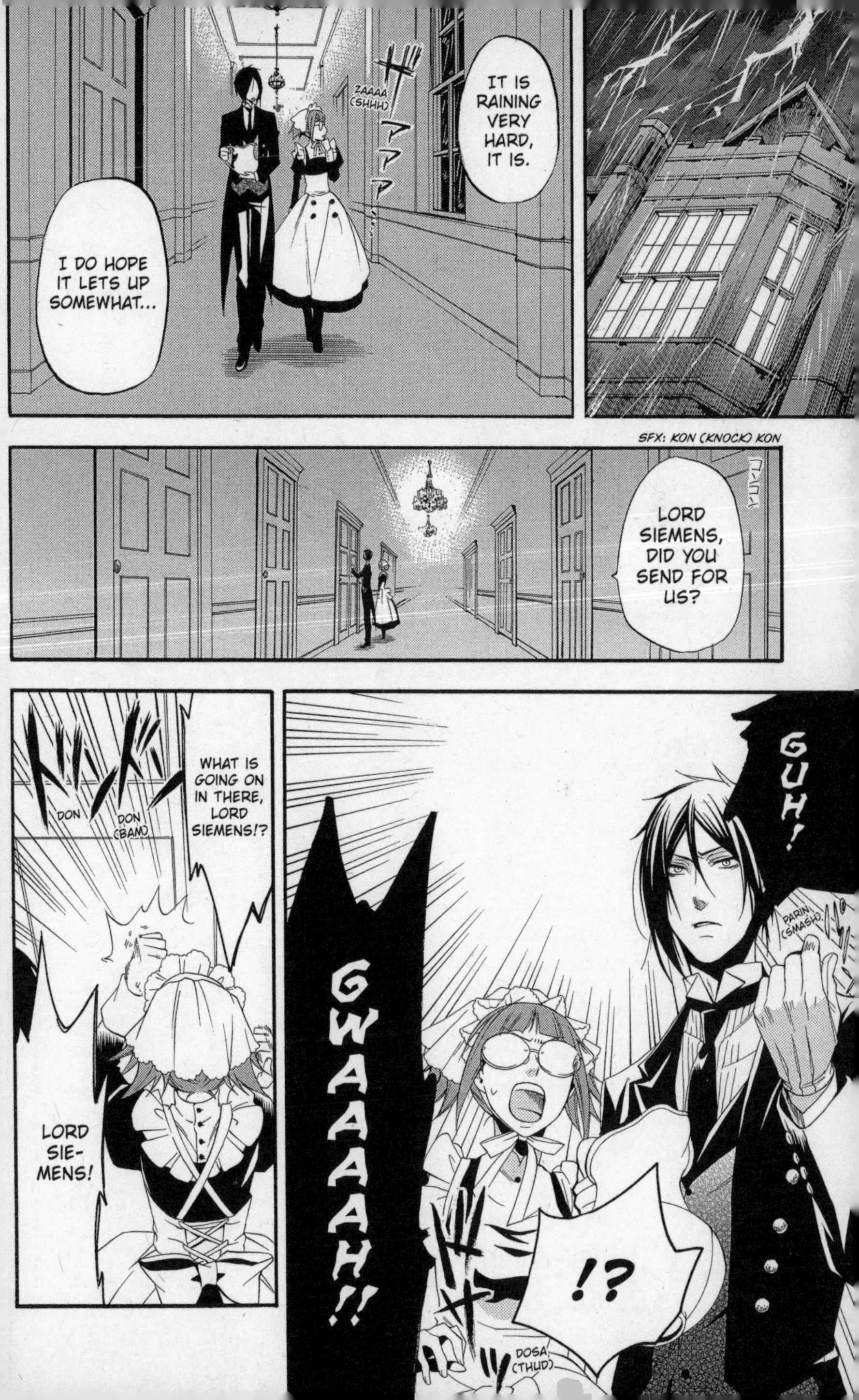
IT IS RAINING VERY HARD, IT IS.
ZAAAA (SHHH)
I DO HOPE IT LETS UP SOMEWHAT...
SFX: KON (KNOCK) KON
LORD SIEMENS, DID YOU SEND FOR US?
GUH!
PARIN (SMASH)
GWAAAAH!!
!?
DOSA (THUD)
WHAT IS GOING ON IN THERE, LORD SIEMENS!?
DON DON (BAM)
LORD SIE-MENS!

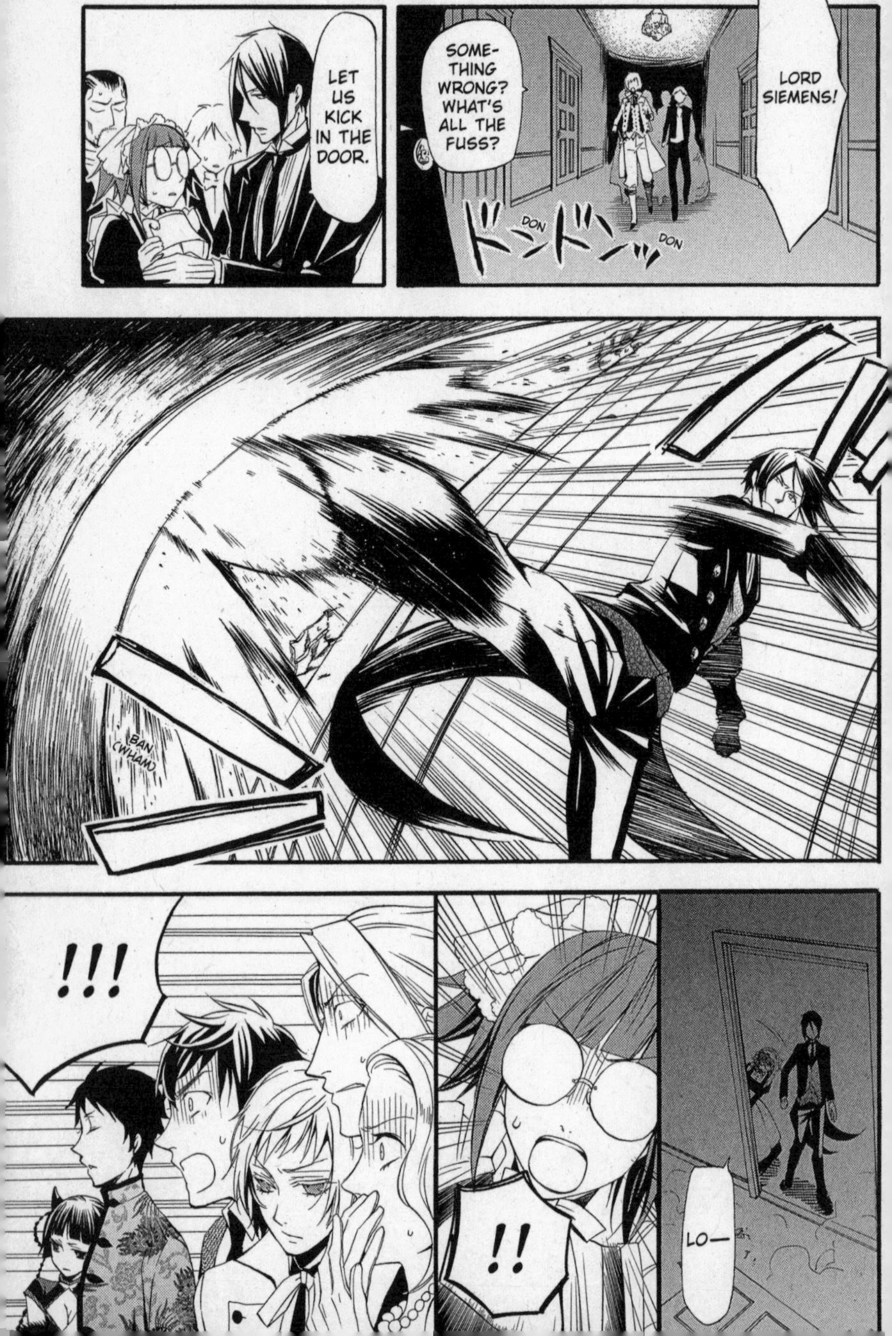
LORD SIEMENS!
SOME-THING WRONG? WHAT'S ALL THE FUSS?
DON
DON
LET US KICK IN THE DOOR.
BAN (WHAM)
LO—
!!
!!!

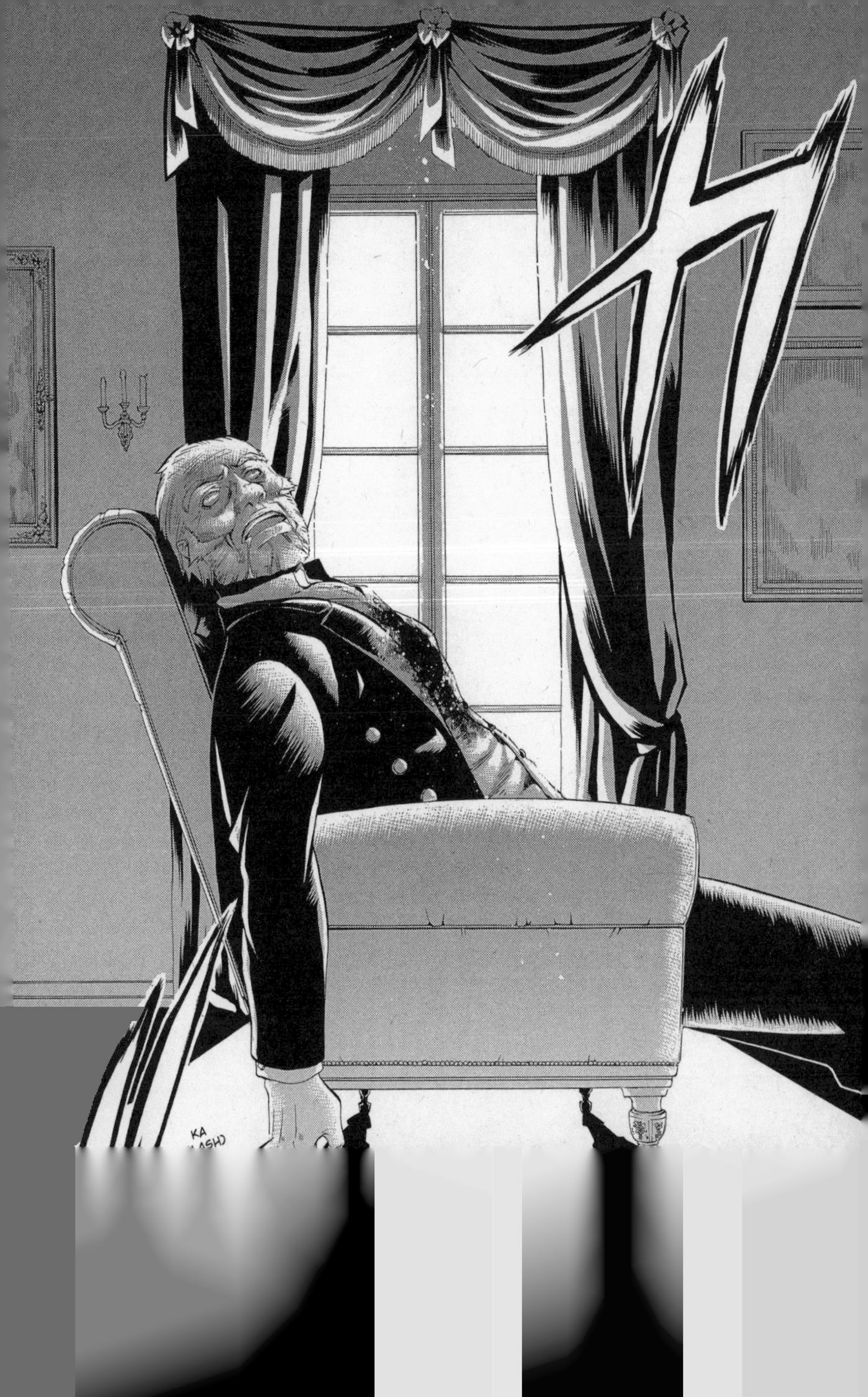
KA

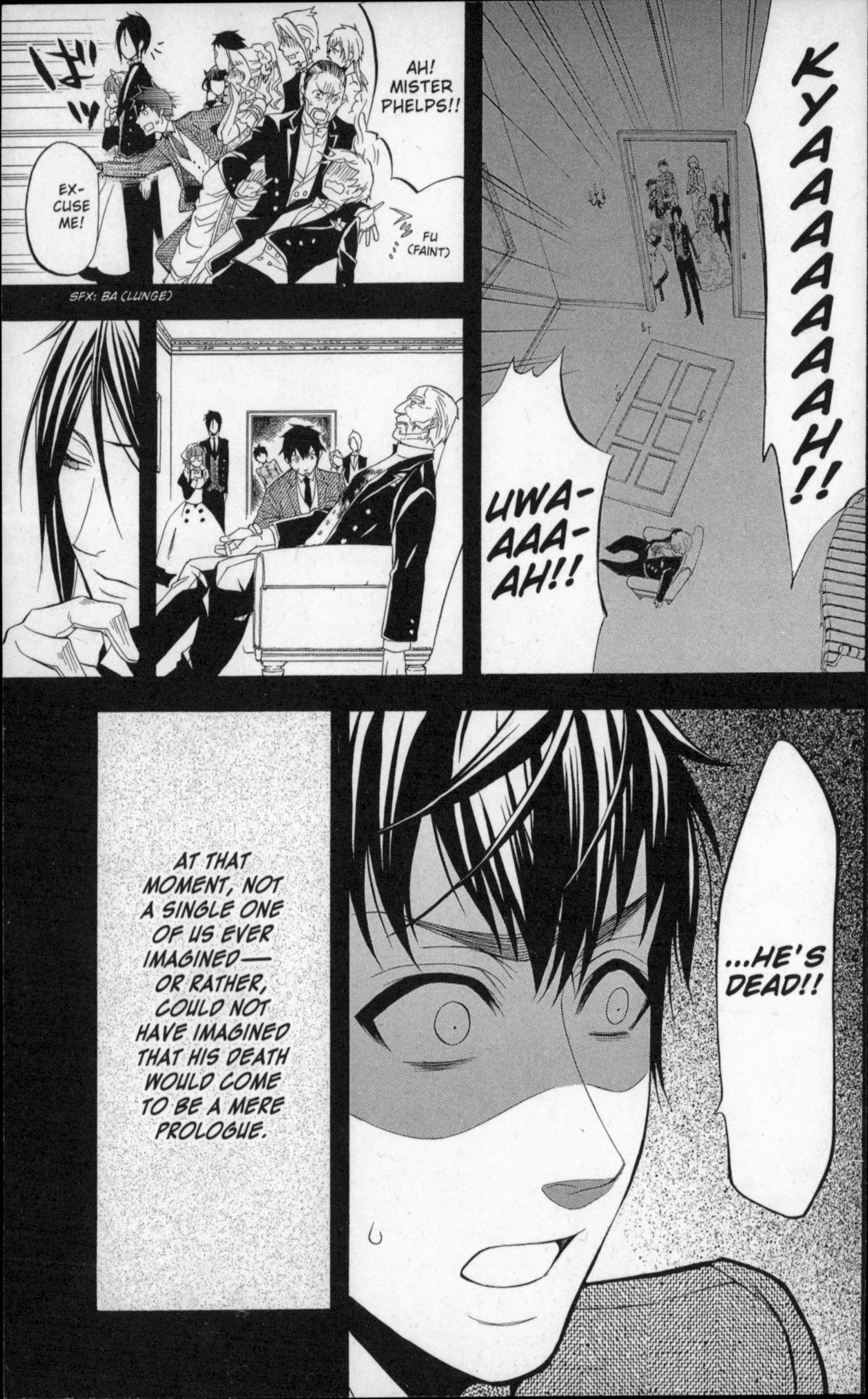
KYAAAAAAAH!!
UWA-AAAA-AH!!
ばッ
AH! MISTER PHELPS!!
EX-CUSE ME!
FU (FAINT)
SFX: BA (LUNGE)
...HE'S DEAD!!
AT THAT MOMENT, NOT A SINGLE ONE OF US EVER IMAGINED—OR RATHER, COULD NOT HAVE IMAGINED THAT HIS DEATH WOULD COME TO BE A MERE PROLOGUE.

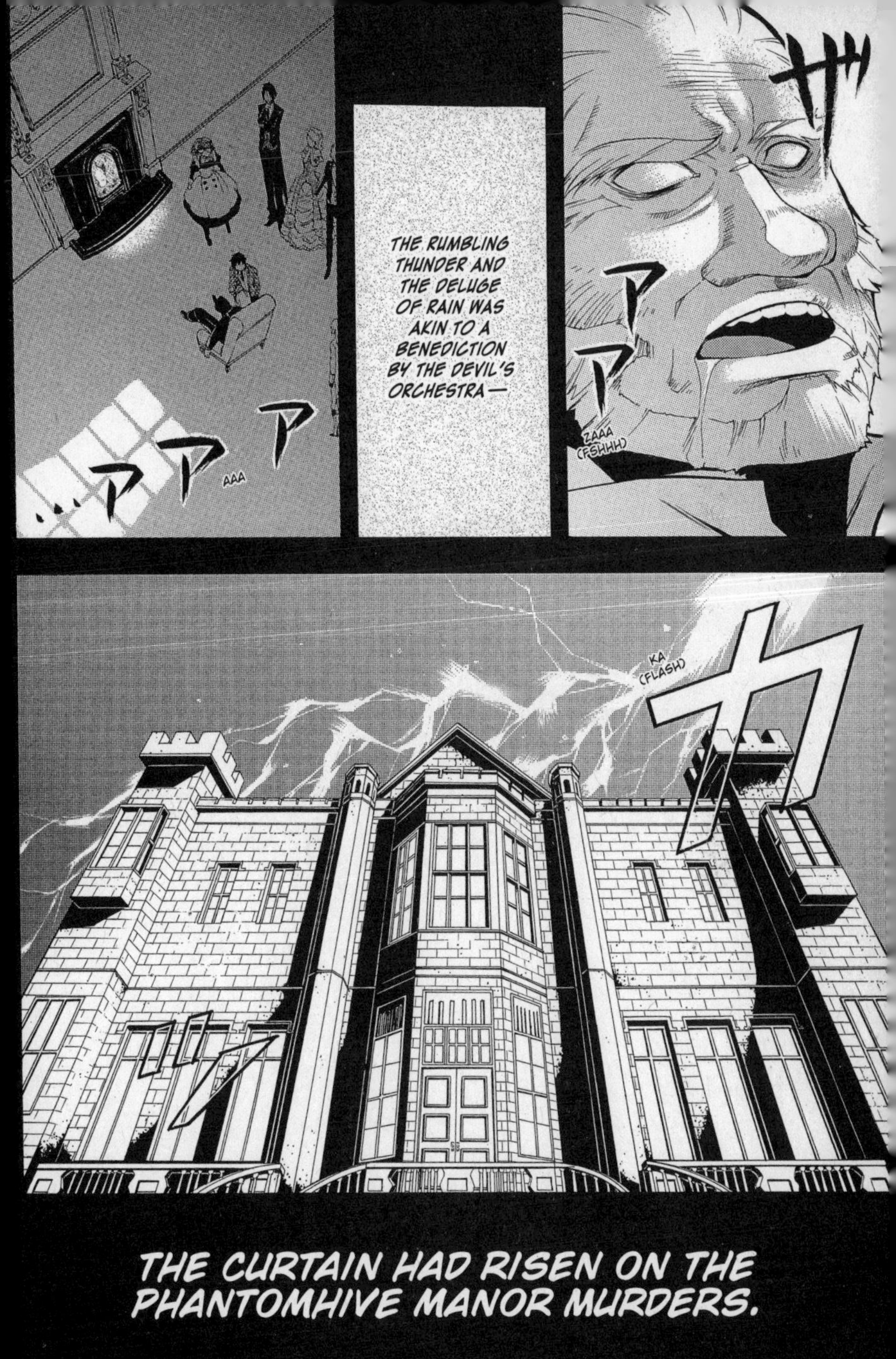
ZAAA (FSHHH)
THE RUMBLING THUNDER AND THE DELUGE OF RAIN WAS AKIN TO A BENEDICTION BY THE DEVIL'S ORCHESTRA—
...AAA
KA (FLASH)
THE CURTAIN HAD RISEN ON THE PHANTOMHIVE MANOR MURDERS.

Black Butler

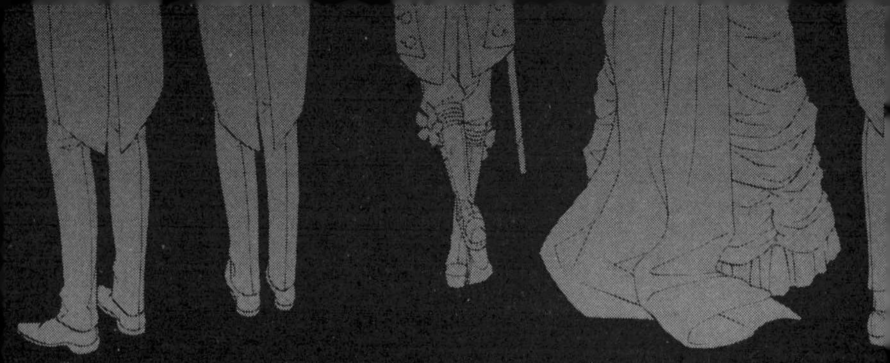

CHAPTER 40

In the afternoon : The Butler, Confining

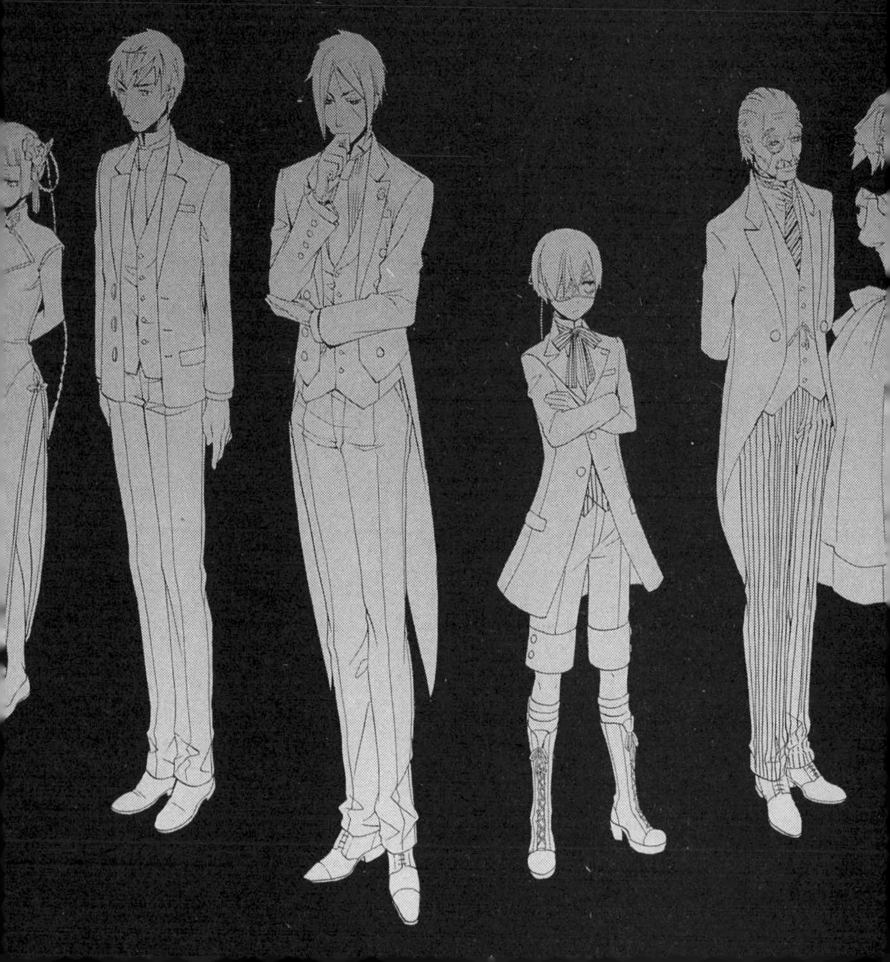

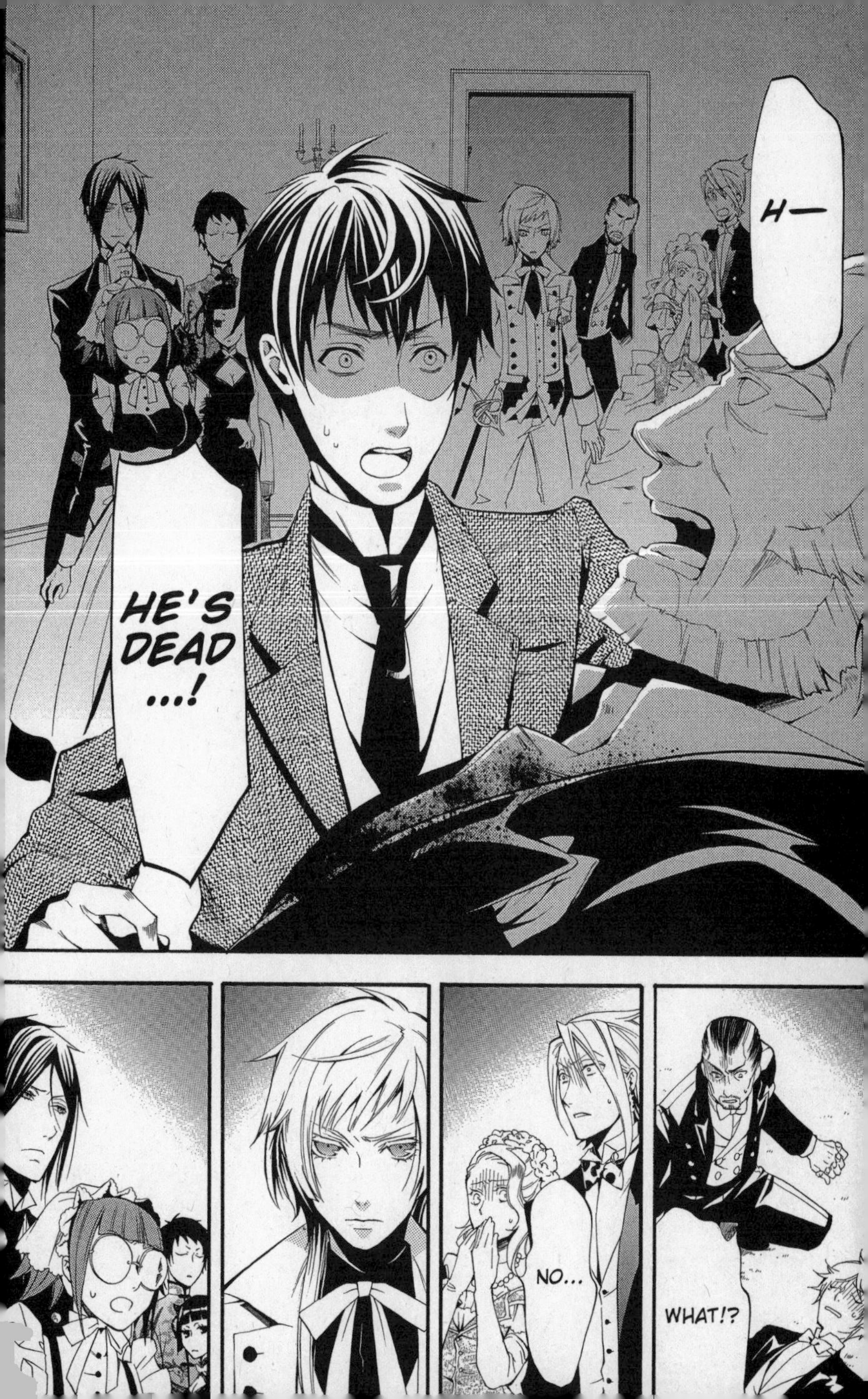

H—
HE'S DEAD ...!
WHAT!?
NO...

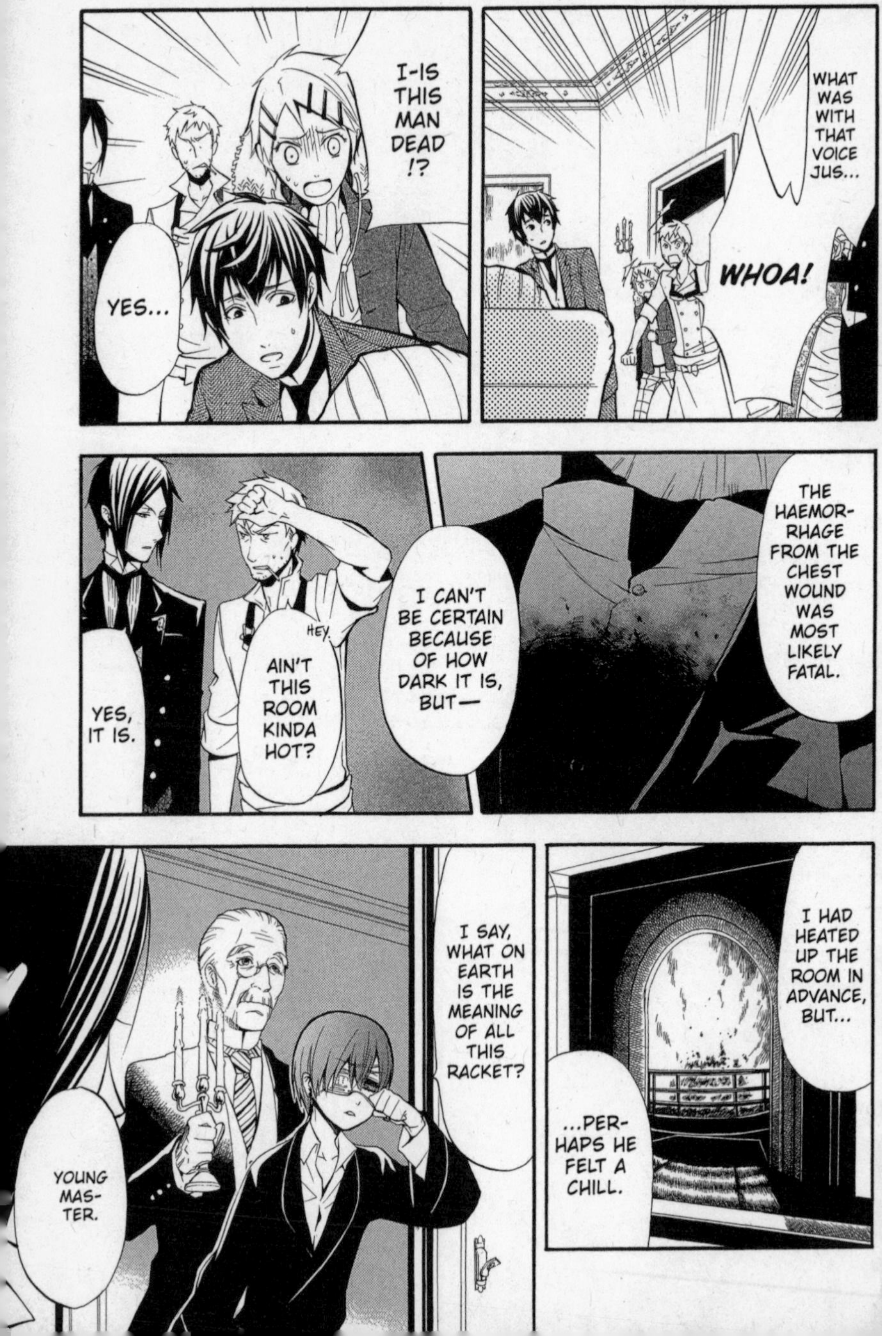
WHAT WAS WITH THAT VOICE JUS...
WHOA!
I-IS THIS MAN DEAD!?
YES...
THE HAEMORRHAGE FROM THE CHEST WOUND WAS MOST LIKELY FATAL.
I CAN'T BE CERTAIN BECAUSE OF HOW DARK IT IS, BUT—
HEY.
AIN'T THIS ROOM KINDA HOT?
YES, IT IS.
I HAD HEATED UP THE ROOM IN ADVANCE, BUT...
...PERHAPS HE FELT A CHILL.
I SAY, WHAT ON EARTH IS THE MEANING OF ALL THIS RACKET?
YOUNG MASTER.

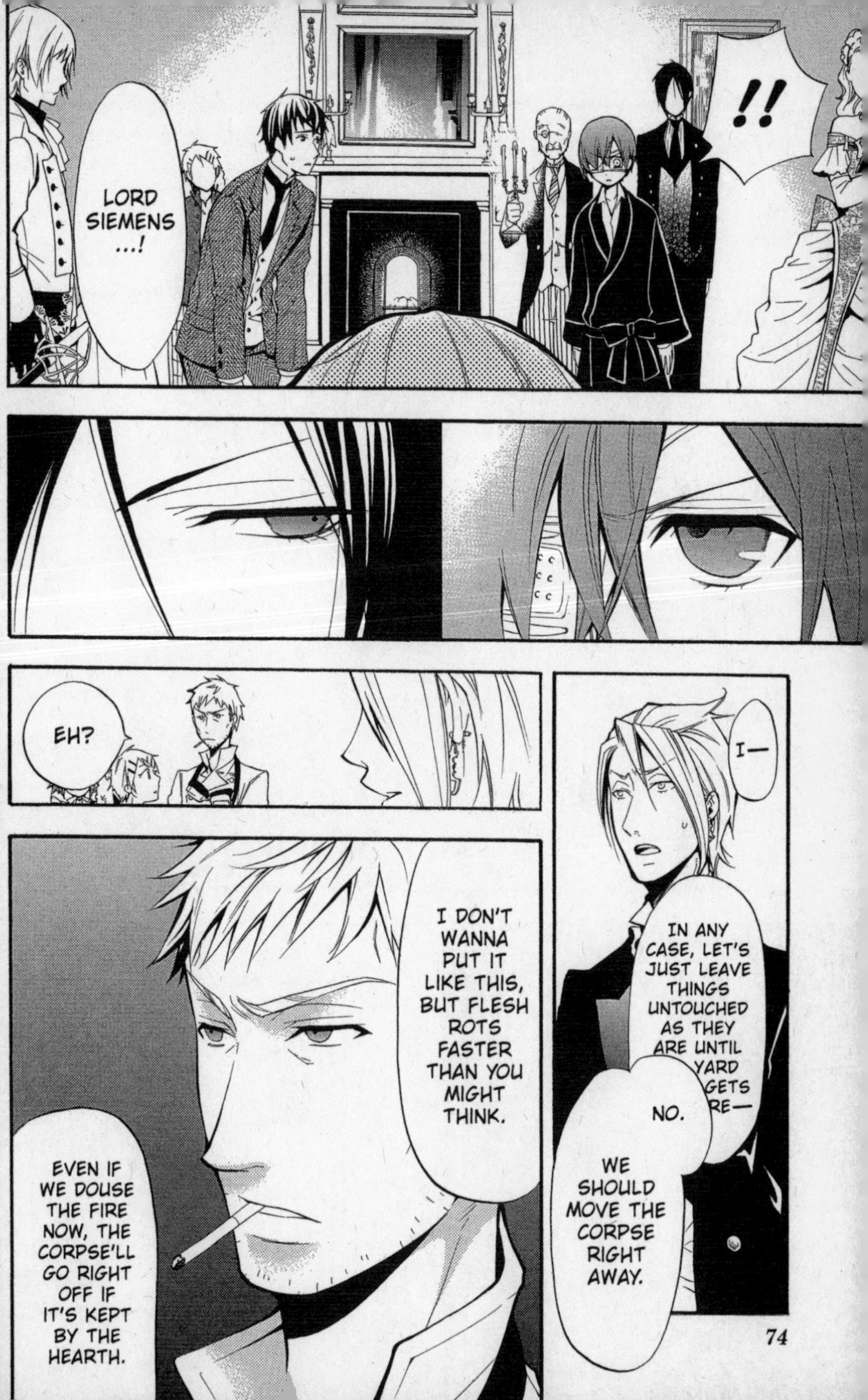
!!
LORD SIEMENS ...!
I—
EH?
IN ANY CASE, LET'S JUST LEAVE THINGS UNTOUCHED AS THEY ARE UNTIL YARD GETS RE—
NO.
WE SHOULD MOVE THE CORPSE RIGHT AWAY.
I DON'T WANNA PUT IT LIKE THIS, BUT FLESH ROTS FASTER THAN YOU MIGHT THINK.
EVEN IF WE DOUSE THE FIRE NOW, THE CORPSE'LL GO RIGHT OFF IF IT'S KEPT BY THE HEARTH.

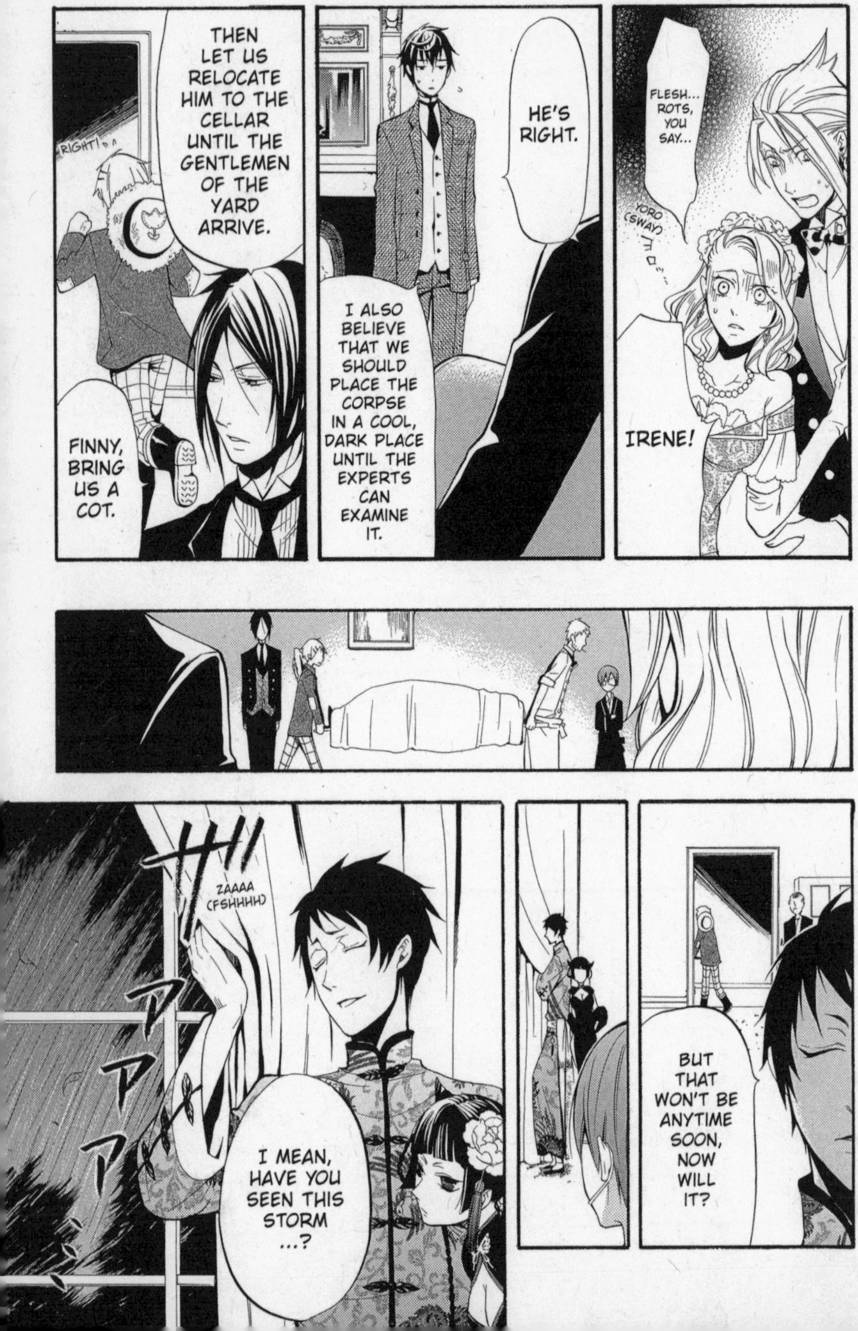
FLESH... ROTS, YOU SAY...
YORO (SWAY)
IRENE!
HE'S RIGHT.
I ALSO BELIEVE THAT WE SHOULD PLACE THE CORPSE IN A COOL, DARK PLACE UNTIL THE EXPERTS CAN EXAMINE IT.
THEN LET US RELOCATE HIM TO THE CELLAR UNTIL THE GENTLEMEN OF THE YARD ARRIVE.
RIGHT!
FINNY, BRING US A COT.
BUT THAT WON'T BE ANYTIME SOON, NOW WILL IT?
ZAAAA (FSHHHH)
I MEAN, HAVE YOU SEEN THIS STORM ...?

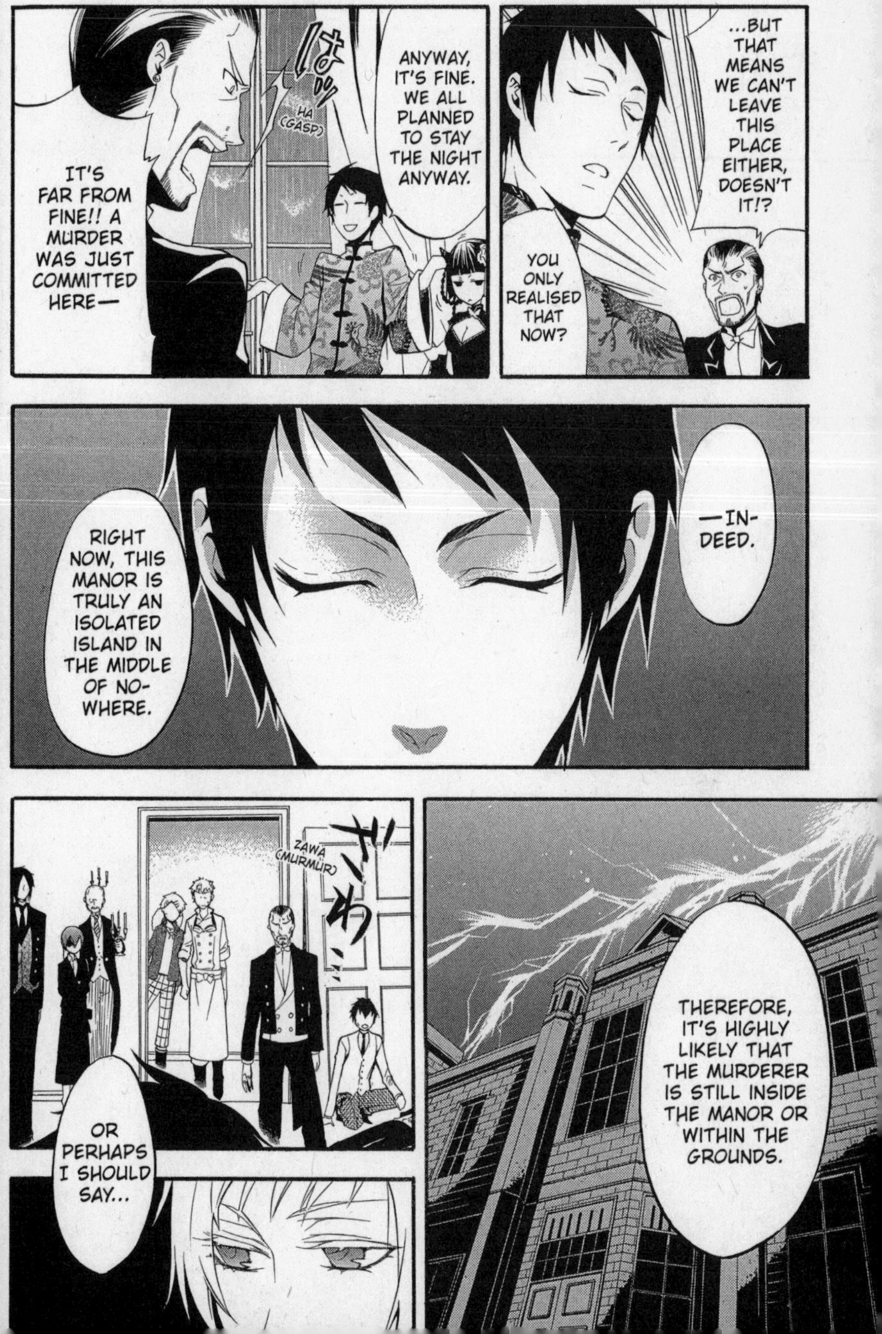
...BUT THAT MEANS WE CAN'T LEAVE THIS PLACE EITHER, DOESN'T IT!?
YOU ONLY REALISED THAT NOW?
ANYWAY, IT'S FINE. WE ALL PLANNED TO STAY THE NIGHT ANYWAY.
HA (GASP)
IT'S FAR FROM FINE!! A MURDER WAS JUST COMMITTED HERE—
—INDEED.
RIGHT NOW, THIS MANOR IS TRULY AN ISOLATED ISLAND IN THE MIDDLE OF NOWHERE.
THEREFORE, IT'S HIGHLY LIKELY THAT THE MURDERER IS STILL INSIDE THE MANOR OR WITHIN THE GROUNDS.
ZAWA (MURMUR)
OR PERHAPS I SHOULD SAY...

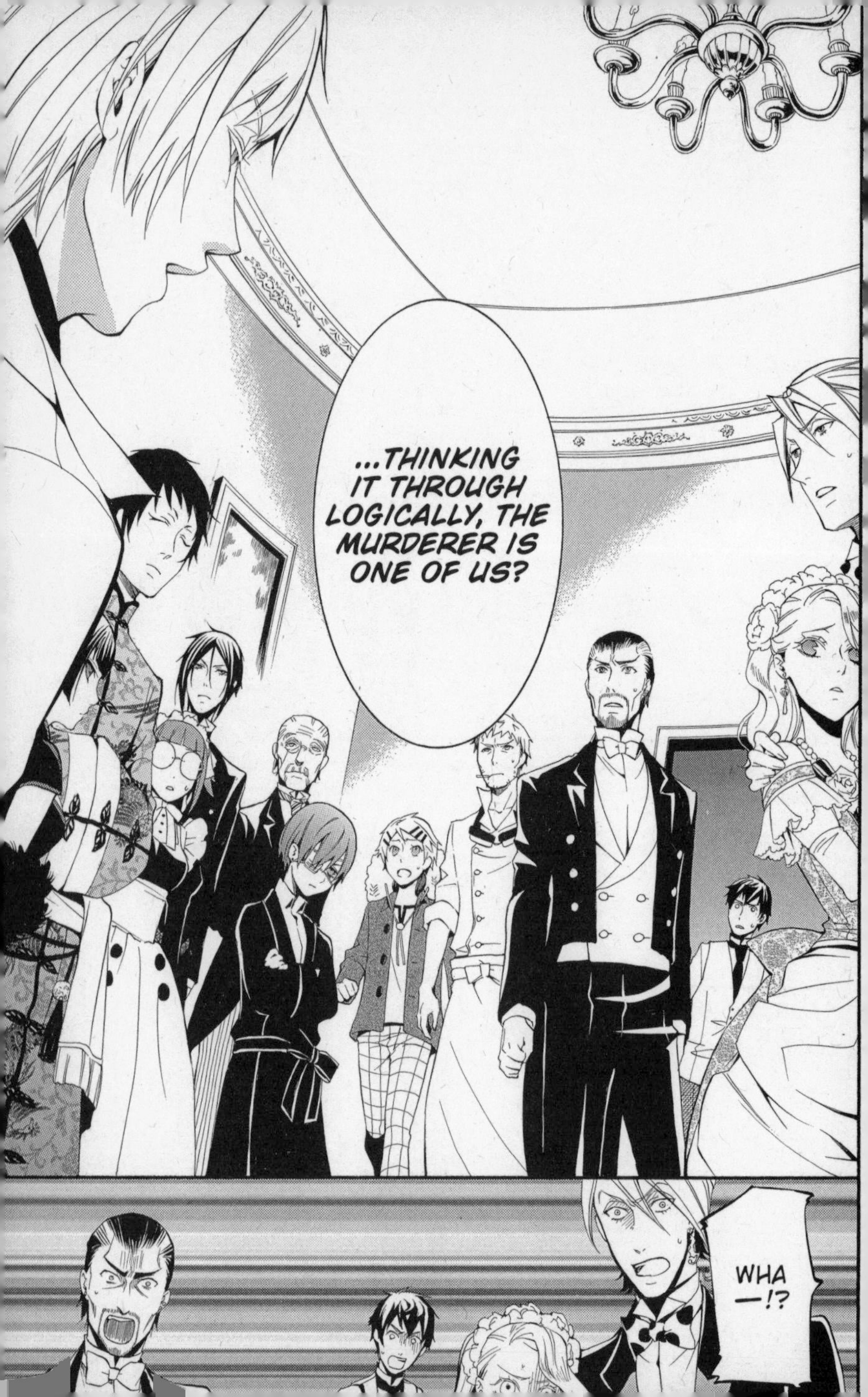
...THINKING IT THROUGH LOGICALLY, THE MURDERER IS ONE OF US?
WHA—!?

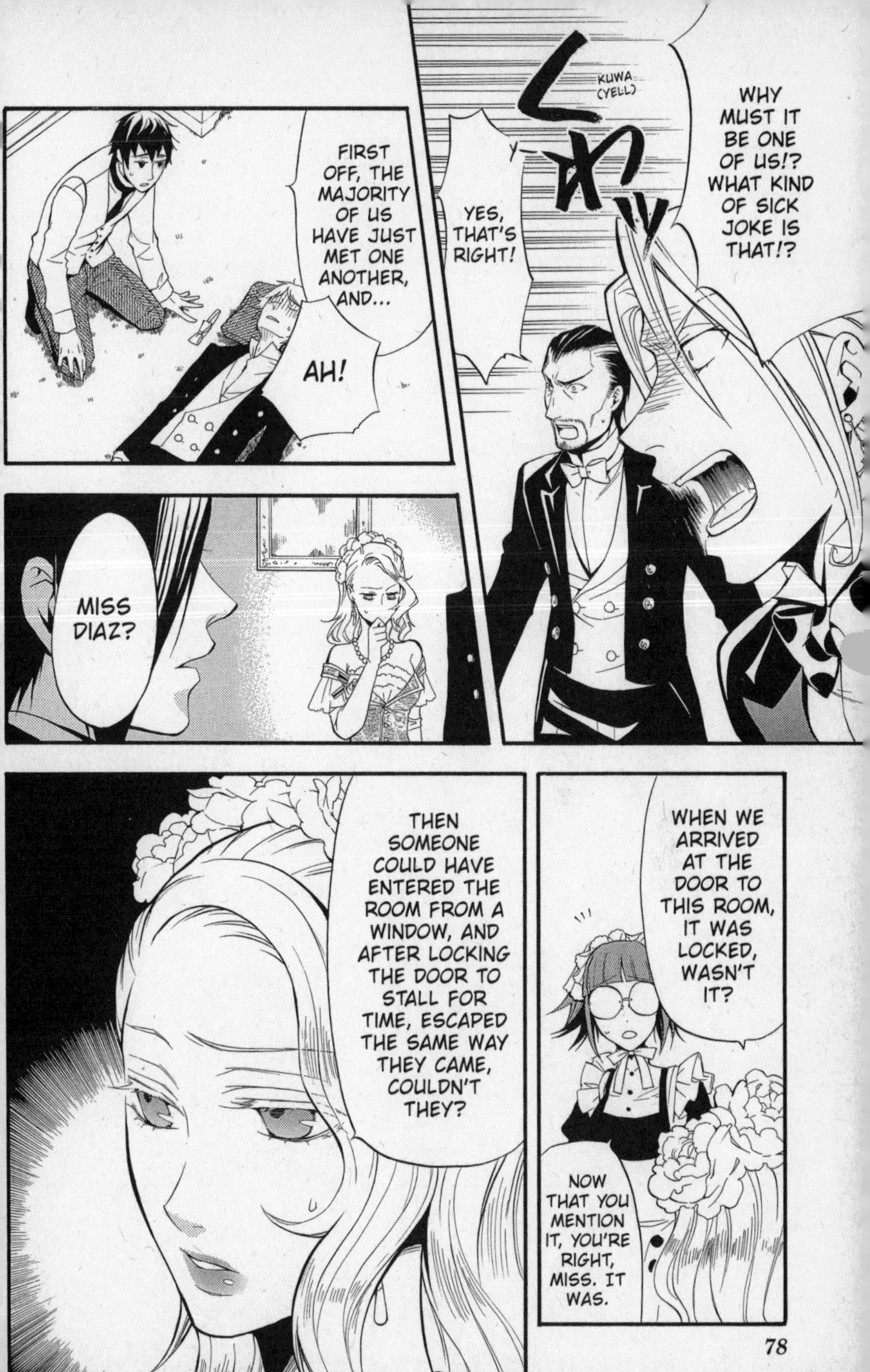
WHY MUST IT BE ONE OF US!? WHAT KIND OF SICK JOKE IS THAT!?
KUWA (YELL)
Y-
YES, THAT'S RIGHT!
FIRST OFF, THE MAJORITY OF US HAVE JUST MET ONE ANOTHER, AND...
AH!
MISS DIAZ?
WHEN WE ARRIVED AT THE DOOR TO THIS ROOM, IT WAS LOCKED, WASN'T IT?
NOW THAT YOU MENTION IT, YOU'RE RIGHT, MISS. IT WAS.
THEN SOMEONE COULD HAVE ENTERED THE ROOM FROM A WINDOW, AND AFTER LOCKING THE DOOR TO STALL FOR TIME, ESCAPED THE SAME WAY THEY CAME, COULDN'T THEY?

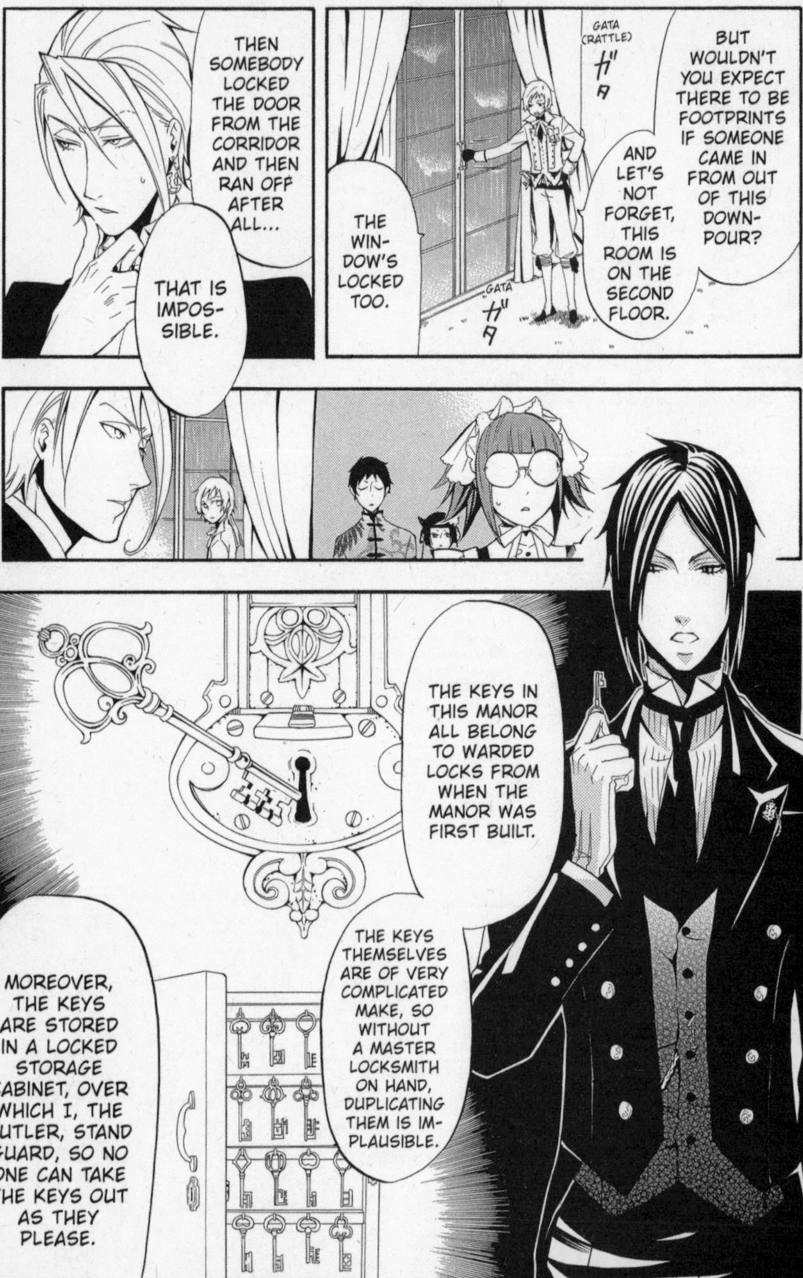
GATA (RATTLE)
ガタ
BUT WOULDN'T YOU EXPECT THERE TO BE FOOTPRINTS IF SOMEONE CAME IN FROM OUT OF THIS DOWNPOUR?
AND LET'S NOT FORGET, THIS ROOM IS ON THE SECOND FLOOR.
THE WINDOW'S LOCKED TOO.
GATA
ガタ
THEN SOMEBODY LOCKED THE DOOR FROM THE CORRIDOR AND THEN RAN OFF AFTER ALL...
THAT IS IMPOSSIBLE.
THE KEYS IN THIS MANOR ALL BELONG TO WARDED LOCKS FROM WHEN THE MANOR WAS FIRST BUILT.
THE KEYS THEMSELVES ARE OF VERY COMPLICATED MAKE, SO WITHOUT A MASTER LOCKSMITH ON HAND, DUPLICATING THEM IS IMPLAUSIBLE.
MOREOVER, THE KEYS ARE STORED IN A LOCKED STORAGE CABINET, OVER WHICH I, THE BUTLER, STAND GUARD, SO NO ONE CAN TAKE THE KEYS OUT AS THEY PLEASE.

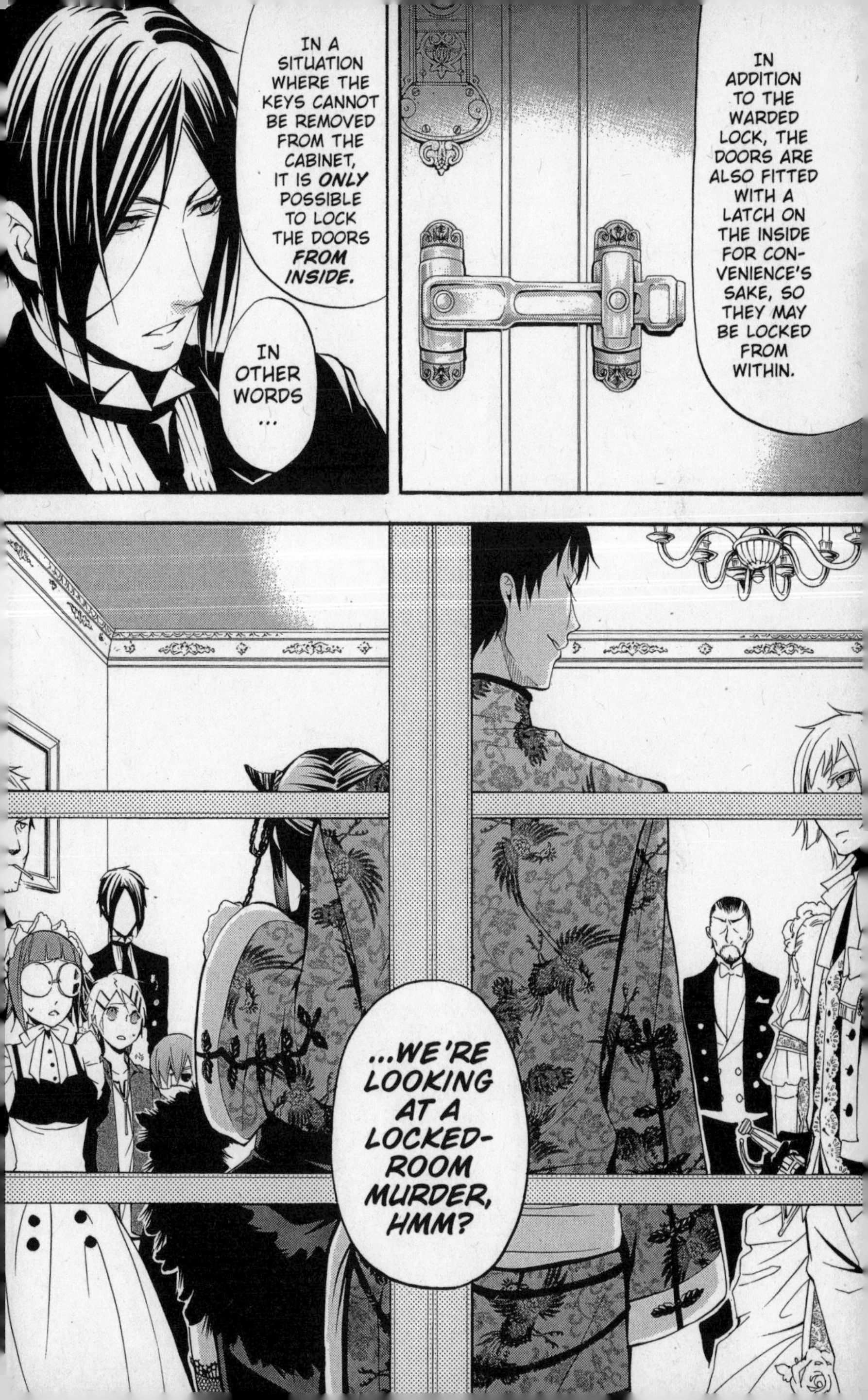
IN ADDITION TO THE WARDED LOCK, THE DOORS ARE ALSO FITTED WITH A LATCH ON THE INSIDE FOR CON-VENIENCE'S SAKE, SO THEY MAY BE LOCKED FROM WITHIN.
IN A SITUATION WHERE THE KEYS CANNOT BE REMOVED FROM THE CABINET, IT IS *ONLY* POSSIBLE TO LOCK THE DOORS ***FROM INSIDE.***
IN OTHER WORDS ...
...WE'RE LOOKING AT A LOCKED-ROOM MURDER, HMM?

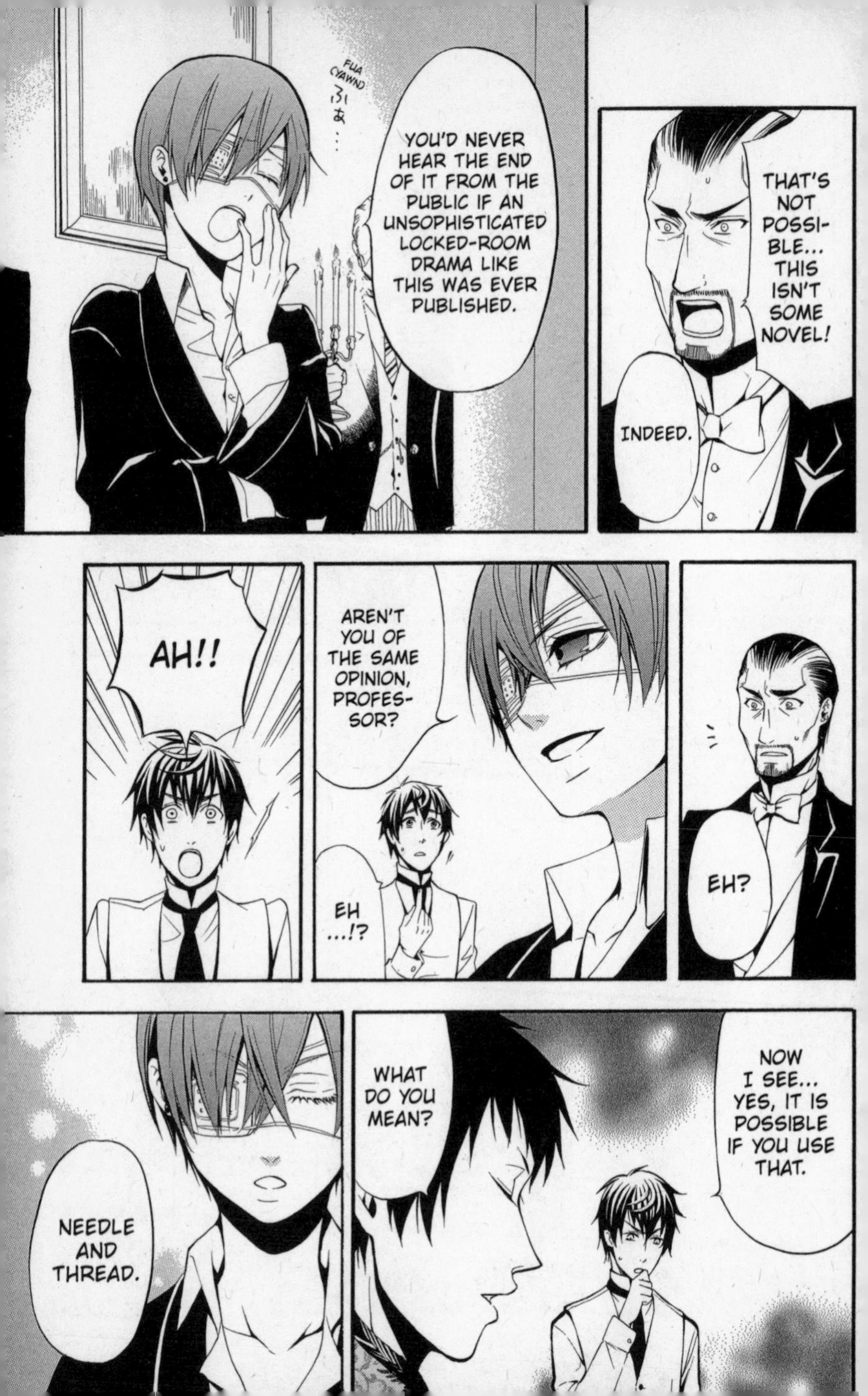
THAT'S NOT POSSIBLE... THIS ISN'T SOME NOVEL!
INDEED.
FUA (YAWN)
ふぁ…
YOU'D NEVER HEAR THE END OF IT FROM THE PUBLIC IF AN UNSOPHISTICATED LOCKED-ROOM DRAMA LIKE THIS WAS EVER PUBLISHED.
EH?
AREN'T YOU OF THE SAME OPINION, PROFESSOR?
EH ...!?
AH!!
NOW I SEE... YES, IT IS POSSIBLE IF YOU USE THAT.
WHAT DO YOU MEAN?
NEEDLE AND THREAD.

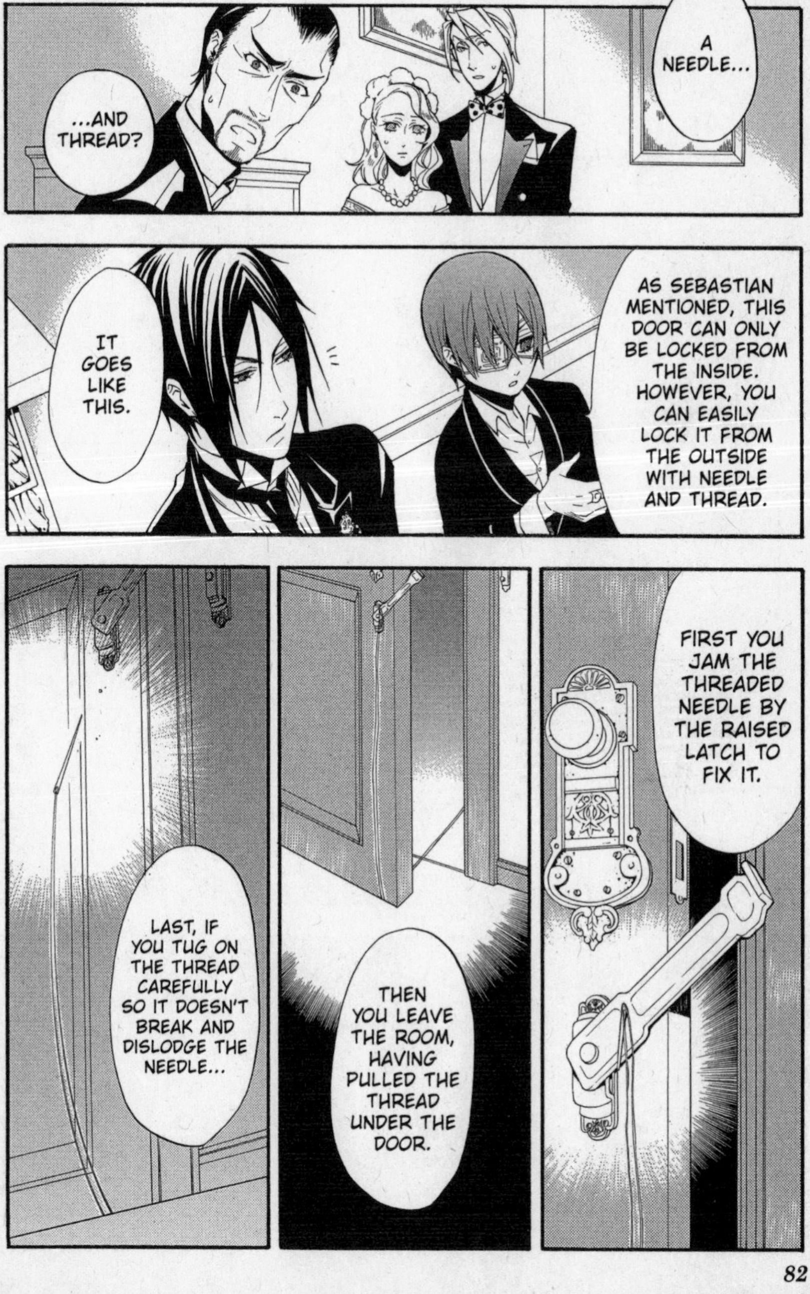
A NEEDLE...
...AND THREAD?
AS SEBASTIAN MENTIONED, THIS DOOR CAN ONLY BE LOCKED FROM THE INSIDE. HOWEVER, YOU CAN EASILY LOCK IT FROM THE OUTSIDE WITH NEEDLE AND THREAD.
IT GOES LIKE THIS.
FIRST YOU JAM THE THREADED NEEDLE BY THE RAISED LATCH TO FIX IT.
THEN YOU LEAVE THE ROOM, HAVING PULLED THE THREAD UNDER THE DOOR.
LAST, IF YOU TUG ON THE THREAD CAREFULLY SO IT DOESN'T BREAK AND DISLODGE THE NEEDLE...

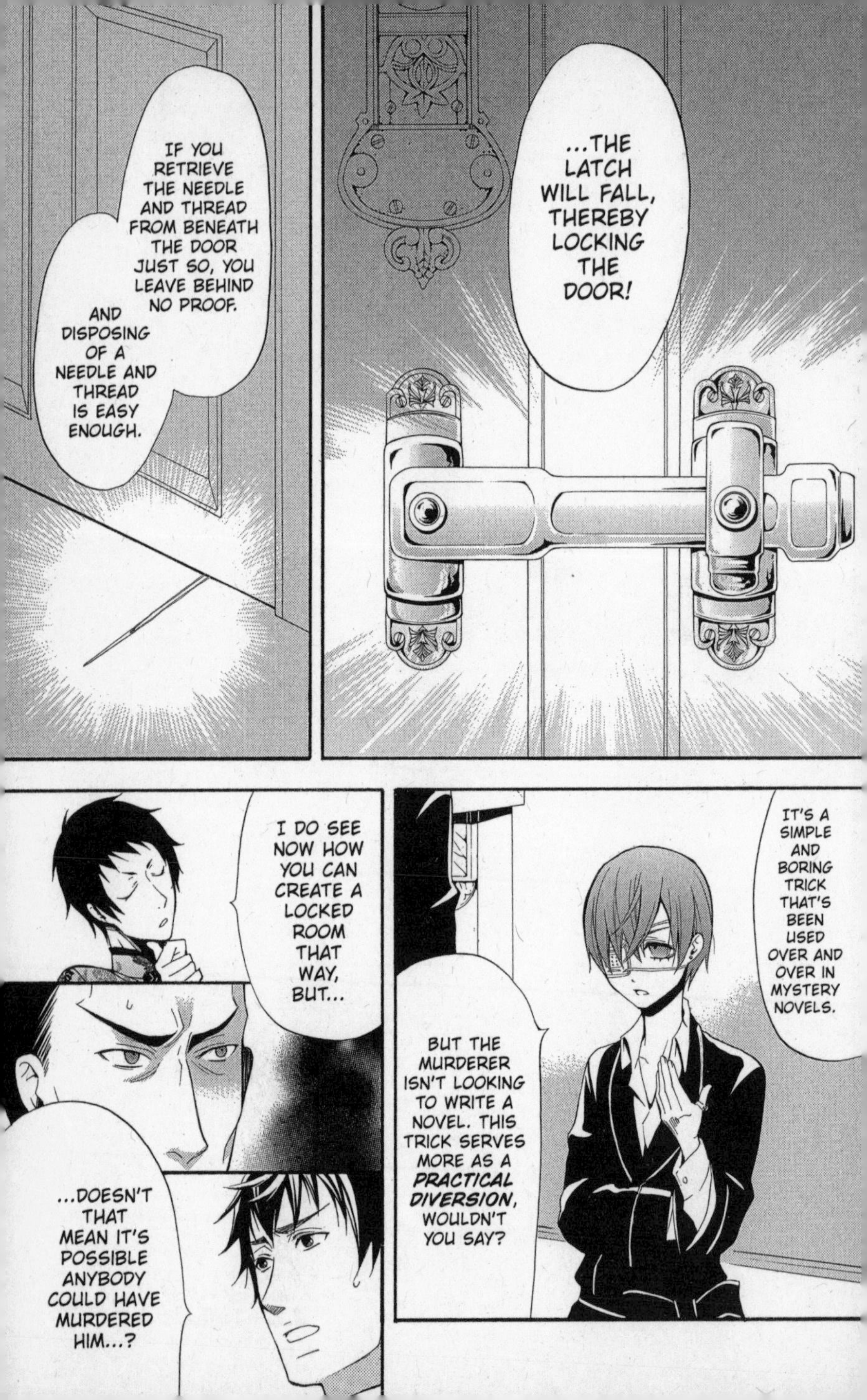
...THE LATCH WILL FALL, THEREBY LOCKING THE DOOR!
IF YOU RETRIEVE THE NEEDLE AND THREAD FROM BENEATH THE DOOR JUST SO, YOU LEAVE BEHIND NO PROOF.
AND DISPOSING OF A NEEDLE AND THREAD IS EASY ENOUGH.
IT'S A SIMPLE AND BORING TRICK THAT'S BEEN USED OVER AND OVER IN MYSTERY NOVELS.
BUT THE MURDERER ISN'T LOOKING TO WRITE A NOVEL. THIS TRICK SERVES MORE AS A *PRACTICAL DIVERSION*, WOULDN'T YOU SAY?
I DO SEE NOW HOW YOU CAN CREATE A LOCKED ROOM THAT WAY, BUT...
...DOESN'T THAT MEAN IT'S POSSIBLE ANYBODY COULD HAVE MURDERED HIM...?

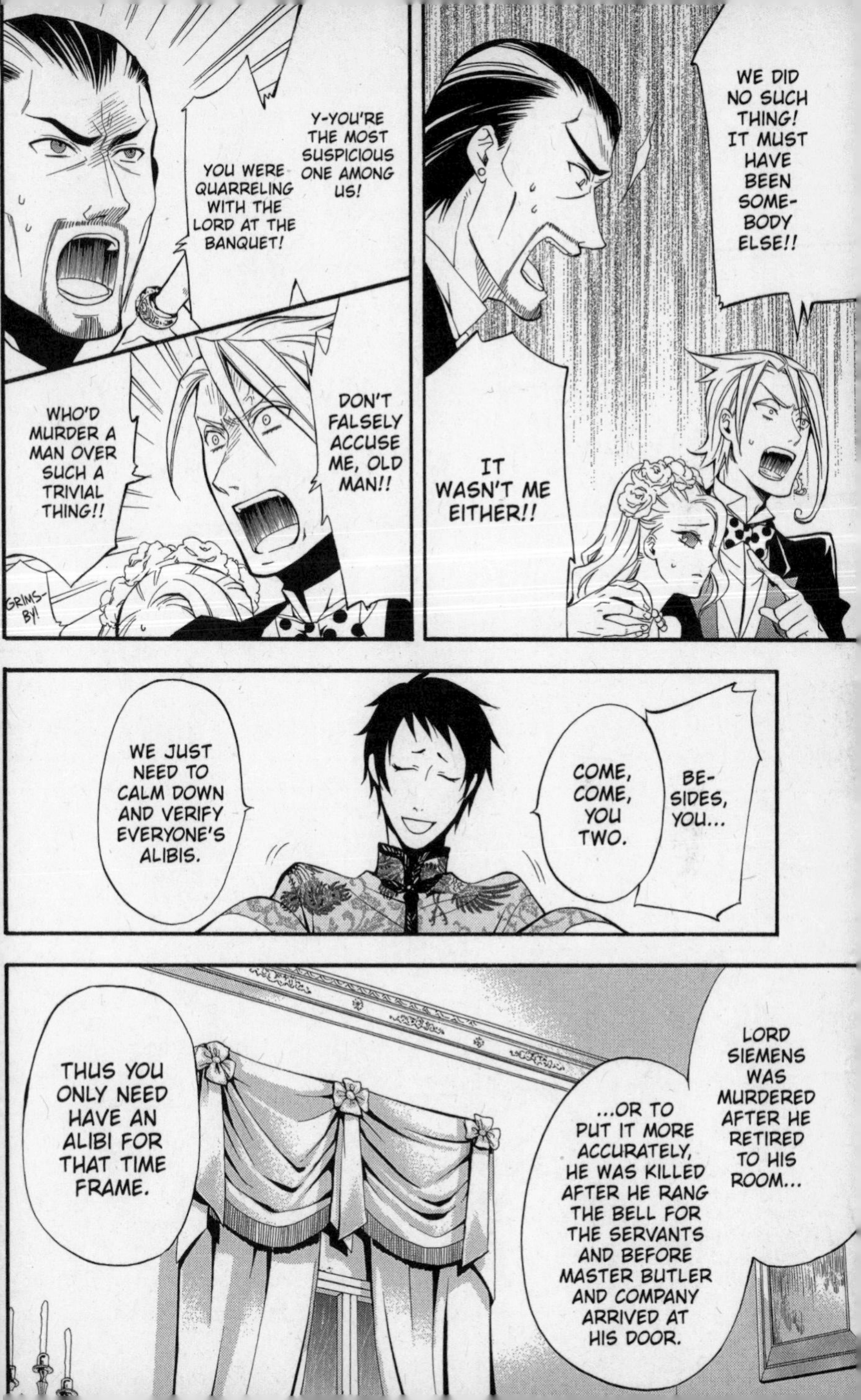
WE DID NO SUCH THING! IT MUST HAVE BEEN SOME-BODY ELSE!!
IT WASN'T ME EITHER!!
Y-YOU'RE THE MOST SUSPICIOUS ONE AMONG US!
YOU WERE QUARRELING WITH THE LORD AT THE BANQUET!
DON'T FALSELY ACCUSE ME, OLD MAN!!
WHO'D MURDER A MAN OVER SUCH A TRIVIAL THING!!
GRIMS-BY!
BE-SIDES, YOU...
COME, COME, YOU TWO.
WE JUST NEED TO CALM DOWN AND VERIFY EVERYONE'S ALIBIS.
LORD SIEMENS WAS MURDERED AFTER HE RETIRED TO HIS ROOM...
...OR TO PUT IT MORE ACCURATELY, HE WAS KILLED AFTER HE RANG THE BELL FOR THE SERVANTS AND BEFORE MASTER BUTLER AND COMPANY ARRIVED AT HIS DOOR.
THUS YOU ONLY NEED HAVE AN ALIBI FOR THAT TIME FRAME.

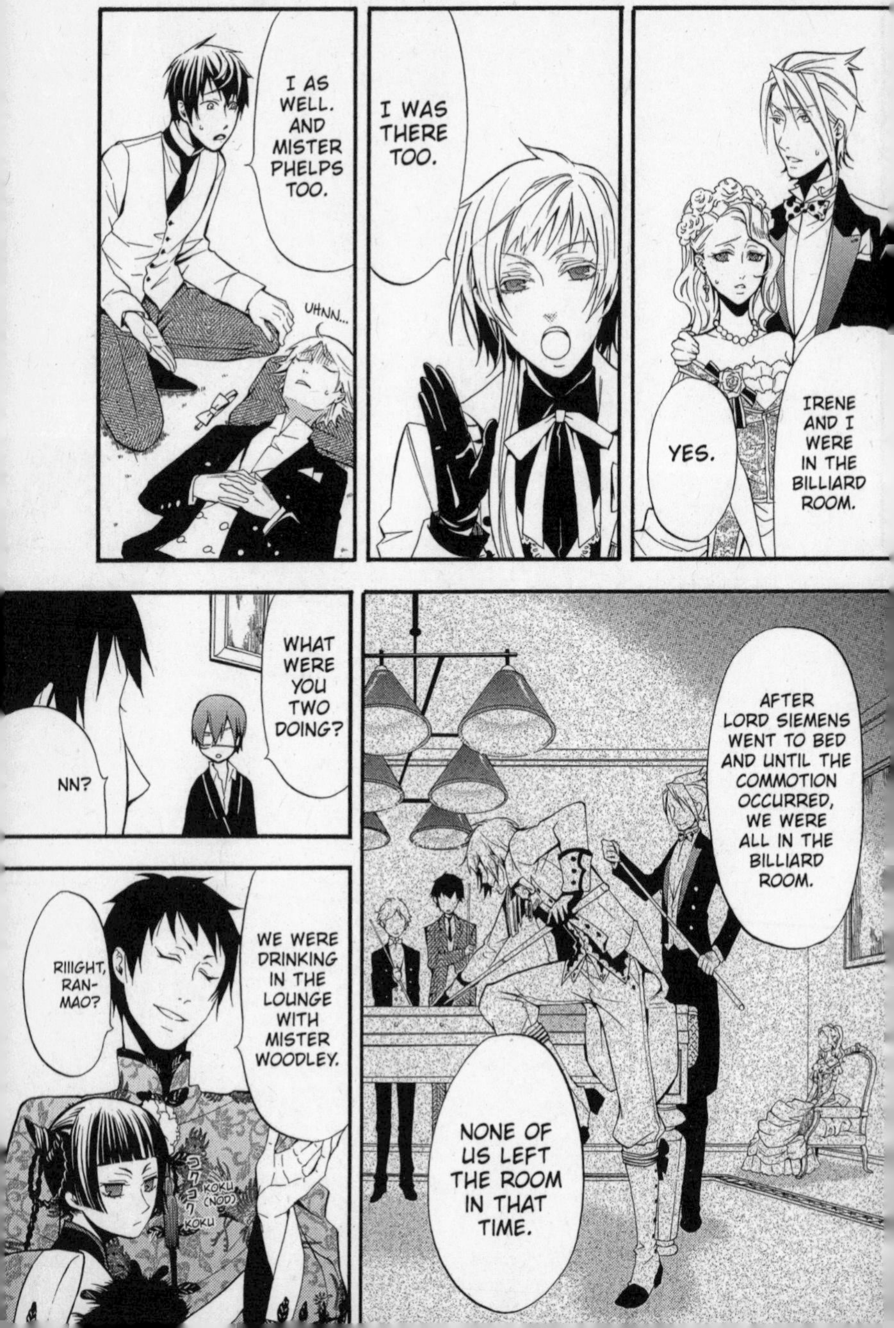
IRENE AND I WERE IN THE BILLIARD ROOM.
YES.
I WAS THERE TOO.
I AS WELL. AND MISTER PHELPS TOO.
UHNN...
AFTER LORD SIEMENS WENT TO BED AND UNTIL THE COMMOTION OCCURRED, WE WERE ALL IN THE BILLIARD ROOM.
NONE OF US LEFT THE ROOM IN THAT TIME.
WHAT WERE YOU TWO DOING?
NN?
WE WERE DRINKING IN THE LOUNGE WITH MISTER WOODLEY.
RIIIGHT, RAN-MAO?
KOKU (NOD) KOKU

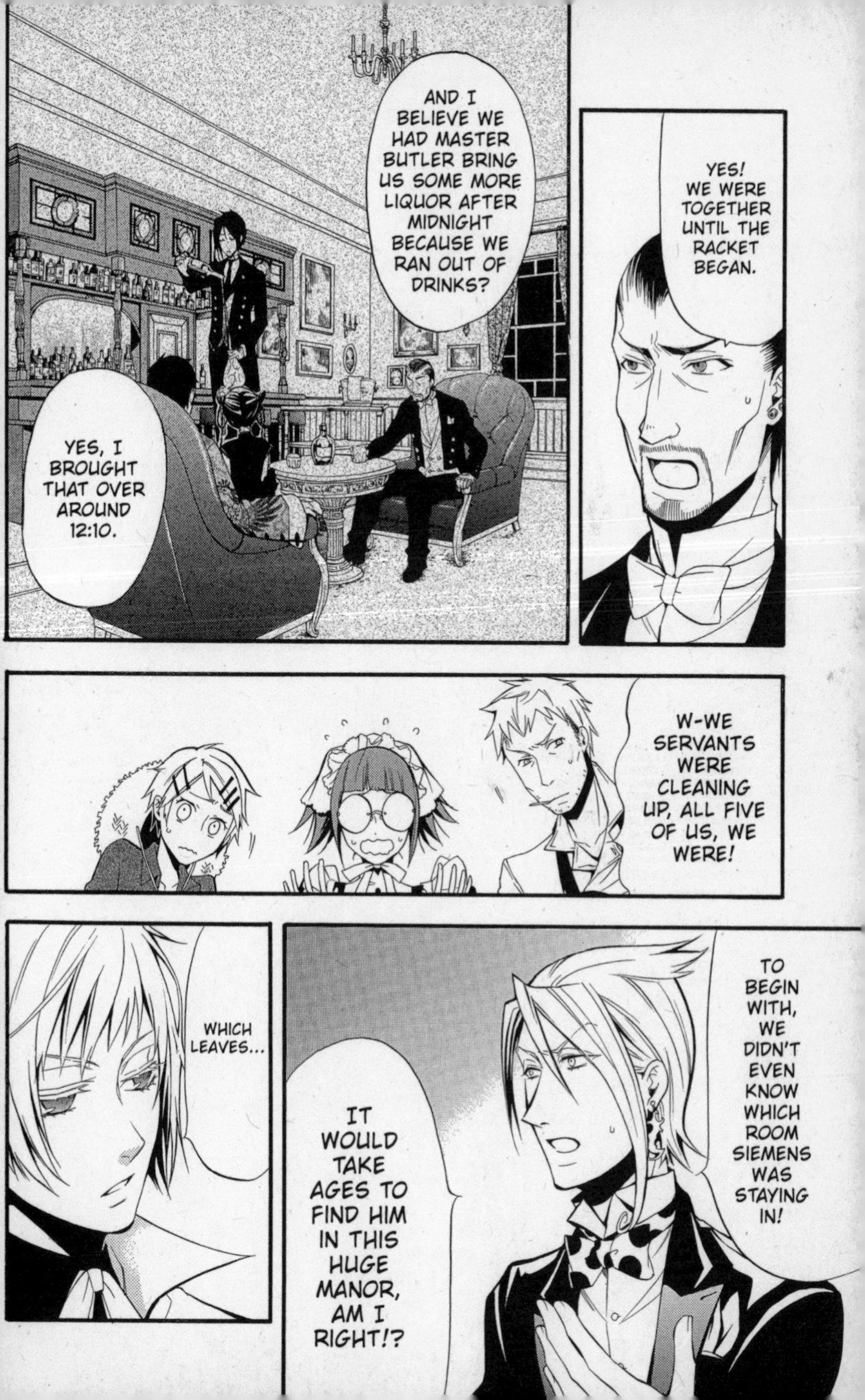
YES! WE WERE TOGETHER UNTIL THE RACKET BEGAN.
AND I BELIEVE WE HAD MASTER BUTLER BRING US SOME MORE LIQUOR AFTER MIDNIGHT BECAUSE WE RAN OUT OF DRINKS?
YES, I BROUGHT THAT OVER AROUND 12:10.
W-WE SERVANTS WERE CLEANING UP, ALL FIVE OF US, WE WERE!
TO BEGIN WITH, WE DIDN'T EVEN KNOW WHICH ROOM SIEMENS WAS STAYING IN!
IT WOULD TAKE AGES TO FIND HIM IN THIS HUGE MANOR, AM I RIGHT!?
WHICH LEAVES...

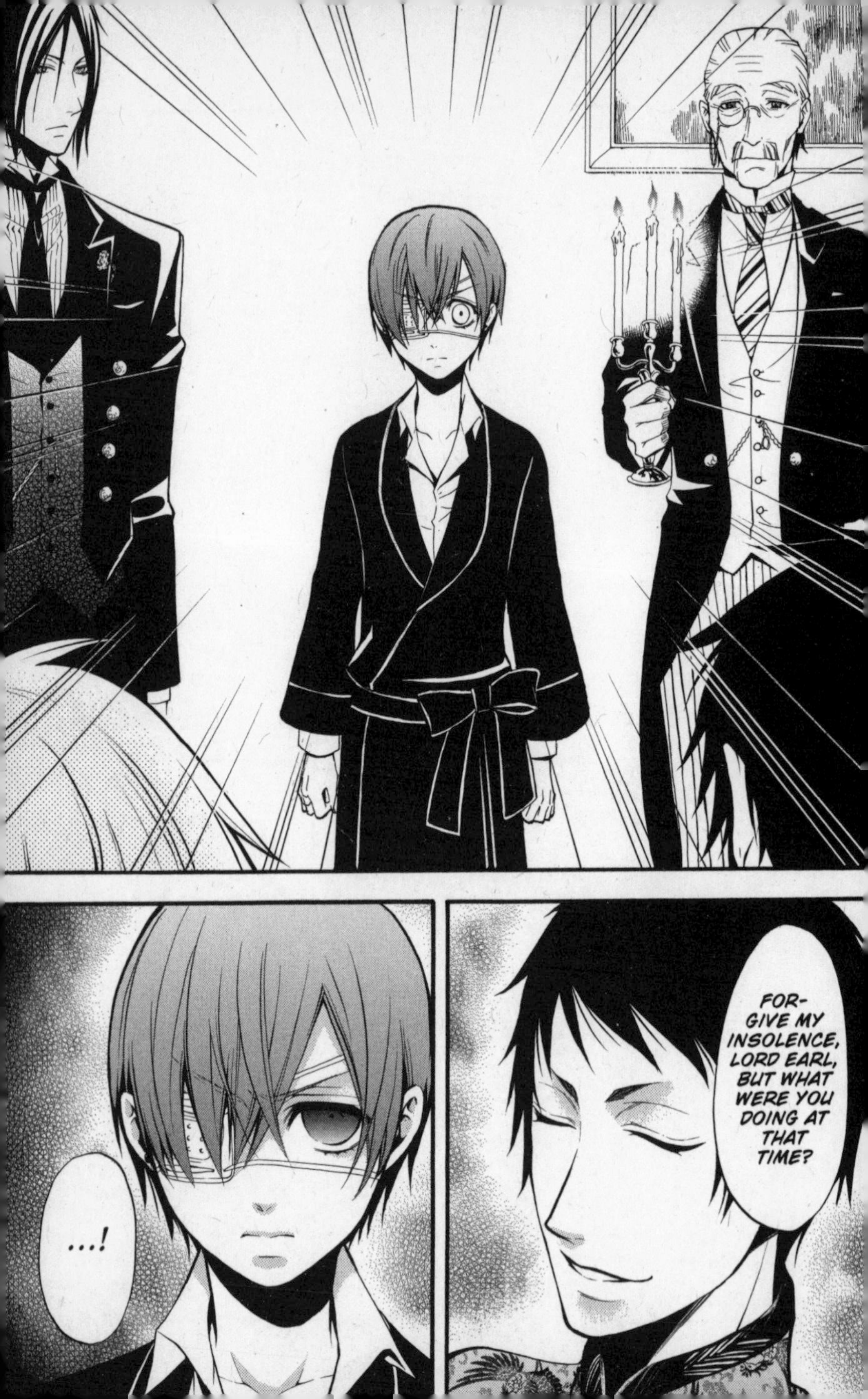
FOR-GIVE MY INSOLENCE, LORD EARL, BUT WHAT WERE YOU DOING AT THAT TIME?
...!

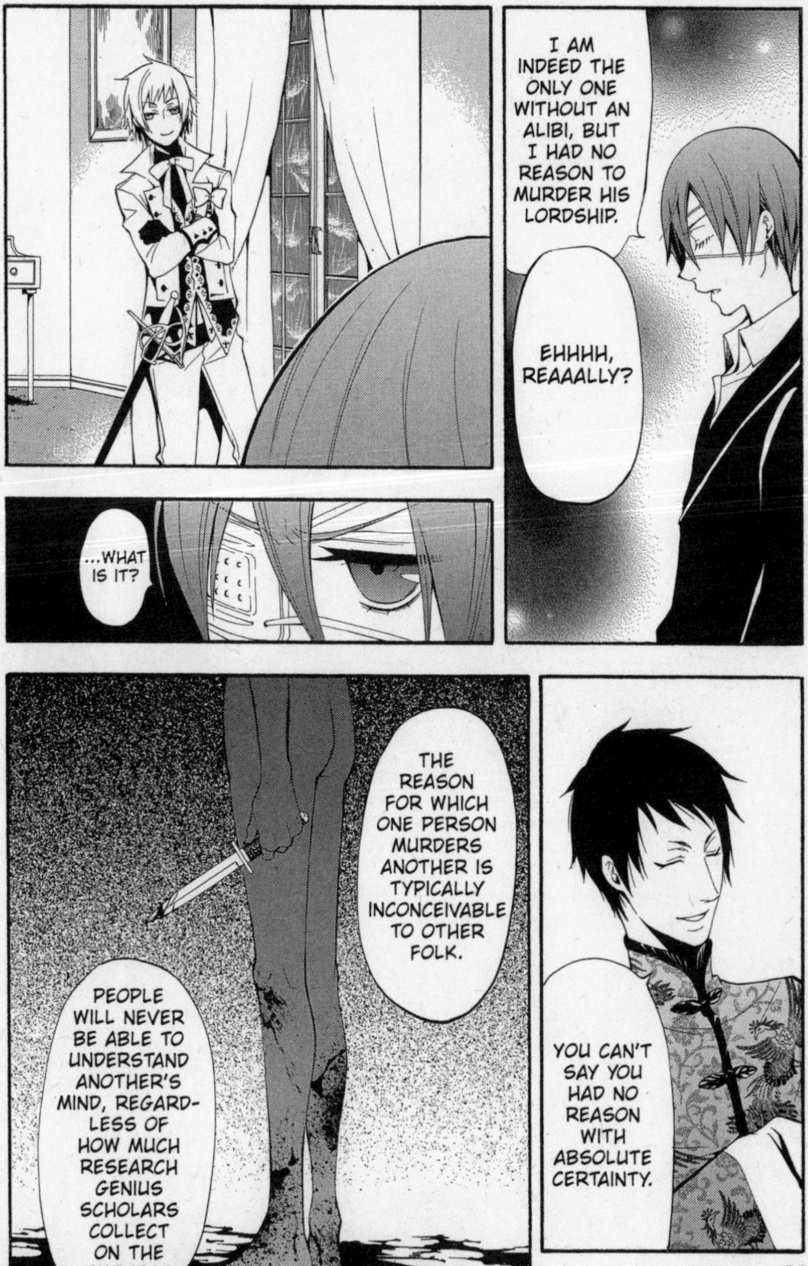
I AM INDEED THE ONLY ONE WITHOUT AN ALIBI, BUT I HAD NO REASON TO MURDER HIS LORDSHIP.
EHHHH, REAAALLY?
...WHAT IS IT?
YOU CAN'T SAY YOU HAD NO REASON WITH ABSOLUTE CERTAINTY.
THE REASON FOR WHICH ONE PERSON MURDERS ANOTHER IS TYPICALLY INCONCEIVABLE TO OTHER FOLK.
PEOPLE WILL NEVER BE ABLE TO UNDERSTAND ANOTHER'S MIND, REGARDLESS OF HOW MUCH RESEARCH GENIUS SCHOLARS COLLECT ON THE SUBJECT.

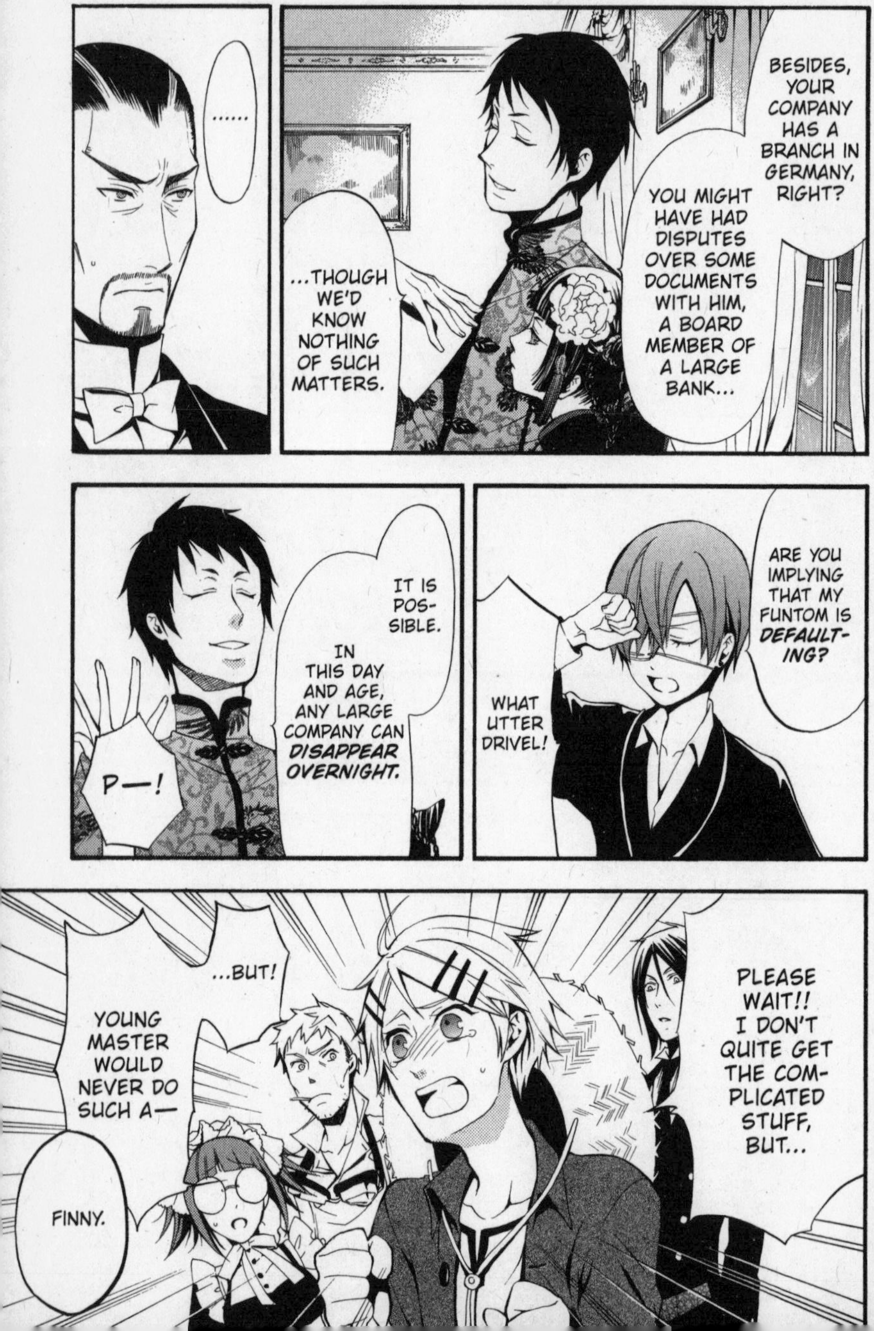
BESIDES, YOUR COMPANY HAS A BRANCH IN GERMANY, RIGHT?
YOU MIGHT HAVE HAD DISPUTES OVER SOME DOCUMENTS WITH HIM, A BOARD MEMBER OF A LARGE BANK...
...THOUGH WE'D KNOW NOTHING OF SUCH MATTERS.
......
ARE YOU IMPLYING THAT MY FUNTOM IS *DEFAULTING?*
WHAT UTTER DRIVEL!
IT IS POSSIBLE.
IN THIS DAY AND AGE, ANY LARGE COMPANY CAN *DISAPPEAR OVERNIGHT.*
P—!
PLEASE WAIT!! I DON'T QUITE GET THE COMPLICATED STUFF, BUT...
...BUT!
YOUNG MASTER WOULD NEVER DO SUCH A—
FINNY.

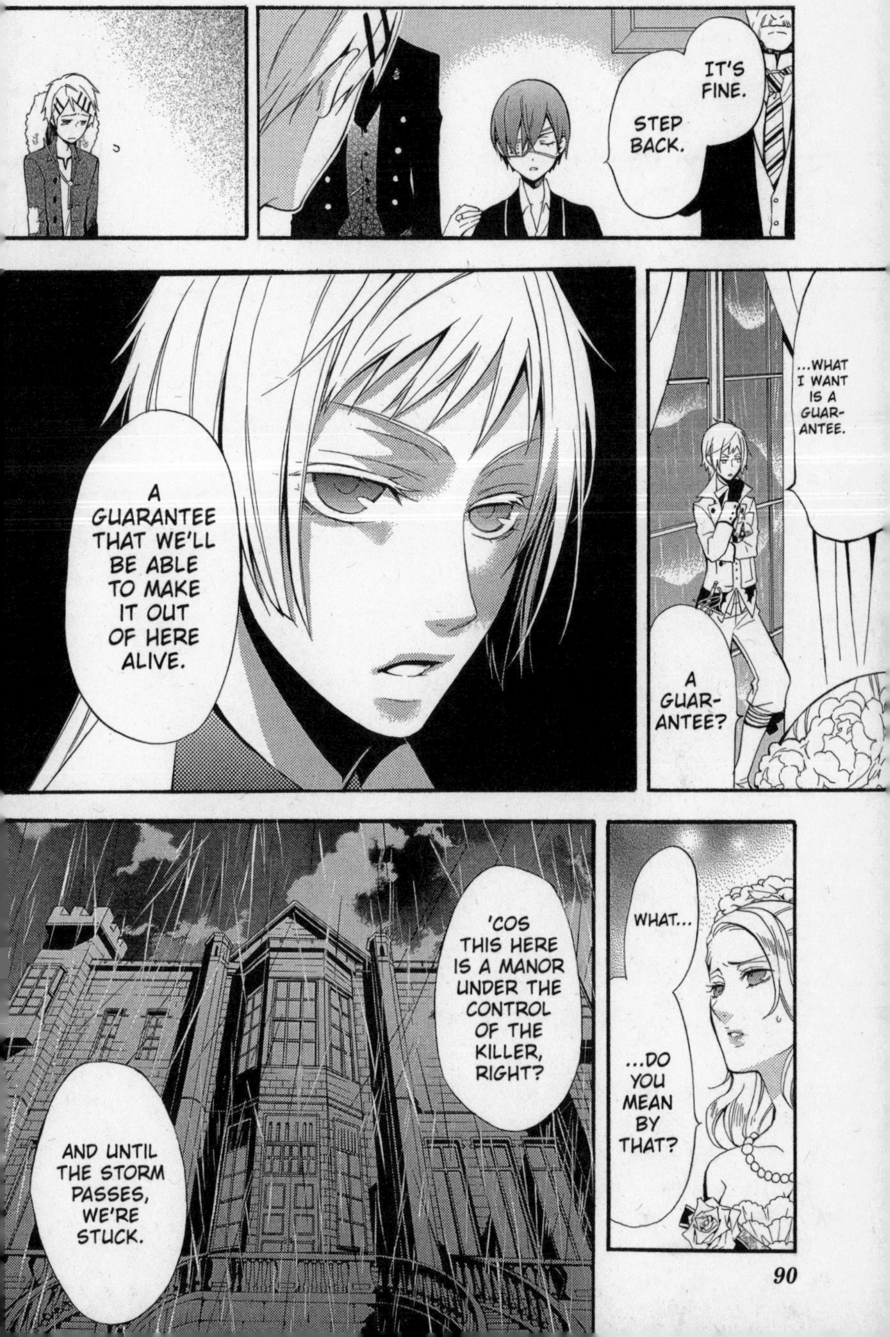
IT'S FINE.
STEP BACK.
...WHAT I WANT IS A GUAR-ANTEE.
A GUAR-ANTEE?
A GUARANTEE THAT WE'LL BE ABLE TO MAKE IT OUT OF HERE ALIVE.
WHAT...
...DO YOU MEAN BY THAT?
'COS THIS HERE IS A MANOR UNDER THE CONTROL OF THE KILLER, RIGHT?
AND UNTIL THE STORM PASSES, WE'RE STUCK.

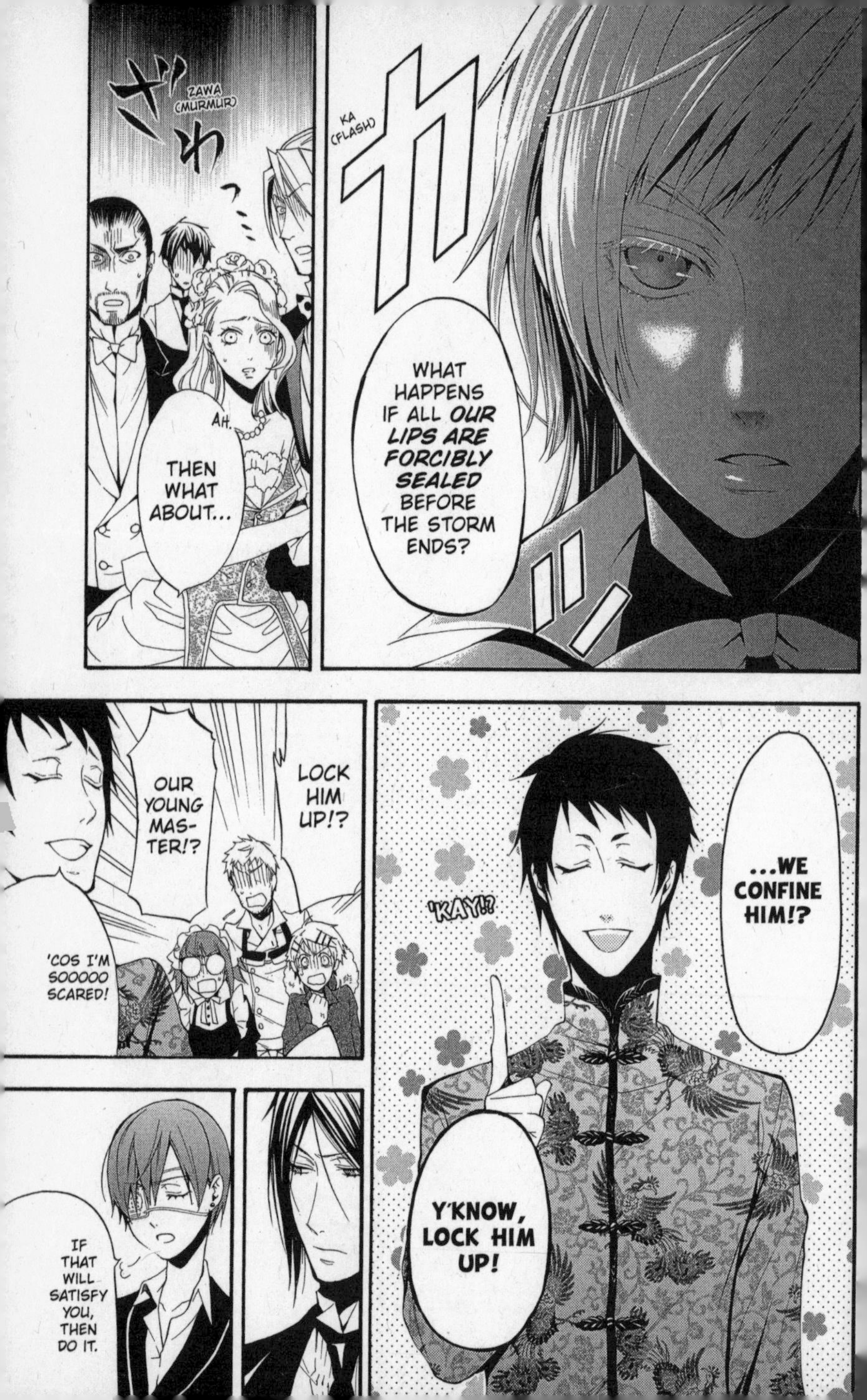
カ
KA (FLASH)
WHAT HAPPENS IF ALL OUR LIPS ARE FORCIBLY SEALED BEFORE THE STORM ENDS?
ざわ
ZAWA (MURMUR)
AH.
THEN WHAT ABOUT...
...WE CONFINE HIM!?
'KAY!?
Y'KNOW, LOCK HIM UP!
LOCK HIM UP!?
OUR YOUNG MAS-TER!?
'COS I'M SOOOOO SCARED!
IF THAT WILL SATISFY YOU, THEN DO IT.

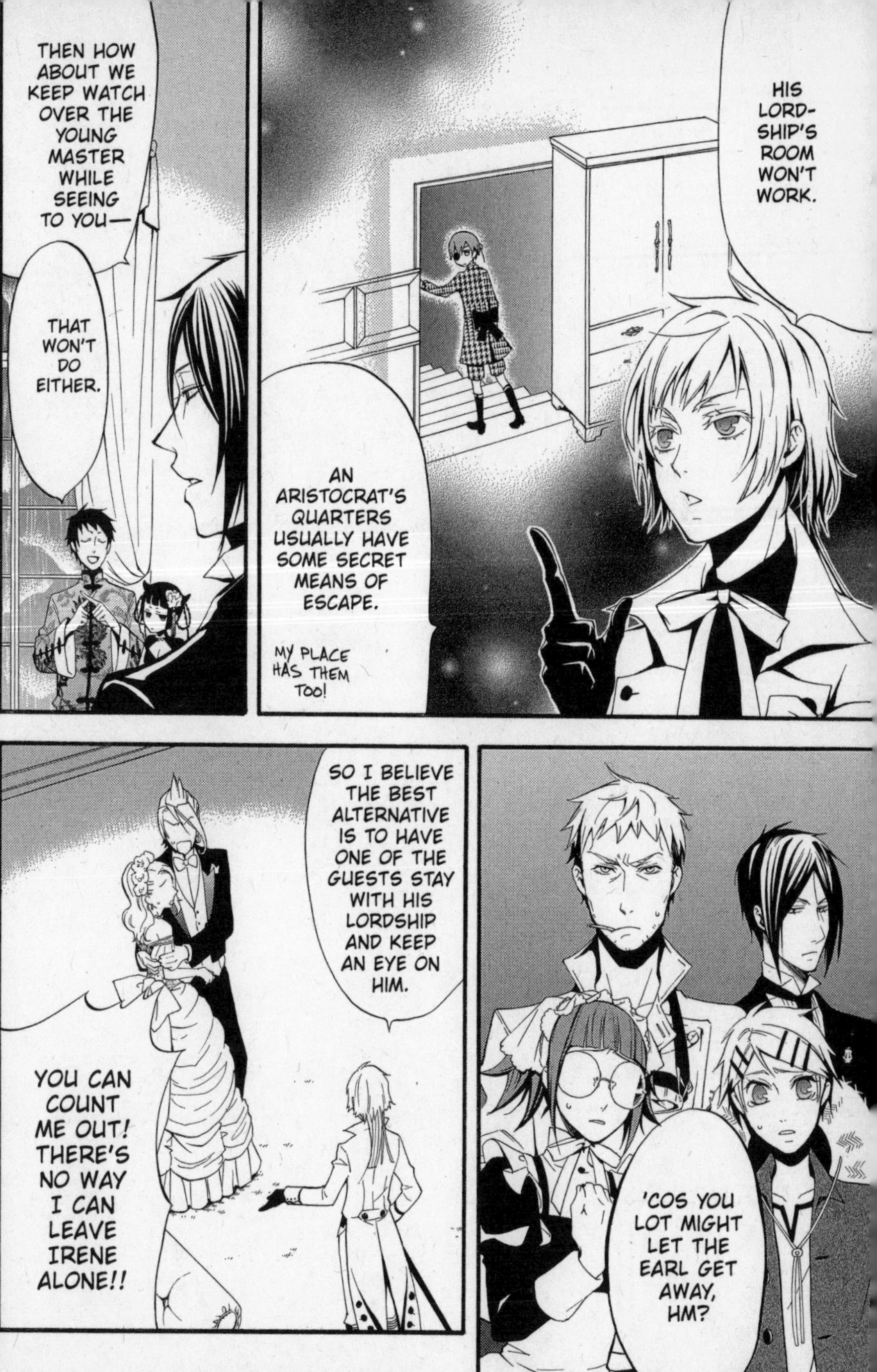
HIS LORDSHIP'S ROOM WON'T WORK.
AN ARISTOCRAT'S QUARTERS USUALLY HAVE SOME SECRET MEANS OF ESCAPE.
MY PLACE HAS THEM TOO!
THEN HOW ABOUT WE KEEP WATCH OVER THE YOUNG MASTER WHILE SEEING TO YOU—
THAT WON'T DO EITHER.
'COS YOU LOT MIGHT LET THE EARL GET AWAY, HM?
SO I BELIEVE THE BEST ALTERNATIVE IS TO HAVE ONE OF THE GUESTS STAY WITH HIS LORDSHIP AND KEEP AN EYE ON HIM.
YOU CAN COUNT ME OUT! THERE'S NO WAY I CAN LEAVE IRENE ALONE!!

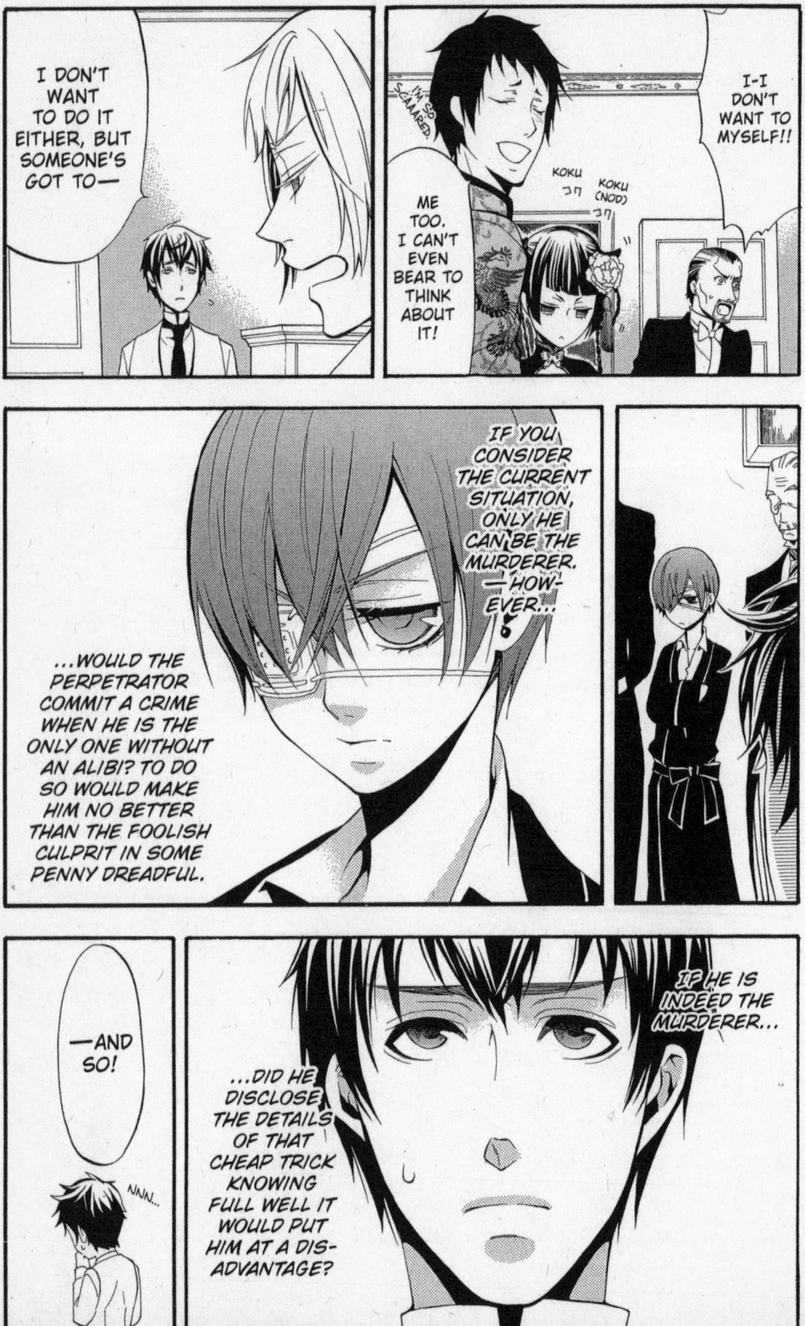
I-I DON'T WANT TO MYSELF!!
ME TOO. I CAN'T EVEN BEAR TO THINK ABOUT IT!
KOKU コク
KOKU (NOD) コク
I'M SO SCAAARED.
I DON'T WANT TO DO IT EITHER, BUT SOMEONE'S GOT TO—
IF YOU CONSIDER THE CURRENT SITUATION, ONLY HE CAN BE THE MURDERER. —HOW-EVER...
...WOULD THE PERPETRATOR COMMIT A CRIME WHEN HE IS THE ONLY ONE WITHOUT AN ALIBI? TO DO SO WOULD MAKE HIM NO BETTER THAN THE FOOLISH CULPRIT IN SOME PENNY DREADFUL.
IF HE IS INDEED THE MURDERER...
...DID HE DISCLOSE THE DETAILS OF THAT CHEAP TRICK KNOWING FULL WELL IT WOULD PUT HIM AT A DIS-ADVANTAGE?
—AND SO!
NNN...

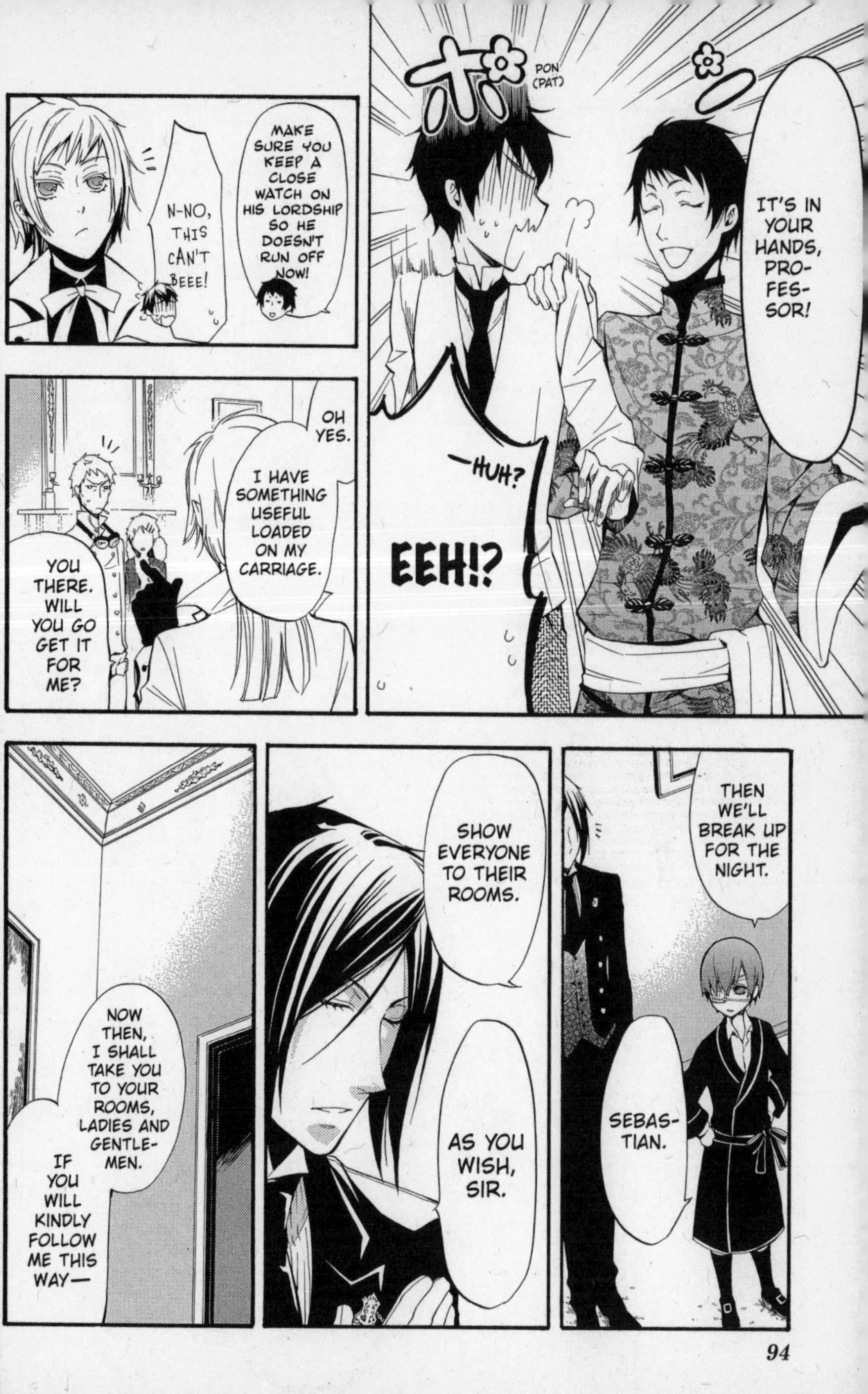
PON (PAT)
IT'S IN YOUR HANDS, PRO-FES-SOR!
—HUH?
EEH!?
MAKE SURE YOU KEEP A CLOSE WATCH ON HIS LORDSHIP SO HE DOESN'T RUN OFF NOW!
N-NO, THIS CAN'T BEEE!
OH YES.
I HAVE SOMETHING USEFUL LOADED ON MY CARRIAGE.
YOU THERE. WILL YOU GO GET IT FOR ME?
THEN WE'LL BREAK UP FOR THE NIGHT.
SEBAS-TIAN.
SHOW EVERYONE TO THEIR ROOMS.
AS YOU WISH, SIR.
NOW THEN, I SHALL TAKE YOU TO YOUR ROOMS, LADIES AND GENTLE-MEN.
IF YOU WILL KINDLY FOLLOW ME THIS WAY—

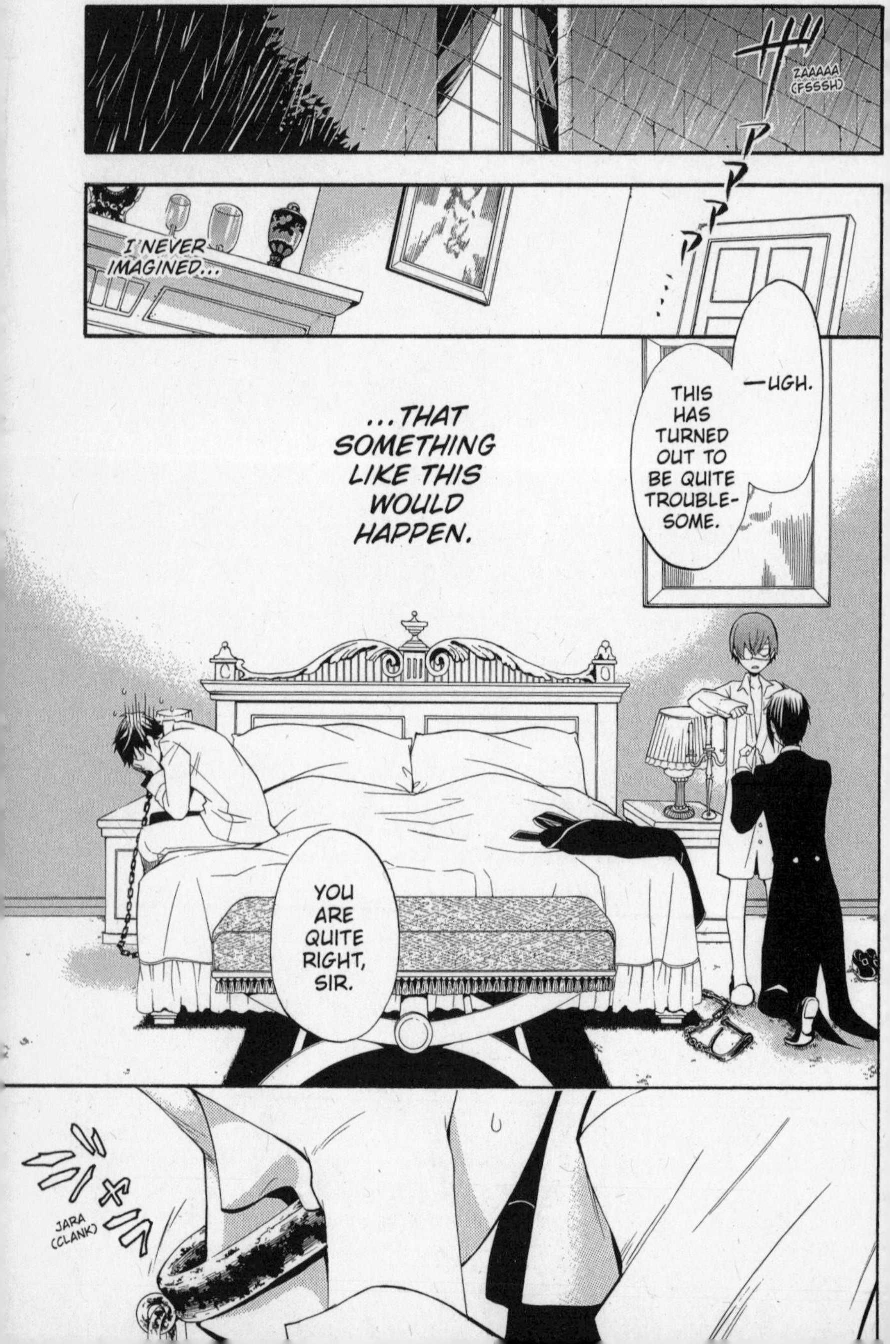
ZAAAAA (FSSSH)
I NEVER IMAGINED...
—UGH.
THIS HAS TURNED OUT TO BE QUITE TROUBLE-SOME.
...THAT SOMETHING LIKE THIS WOULD HAPPEN.
YOU ARE QUITE RIGHT, SIR.
JARA (CLANK)

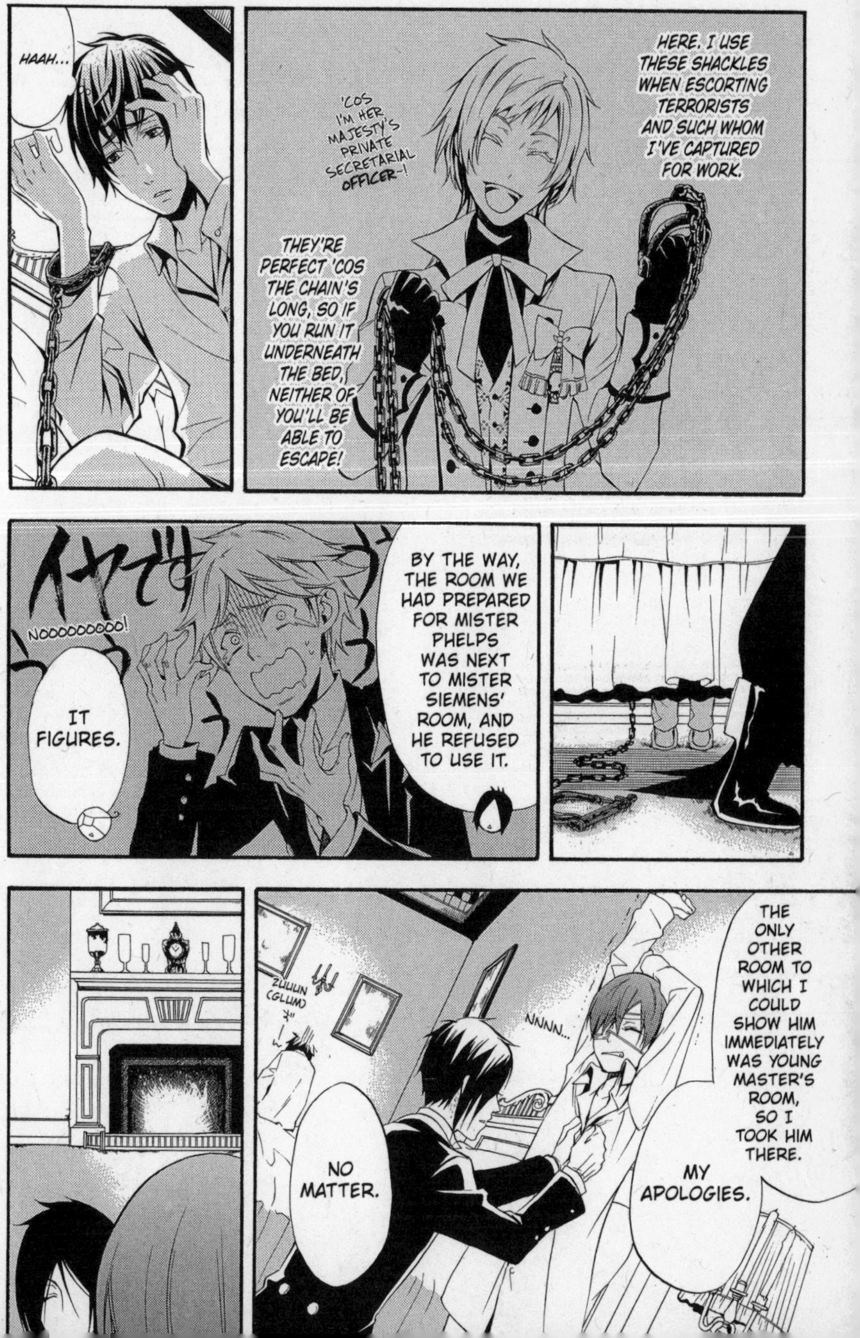
HERE. I USE THESE SHACKLES WHEN ESCORTING TERRORISTS AND SUCH WHOM I'VE CAPTURED FOR WORK.
'COS I'M HER MAJESTY'S PRIVATE SECRETARIAL OFFICER~!
THEY'RE PERFECT 'COS THE CHAIN'S LONG, SO IF YOU RUN IT UNDERNEATH THE BED, NEITHER OF YOU'LL BE ABLE TO ESCAPE!
HAAH...
BY THE WAY, THE ROOM WE HAD PREPARED FOR MISTER PHELPS WAS NEXT TO MISTER SIEMENS' ROOM, AND HE REFUSED TO USE IT.
イヤです
NOOOOOOOOO!
IT FIGURES.
THE ONLY OTHER ROOM TO WHICH I COULD SHOW HIM IMMEDIATELY WAS YOUNG MASTER'S ROOM, SO I TOOK HIM THERE.
NNNN...
MY APOLOGIES.
ZUUUN (GLUM)
NO MATTER.

PASU (FWAP)

IT'S TO BE COLD TONIGHT.

MAKE SURE THE GUEST ROOMS HAVE ENOUGH COKE TO KEEP THE FIRES GOING THROUGH THE NIGHT.

EVEN IF I'M NOT AROUND, MAKE SURE OUR GUESTS GET THE FINEST PHANTOM-HIVE HAS TO OFFER.

YES, MY LORD.

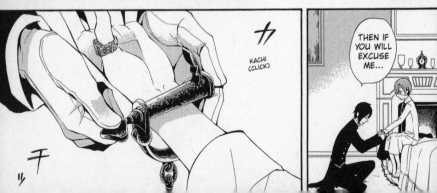

KACHI (CLICK)

THEN IF YOU WILL EXCUSE ME...

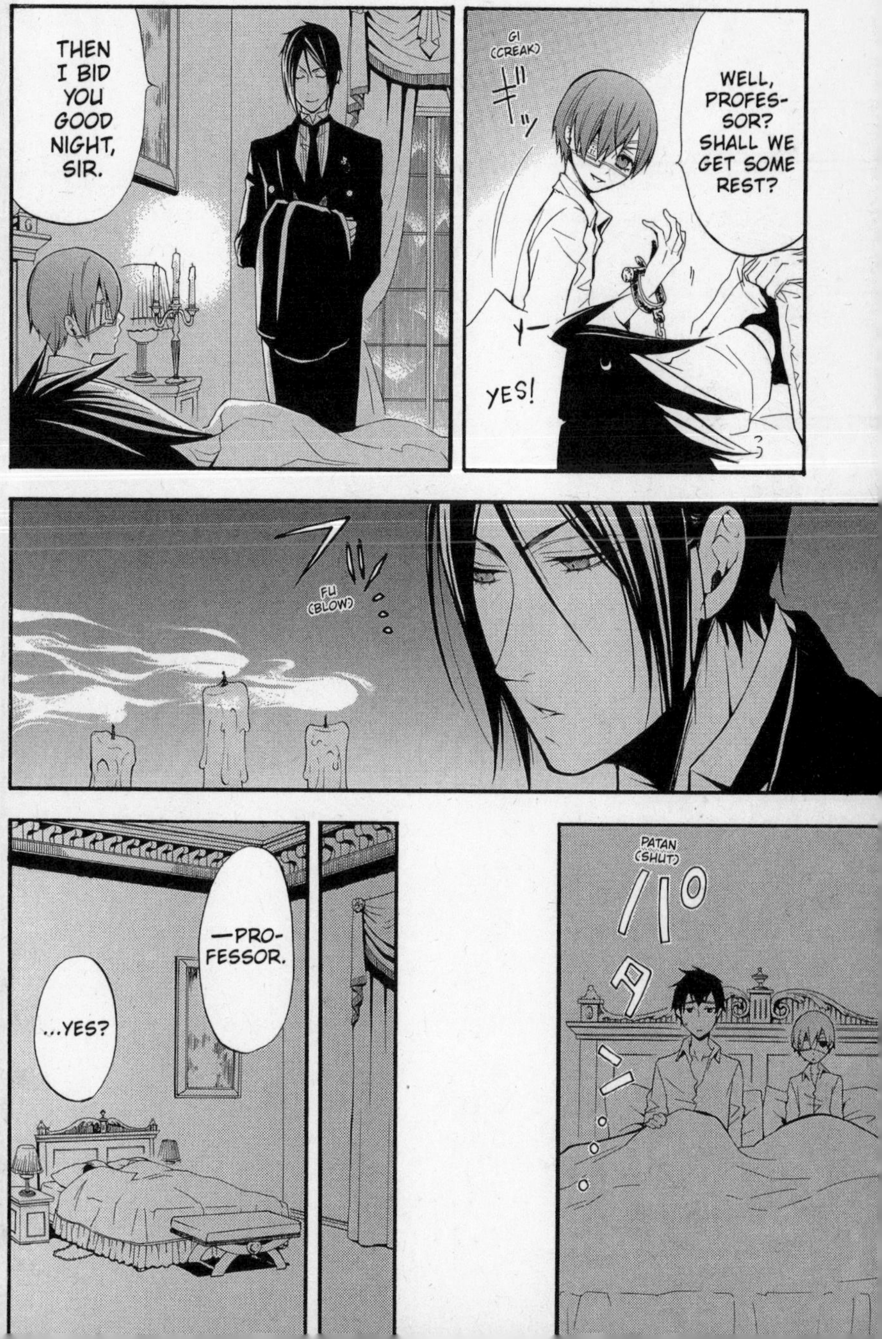
GI (CREAK)
WELL, PROFES-SOR? SHALL WE GET SOME REST?
YES!
THEN I BID YOU GOOD NIGHT, SIR.
FU (BLOW)
PATAN (SHUT)
—PRO-FESSOR.
...YES?

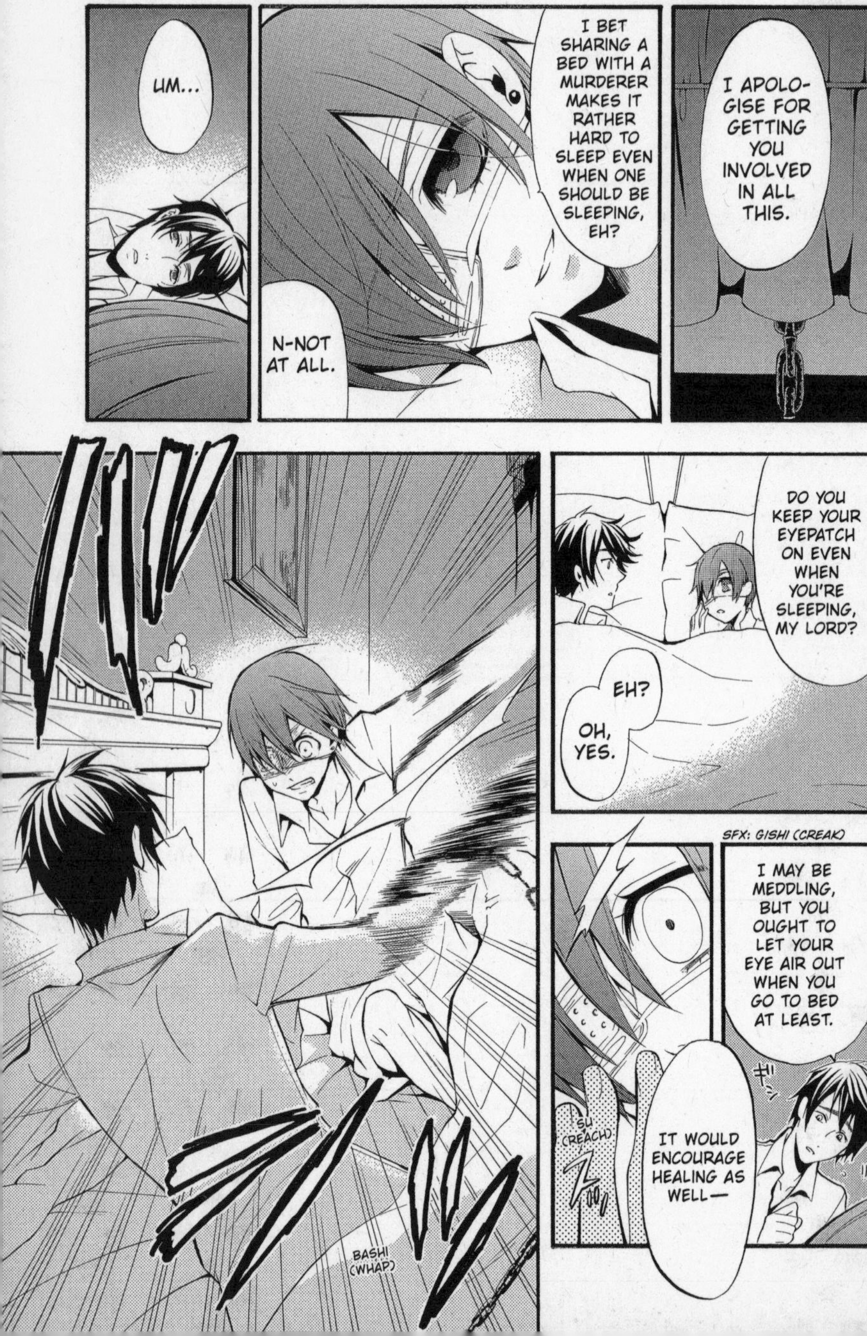
I APOLOGISE FOR GETTING YOU INVOLVED IN ALL THIS.
I BET SHARING A BED WITH A MURDERER MAKES IT RATHER HARD TO SLEEP EVEN WHEN ONE SHOULD BE SLEEPING, EH?
N-NOT AT ALL.
UM...
DO YOU KEEP YOUR EYEPATCH ON EVEN WHEN YOU'RE SLEEPING, MY LORD?
EH?
OH, YES.
SFX: GISHI (CREAK)
I MAY BE MEDDLING, BUT YOU OUGHT TO LET YOUR EYE AIR OUT WHEN YOU GO TO BED AT LEAST.
SU (REACH)
IT WOULD ENCOURAGE HEALING AS WELL—
BASHI (WHAP)

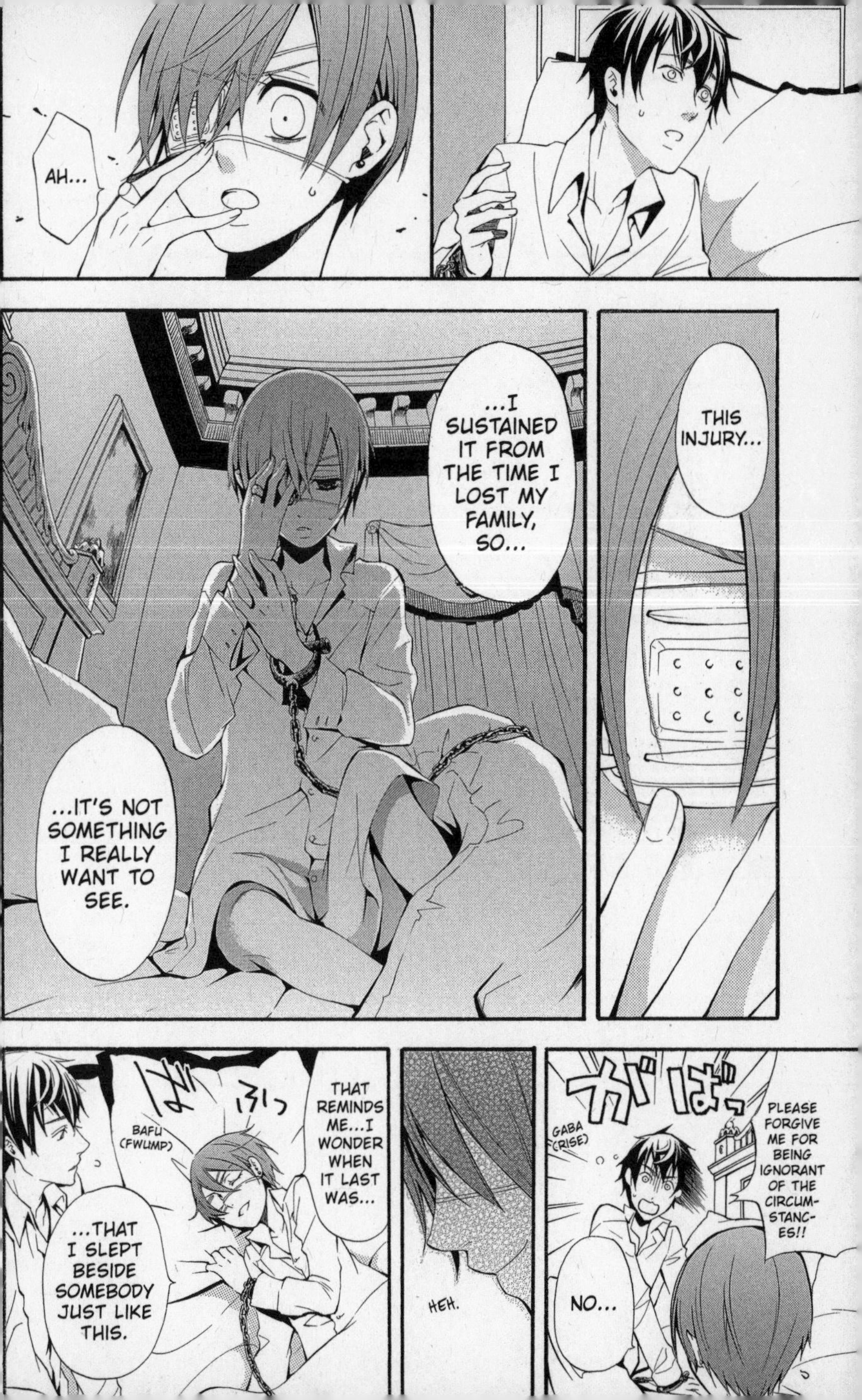
AH...
THIS INJURY...
...I SUSTAINED IT FROM THE TIME I LOST MY FAMILY, SO...
...IT'S NOT SOMETHING I REALLY WANT TO SEE.
がばっ
GABA (RISE)
PLEASE FORGIVE ME FOR BEING IGNORANT OF THE CIRCUM-STANC-ES!!
NO...
HEH.
ばふっ
BAFU (FWUMP)
THAT REMINDS ME...I WONDER WHEN IT LAST WAS...
...THAT I SLEPT BESIDE SOMEBODY JUST LIKE THIS.

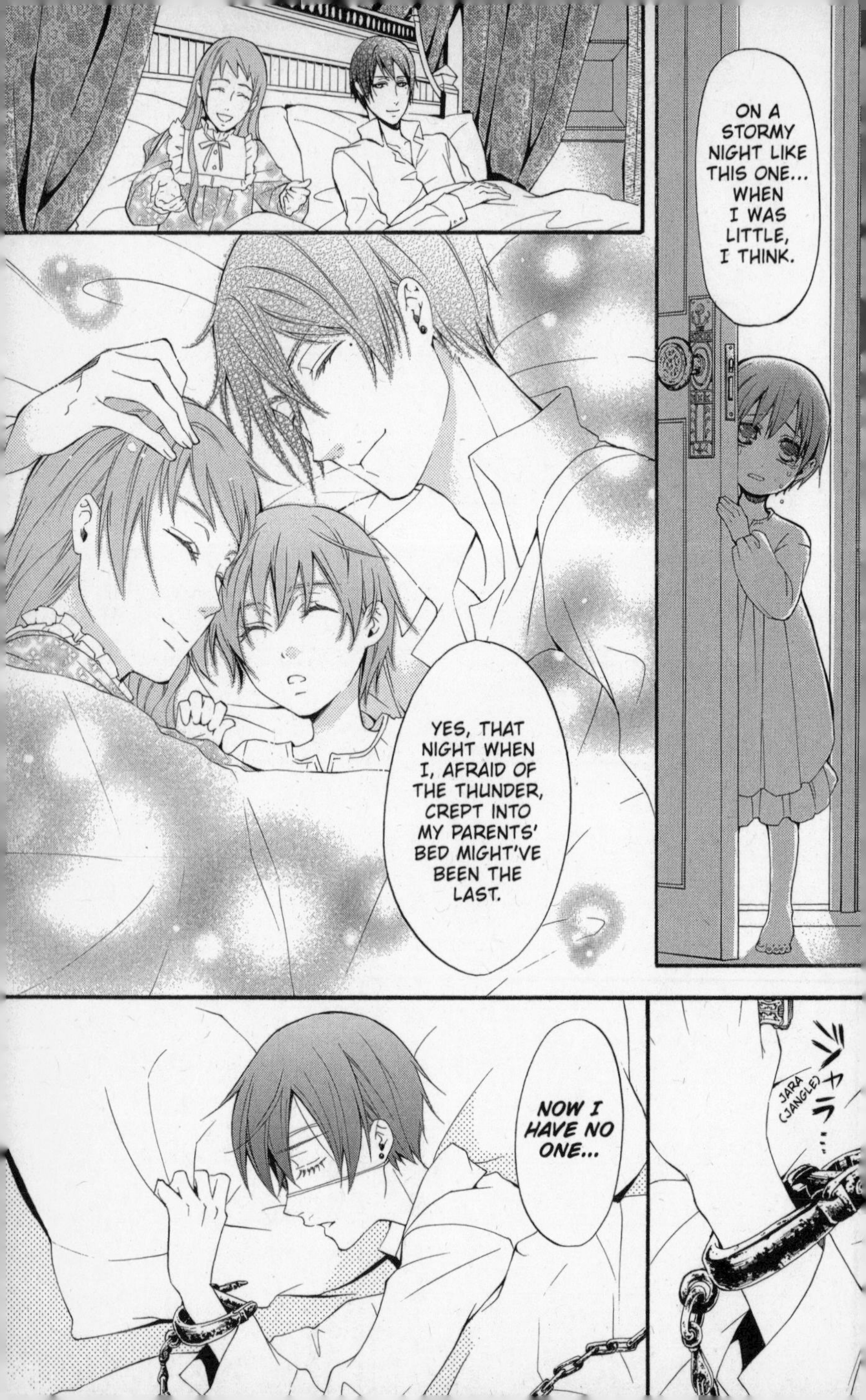
ON A STORMY NIGHT LIKE THIS ONE... WHEN I WAS LITTLE, I THINK.
YES, THAT NIGHT WHEN I, AFRAID OF THE THUNDER, CREPT INTO MY PARENTS' BED MIGHT'VE BEEN THE LAST.
JARA (JANGLE)
NOW I HAVE NO ONE...

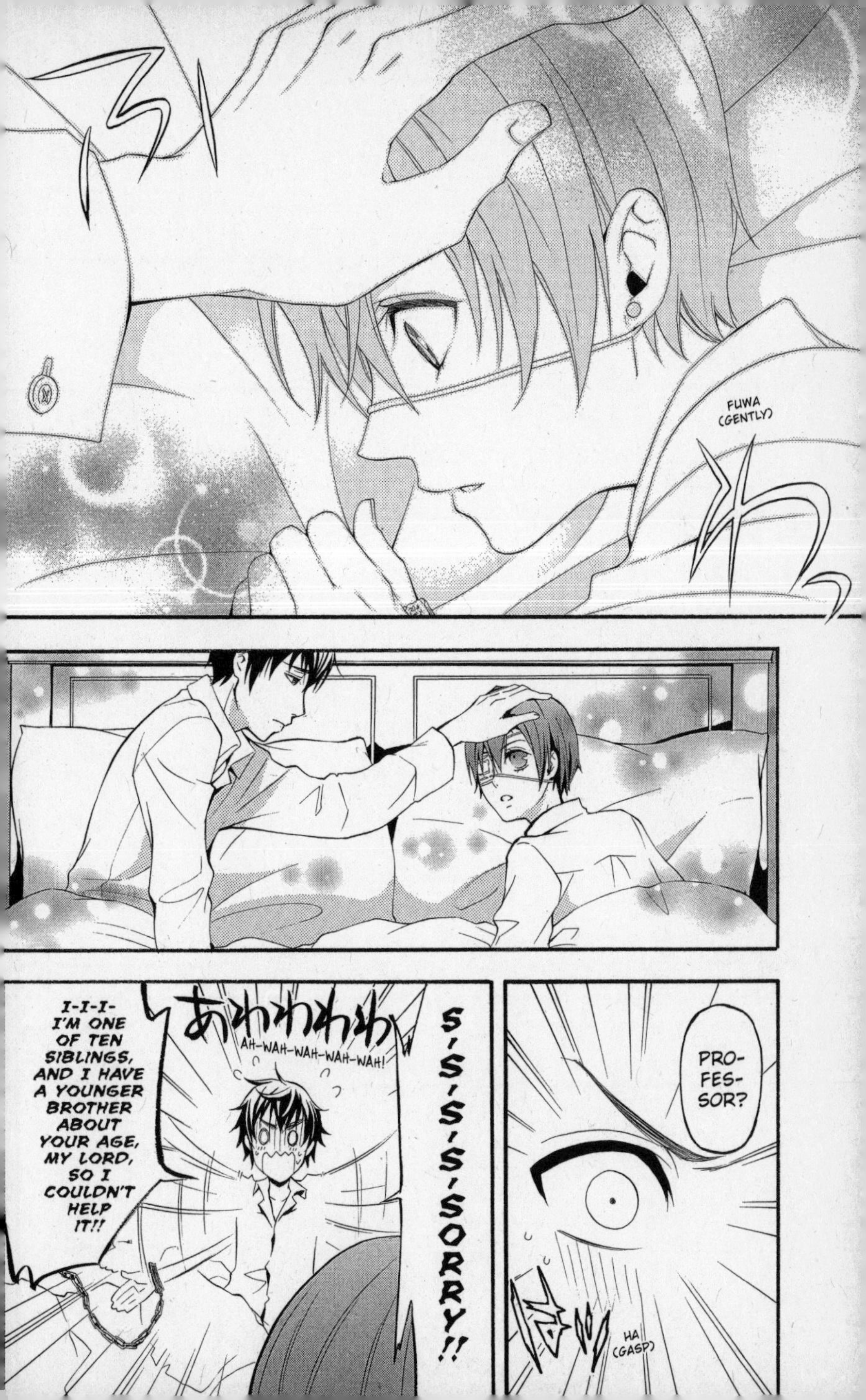
FUWA (GENTLY)
PRO-FES-SOR?
HA (GASP)
S-S-S-S-SORRY!!
あわわわわ
AH-WAH-WAH-WAH-WAH!
I-I-I-I'M ONE OF TEN SIBLINGS, AND I HAVE A YOUNGER BROTHER ABOUT YOUR AGE, MY LORD, SO I COULDN'T HELP IT!!

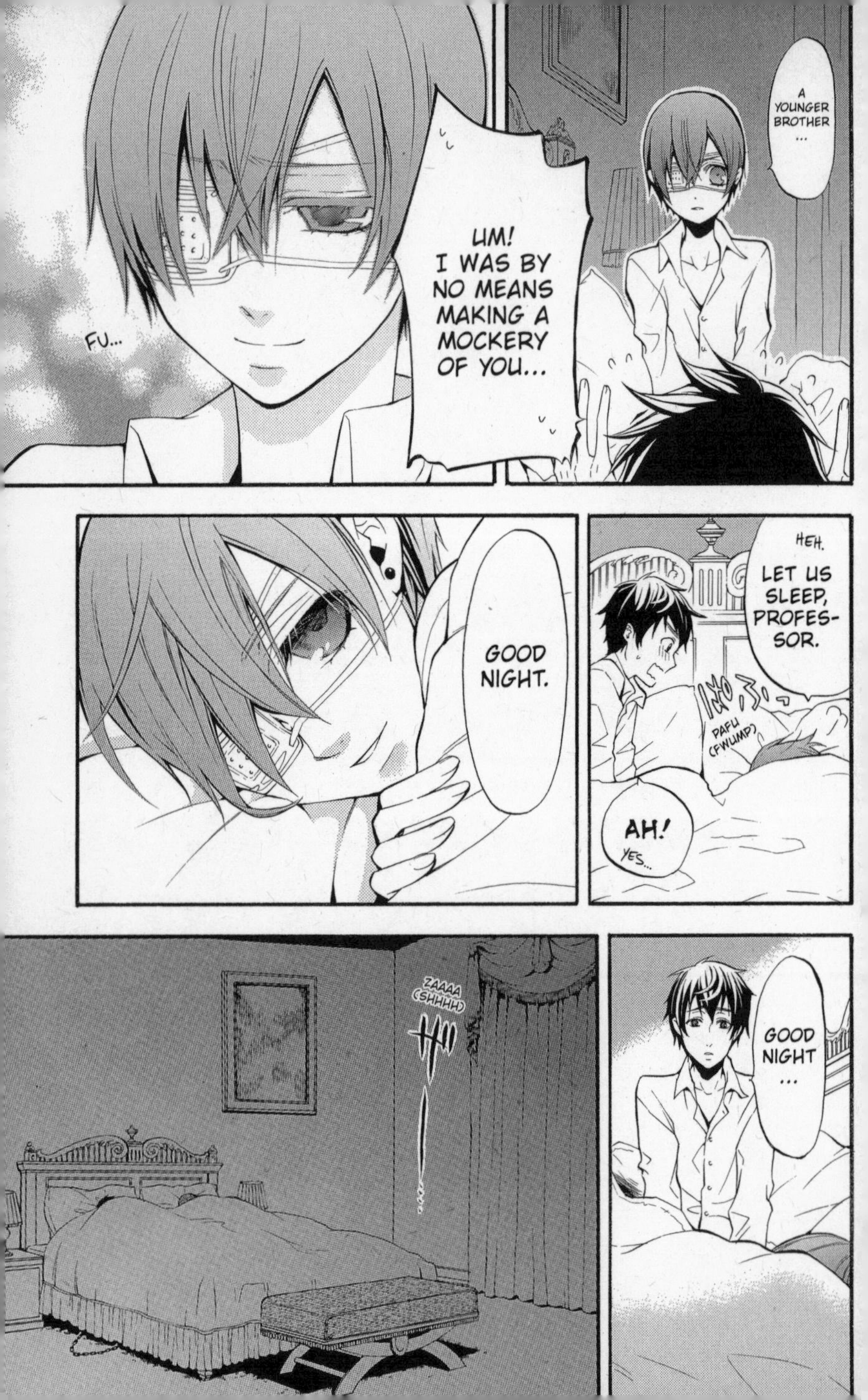
A YOUNGER BROTHER...
UM! I WAS BY NO MEANS MAKING A MOCKERY OF YOU...
FU...
HEH.
LET US SLEEP, PROFES-SOR.
PAFU (FWUMP)
AH! YES...
GOOD NIGHT.
GOOD NIGHT...
ZAAAA (SHHHH)

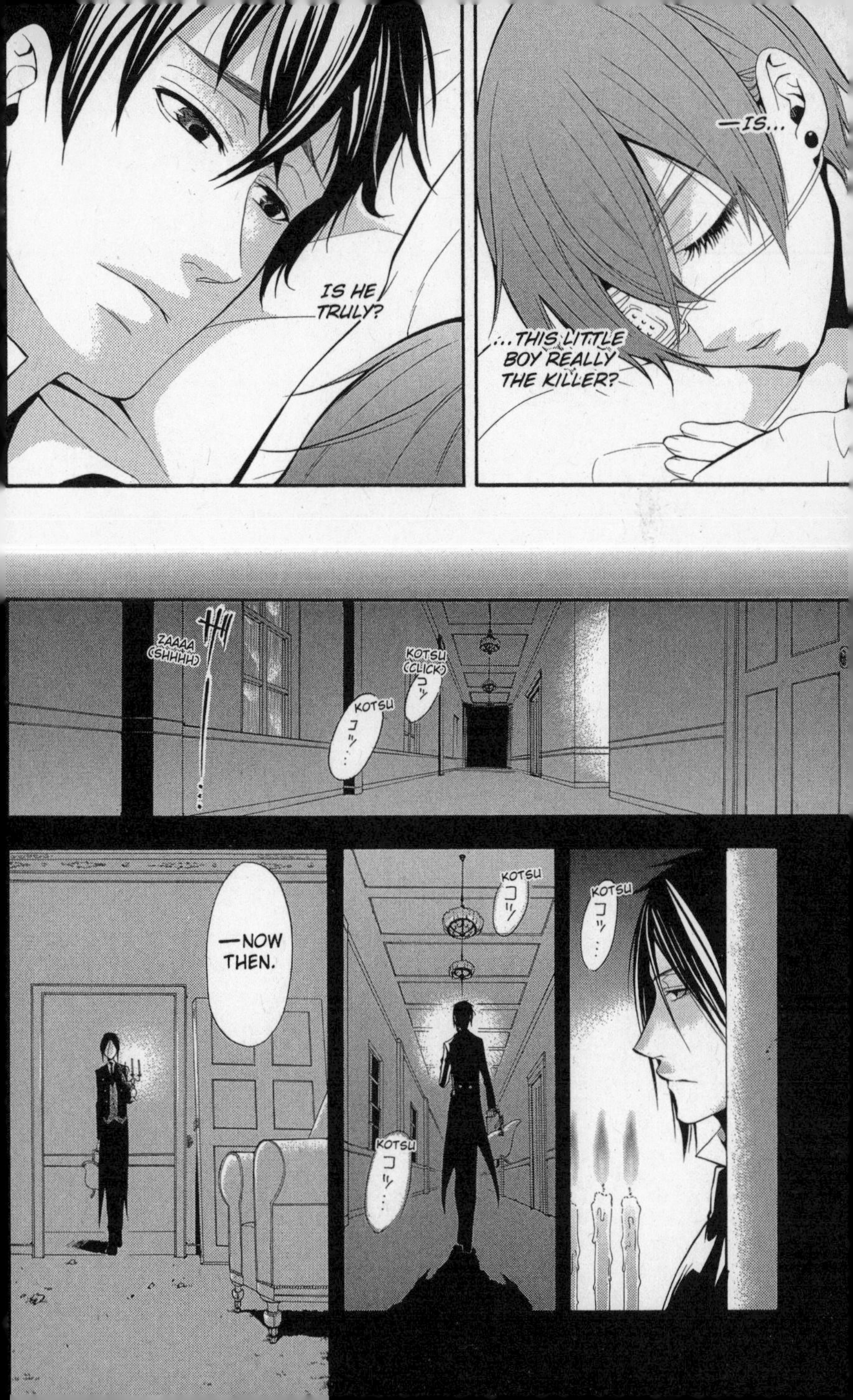
—IS...
...THIS LITTLE BOY REALLY THE KILLER?
IS HE TRULY?
KOTSU (CLICK)
コッ
KOTSU
コッ...
ZAAAA (SHHHH)
KOTSU
コッ...
KOTSU
コッ
KOTSU
コッ...
—NOW THEN.

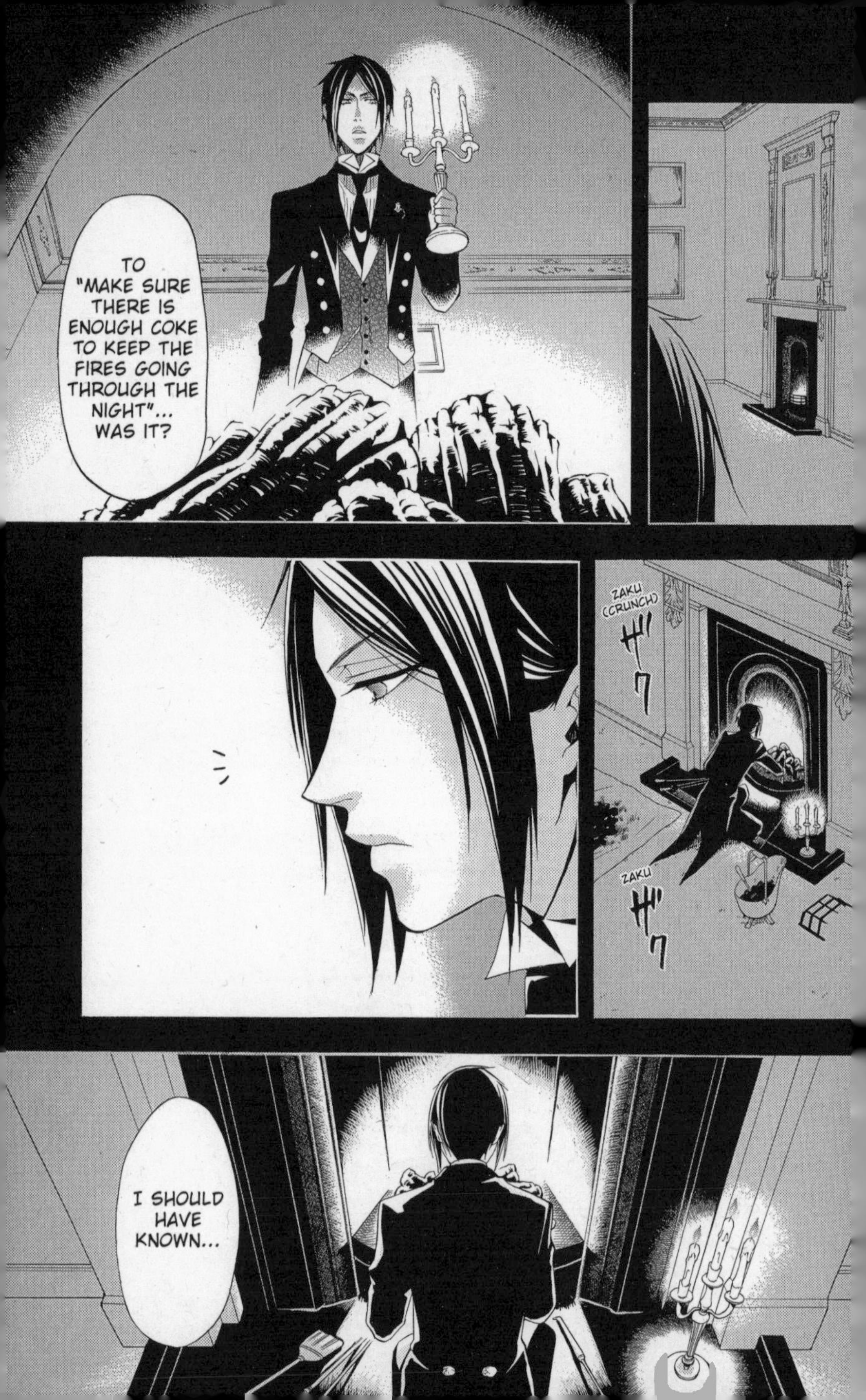
TO "MAKE SURE THERE IS ENOUGH COKE TO KEEP THE FIRES GOING THROUGH THE NIGHT"... WAS IT?
ZAKU (CRUNCH)
ザク
ZAKU
ザク
I SHOULD HAVE KNOWN...

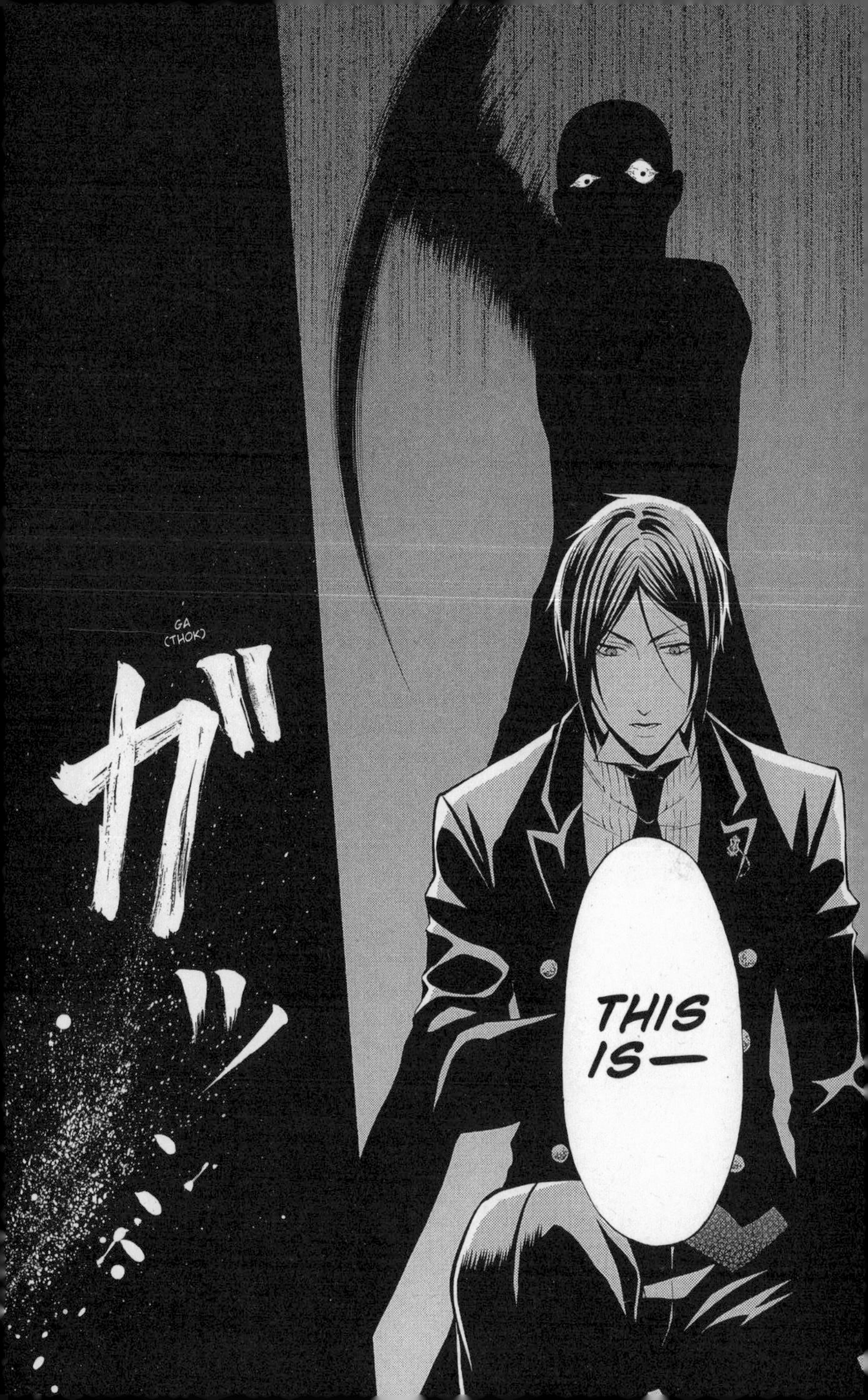
THIS IS—
GA (THOK)

Black Butler

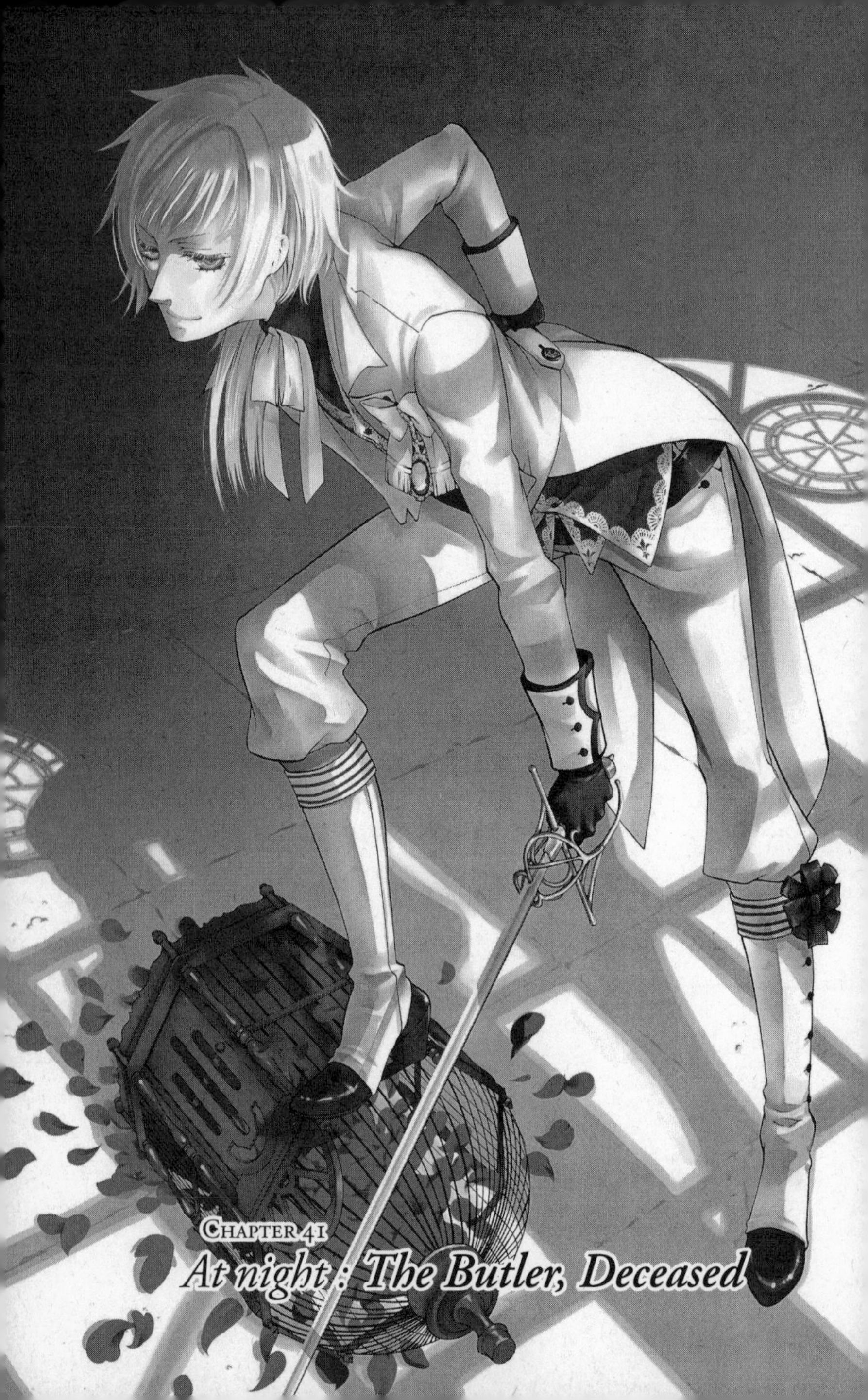
CHAPTER 41
At night : The Butler, Deceased

Black Butler

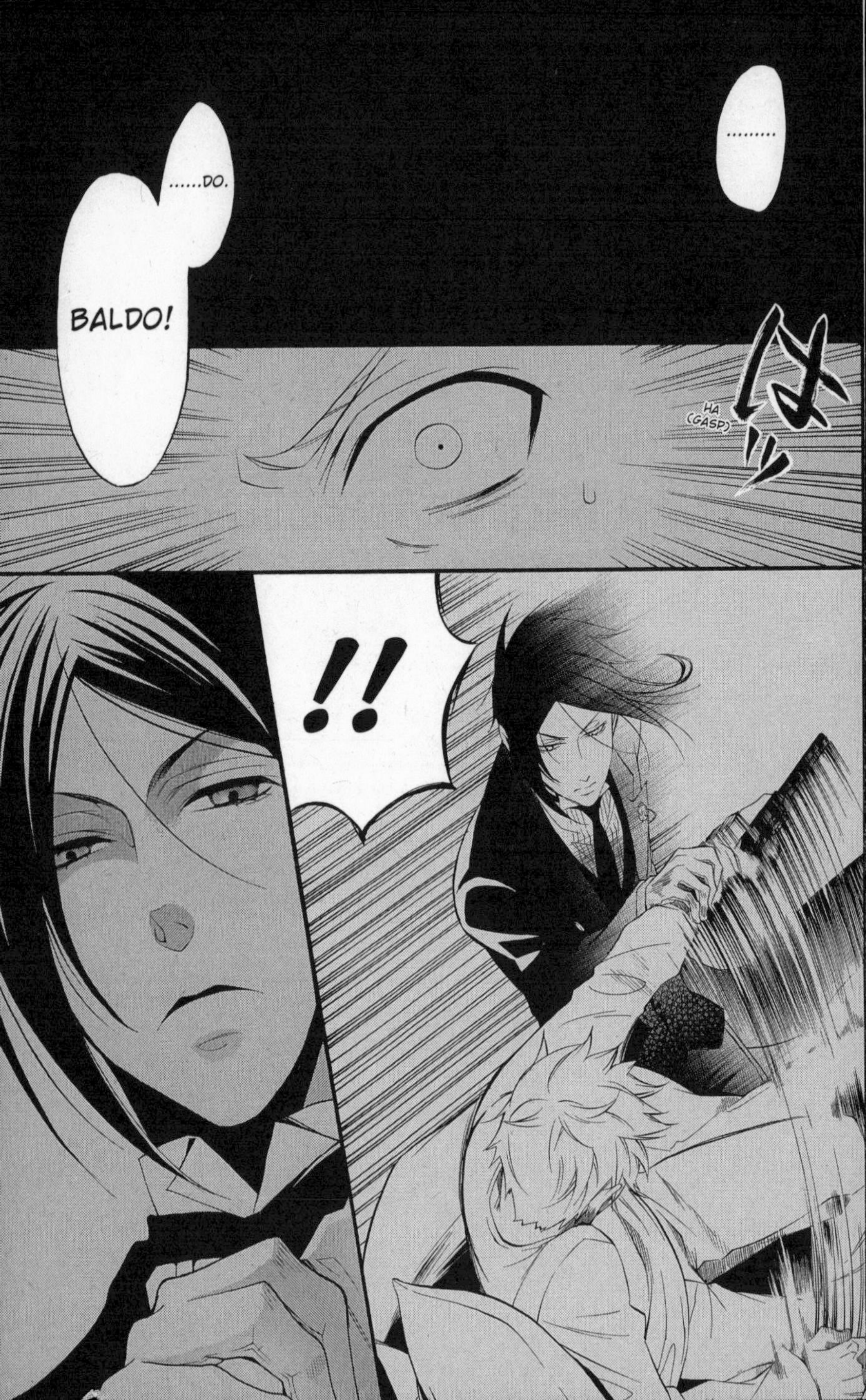

....
......DO.
BALDO!
はッ
HA (GASP)
!!

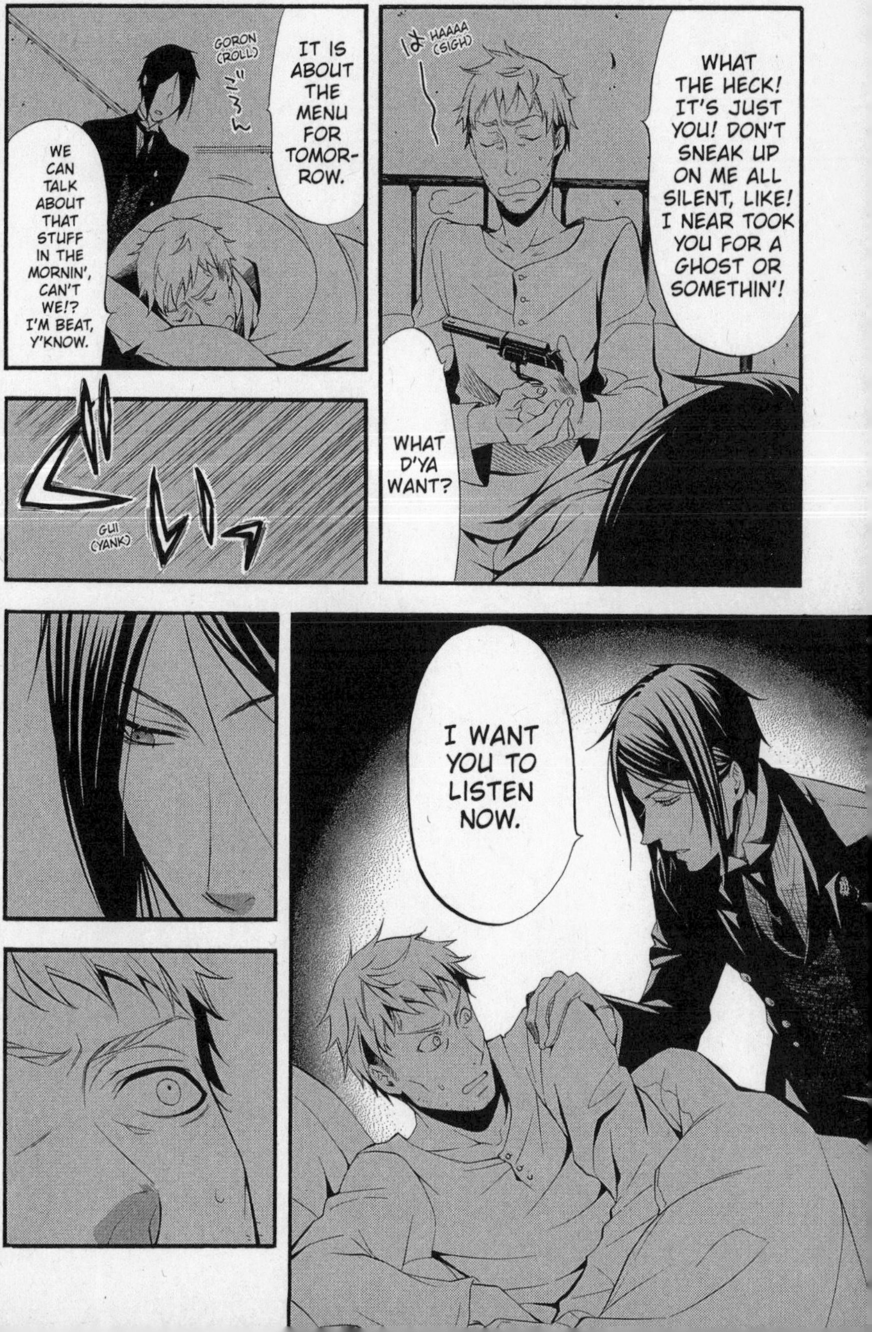
HAAAA (SIGH)
WHAT THE HECK! IT'S JUST YOU! DON'T SNEAK UP ON ME ALL SILENT, LIKE! I NEAR TOOK YOU FOR A GHOST OR SOMETHIN'!
WHAT D'YA WANT?
IT IS ABOUT THE MENU FOR TOMORROW.
GORON (ROLL)
WE CAN TALK ABOUT THAT STUFF IN THE MORNIN', CAN'T WE!? I'M BEAT, Y'KNOW.
GUI (YANK)
I WANT YOU TO LISTEN NOW.

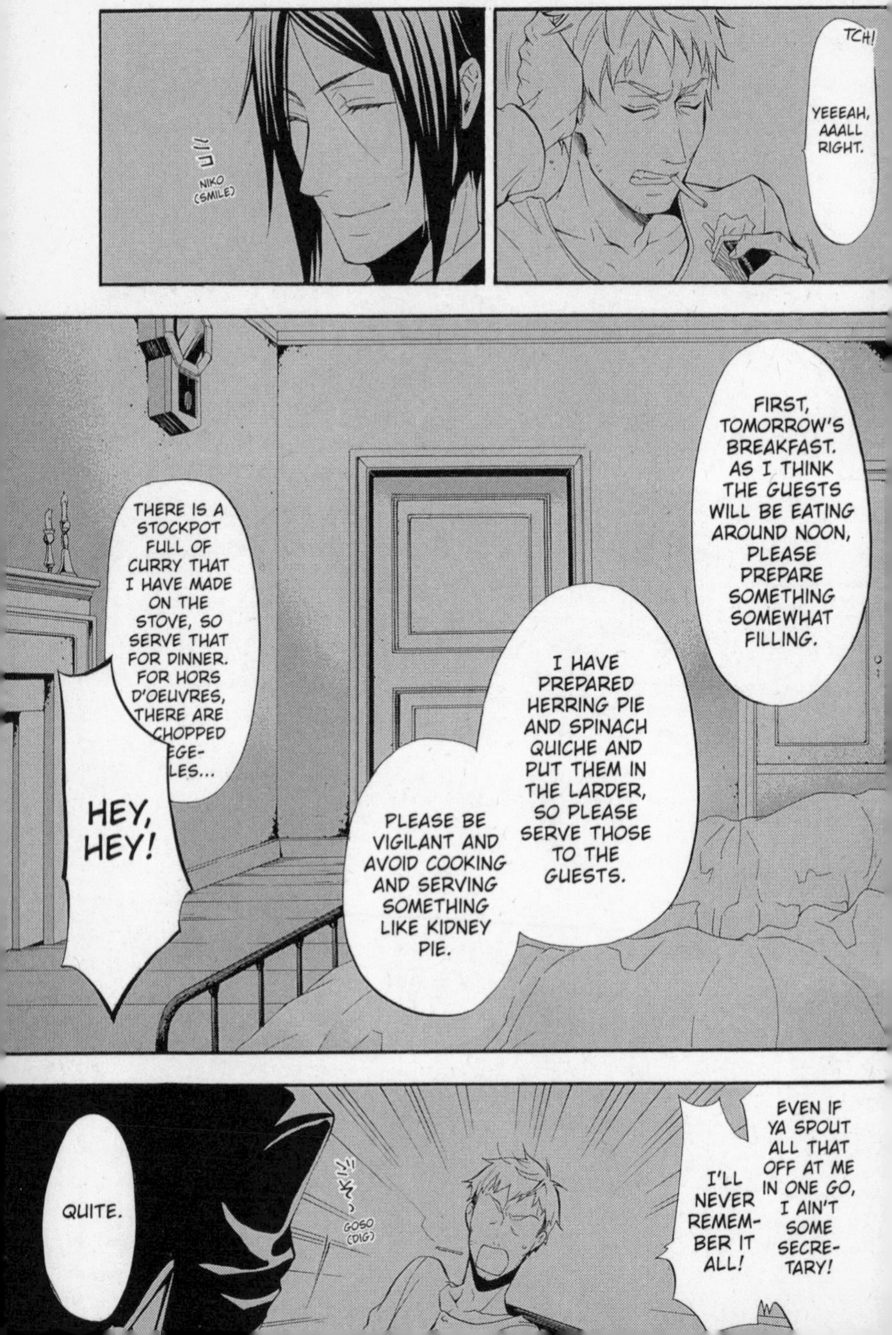
TCH!
YEEEAH, AAALL RIGHT.
NIKO (SMILE)
FIRST, TOMORROW'S BREAKFAST. AS I THINK THE GUESTS WILL BE EATING AROUND NOON, PLEASE PREPARE SOMETHING SOMEWHAT FILLING.
I HAVE PREPARED HERRING PIE AND SPINACH QUICHE AND PUT THEM IN THE LARDER, SO PLEASE SERVE THOSE TO THE GUESTS.
PLEASE BE VIGILANT AND AVOID COOKING AND SERVING SOMETHING LIKE KIDNEY PIE.
THERE IS A STOCKPOT FULL OF CURRY THAT I HAVE MADE ON THE STOVE, SO SERVE THAT FOR DINNER. FOR HORS D'OEUVRES, THERE ARE CHOPPED EGE- LES...
HEY, HEY!
EVEN IF YA SPOUT ALL THAT OFF AT ME IN ONE GO, I AIN'T SOME SECRE- TARY!
I'LL NEVER REMEM- BER IT ALL!
GOSO (DIG)
QUITE.

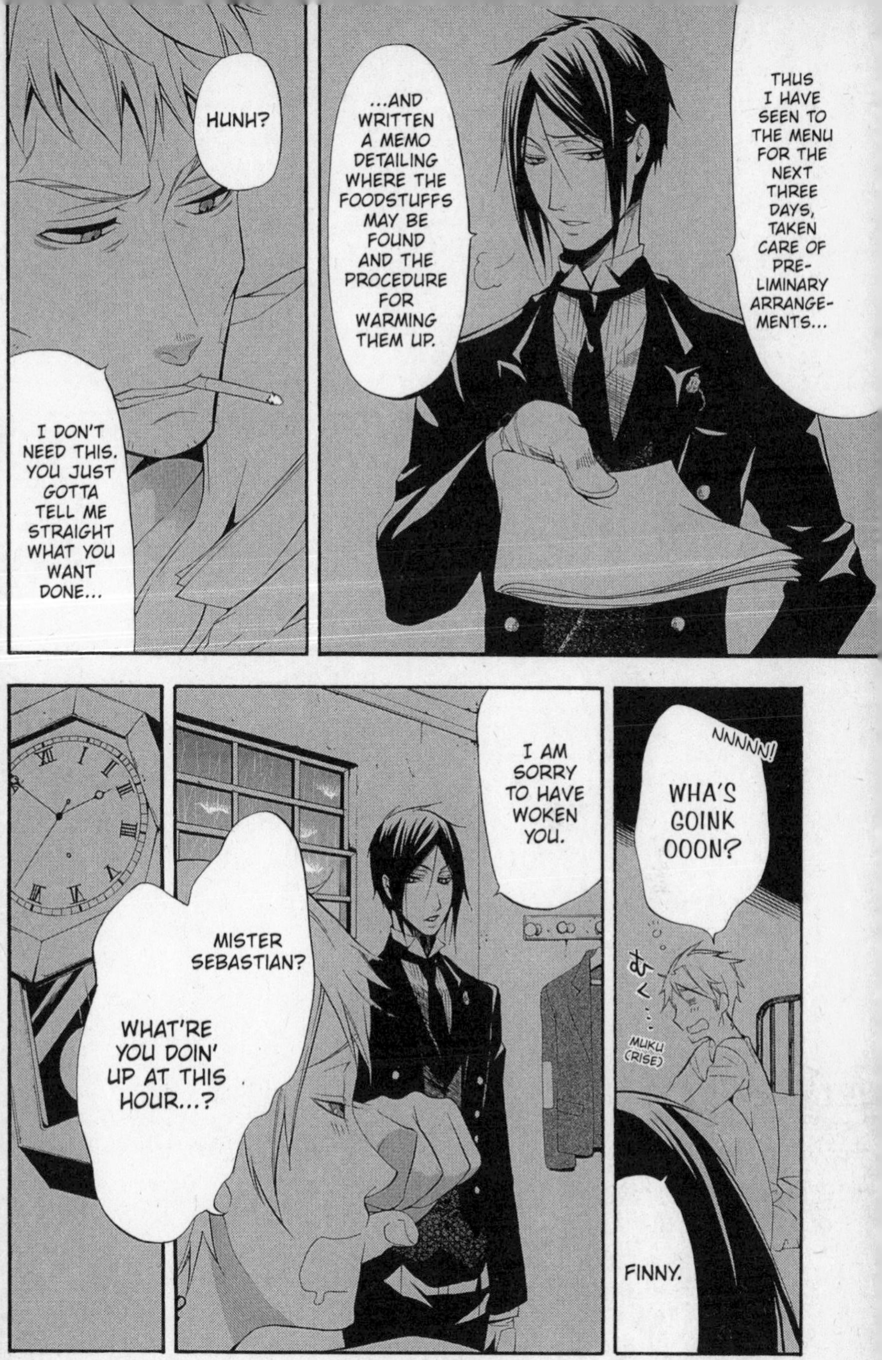
THUS I HAVE SEEN TO THE MENU FOR THE NEXT THREE DAYS, TAKEN CARE OF PRE-LIMINARY ARRANGE-MENTS...
...AND WRITTEN A MEMO DETAILING WHERE THE FOODSTUFFS MAY BE FOUND AND THE PROCEDURE FOR WARMING THEM UP.
HUNH?
I DON'T NEED THIS. YOU JUST GOTTA TELL ME STRAIGHT WHAT YOU WANT DONE...
NNNNN!
WHA'S GOINK OOON?
むく…
MUKU (RISE)
FINNY.
I AM SORRY TO HAVE WOKEN YOU.
MISTER SEBASTIAN?
WHAT'RE YOU DOIN' UP AT THIS HOUR...?

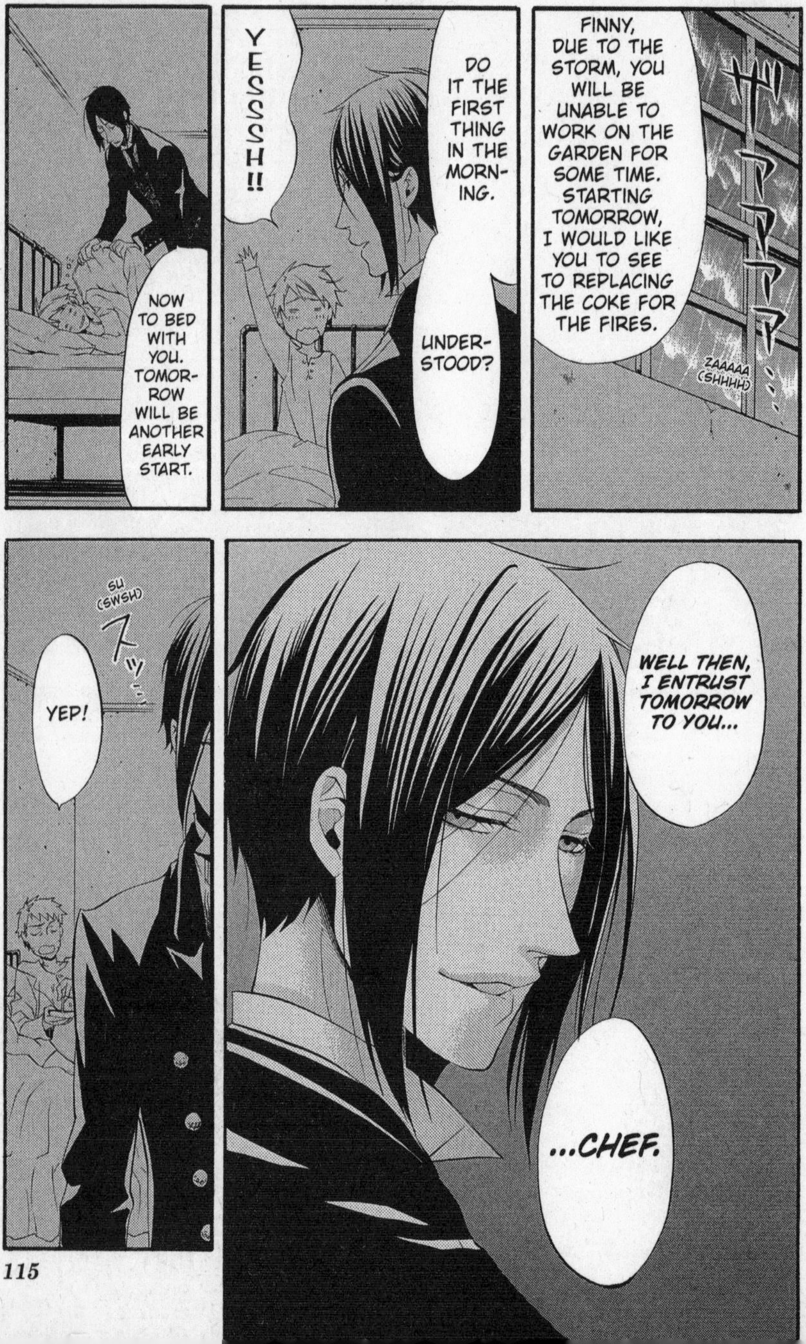
FINNY, DUE TO THE STORM, YOU WILL BE UNABLE TO WORK ON THE GARDEN FOR SOME TIME. STARTING TOMORROW, I WOULD LIKE YOU TO SEE TO REPLACING THE COKE FOR THE FIRES.
ZAAAAA (SHHHH)
DO IT THE FIRST THING IN THE MORN-ING.
UNDER-STOOD?
YESSSH!!
NOW TO BED WITH YOU. TOMOR-ROW WILL BE ANOTHER EARLY START.
WELL THEN, I ENTRUST TOMORROW TO YOU...
...CHEF.
SU (SWSH)
YEP!

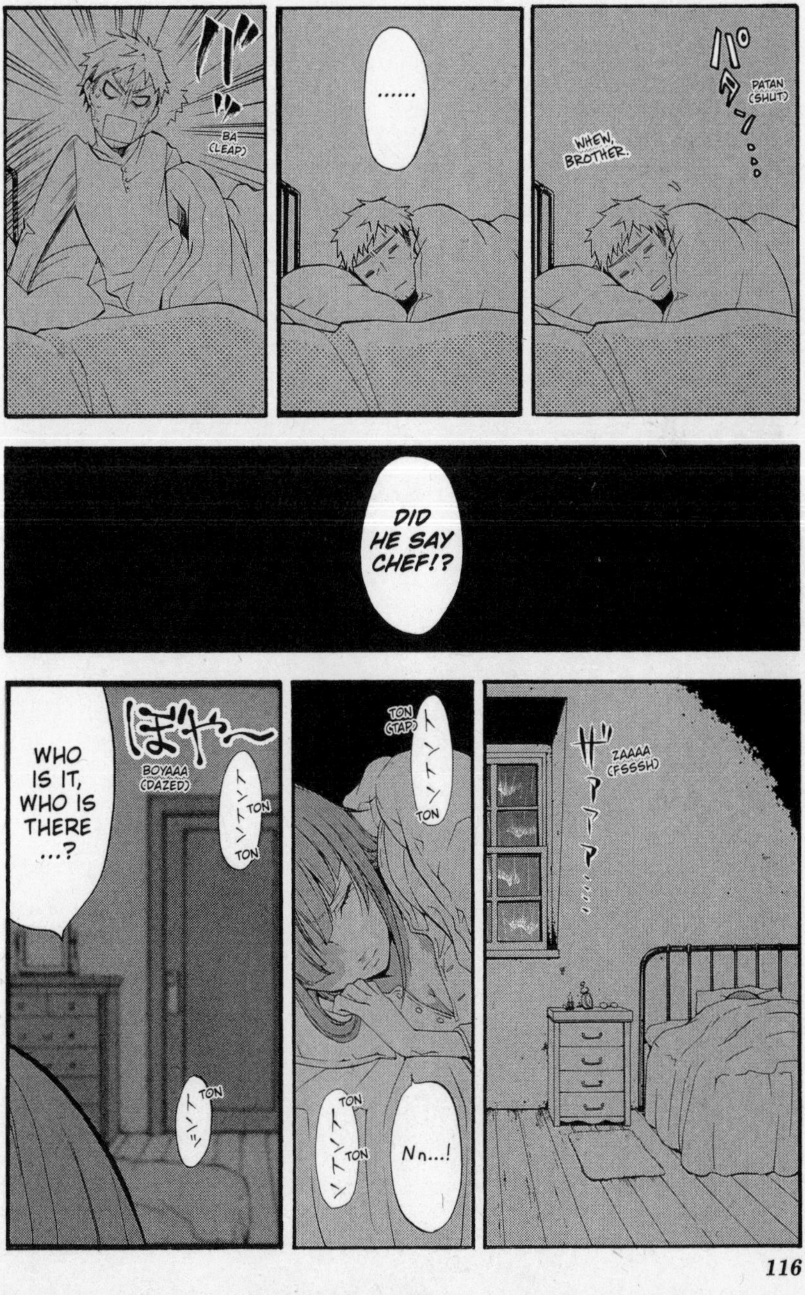
PATAN (SHUT)
WHEW, BROTHER.
......
BA (LEAP)
DID HE SAY CHEF!?
ZAAAA (FSSSH)
TON (TAP)
TON
TON
TON
Nn...!
BOYAAA (DAZED)
TON
TON
TON
WHO IS IT, WHO IS THERE ...?

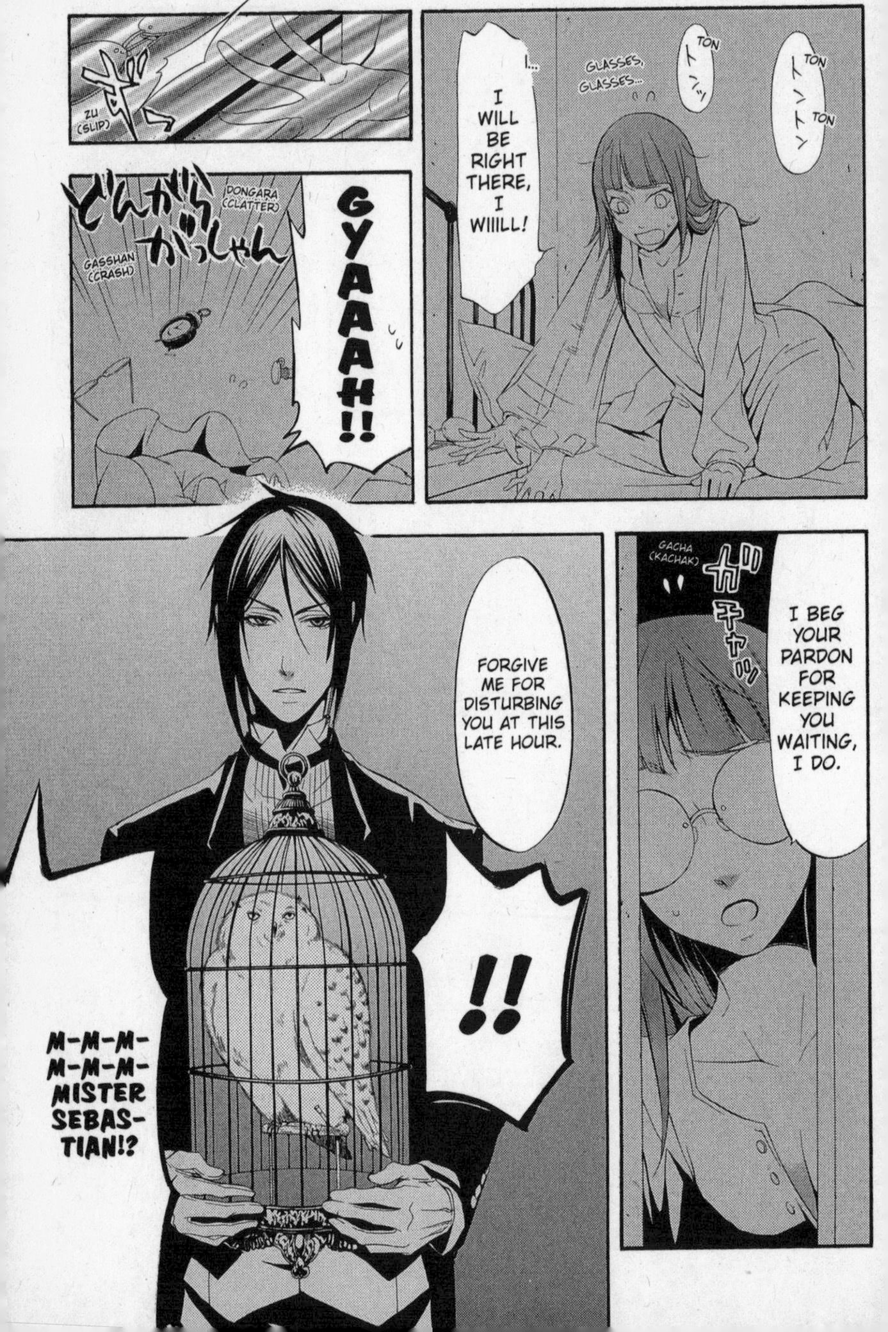
トントン TON TON
トンッ TON
GLASSES, GLASSES...
I... I WILL BE RIGHT THERE, I WIIILL!
ZU (SLIP)
どんがら DONGARA (CLATTER)
がっしゃん GASSHAN (CRASH)
GYAAAAH!!
ガチャッ GACHA (KACHAK)
I BEG YOUR PARDON FOR KEEPING YOU WAITING, I DO.
FORGIVE ME FOR DISTURBING YOU AT THIS LATE HOUR.
!!
M-M-M-M-M-M-MISTER SEBASTIAN!?

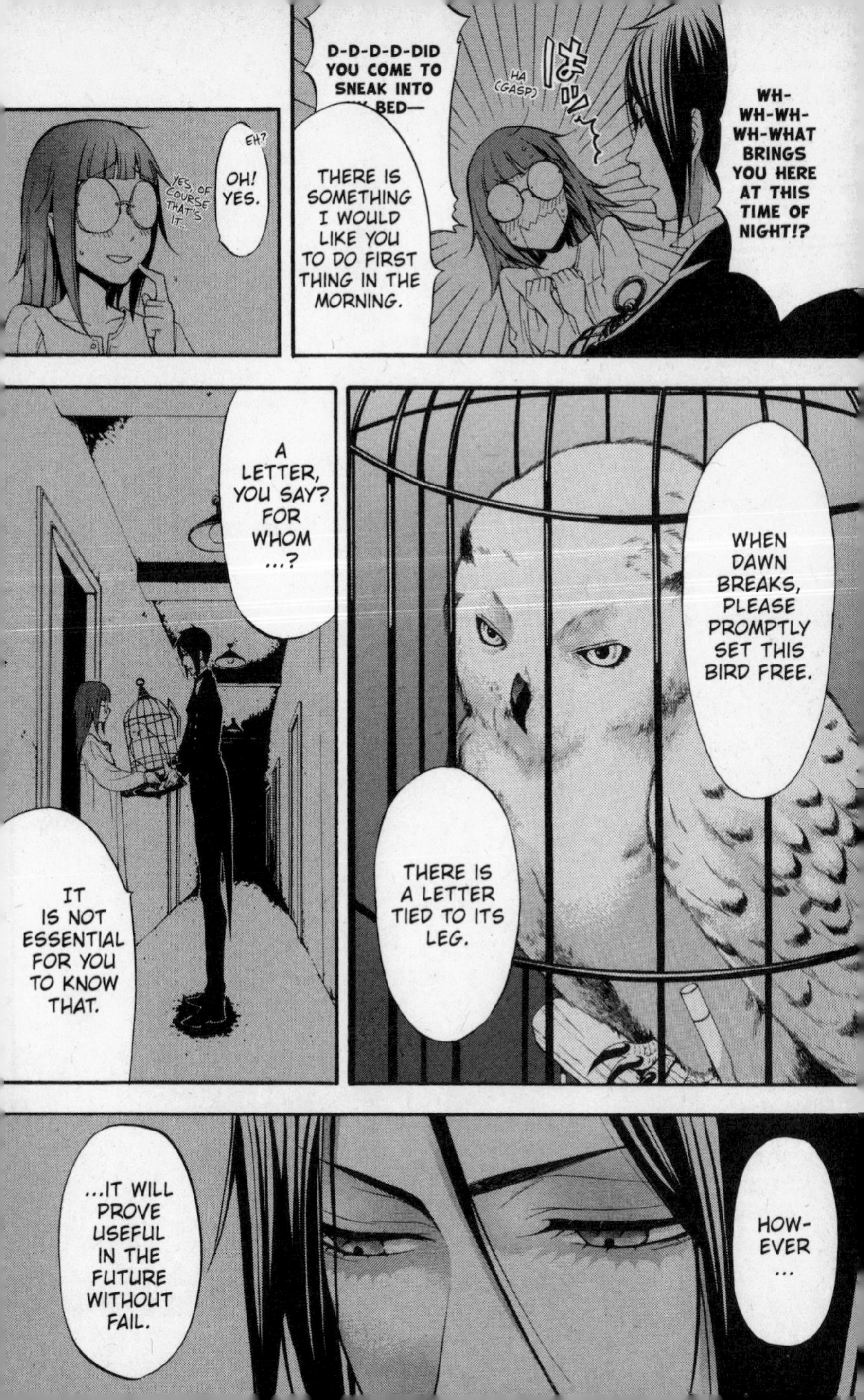
WH-WH-WH-WH-WHAT BRINGS YOU HERE AT THIS TIME OF NIGHT!?
はっ
HA (GASP)
D-D-D-D-DID YOU COME TO SNEAK INTO
BED—
THERE IS SOMETHING I WOULD LIKE YOU TO DO FIRST THING IN THE MORNING.
EH?
OH! YES.
YES, OF COURSE THAT'S IT...
WHEN DAWN BREAKS, PLEASE PROMPTLY SET THIS BIRD FREE.
THERE IS A LETTER TIED TO ITS LEG.
A LETTER, YOU SAY? FOR WHOM...?
IT IS NOT ESSENTIAL FOR YOU TO KNOW THAT.
HOW-EVER...
...IT WILL PROVE USEFUL IN THE FUTURE WITHOUT FAIL.

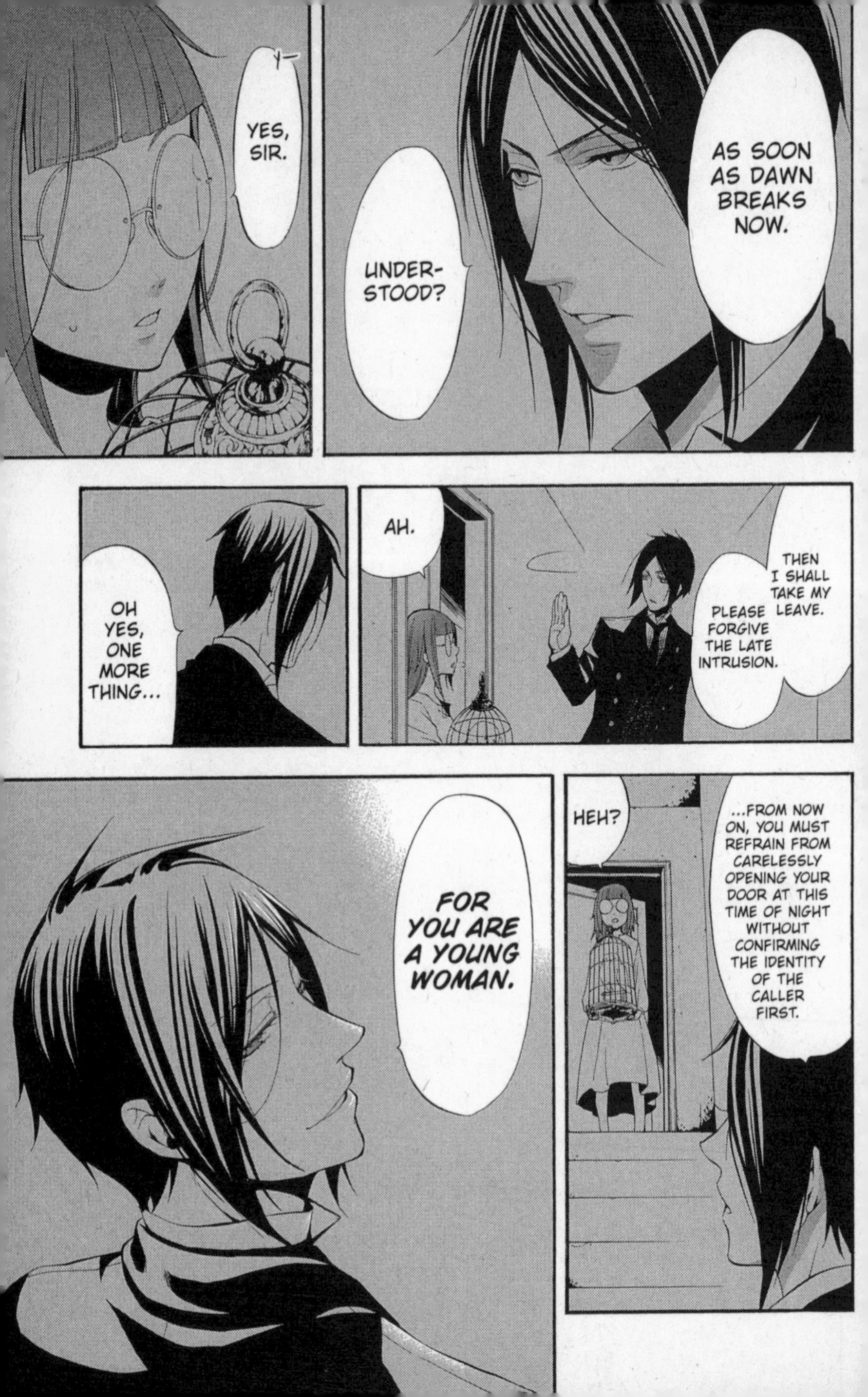
AS SOON AS DAWN BREAKS NOW.
UNDER-STOOD?
Y—
YES, SIR.
THEN I SHALL TAKE MY LEAVE.
PLEASE FORGIVE THE LATE INTRUSION.
AH.
OH YES, ONE MORE THING...
...FROM NOW ON, YOU MUST REFRAIN FROM CARELESSLY OPENING YOUR DOOR AT THIS TIME OF NIGHT WITHOUT CONFIRMING THE IDENTITY OF THE CALLER FIRST.
HEH?
FOR YOU ARE A YOUNG WOMAN.

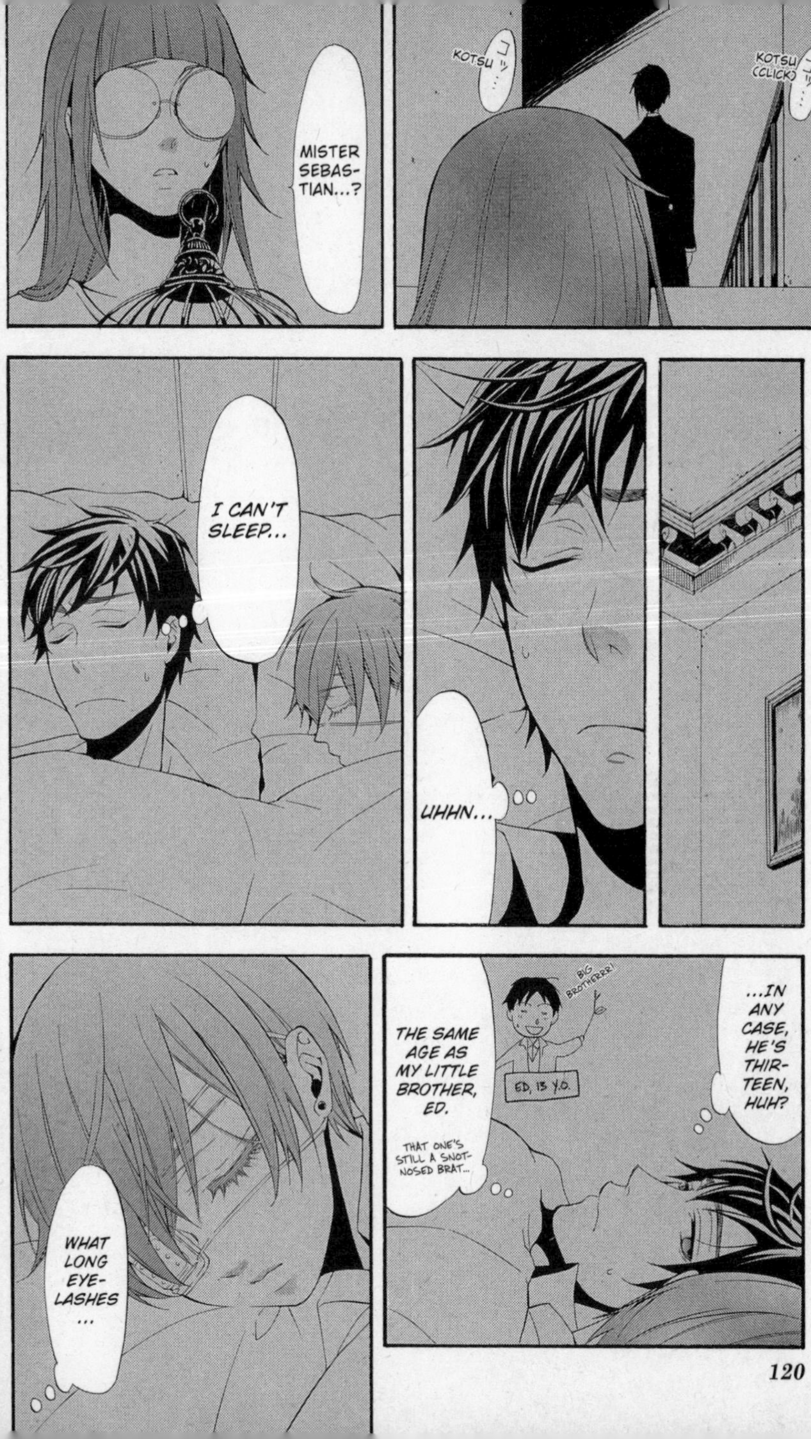

KOTSU (CLICK)
コツ…
KOTSU
コツ…
MISTER SEBASTIAN...?
UHHN...
I CAN'T SLEEP...
...IN ANY CASE, HE'S THIRTEEN, HUH?
THE SAME AGE AS MY LITTLE BROTHER, ED.
BIG BROTHERRR!
ED, 13 Y.O.
THAT ONE'S STILL A SNOT-NOSED BRAT...
WHAT LONG EYELASHES...

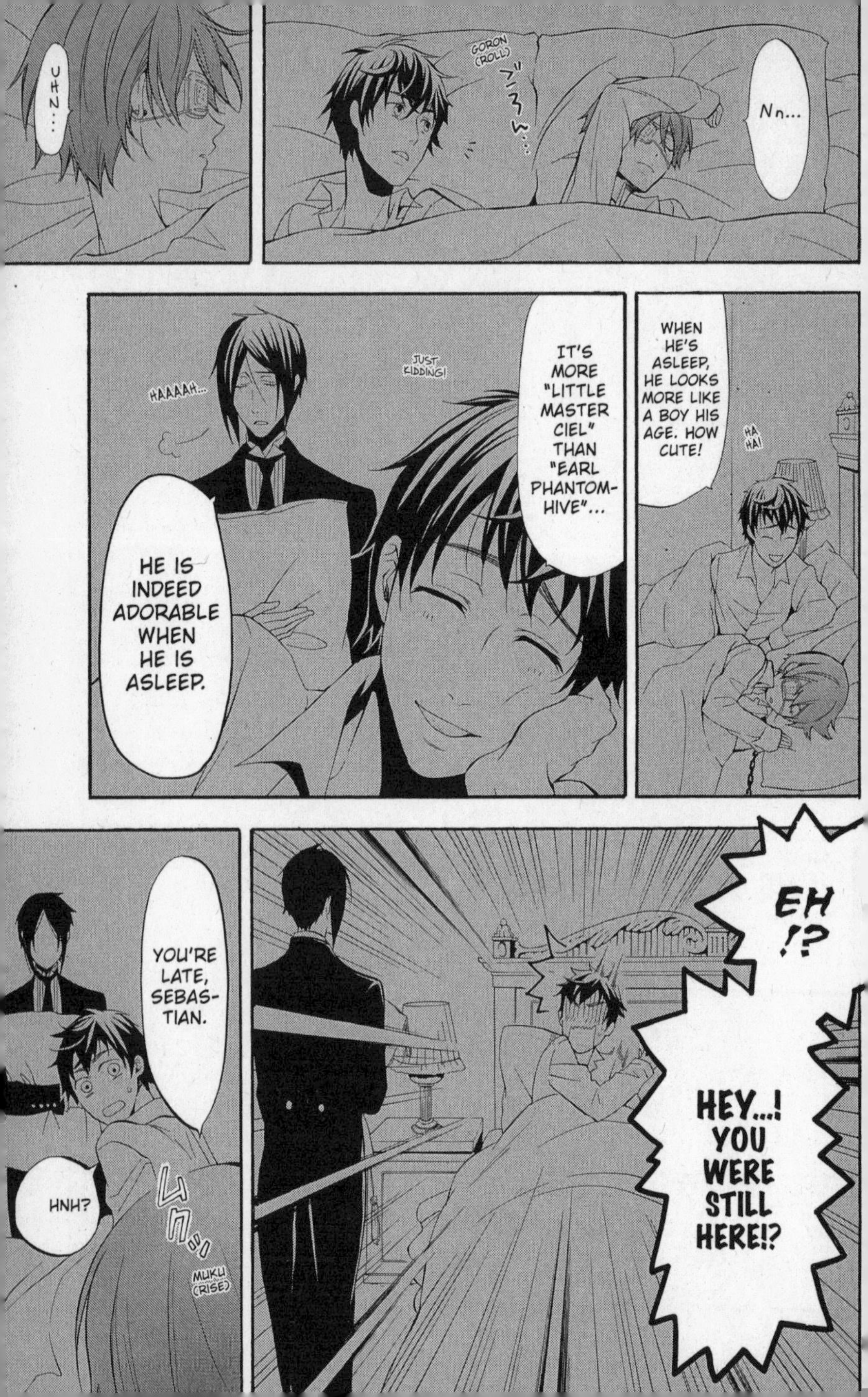
Nn...
GORON (ROLL)
UHN...
WHEN HE'S ASLEEP, HE LOOKS MORE LIKE A BOY HIS AGE. HOW CUTE!
HA HA!
IT'S MORE "LITTLE MASTER CIEL" THAN "EARL PHANTOM-HIVE"...
JUST KIDDING!
HAAAAH...
HE IS INDEED ADORABLE WHEN HE IS ASLEEP.
EH!?
HEY...! YOU WERE STILL HERE!?
YOU'RE LATE, SEBAS-TIAN.
HNH?
MUKU (RISE)

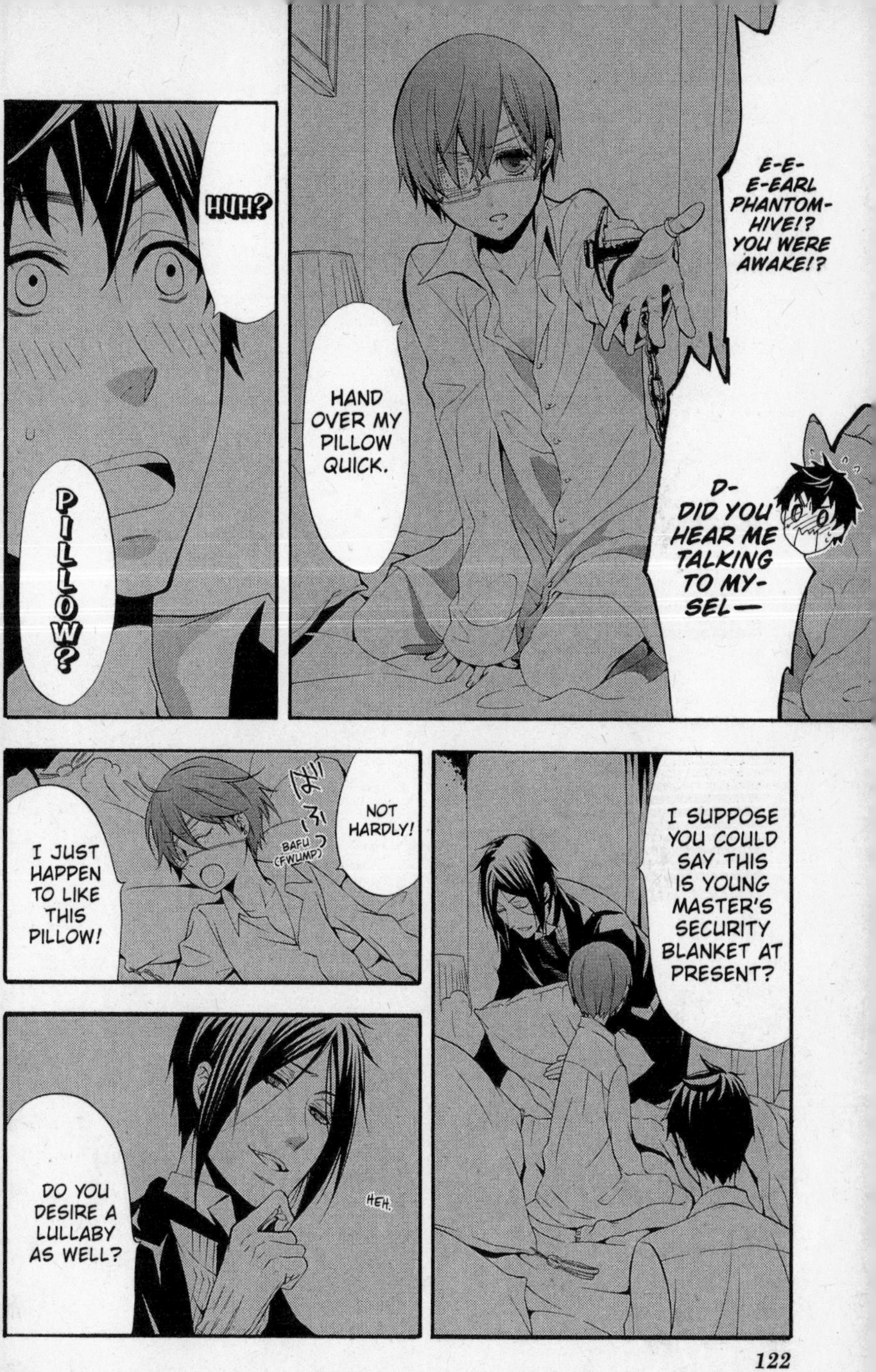
E-E-E-EARL PHANTOMHIVE!? YOU WERE AWAKE!?
D-DID YOU HEAR ME TALKING TO MY-SEL—
HAND OVER MY PILLOW QUICK.
HUH?
PILLOW?
I SUPPOSE YOU COULD SAY THIS IS YOUNG MASTER'S SECURITY BLANKET AT PRESENT?
NOT HARDLY!
ばふっ
BAFU (FWUMP)
I JUST HAPPEN TO LIKE THIS PILLOW!
HEH.
DO YOU DESIRE A LULLABY AS WELL?

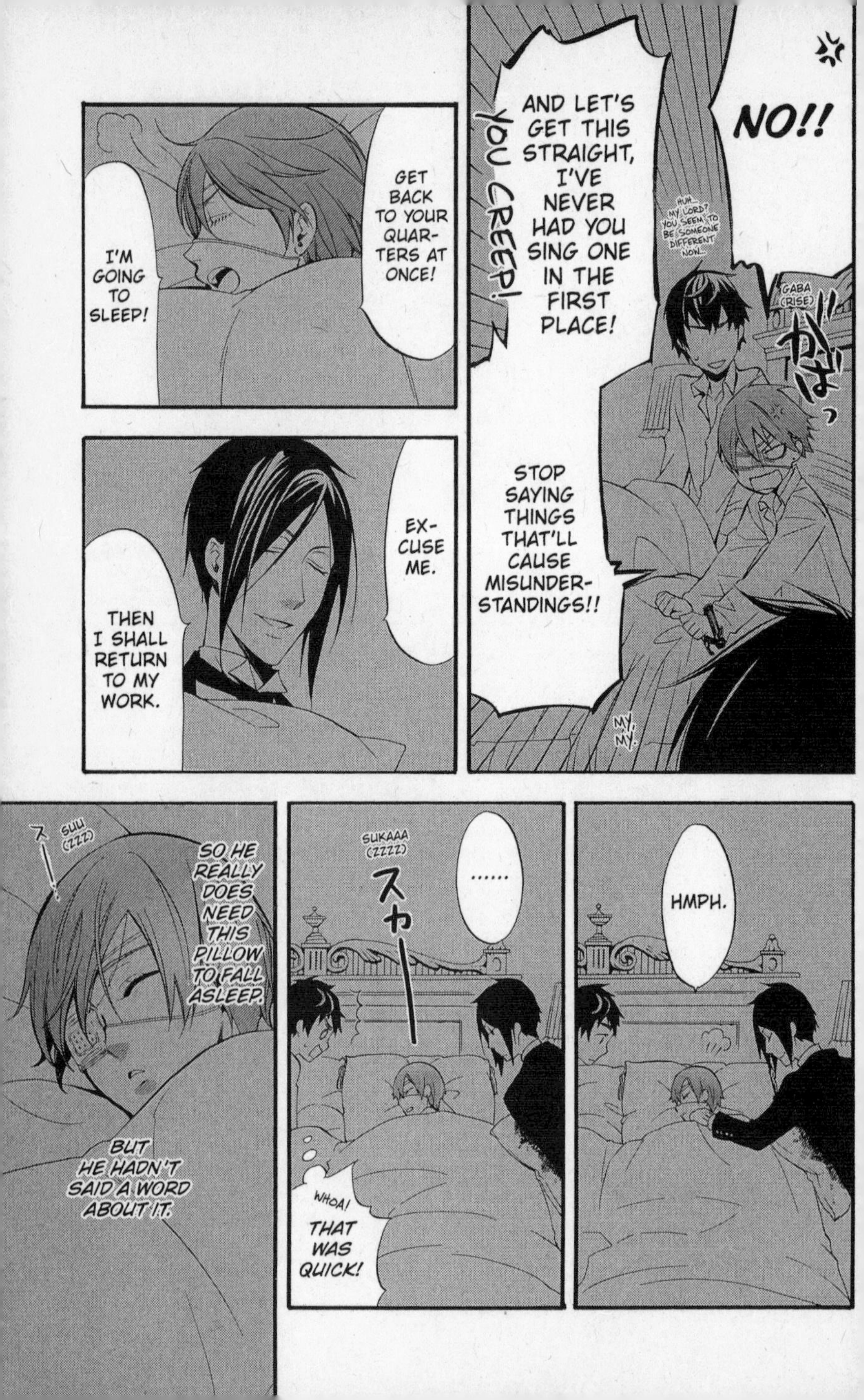
NO!!
HUH... MY LORD? YOU SEEM TO BE SOMEONE DIFFERENT NOW...
GABA (RISE)
AND LET'S GET THIS STRAIGHT, I'VE NEVER HAD YOU SING ONE IN THE FIRST PLACE!
YOU CREEP!
STOP SAYING THINGS THAT'LL CAUSE MISUNDER-STANDINGS!!
MY, MY.
GET BACK TO YOUR QUAR-TERS AT ONCE!
I'M GOING TO SLEEP!
EX-CUSE ME.
THEN I SHALL RETURN TO MY WORK.
HMPH.
......
SUKAAA (ZZZZ)
WHOA! THAT WAS QUICK!
SUU (ZZZ)
SO HE REALLY DOES NEED THIS PILLOW TO FALL ASLEEP.
BUT HE HADN'T SAID A WORD ABOUT IT.

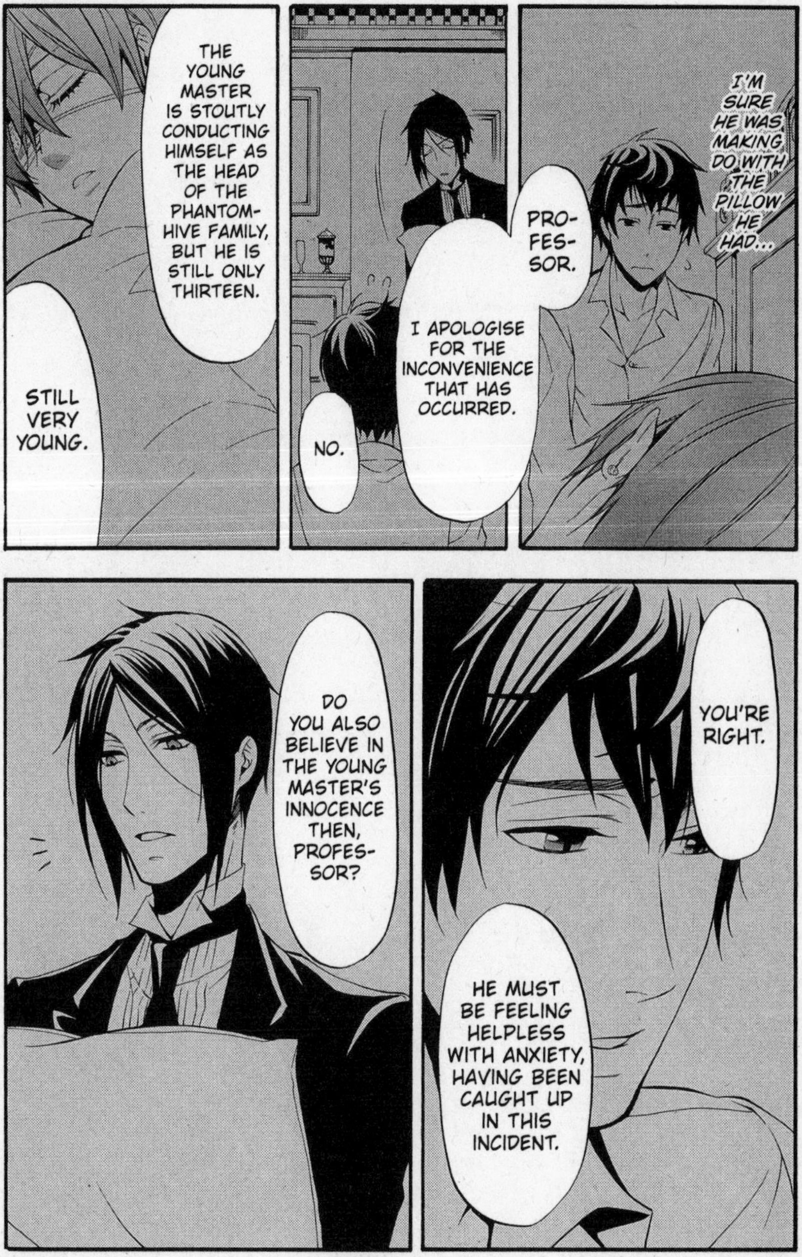
I'M SURE HE WAS MAKING DO WITH THE PILLOW HE HAD...
PRO-FES-SOR.
I APOLOGISE FOR THE INCONVENIENCE THAT HAS OCCURRED.
NO.
THE YOUNG MASTER IS STOUTLY CONDUCTING HIMSELF AS THE HEAD OF THE PHANTOM-HIVE FAMILY, BUT HE IS STILL ONLY THIRTEEN.
STILL VERY YOUNG.
YOU'RE RIGHT.
HE MUST BE FEELING HELPLESS WITH ANXIETY, HAVING BEEN CAUGHT UP IN THIS INCIDENT.
DO YOU ALSO BELIEVE IN THE YOUNG MASTER'S INNOCENCE THEN, PROFES-SOR?

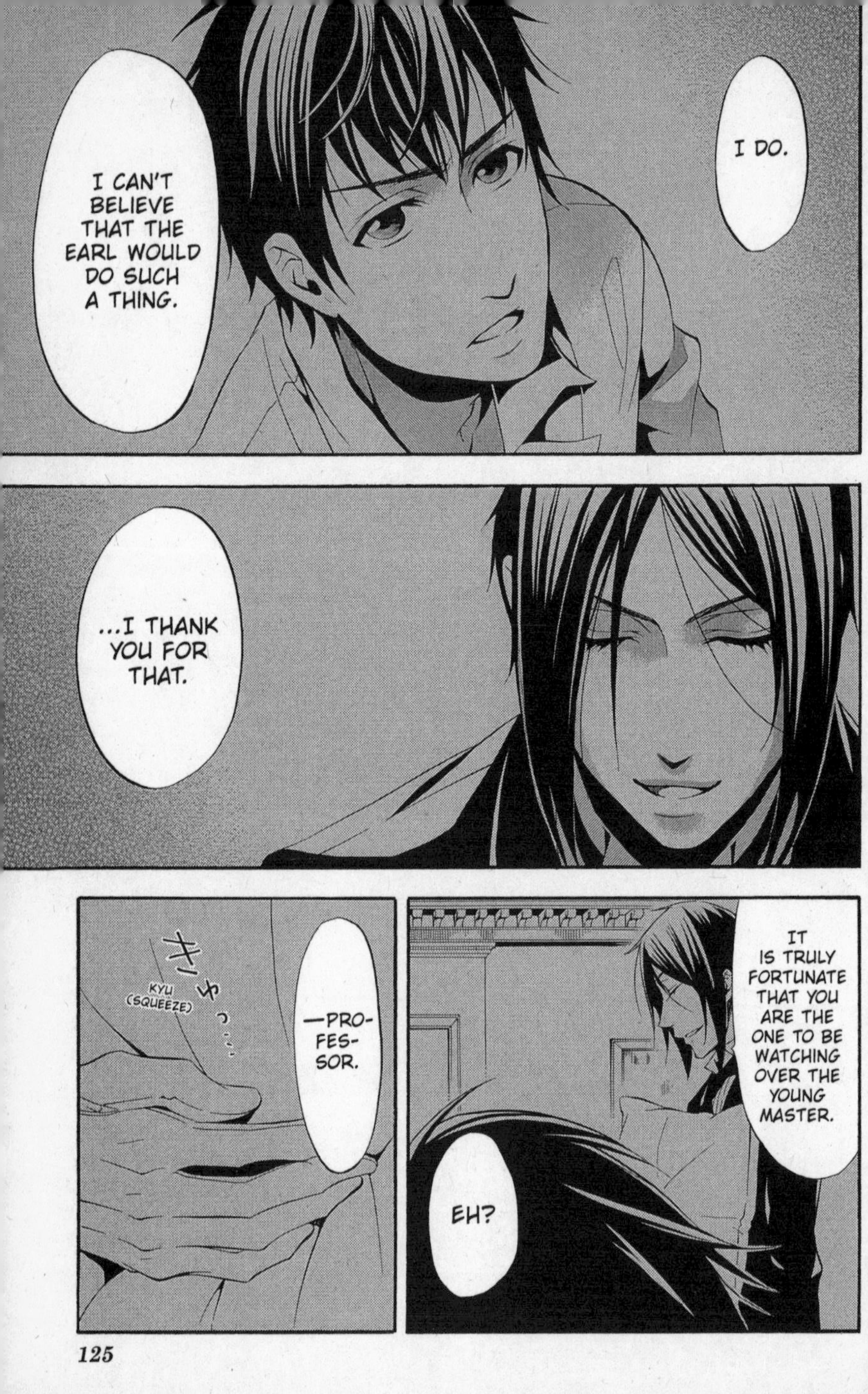
I DO.
I CAN'T BELIEVE THAT THE EARL WOULD DO SUCH A THING.
...I THANK YOU FOR THAT.
IT IS TRULY FORTUNATE THAT YOU ARE THE ONE TO BE WATCHING OVER THE YOUNG MASTER.
EH?
—PRO-FES-SOR.
キュッ...
KYU (SQUEEZE)

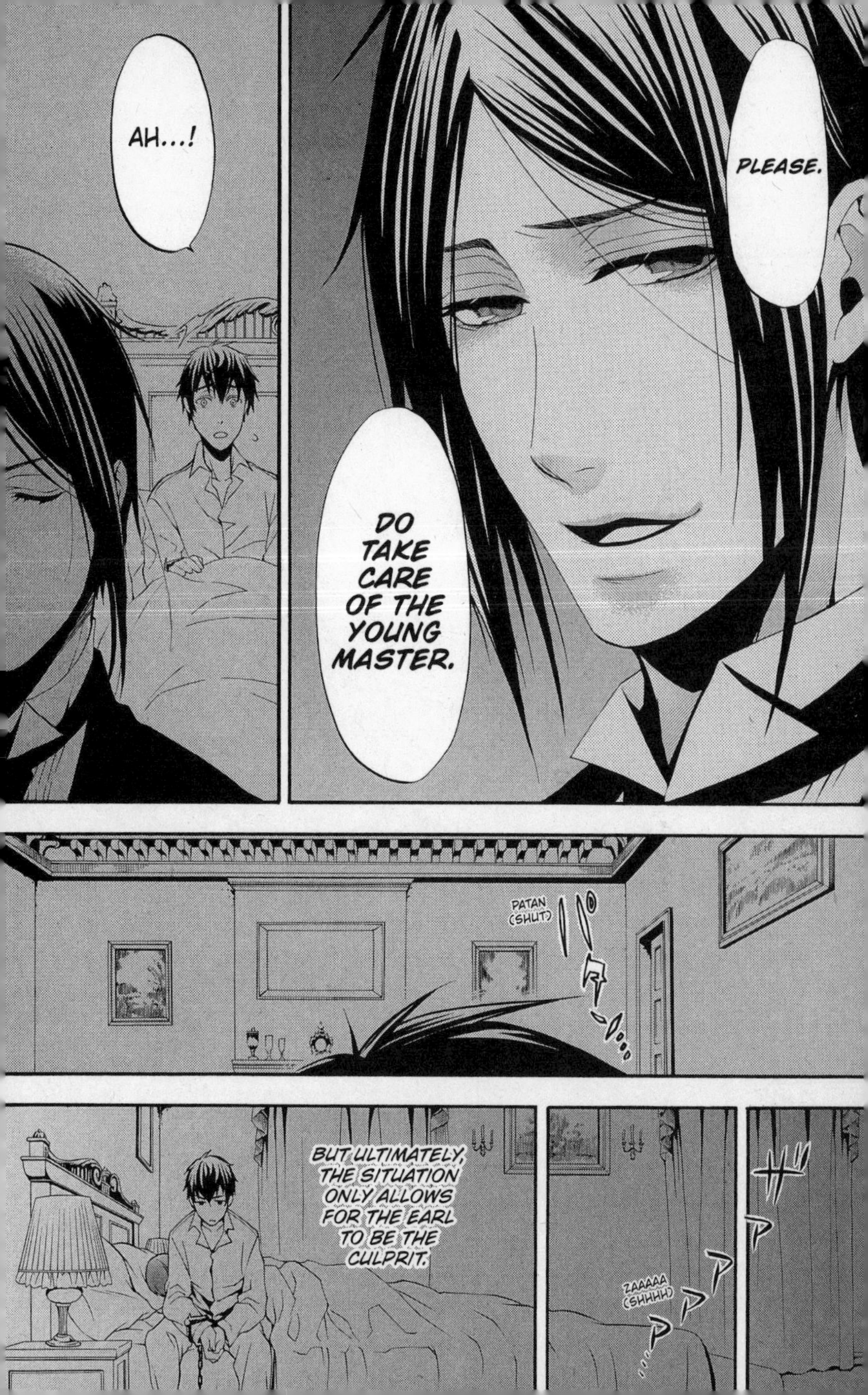
PLEASE.
DO TAKE CARE OF THE YOUNG MASTER.
AH...!
PATAN (SHUT)
ZAAAAA (SHHHH)
BUT ULTIMATELY, THE SITUATION ONLY ALLOWS FOR THE EARL TO BE THE CULPRIT.

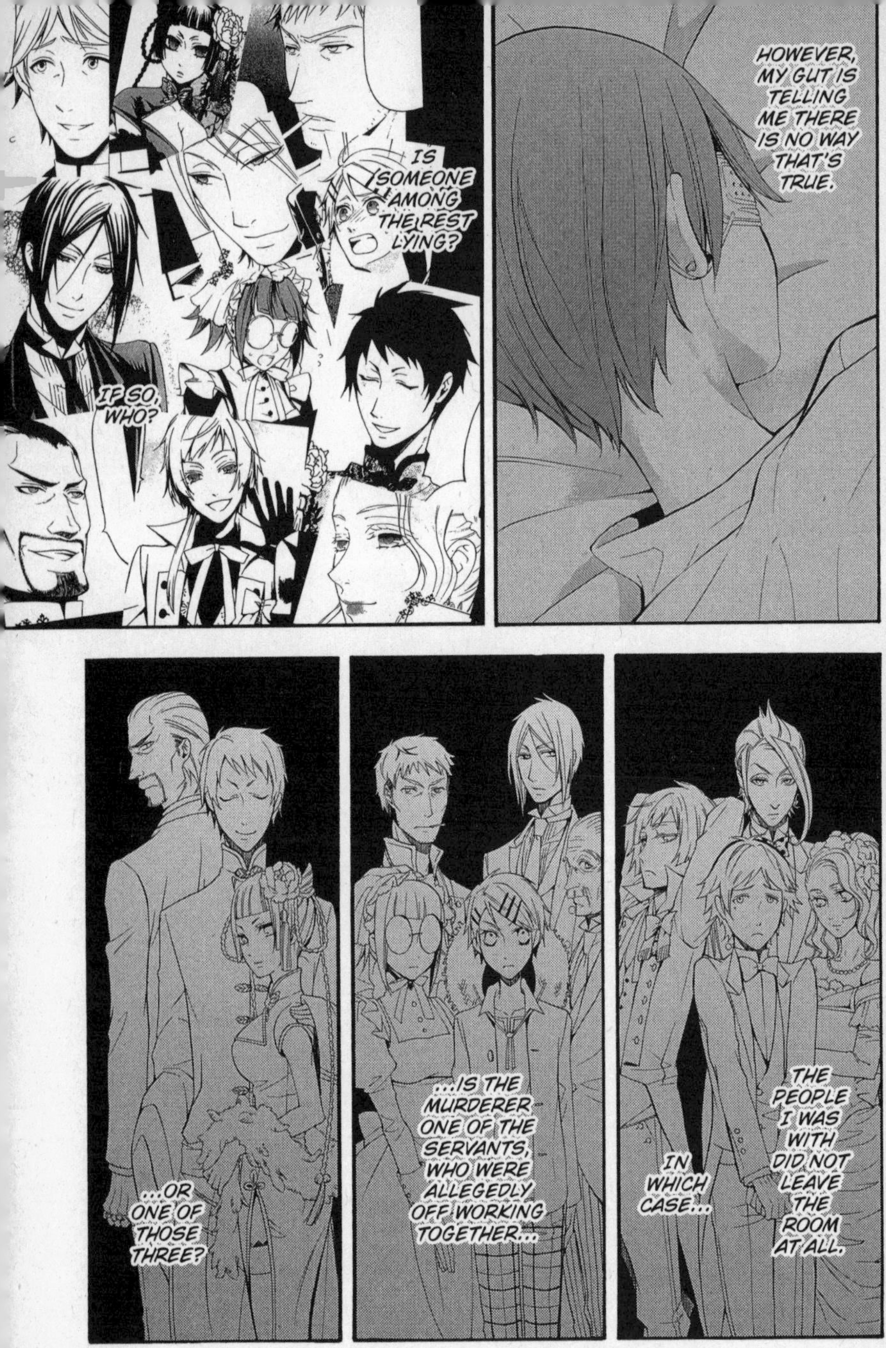
HOWEVER, MY GUT IS TELLING ME THERE IS NO WAY THAT'S TRUE.
IS SOMEONE AMONG THE REST LYING?
IF SO, WHO?
THE PEOPLE I WAS WITH DID NOT LEAVE THE ROOM AT ALL.
IN WHICH CASE...
...IS THE MURDERER ONE OF THE SERVANTS, WHO WERE ALLEGEDLY OFF WORKING TOGETHER...
...OR ONE OF THOSE THREE?

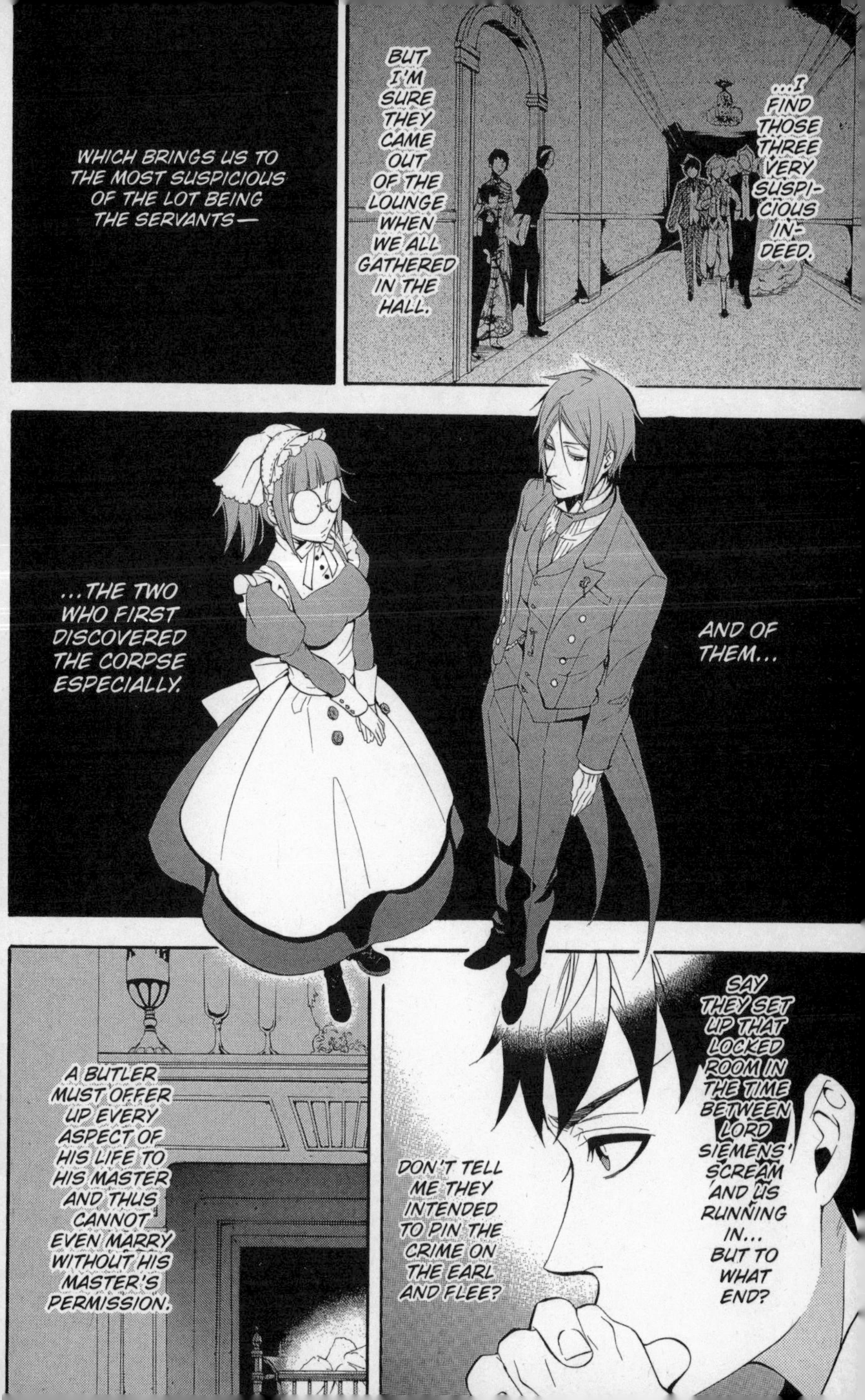
...I FIND THOSE THREE VERY SUSPICIOUS INDEED.
BUT I'M SURE THEY CAME OUT OF THE LOUNGE WHEN WE ALL GATHERED IN THE HALL.
WHICH BRINGS US TO THE MOST SUSPICIOUS OF THE LOT BEING THE SERVANTS—
AND OF THEM...
...THE TWO WHO FIRST DISCOVERED THE CORPSE ESPECIALLY.
SAY THEY SET UP THAT LOCKED ROOM IN THE TIME BETWEEN LORD SIEMENS' SCREAM AND US RUNNING IN... BUT TO WHAT END?
DON'T TELL ME THEY INTENDED TO PIN THE CRIME ON THE EARL AND FLEE?
A BUTLER MUST OFFER UP EVERY ASPECT OF HIS LIFE TO HIS MASTER AND THUS CANNOT EVEN MARRY WITHOUT HIS MASTER'S PERMISSION.

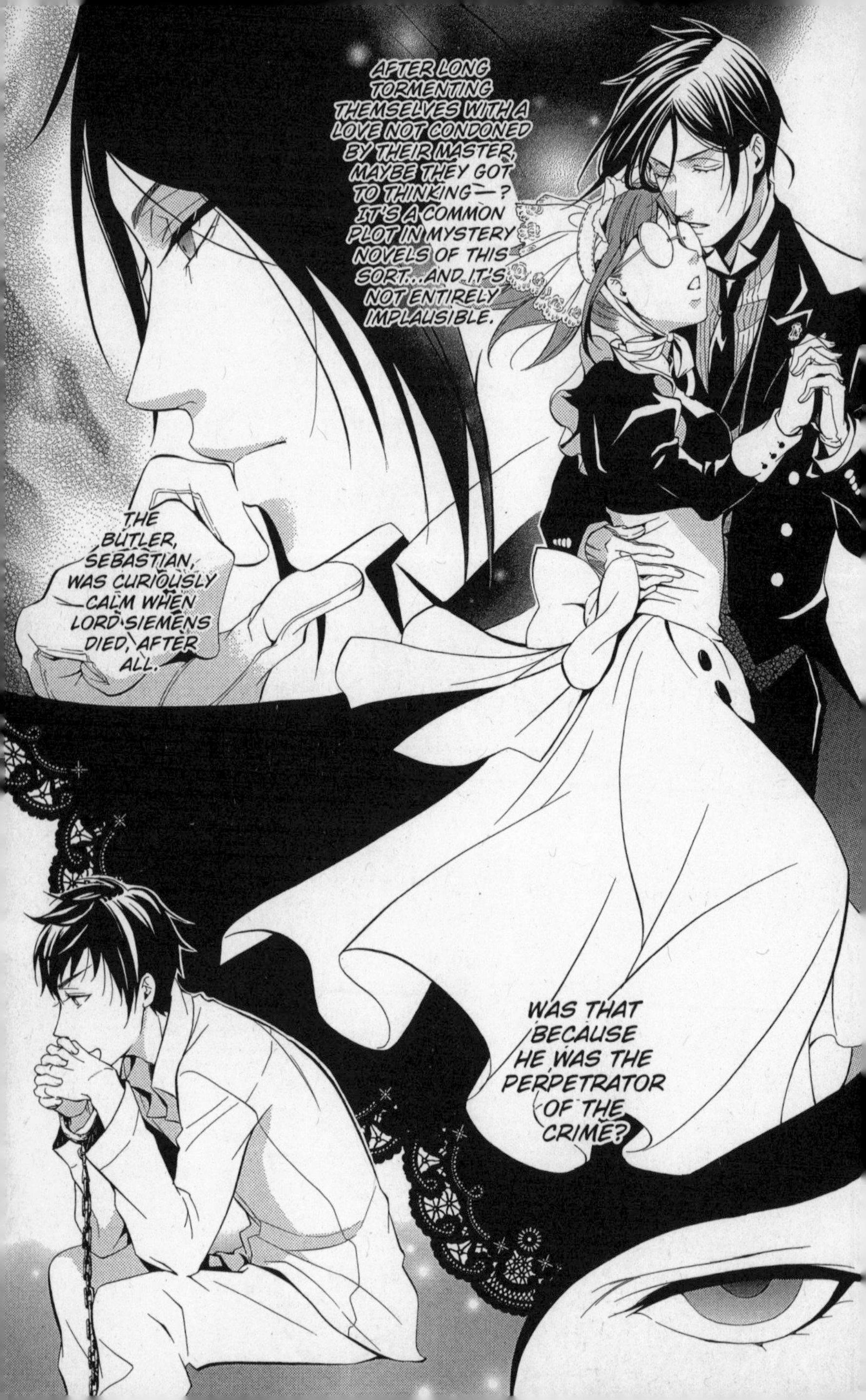
AFTER LONG TORMENTING THEMSELVES WITH A LOVE NOT CONDONED BY THEIR MASTER, MAYBE THEY GOT TO THINKING—? IT'S A COMMON PLOT IN MYSTERY NOVELS OF THIS SORT...AND IT'S NOT ENTIRELY IMPLAUSIBLE.
THE BUTLER, SEBASTIAN, WAS CURIOUSLY CALM WHEN LORD SIEMENS DIED, AFTER ALL.
WAS THAT BECAUSE HE WAS THE PERPETRATOR OF THE CRIME?

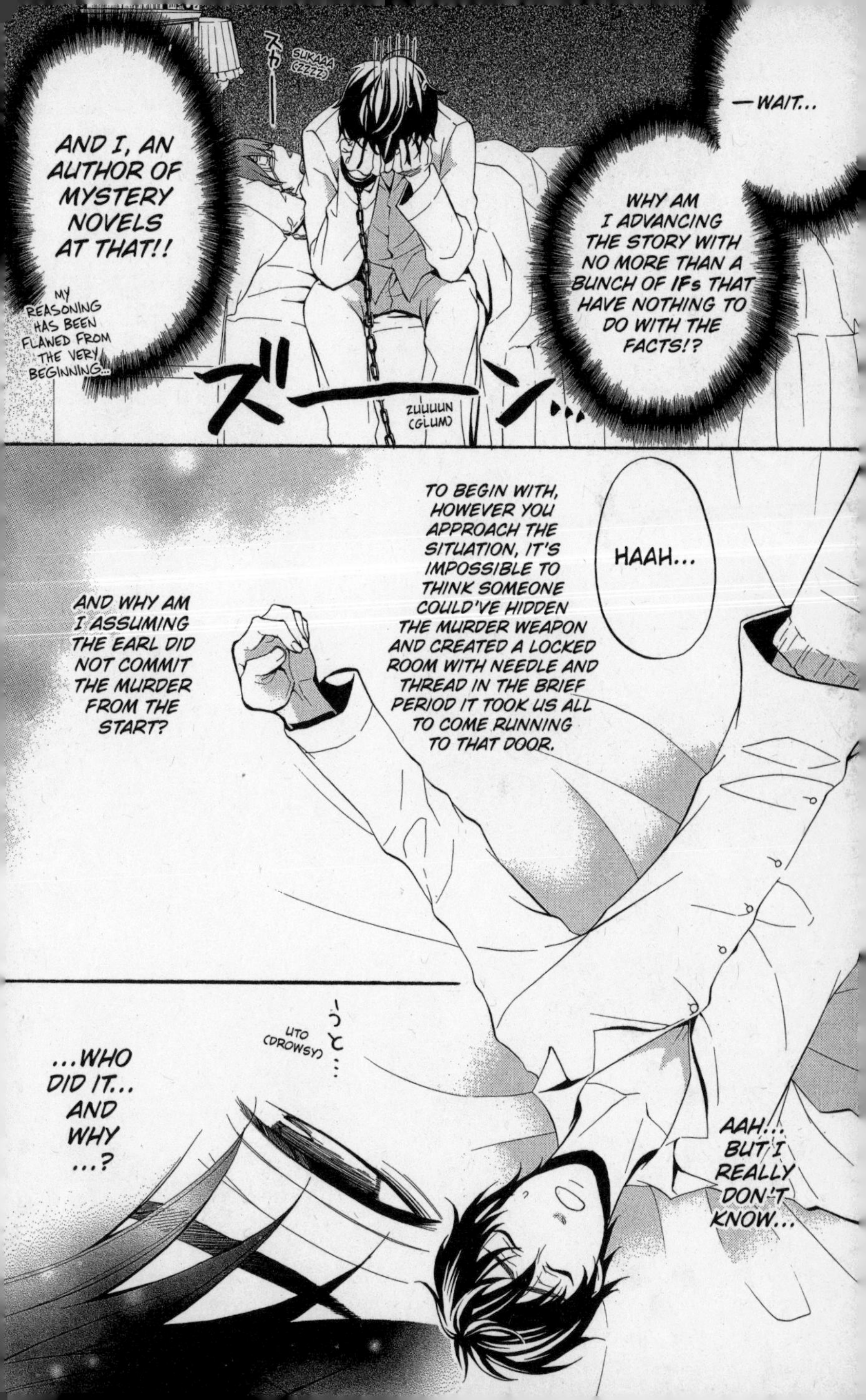
—WAIT...
WHY AM I ADVANCING THE STORY WITH NO MORE THAN A BUNCH OF IFs THAT HAVE NOTHING TO DO WITH THE FACTS!?
スカー
SUKAAA (ZZZZ)
AND I, AN AUTHOR OF MYSTERY NOVELS AT THAT!!
MY REASONING HAS BEEN FLAWED FROM THE VERY BEGINNING...
ズーーン…
ZUUUUN (GLUM)
HAAH...
TO BEGIN WITH, HOWEVER YOU APPROACH THE SITUATION, IT'S IMPOSSIBLE TO THINK SOMEONE COULD'VE HIDDEN THE MURDER WEAPON AND CREATED A LOCKED ROOM WITH NEEDLE AND THREAD IN THE BRIEF PERIOD IT TOOK US ALL TO COME RUNNING TO THAT DOOR.
AND WHY AM I ASSUMING THE EARL DID NOT COMMIT THE MURDER FROM THE START?
AAH... BUT I REALLY DON'T KNOW...
うと…
UTO (DROWSY)
...WHO DID IT... AND WHY ...?

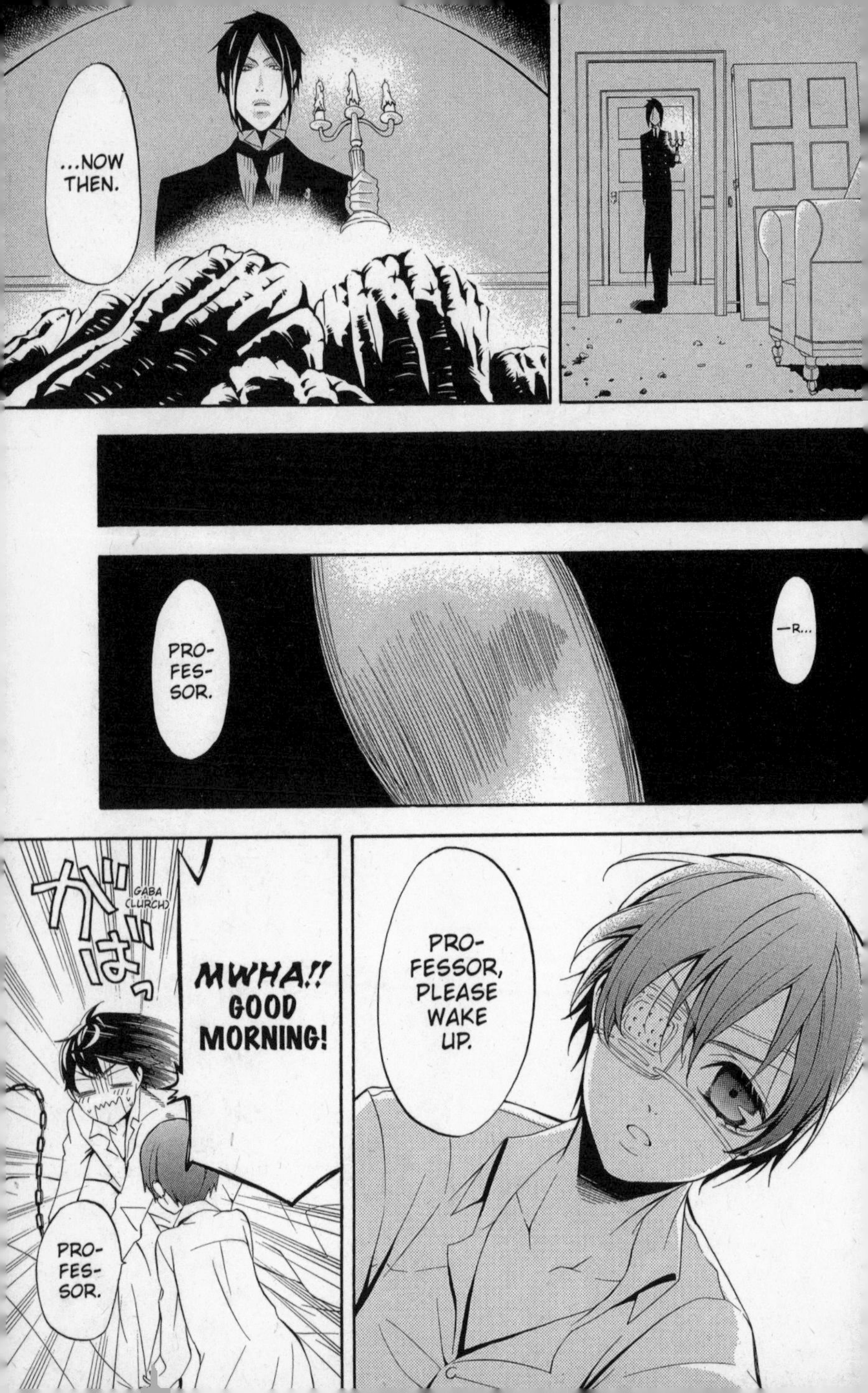
...NOW THEN.
—R...
PRO-FES-SOR.
PRO-FESSOR, PLEASE WAKE UP.
MWHA!! GOOD MORNING!
がばっ
GABA (LURCH)
PRO-FES-SOR.

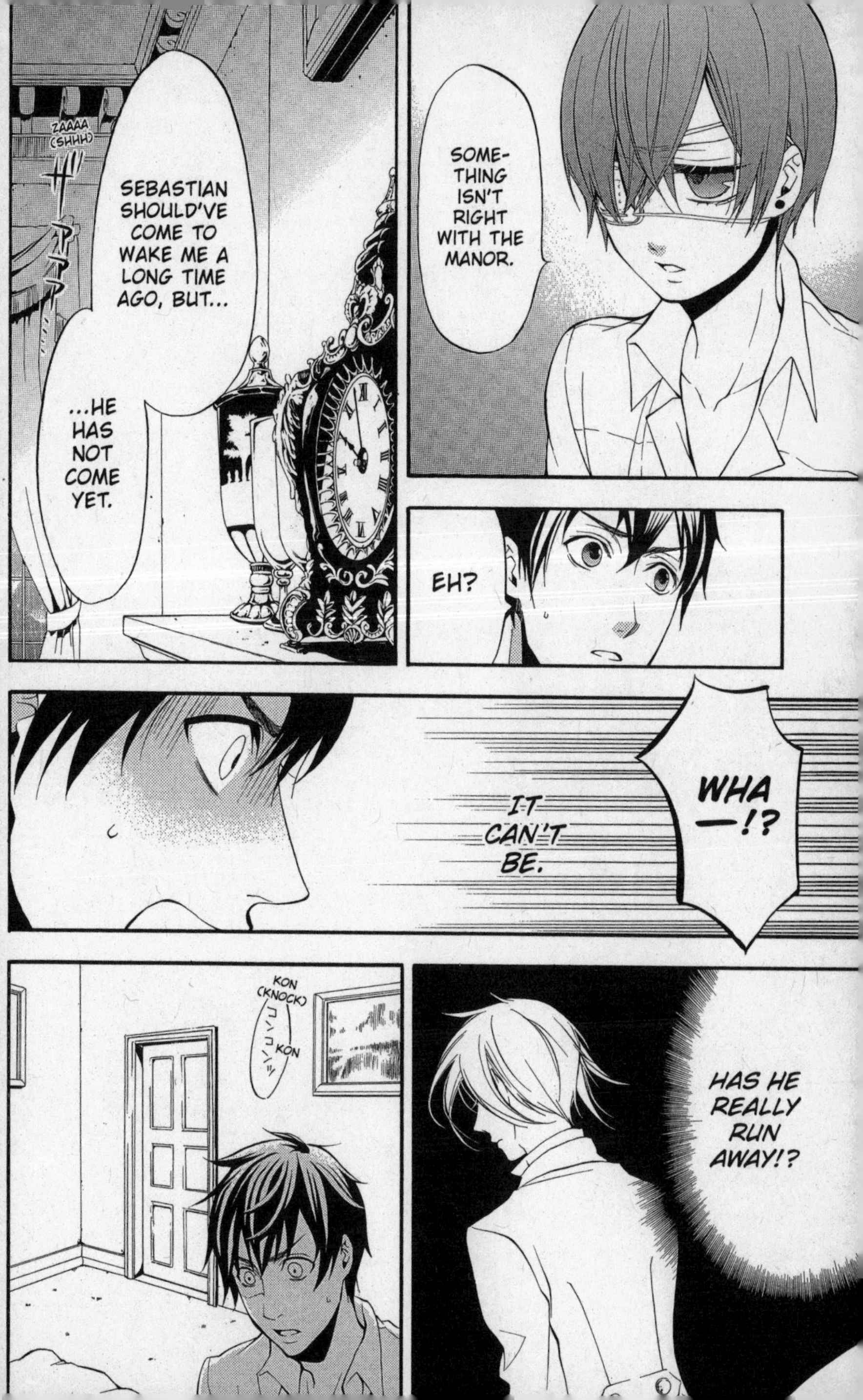
SOME-THING ISN'T RIGHT WITH THE MANOR.
EH?
ZAAAA (SHHH)
SEBASTIAN SHOULD'VE COME TO WAKE ME A LONG TIME AGO, BUT...
...HE HAS NOT COME YET.
WHA—!?
IT CAN'T BE.
HAS HE REALLY RUN AWAY!?
KON (KNOCK)
KON

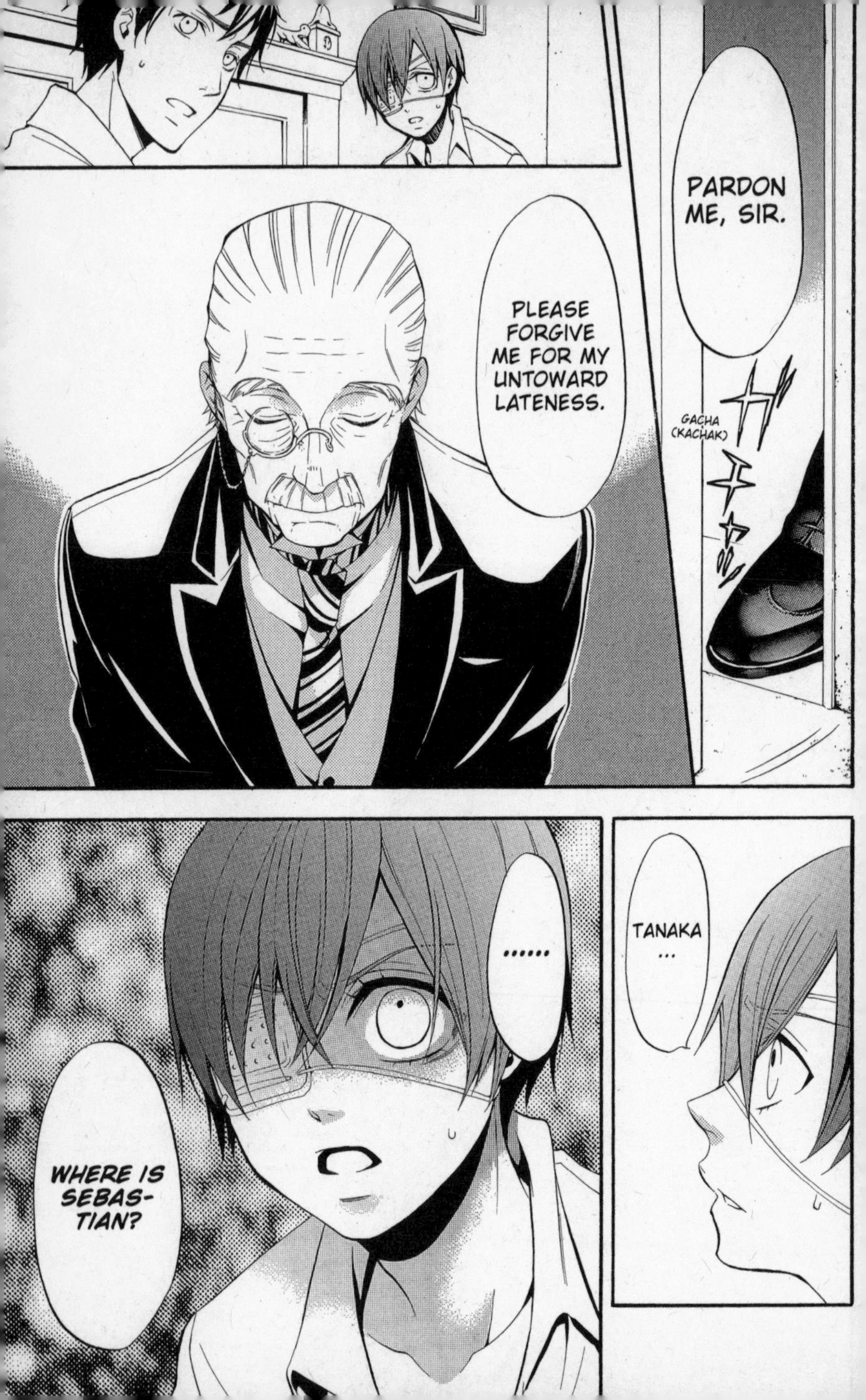
PARDON ME, SIR.
GACHA (KACHAK)
PLEASE FORGIVE ME FOR MY UNTOWARD LATENESS.
TANAKA ...
......
WHERE IS SEBAS-TIAN?

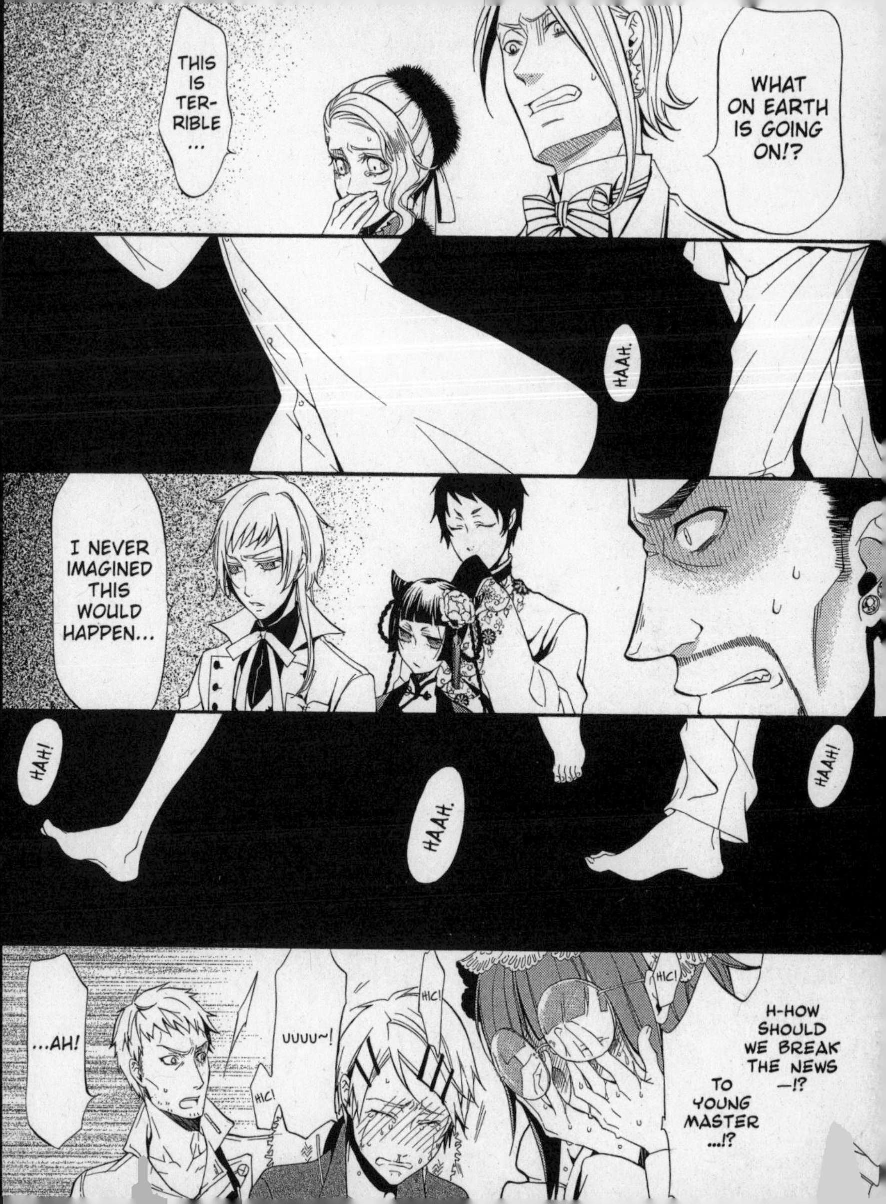
WHAT ON EARTH IS GOING ON!?
THIS IS TER-RIBLE ...
HAAH.
I NEVER IMAGINED THIS WOULD HAPPEN...
HAAH!
HAAH.
HAAH!
H-HOW SHOULD WE BREAK THE NEWS —!?
TO YOUNG MASTER ...!?
HIC!
HIC!
UUUU~!
HIC!
...AH!

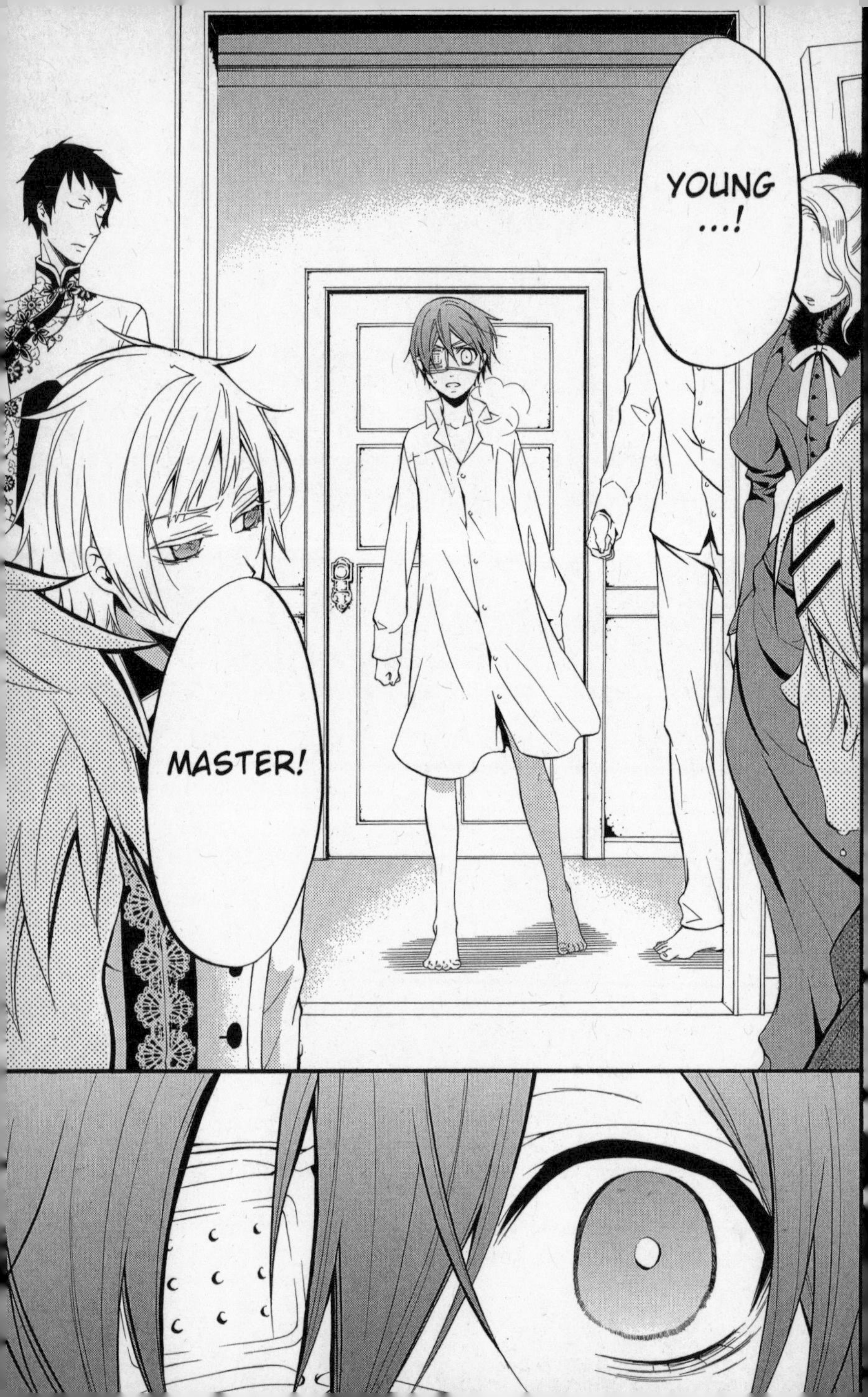
YOUNG ...!
MASTER!

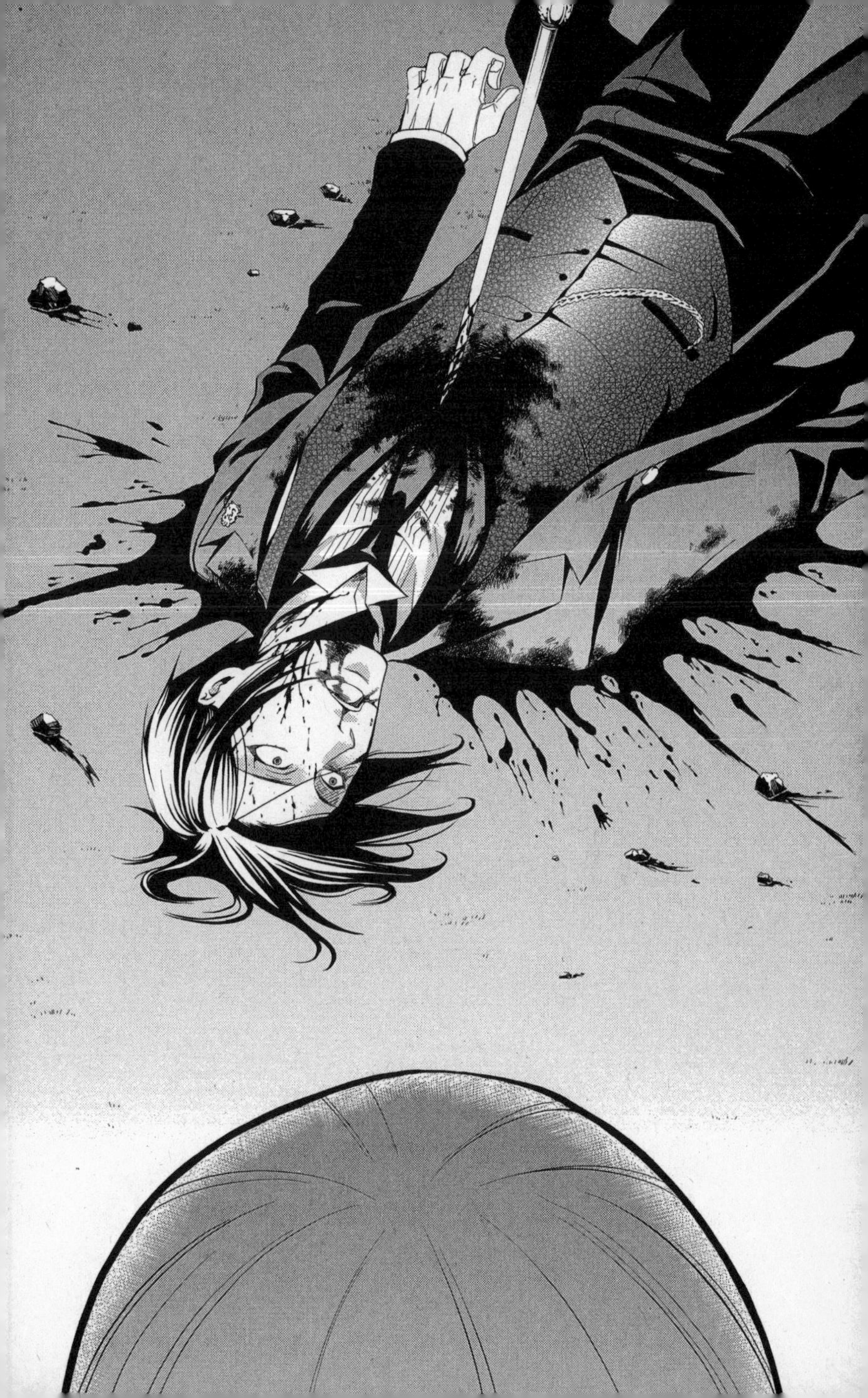

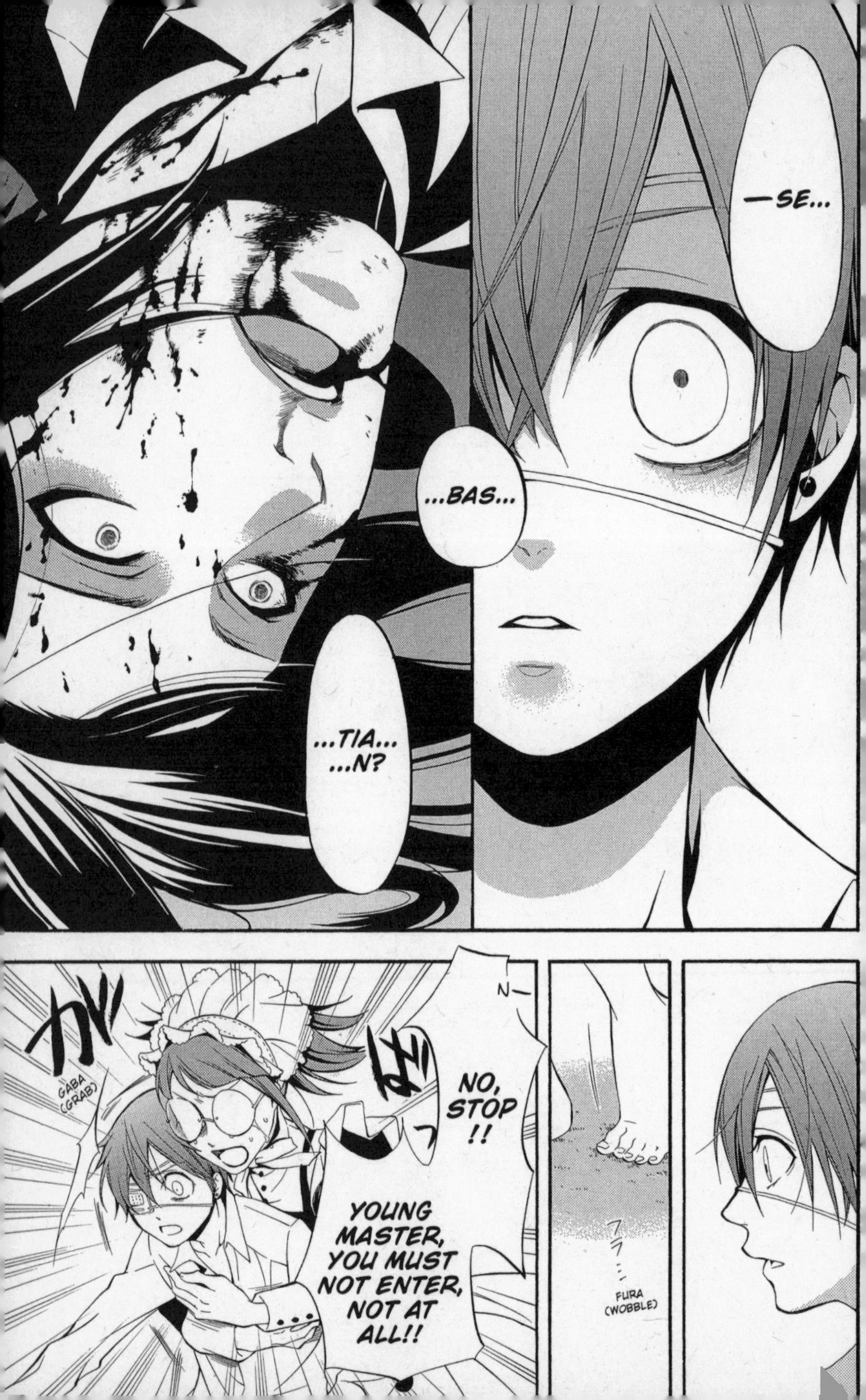
—SE...
...BAS...
...TIA...
...N?
FURA
(WOBBLE)
N—
NO, STOP!!
YOUNG MASTER, YOU MUST NOT ENTER, NOT AT ALL!!
GABA
(GRAB)

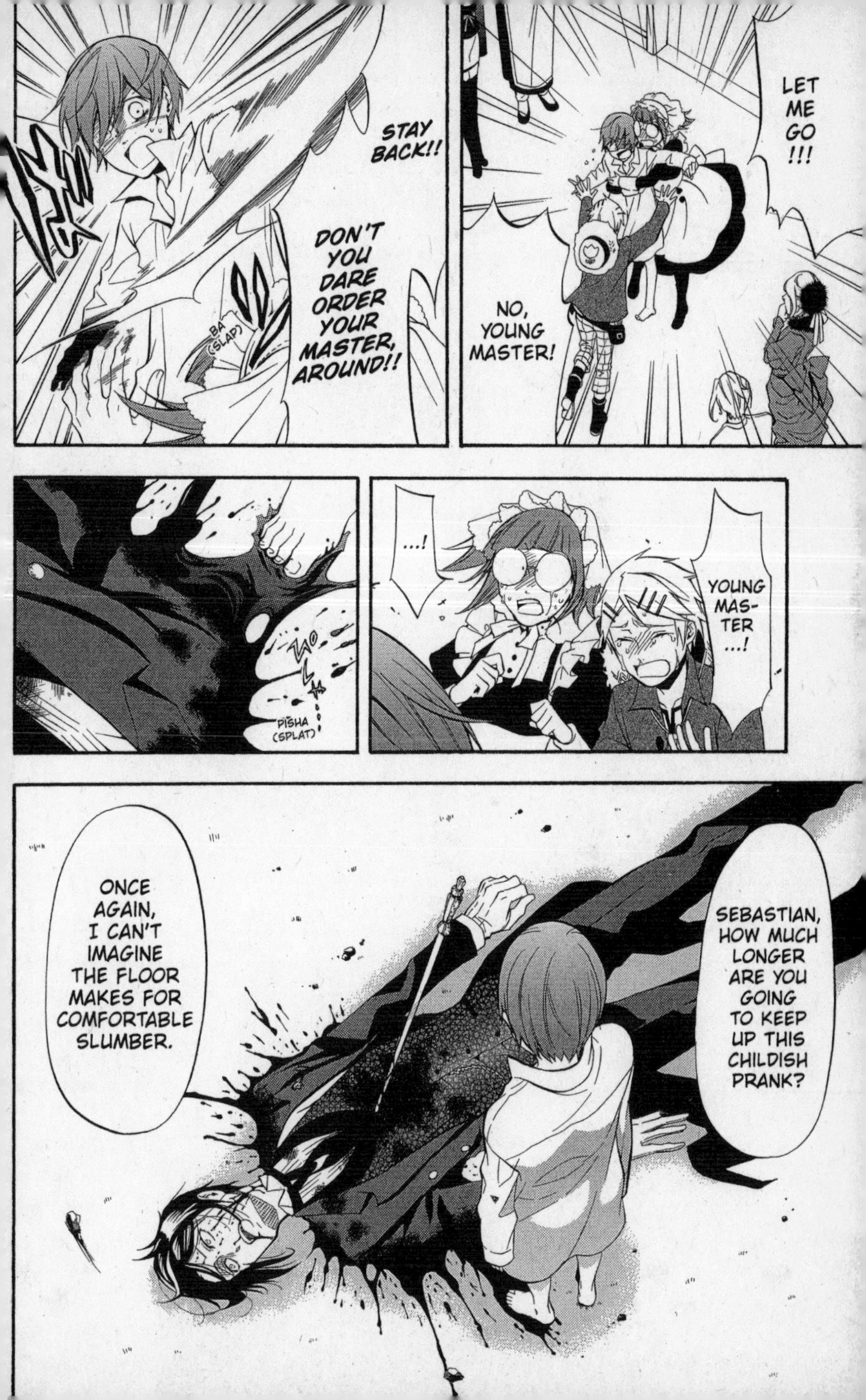
LET ME GO!!!
NO, YOUNG MASTER!
STAY BACK!!
DON'T YOU DARE ORDER YOUR MASTER AROUND!!
BA (SLAP)
YOUNG MASTER...!
...!
PISHA (SPLAT)
SEBASTIAN, HOW MUCH LONGER ARE YOU GOING TO KEEP UP THIS CHILDISH PRANK?
ONCE AGAIN, I CAN'T IMAGINE THE FLOOR MAKES FOR COMFORTABLE SLUMBER.

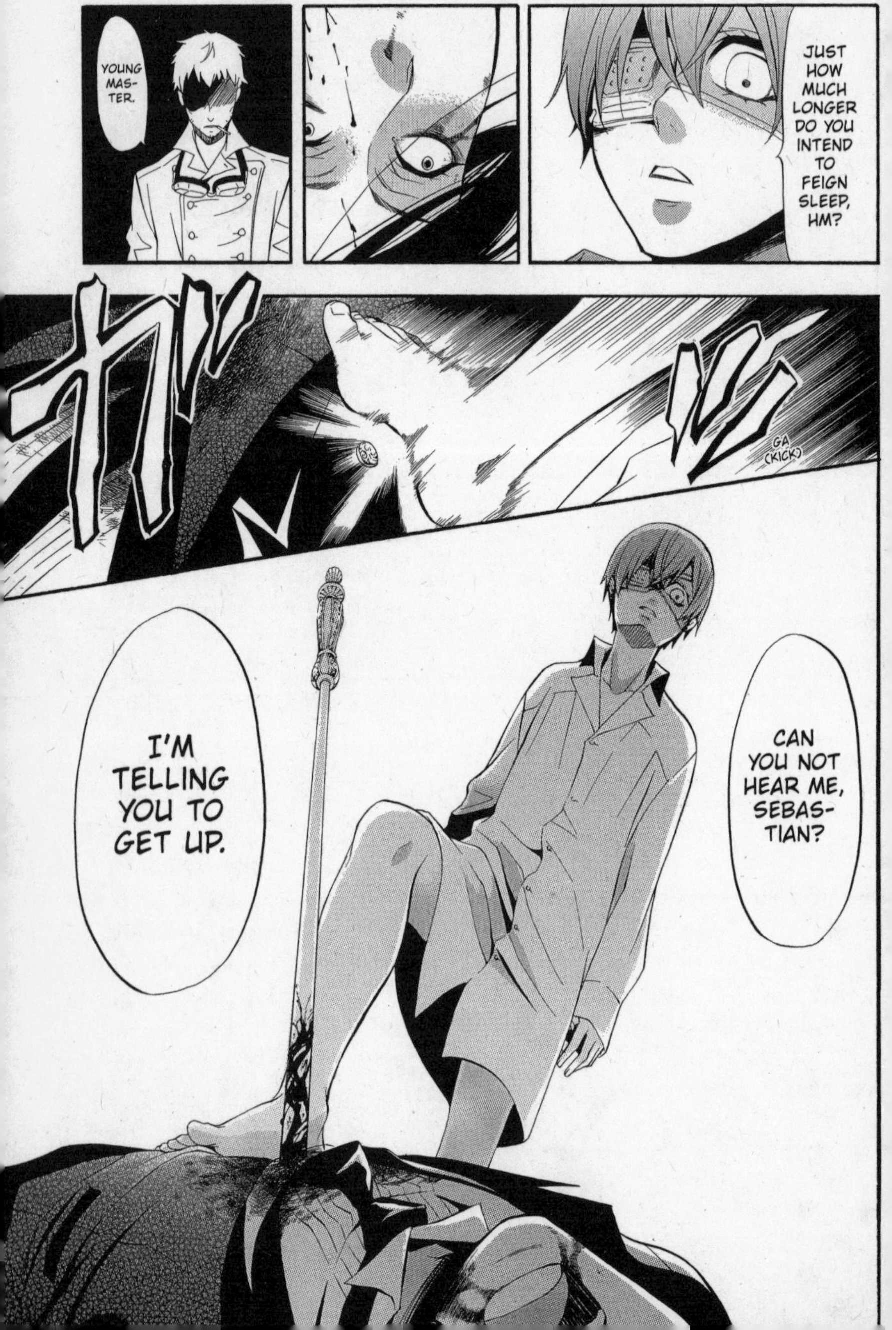
JUST HOW MUCH LONGER DO YOU INTEND TO FEIGN SLEEP, HM?
YOUNG MAS-TER.
GA (KICK)
CAN YOU NOT HEAR ME, SEBAS-TIAN?
I'M TELLING YOU TO GET UP.

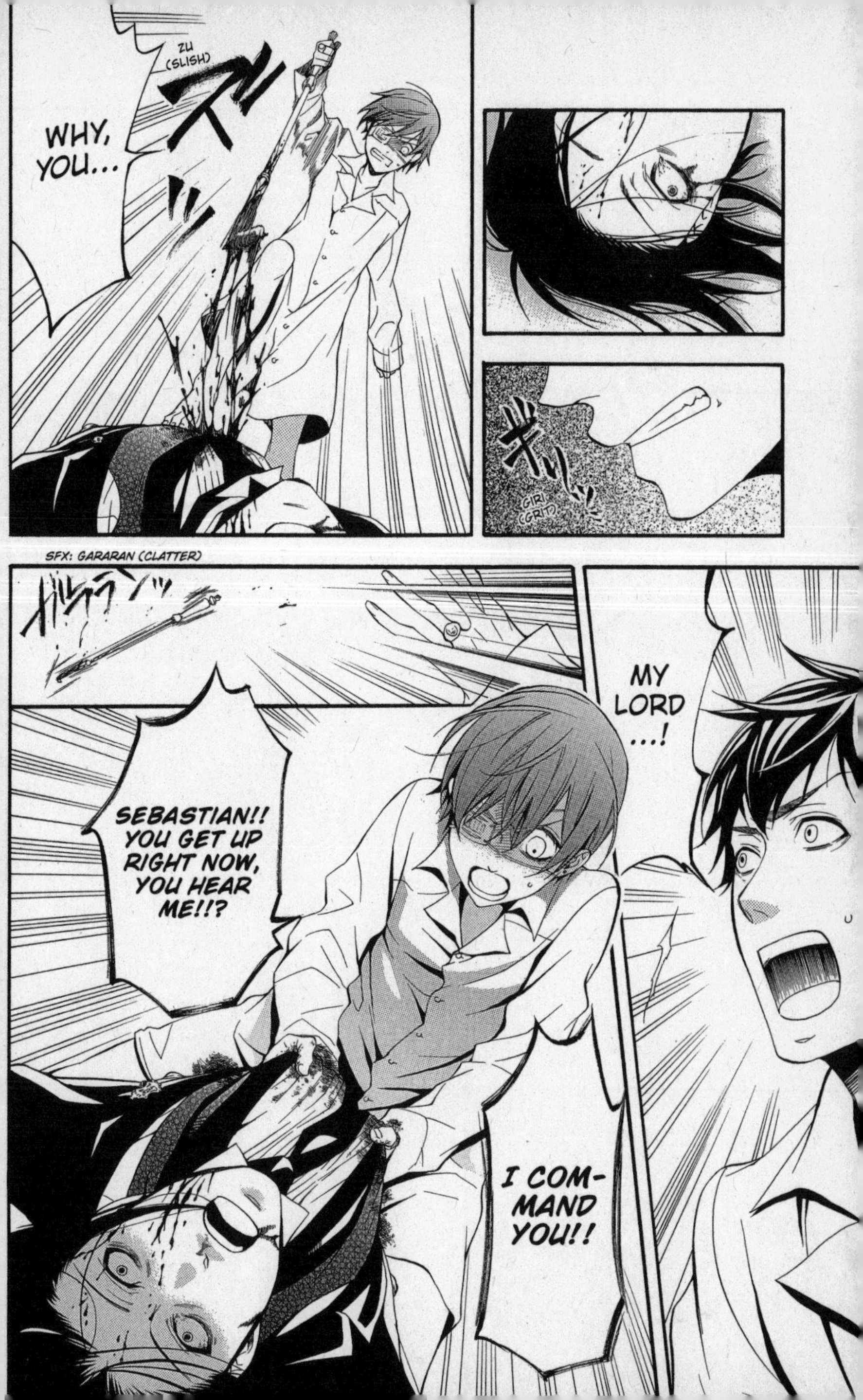
GIRI (GRIT)
ZU (SLISH)
WHY, YOU...
SFX: GARARAN (CLATTER)
MY LORD ...!
SEBASTIAN!! YOU GET UP RIGHT NOW, YOU HEAR ME!!?
I COMMAND YOU!!

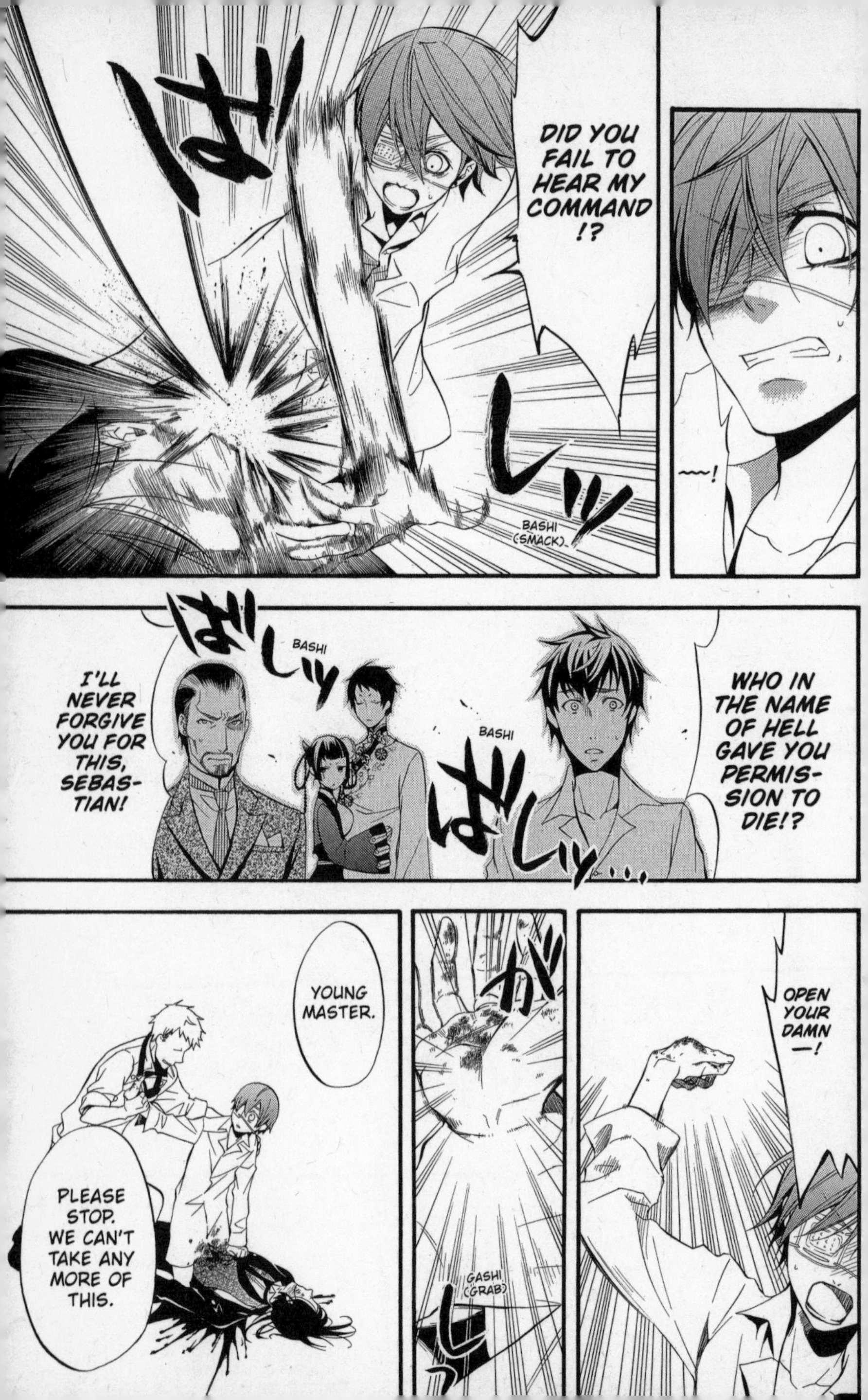
~~!
DID YOU FAIL TO HEAR MY COMMAND !?
BASHI (SMACK)
WHO IN THE NAME OF HELL GAVE YOU PERMISSION TO DIE!?
BASHI
BASHI
I'LL NEVER FORGIVE YOU FOR THIS, SEBASTIAN!
OPEN YOUR DAMN —!
GASHI (GRAB)
YOUNG MASTER.
PLEASE STOP. WE CAN'T TAKE ANY MORE OF THIS.

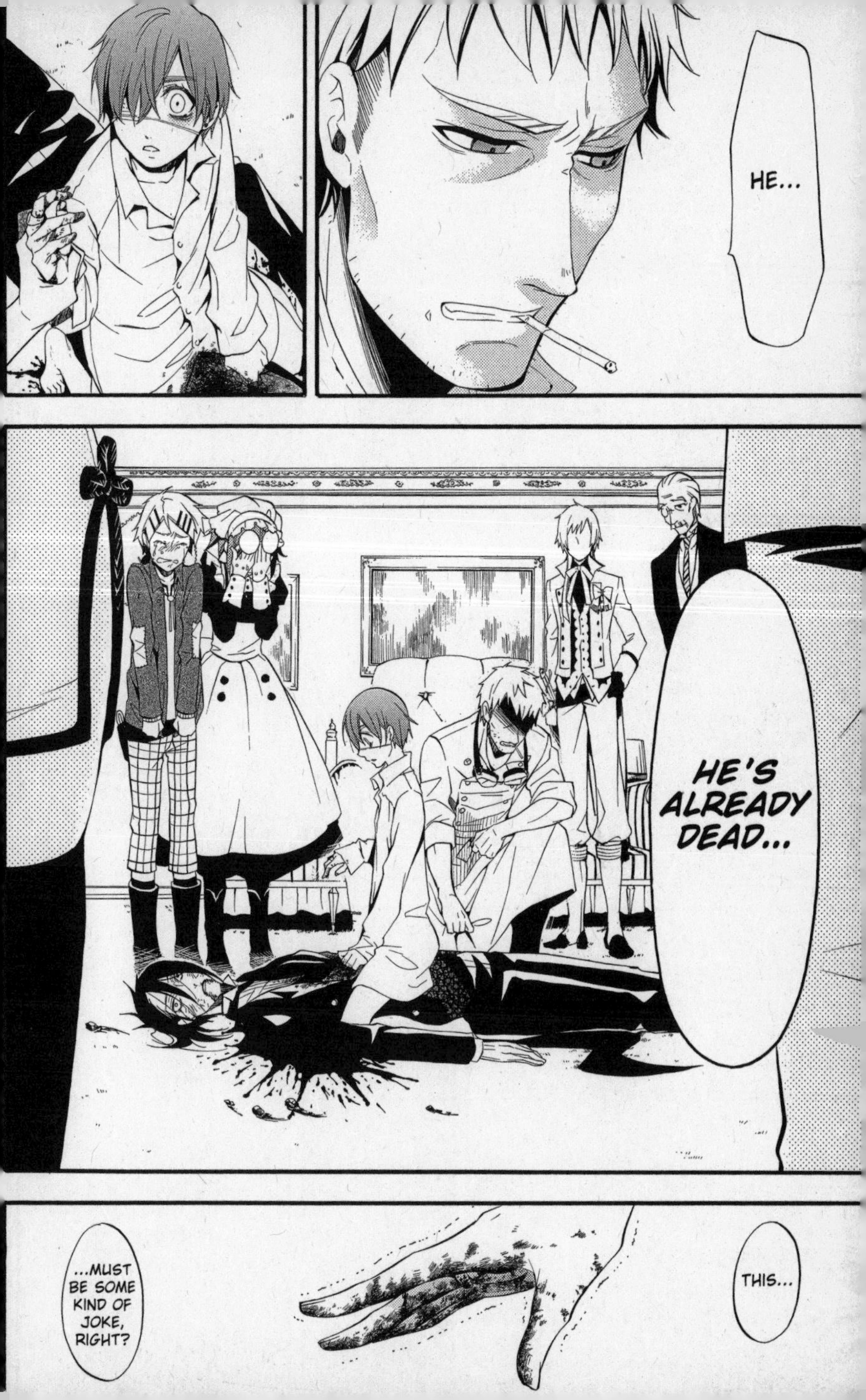
HE...
HE'S ALREADY DEAD...
THIS...
...MUST BE SOME KIND OF JOKE, RIGHT?

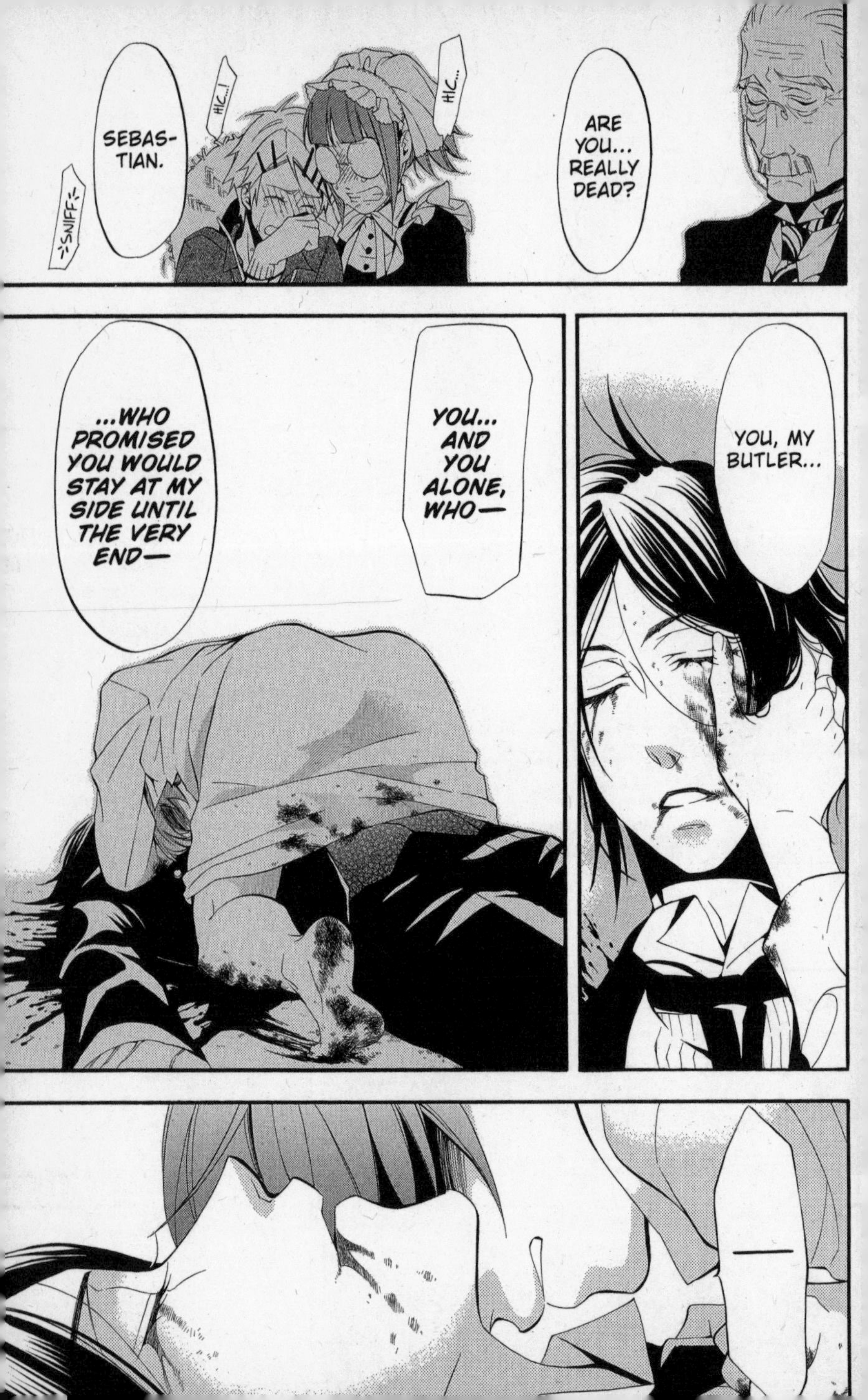
ARE YOU... REALLY DEAD?
HIC...
HIC...!
SEBAS-TIAN.
SNIFF
YOU, MY BUTLER...
YOU... AND YOU ALONE, WHO—
...WHO PROMISED YOU WOULD STAY AT MY SIDE UNTIL THE VERY END—
—

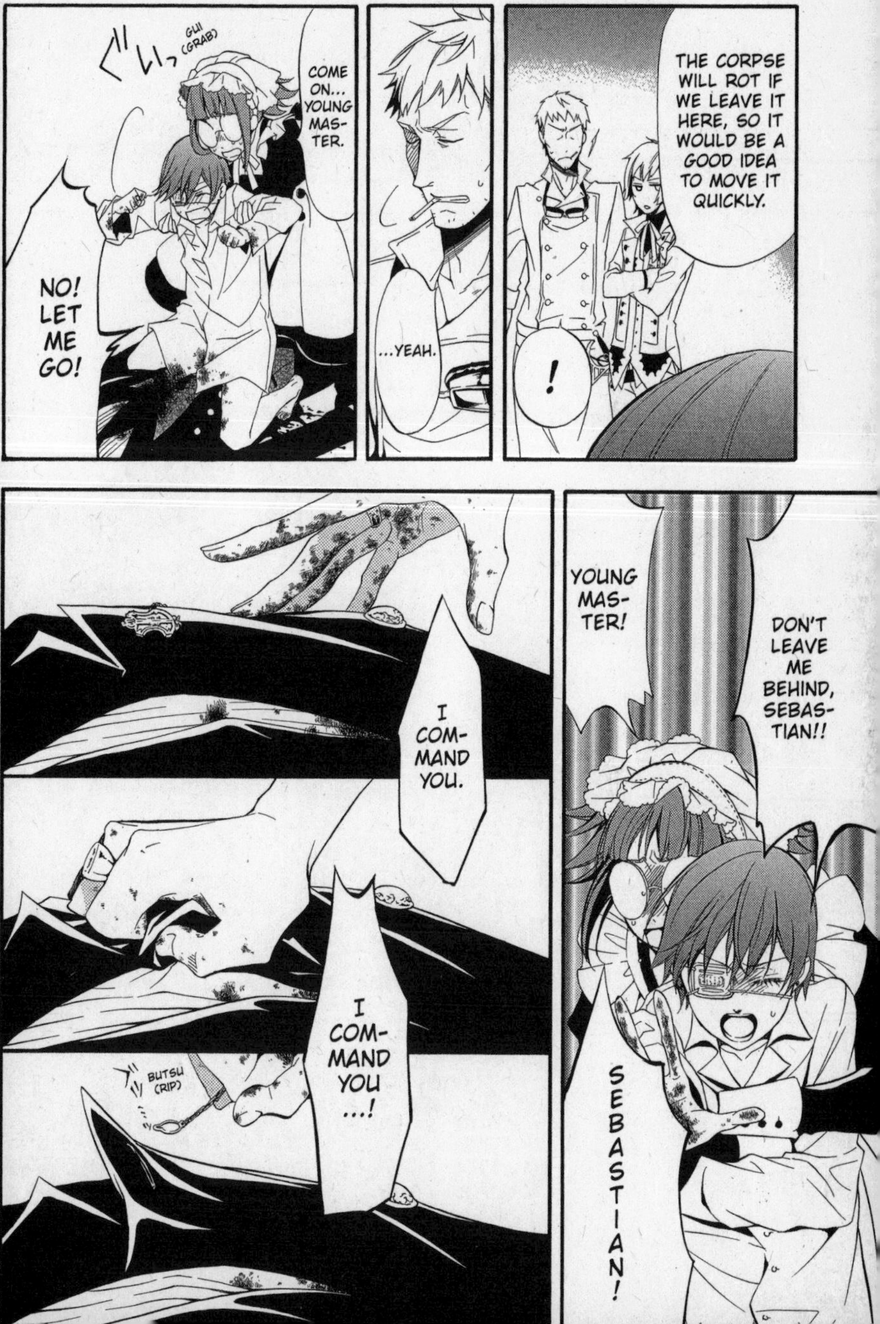
THE CORPSE WILL ROT IF WE LEAVE IT HERE, SO IT WOULD BE A GOOD IDEA TO MOVE IT QUICKLY.
!
...YEAH.
COME ON... YOUNG MAS-TER.
GUI (GRAB)
NO! LET ME GO!
YOUNG MAS-TER!
DON'T LEAVE ME BEHIND, SEBAS-TIAN!!
SEBASTIAN!
I COM-MAND YOU.
I COM-MAND YOU ...!
BUTSU (RIP)

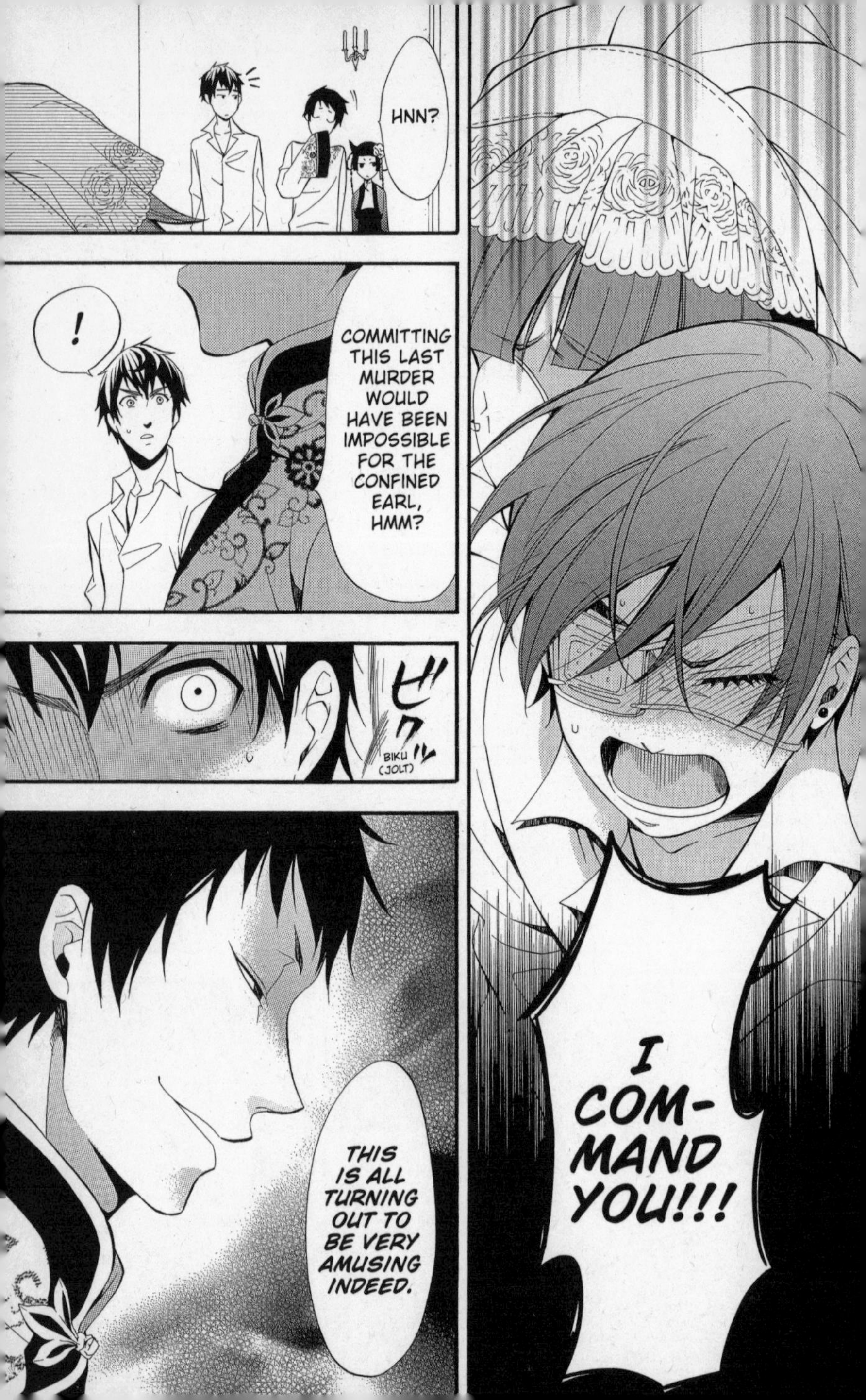
I COM-MAND YOU!!!
HNN?
!
COMMITTING THIS LAST MURDER WOULD HAVE BEEN IMPOSSIBLE FOR THE CONFINED EARL, HMM?
ビクッ
BIKU (JOLT)
THIS IS ALL TURNING OUT TO BE VERY AMUSING INDEED.

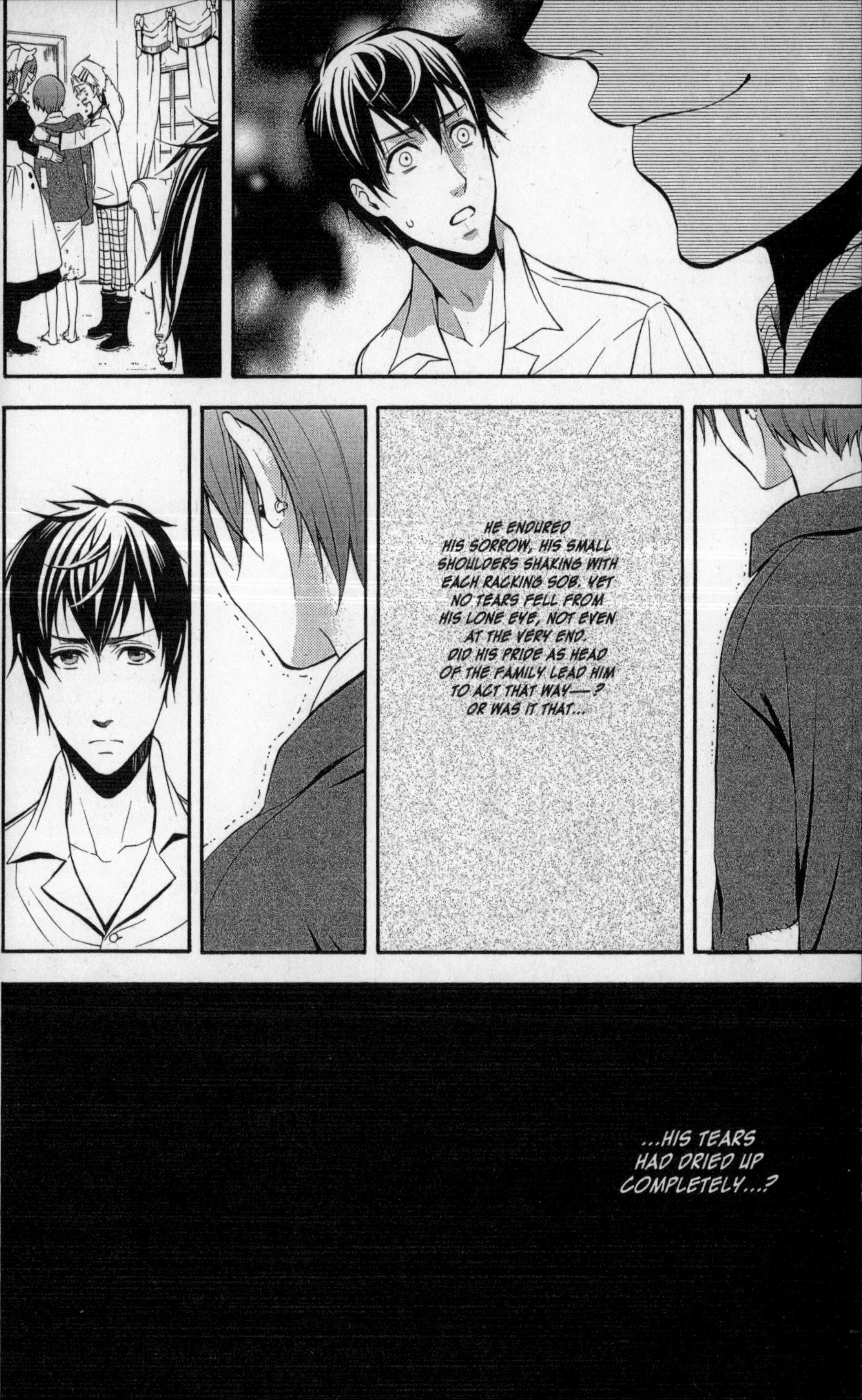
HE ENDURED HIS SORROW, HIS SMALL SHOULDERS SHAKING WITH EACH RACKING SOB. YET NO TEARS FELL FROM HIS LONE EYE, NOT EVEN AT THE VERY END. DID HIS PRIDE AS HEAD OF THE FAMILY LEAD HIM TO ACT THAT WAY—? OR WAS IT THAT...
...HIS TEARS HAD DRIED UP COMPLETELY...?

Black Butler

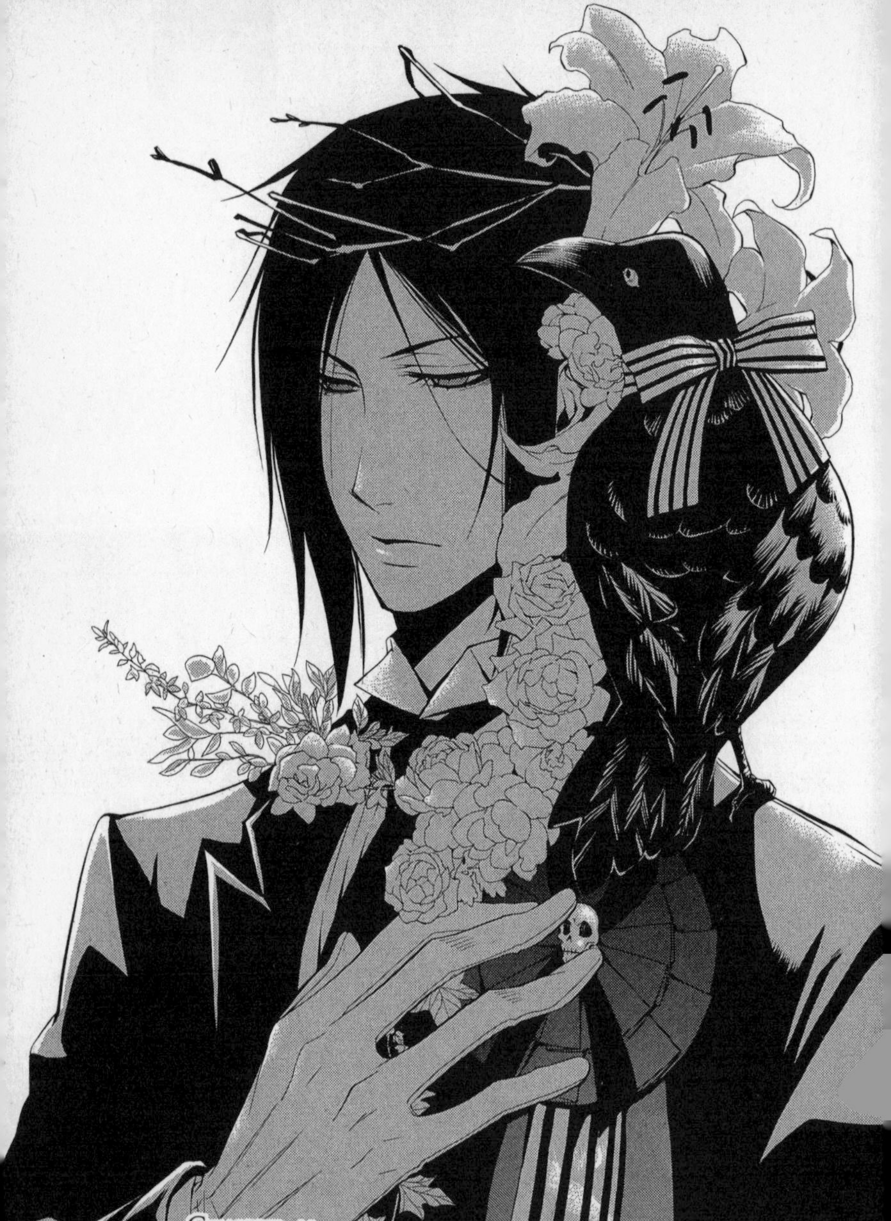

CHAPTER 42

At midnight: The Butler, Substituted

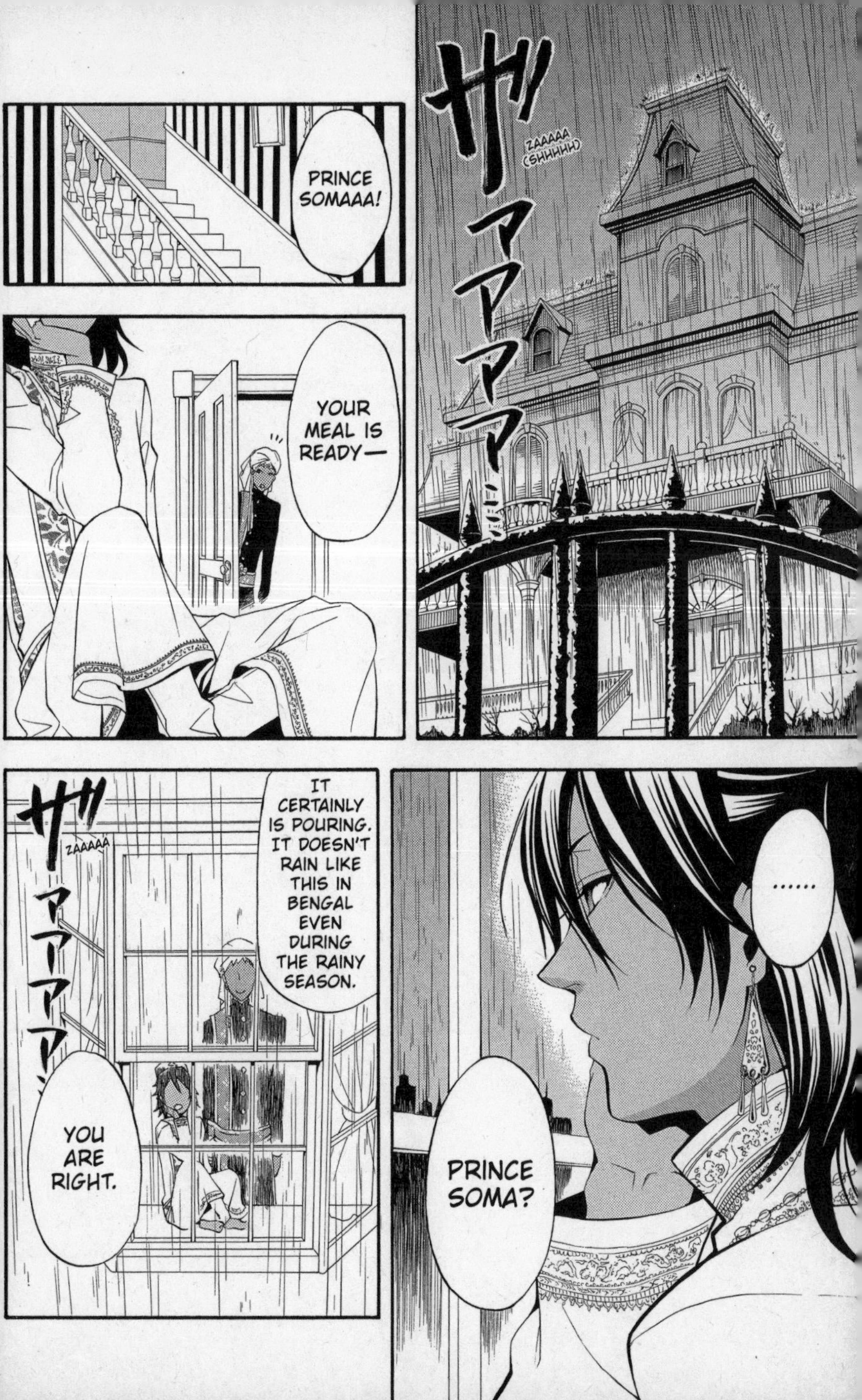
ZAAAAA (SHHHHH)
PRINCE SOMAAA!
YOUR MEAL IS READY—
......
PRINCE SOMA?
ZAAAAA
IT CERTAINLY IS POURING. IT DOESN'T RAIN LIKE THIS IN BENGAL EVEN DURING THE RAINY SEASON.
YOU ARE RIGHT.

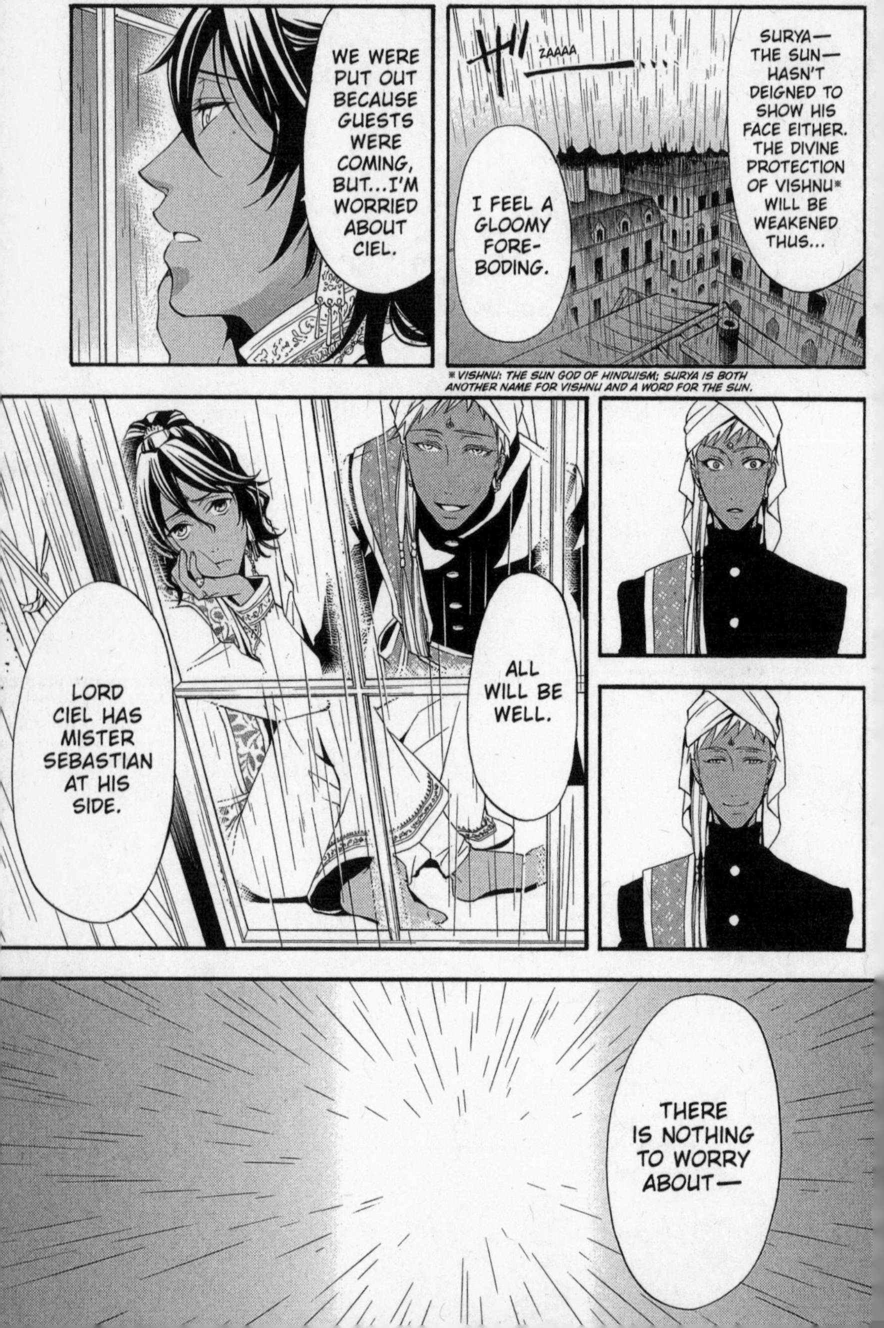
ZAAAA
SURYA—THE SUN—HASN'T DEIGNED TO SHOW HIS FACE EITHER. THE DIVINE PROTECTION OF VISHNU* WILL BE WEAKENED THUS...
I FEEL A GLOOMY FORE-BODING.
WE WERE PUT OUT BECAUSE GUESTS WERE COMING, BUT...I'M WORRIED ABOUT CIEL.
LORD CIEL HAS MISTER SEBASTIAN AT HIS SIDE.
ALL WILL BE WELL.
THERE IS NOTHING TO WORRY ABOUT—

* VISHNU: THE SUN GOD OF HINDUISM; SURYA IS BOTH ANOTHER NAME FOR VISHNU AND A WORD FOR THE SUN.

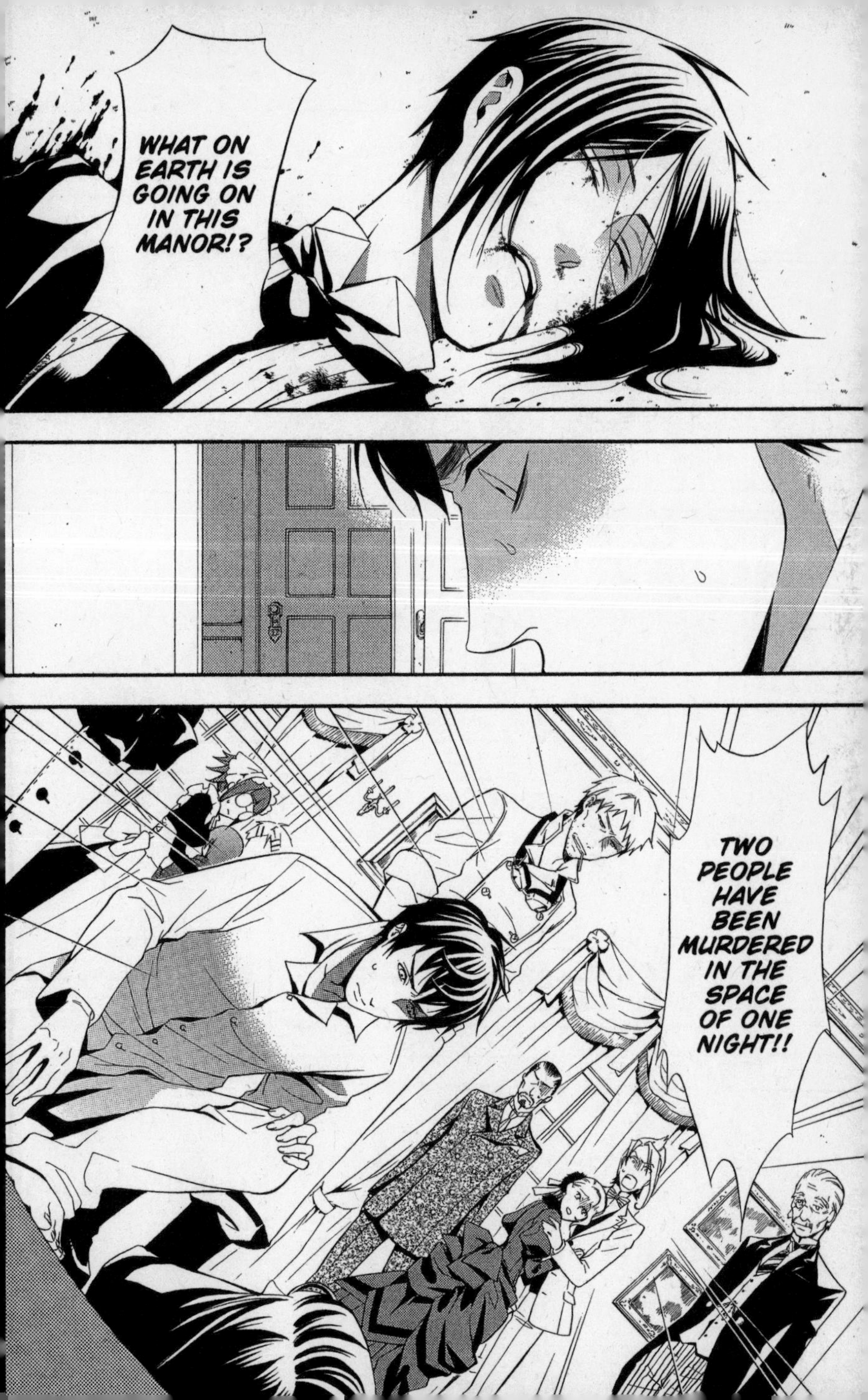
WHAT ON EARTH IS GOING ON IN THIS MANOR!?
TWO PEOPLE HAVE BEEN MURDERED IN THE SPACE OF ONE NIGHT!!

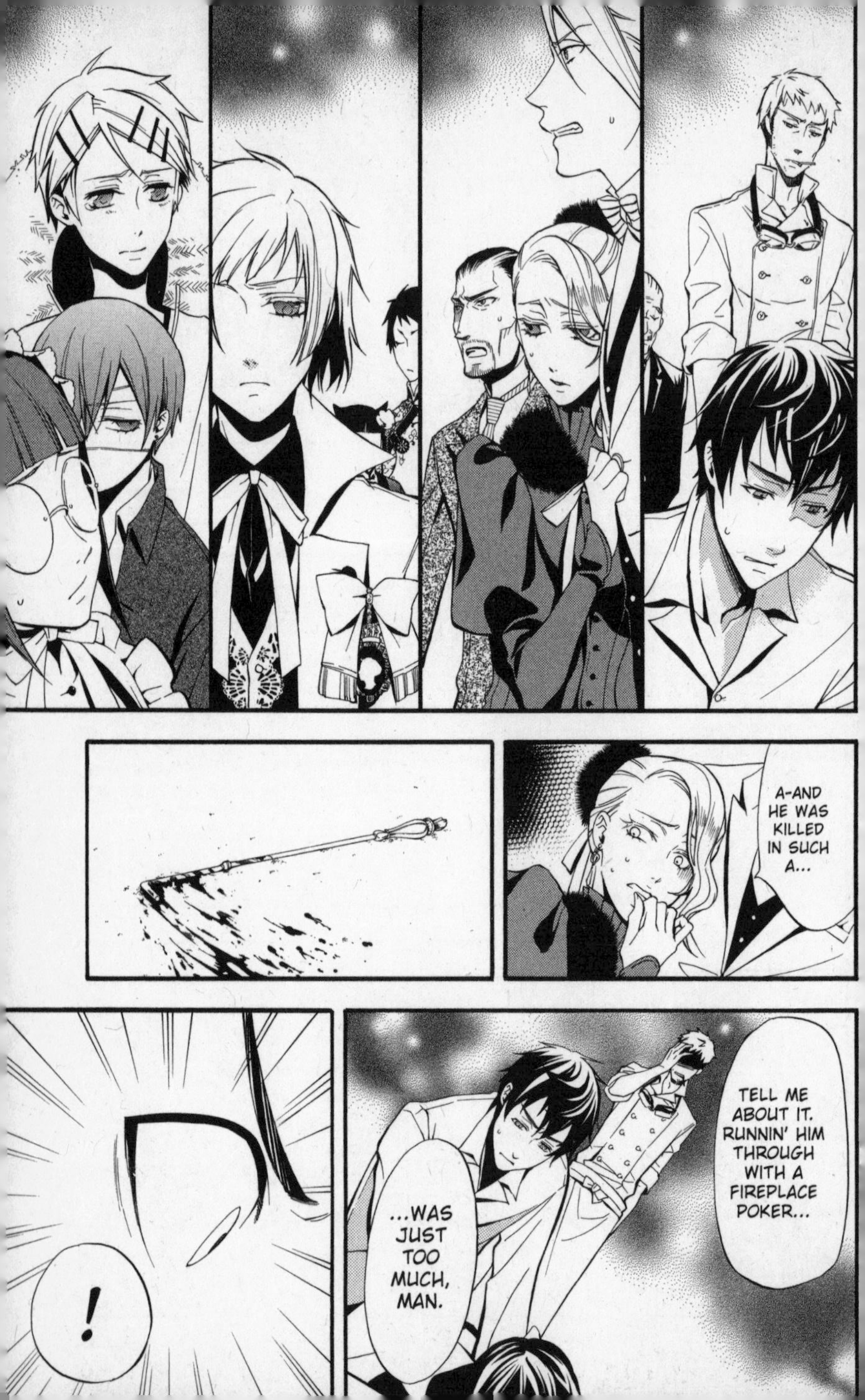
A-AND HE WAS KILLED IN SUCH A...
TELL ME ABOUT IT. RUNNIN' HIM THROUGH WITH A FIREPLACE POKER...
...WAS JUST TOO MUCH, MAN.
!

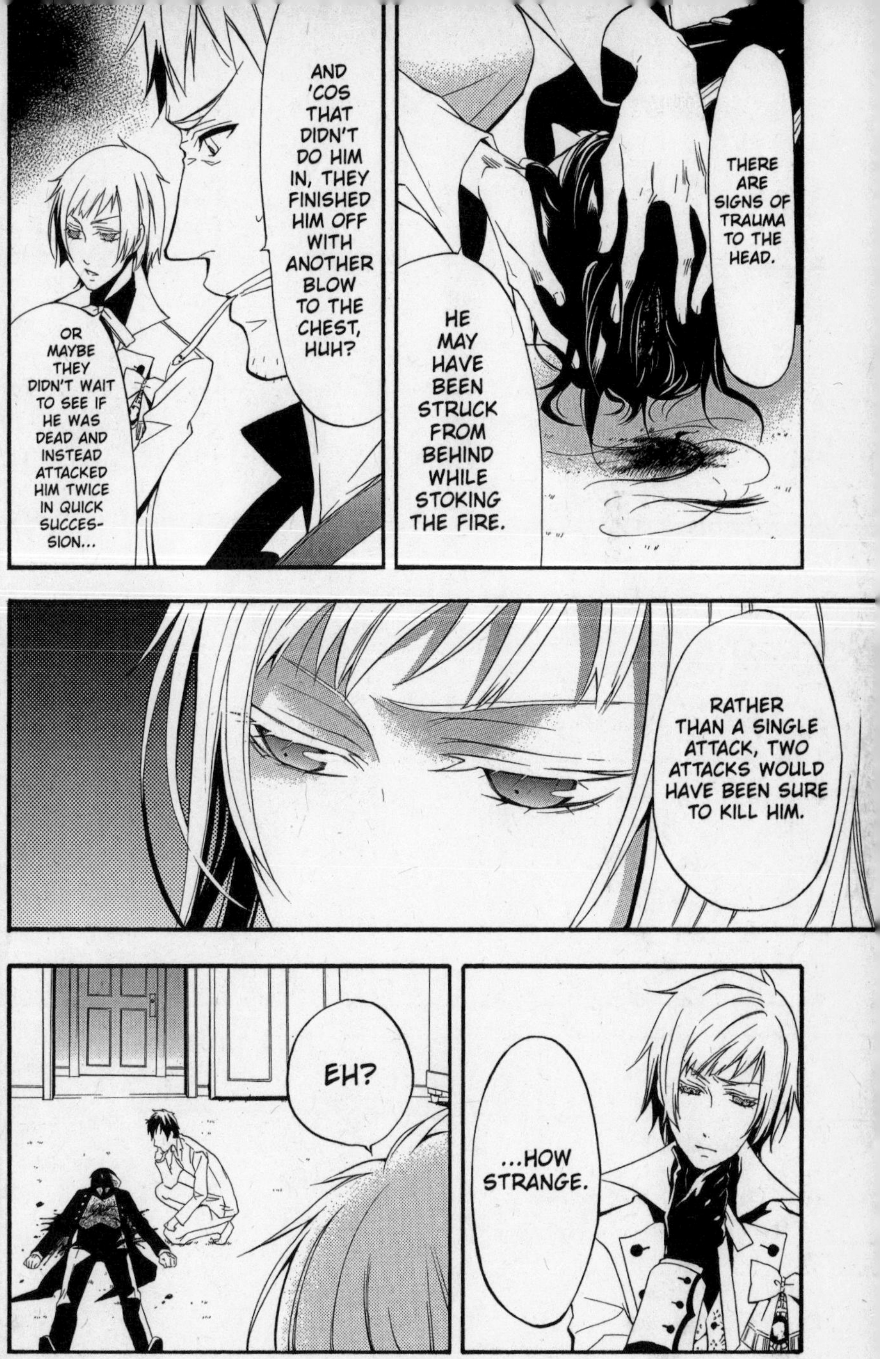
THERE ARE SIGNS OF TRAUMA TO THE HEAD.
HE MAY HAVE BEEN STRUCK FROM BEHIND WHILE STOKING THE FIRE.
AND 'COS THAT DIDN'T DO HIM IN, THEY FINISHED HIM OFF WITH ANOTHER BLOW TO THE CHEST, HUH?
OR MAYBE THEY DIDN'T WAIT TO SEE IF HE WAS DEAD AND INSTEAD ATTACKED HIM TWICE IN QUICK SUCCES-SION...
RATHER THAN A SINGLE ATTACK, TWO ATTACKS WOULD HAVE BEEN SURE TO KILL HIM.
...HOW STRANGE.
EH?

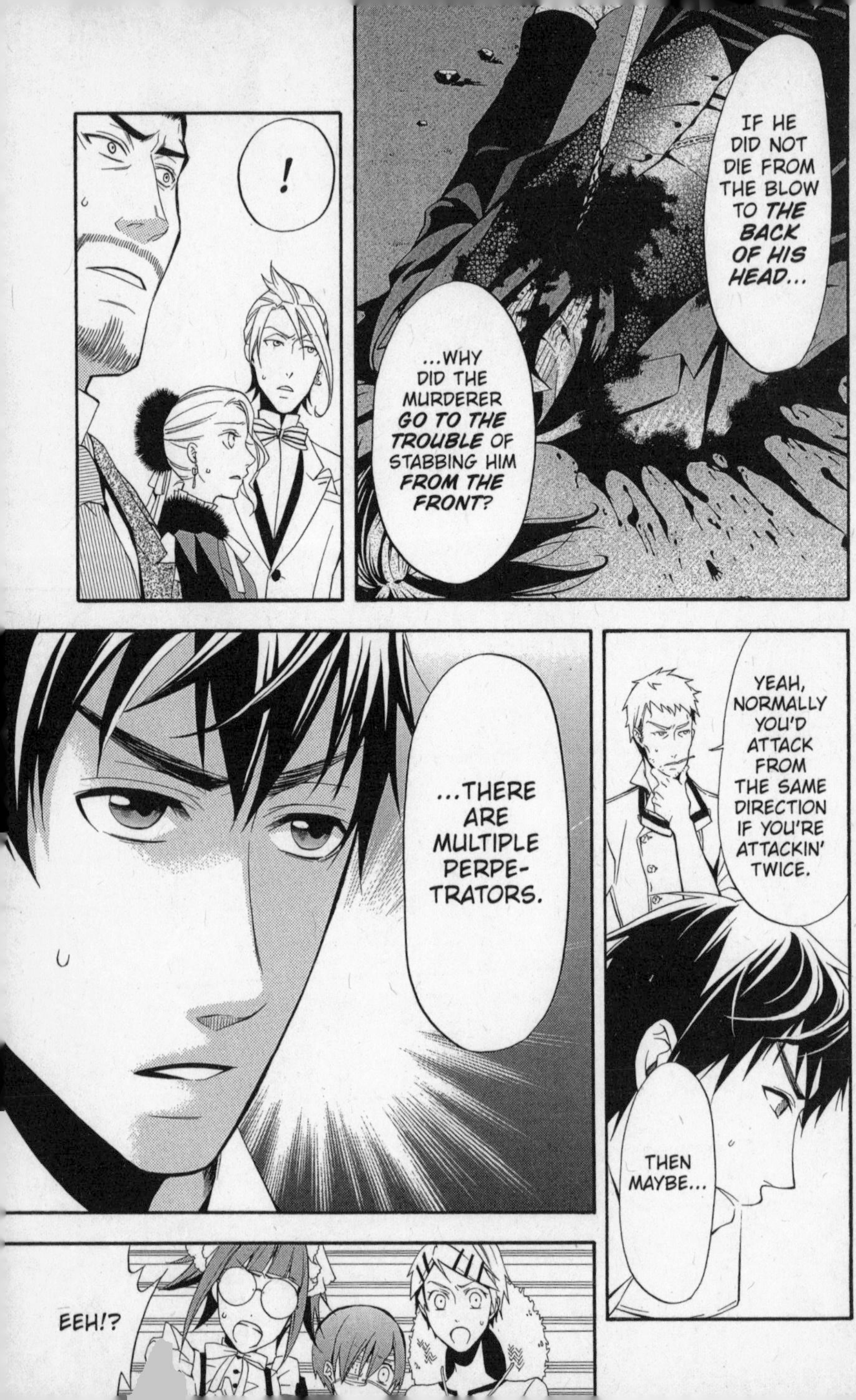
IF HE DID NOT DIE FROM THE BLOW TO THE BACK OF HIS HEAD...
...WHY DID THE MURDERER GO TO THE TROUBLE OF STABBING HIM FROM THE FRONT?
!
YEAH, NORMALLY YOU'D ATTACK FROM THE SAME DIRECTION IF YOU'RE ATTACKIN' TWICE.
THEN MAYBE...
...THERE ARE MULTIPLE PERPE-TRATORS.
EEH!?

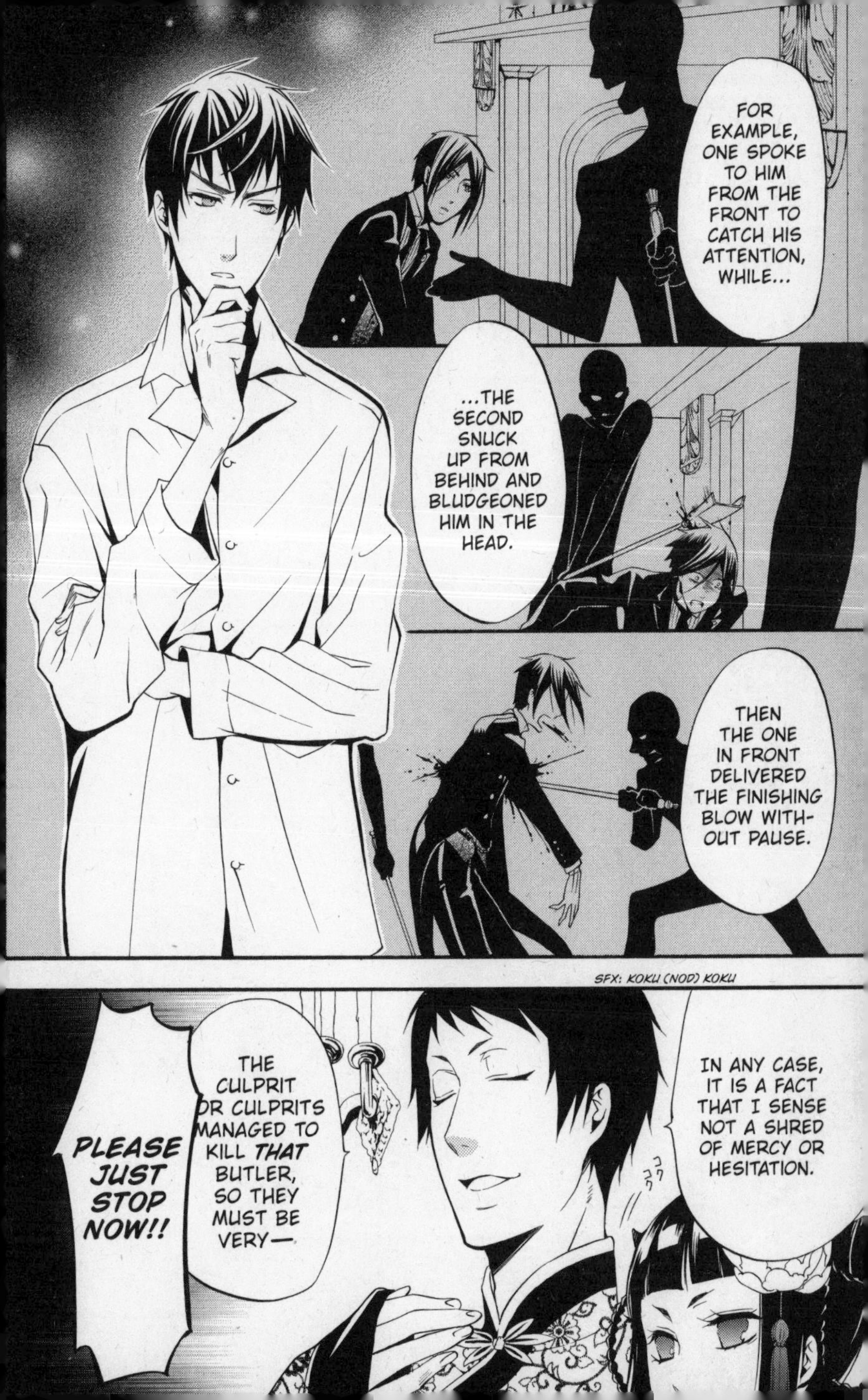
FOR EXAMPLE, ONE SPOKE TO HIM FROM THE FRONT TO CATCH HIS ATTENTION, WHILE...
...THE SECOND SNUCK UP FROM BEHIND AND BLUDGEONED HIM IN THE HEAD.
THEN THE ONE IN FRONT DELIVERED THE FINISHING BLOW WITH-OUT PAUSE.
SFX: KOKU (NOD) KOKU
IN ANY CASE, IT IS A FACT THAT I SENSE NOT A SHRED OF MERCY OR HESITATION.
THE CULPRIT OR CULPRITS MANAGED TO KILL *THAT* BUTLER, SO THEY MUST BE VERY—
PLEASE JUST STOP NOW!!

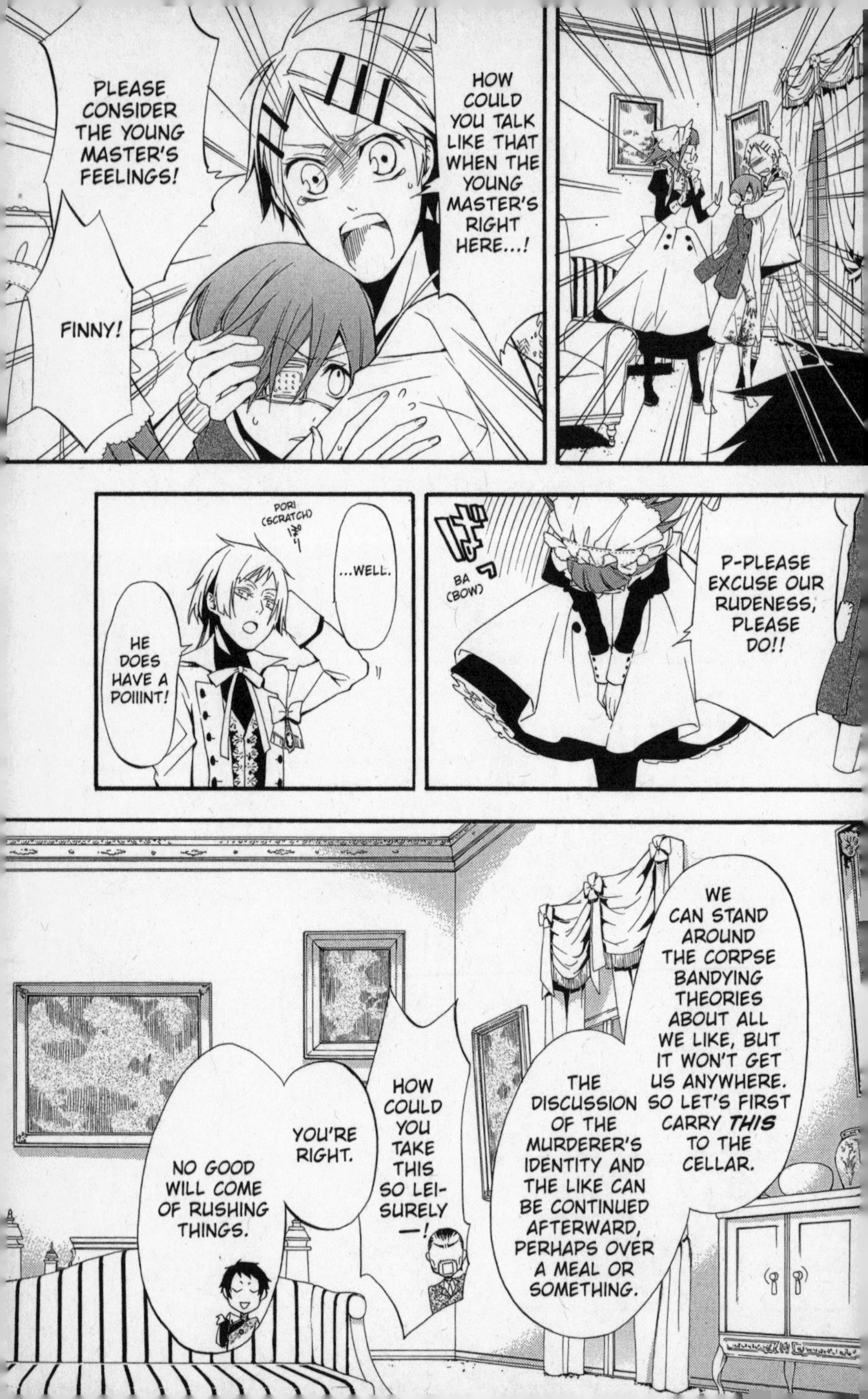

HOW COULD YOU TALK LIKE THAT WHEN THE YOUNG MASTER'S RIGHT HERE...!
PLEASE CONSIDER THE YOUNG MASTER'S FEELINGS!
FINNY!
P-PLEASE EXCUSE OUR RUDENESS, PLEASE DO!!
BA (BOW)
PORI (SCRATCH)
...WELL.
HE DOES HAVE A POIIINT!
WE CAN STAND AROUND THE CORPSE BANDYING THEORIES ABOUT ALL WE LIKE, BUT IT WON'T GET US ANYWHERE. SO LET'S FIRST CARRY *THIS* TO THE CELLAR.
THE DISCUSSION OF THE MURDERER'S IDENTITY AND THE LIKE CAN BE CONTINUED AFTERWARD, PERHAPS OVER A MEAL OR SOMETHING.
HOW COULD YOU TAKE THIS SO LEI-SURELY—!
YOU'RE RIGHT.
NO GOOD WILL COME OF RUSHING THINGS.

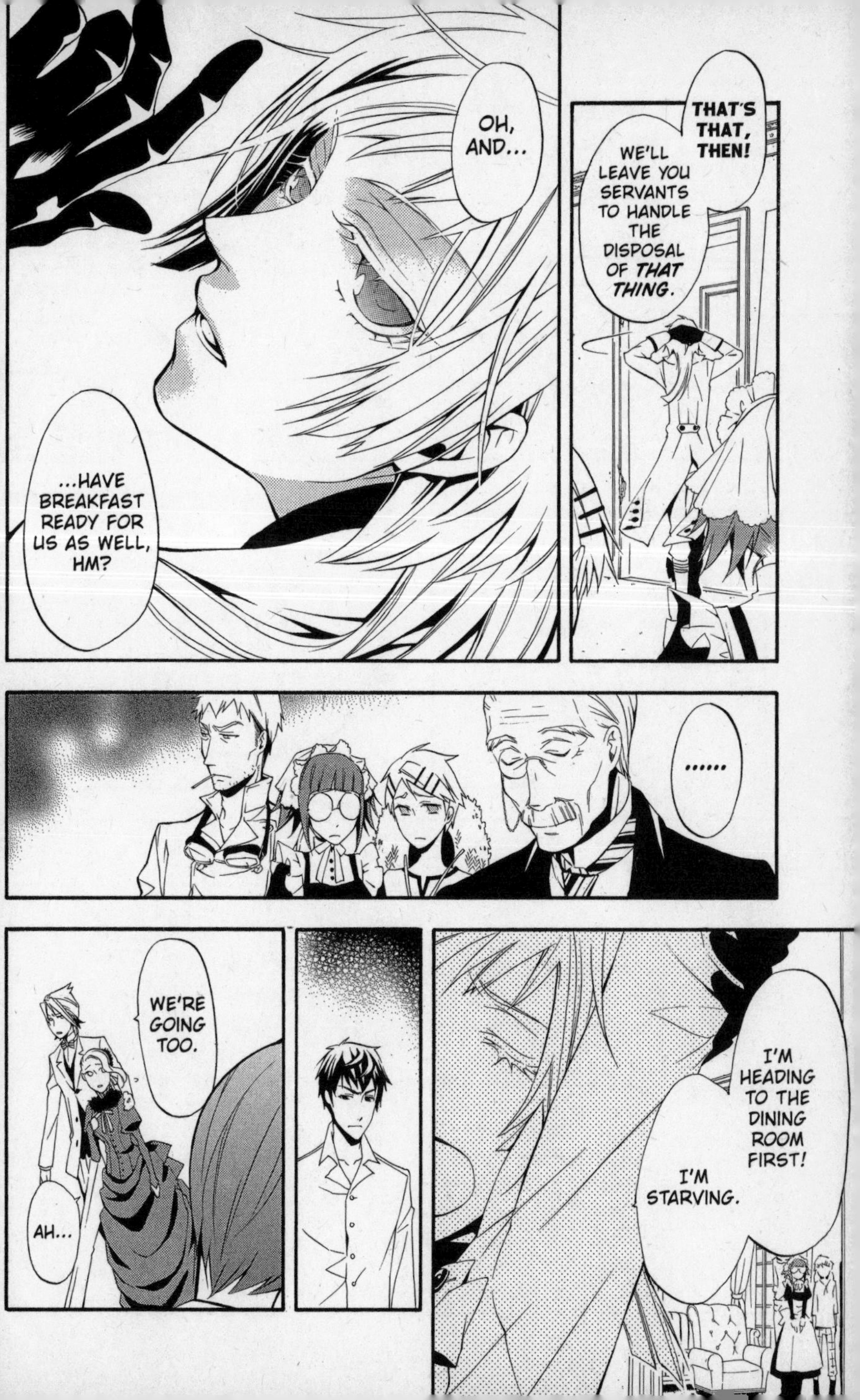
THAT'S THAT, THEN!
WE'LL LEAVE YOU SERVANTS TO HANDLE THE DISPOSAL OF *THAT THING*.
OH, AND...
...HAVE BREAKFAST READY FOR US AS WELL, HM?
......
I'M HEADING TO THE DINING ROOM FIRST!
I'M STARVING.
WE'RE GOING TOO.
AH...

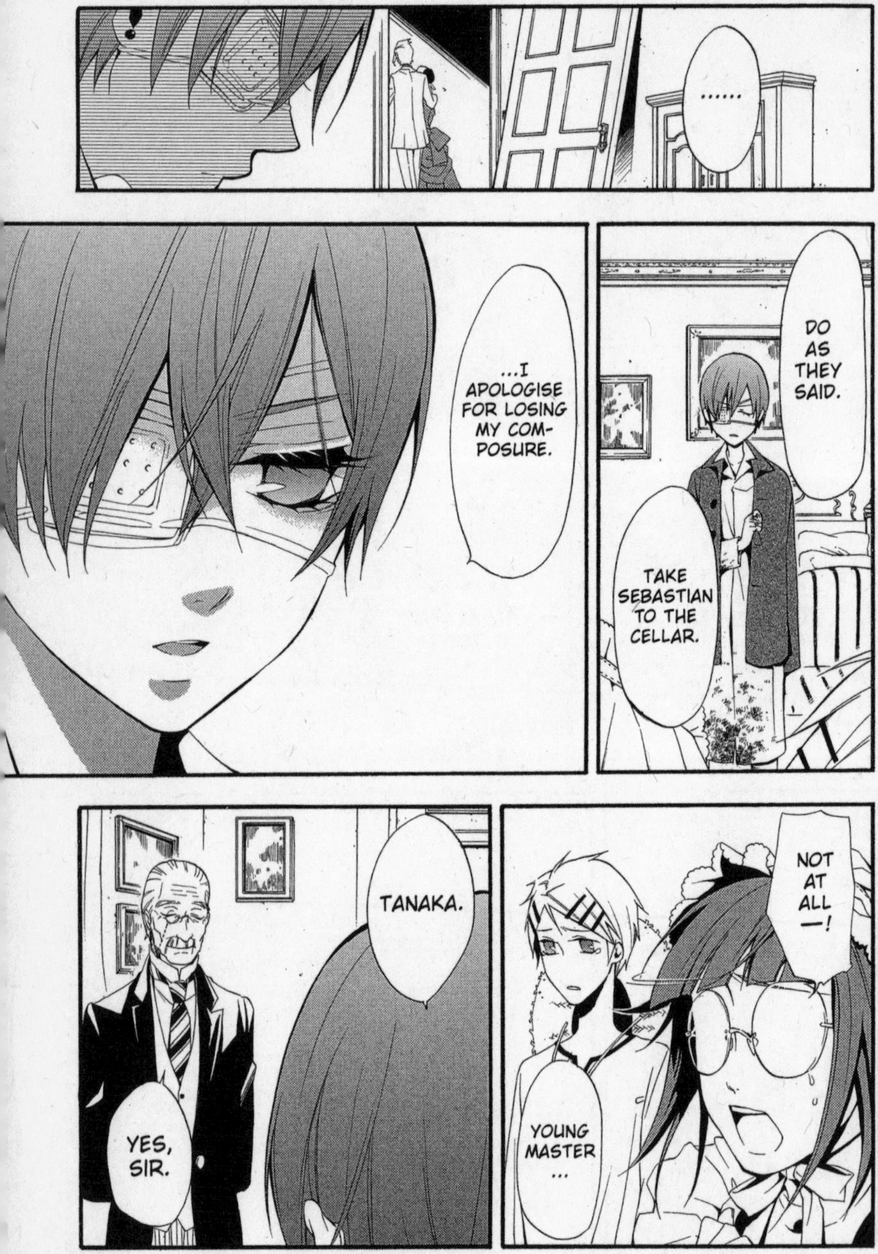
......
DO AS THEY SAID.
TAKE SEBASTIAN TO THE CELLAR.
...I APOLOGISE FOR LOSING MY COM-POSURE.
NOT AT ALL—!
YOUNG MASTER ...
TANAKA.
YES, SIR.

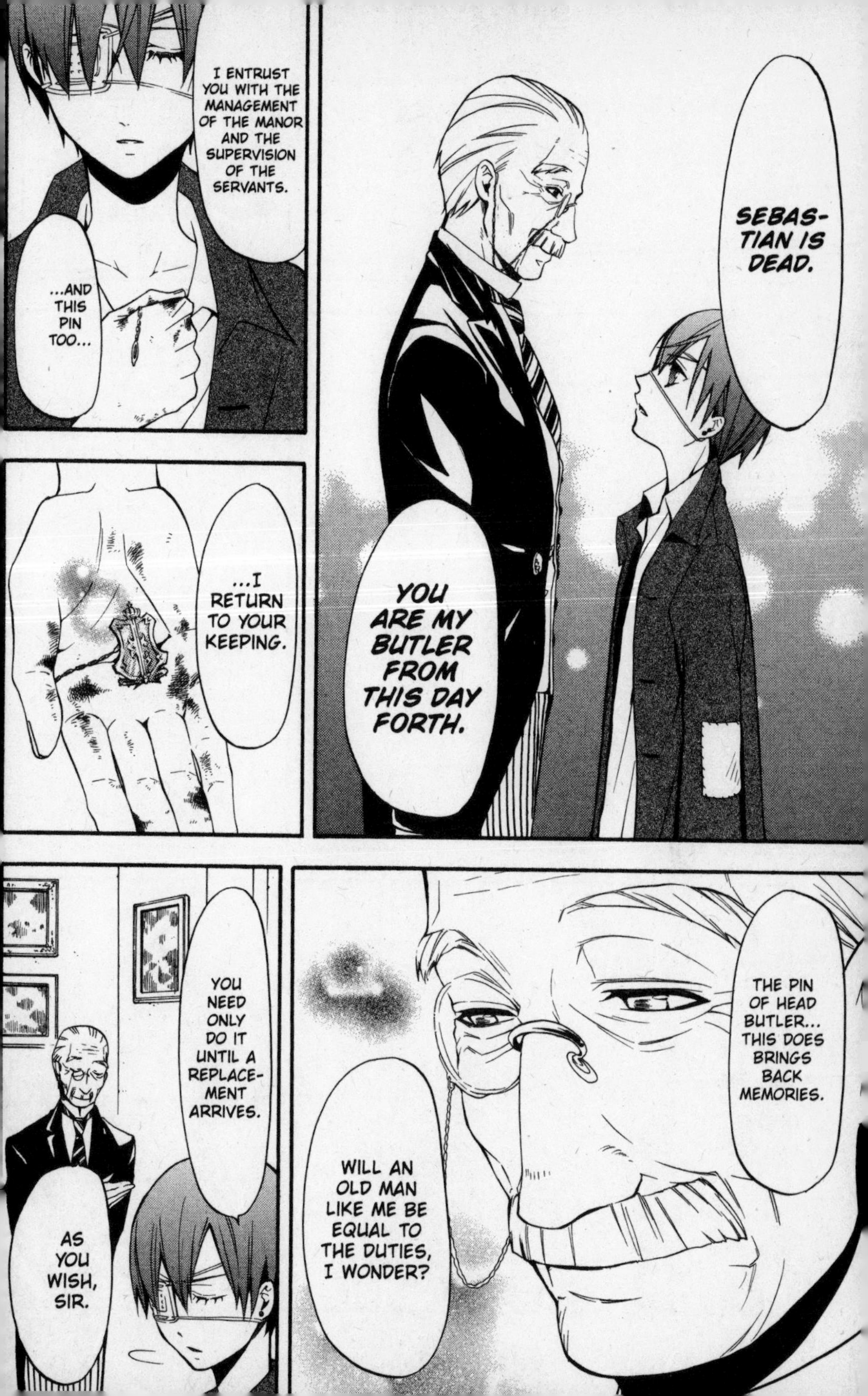
SEBASTIAN IS DEAD.
YOU ARE MY BUTLER FROM THIS DAY FORTH.
I ENTRUST YOU WITH THE MANAGEMENT OF THE MANOR AND THE SUPERVISION OF THE SERVANTS.
...AND THIS PIN TOO...
...I RETURN TO YOUR KEEPING.
THE PIN OF HEAD BUTLER... THIS DOES BRINGS BACK MEMORIES.
WILL AN OLD MAN LIKE ME BE EQUAL TO THE DUTIES, I WONDER?
YOU NEED ONLY DO IT UNTIL A REPLACEMENT ARRIVES.
AS YOU WISH, SIR.

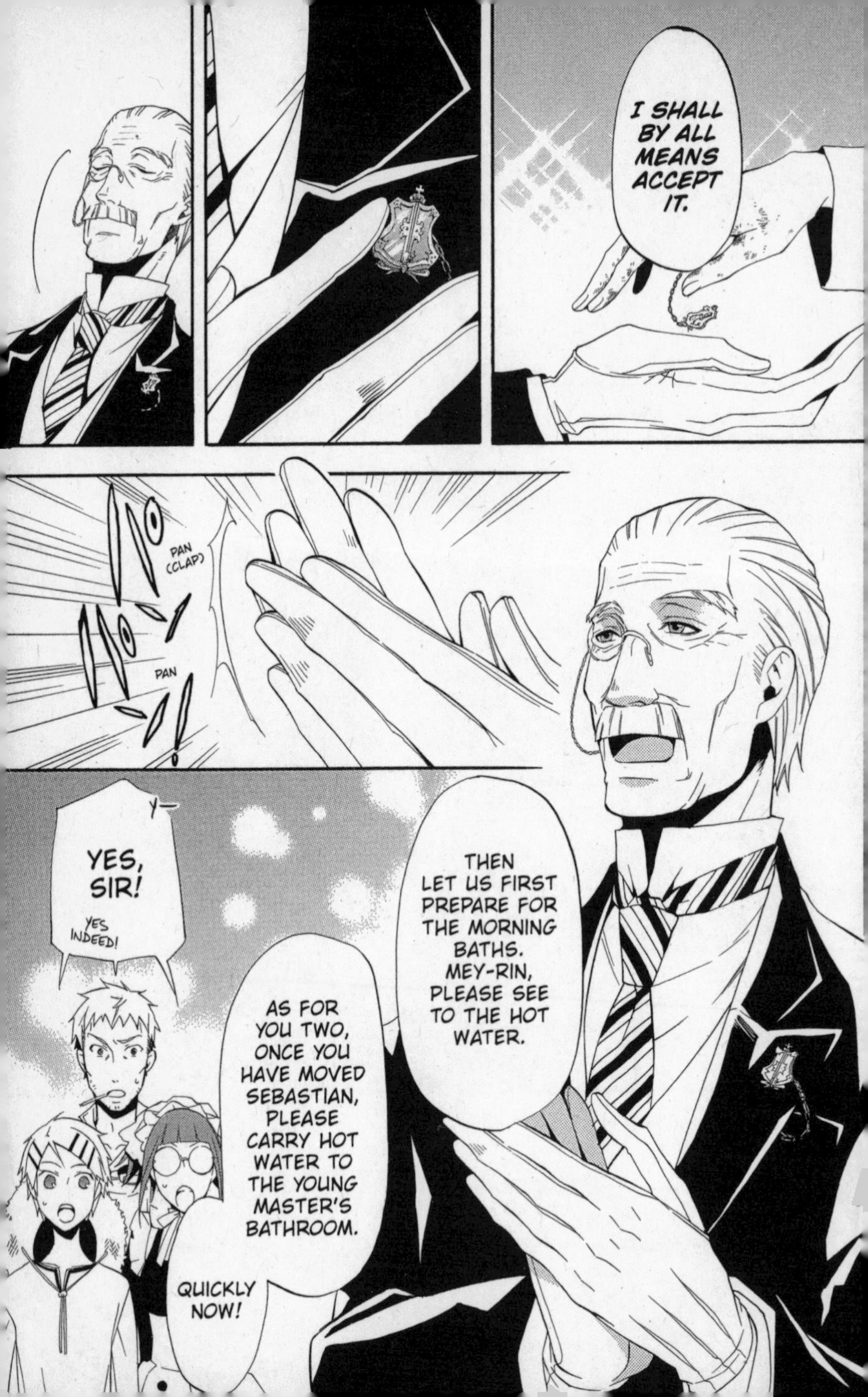
I SHALL BY ALL MEANS ACCEPT IT.
PAN (CLAP)
PAN
THEN LET US FIRST PREPARE FOR THE MORNING BATHS. MEY-RIN, PLEASE SEE TO THE HOT WATER.
AS FOR YOU TWO, ONCE YOU HAVE MOVED SEBASTIAN, PLEASE CARRY HOT WATER TO THE YOUNG MASTER'S BATHROOM.
QUICKLY NOW!
Y—
YES, SIR!
YES INDEED!

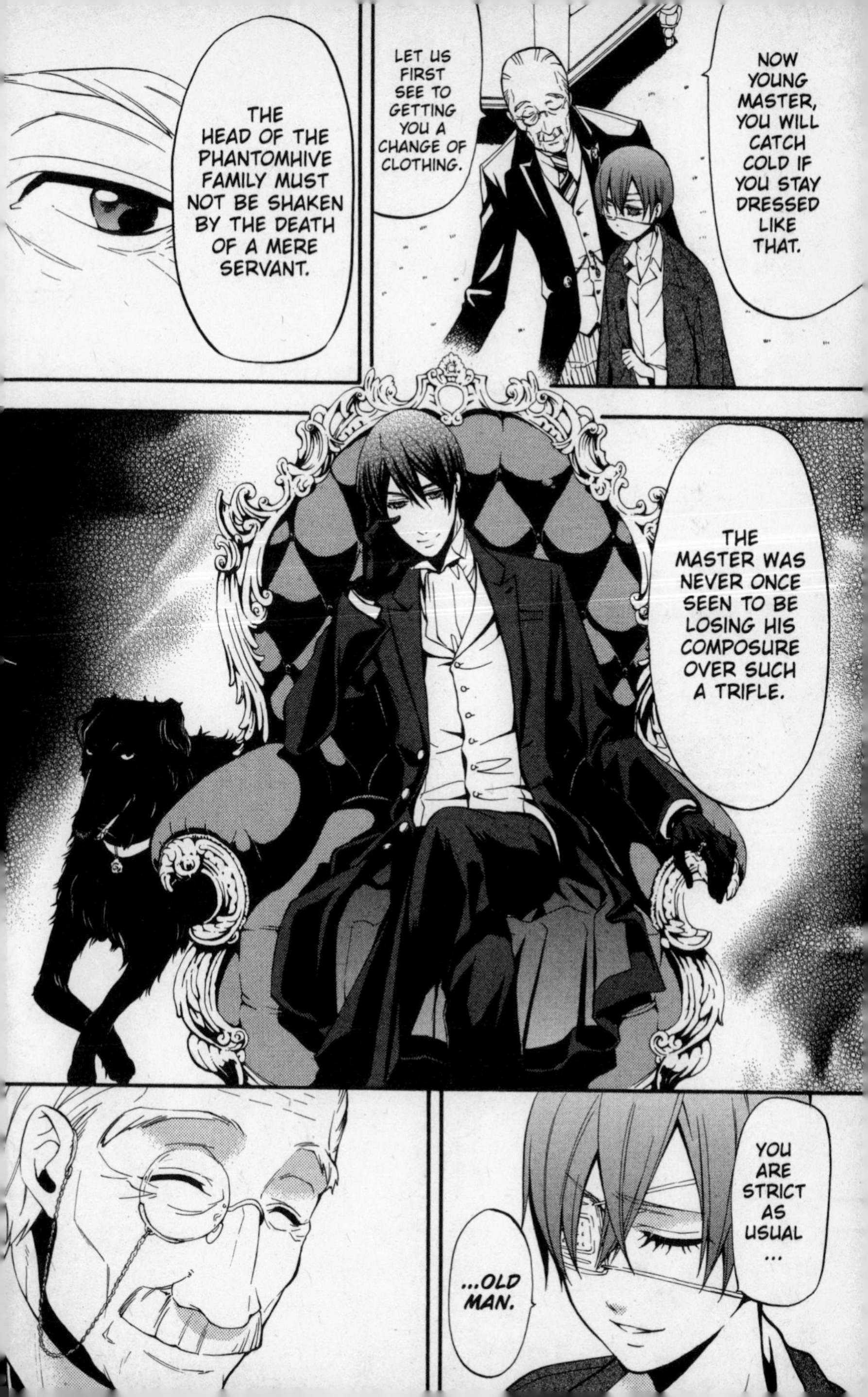
NOW YOUNG MASTER, YOU WILL CATCH COLD IF YOU STAY DRESSED LIKE THAT.
LET US FIRST SEE TO GETTING YOU A CHANGE OF CLOTHING.
THE HEAD OF THE PHANTOMHIVE FAMILY MUST NOT BE SHAKEN BY THE DEATH OF A MERE SERVANT.
THE MASTER WAS NEVER ONCE SEEN TO BE LOSING HIS COMPOSURE OVER SUCH A TRIFLE.
YOU ARE STRICT AS USUAL ...
...OLD MAN.

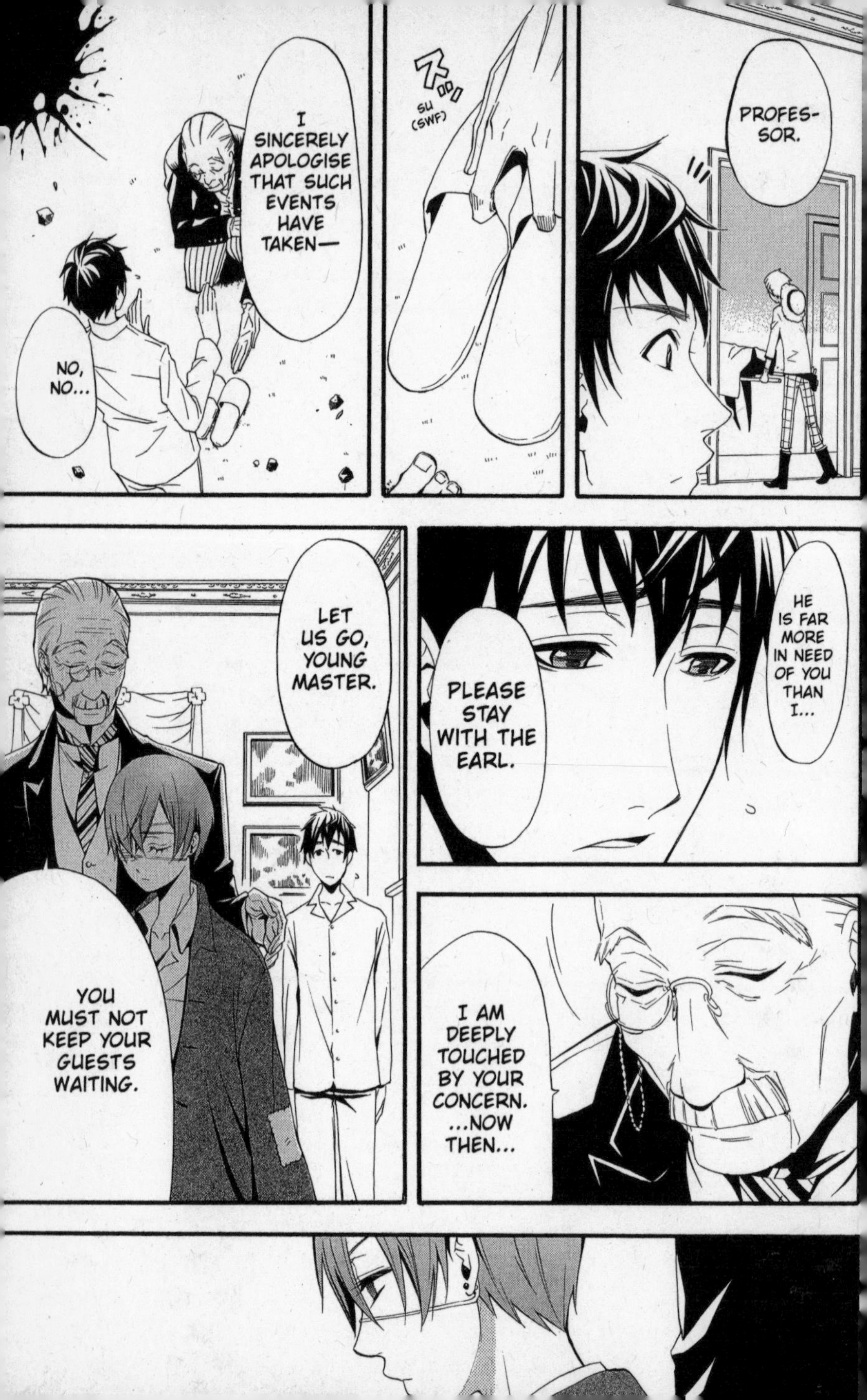
PROFES-SOR.
SU (SWF)
I SINCERELY APOLOGISE THAT SUCH EVENTS HAVE TAKEN—
NO, NO...
HE IS FAR MORE IN NEED OF YOU THAN I...
PLEASE STAY WITH THE EARL.
I AM DEEPLY TOUCHED BY YOUR CONCERN. ...NOW THEN...
LET US GO, YOUNG MASTER.
YOU MUST NOT KEEP YOUR GUESTS WAITING.

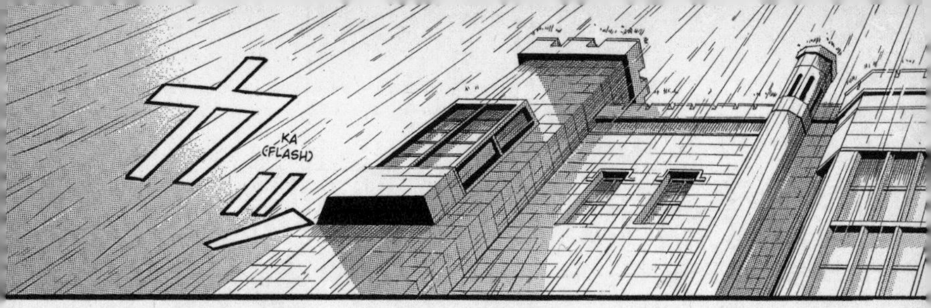
カッ
KA (FLASH)

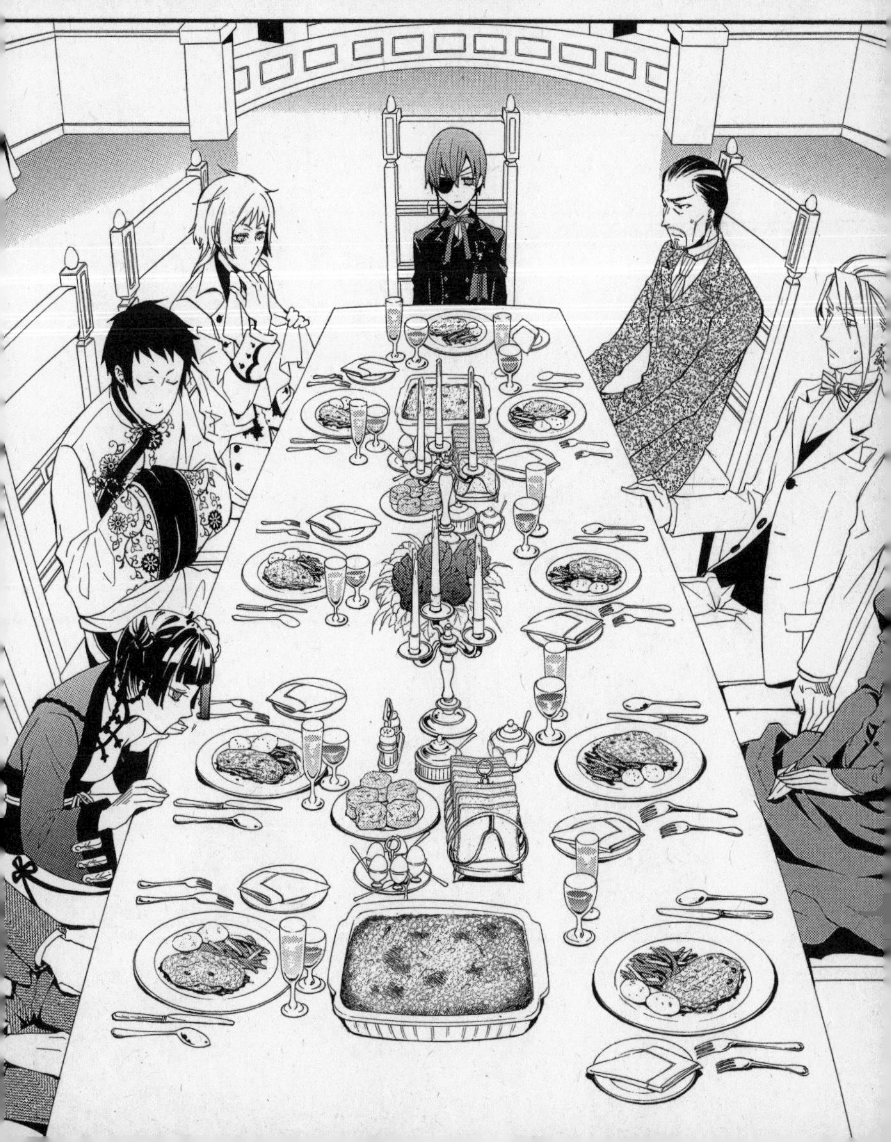

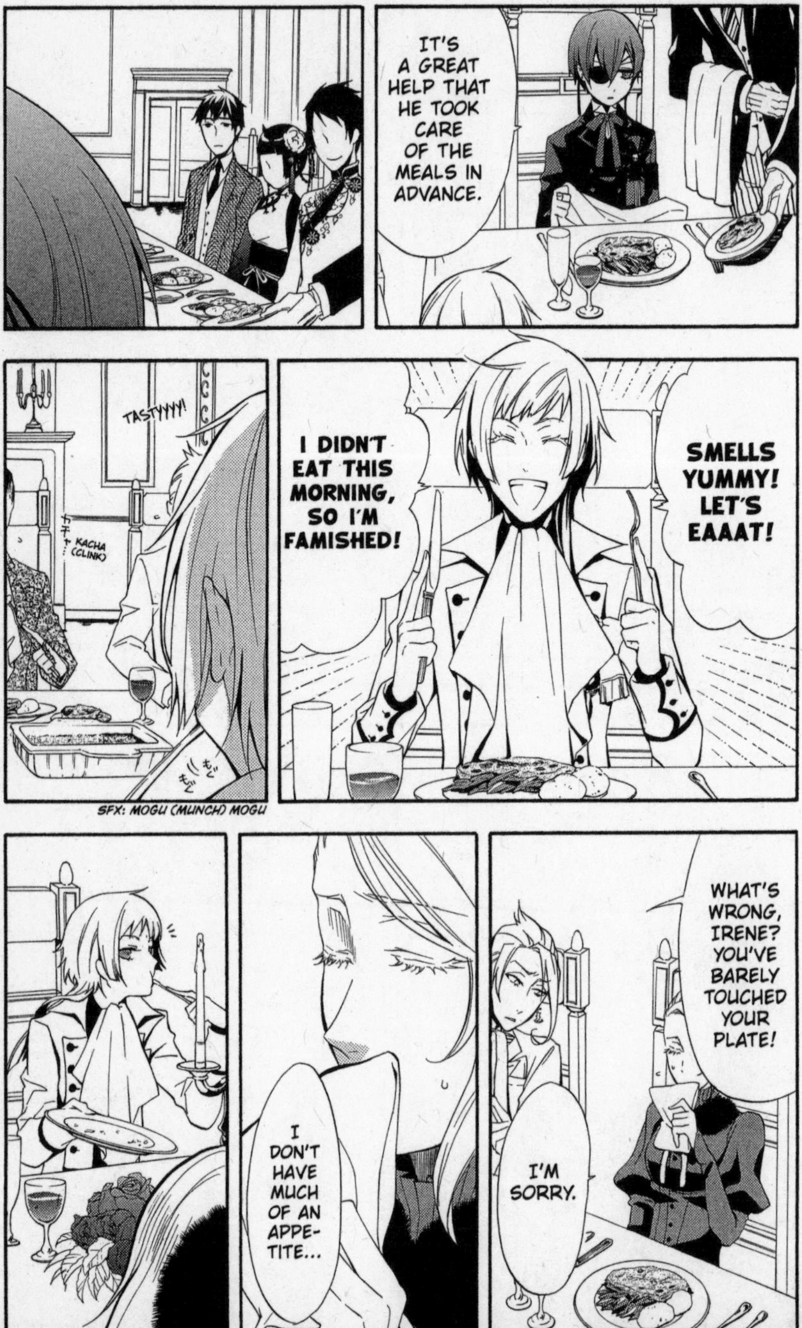
IT'S A GREAT HELP THAT HE TOOK CARE OF THE MEALS IN ADVANCE.
SMELLS YUMMY! LET'S EAAAT!
I DIDN'T EAT THIS MORNING, SO I'M FAMISHED!
TASTYYYY!
KACHA (CLINK)
SFX: MOGU (MUNCH) MOGU
WHAT'S WRONG, IRENE? YOU'VE BARELY TOUCHED YOUR PLATE!
I'M SORRY.
I DON'T HAVE MUCH OF AN APPE-TITE...

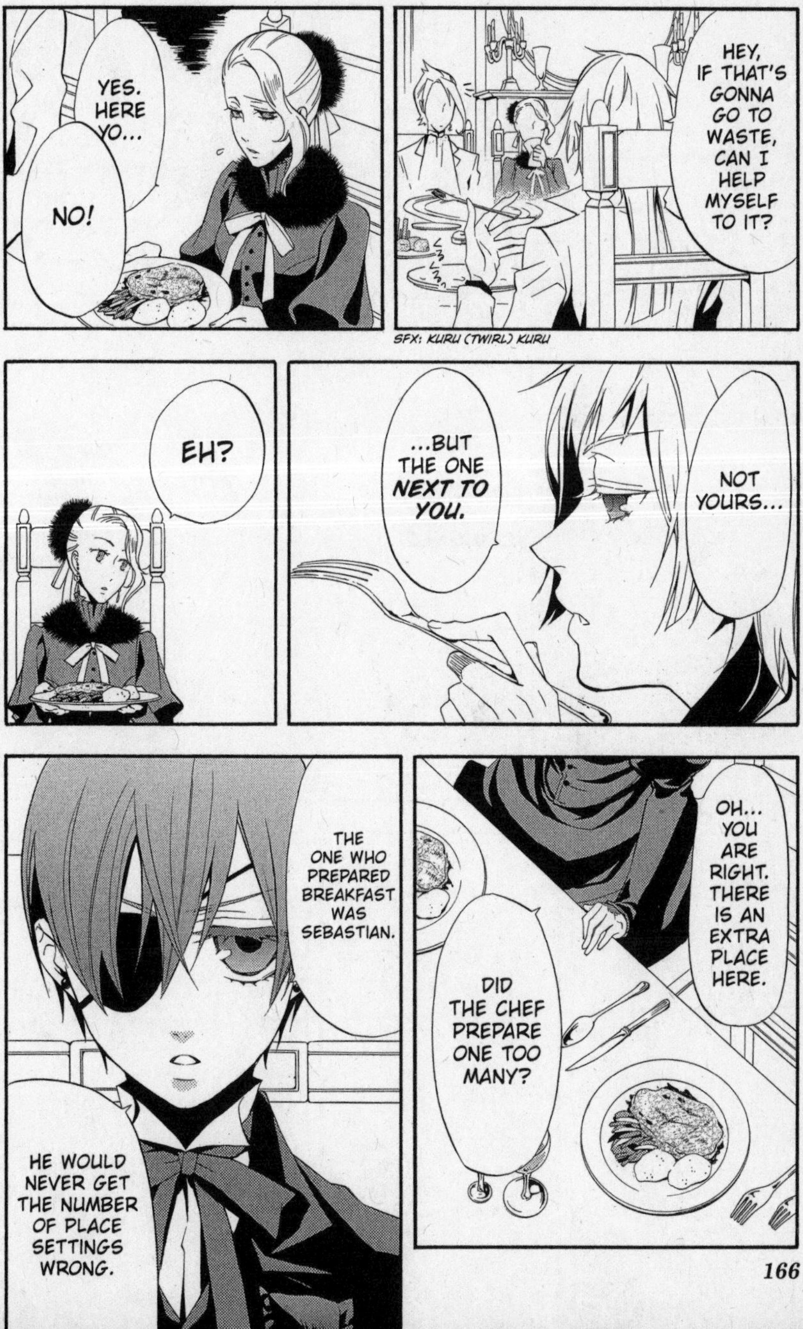

HEY, IF THAT'S GONNA GO TO WASTE, CAN I HELP MYSELF TO IT?
SFX: KURU (TWIRL) KURU
YES. HERE YO...
NO!
NOT YOURS...
...BUT THE ONE *NEXT TO YOU.*
EH?
OH... YOU ARE RIGHT. THERE IS AN EXTRA PLACE HERE.
DID THE CHEF PREPARE ONE TOO MANY?
THE ONE WHO PREPARED BREAKFAST WAS SEBASTIAN.
HE WOULD NEVER GET THE NUMBER OF PLACE SETTINGS WRONG.

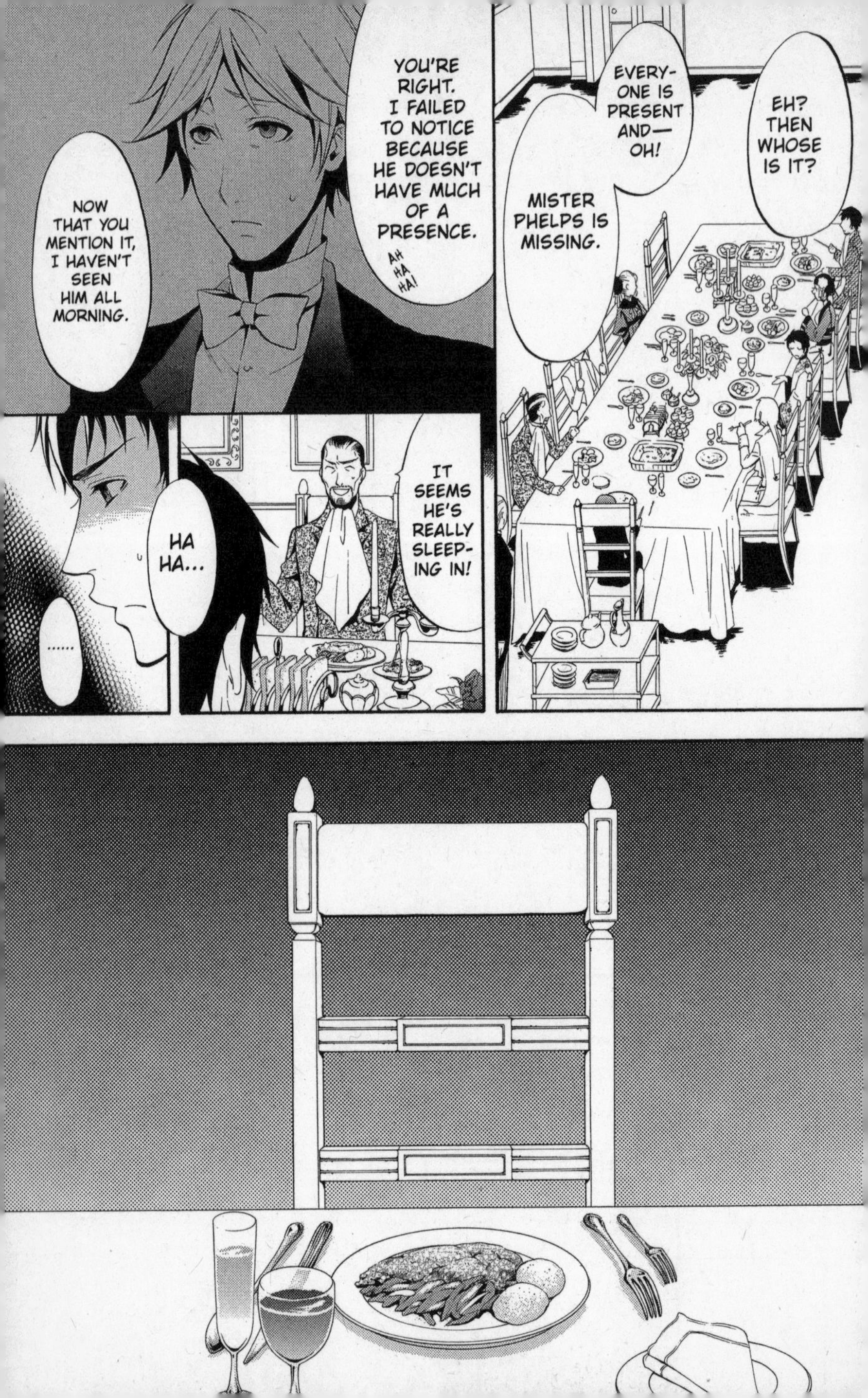
EH? THEN WHOSE IS IT?
EVERY-ONE IS PRESENT AND—OH!
MISTER PHELPS IS MISSING.
YOU'RE RIGHT. I FAILED TO NOTICE BECAUSE HE DOESN'T HAVE MUCH OF A PRESENCE.
AH HA HA!
NOW THAT YOU MENTION IT, I HAVEN'T SEEN HIM ALL MORNING.
IT SEEMS HE'S REALLY SLEEP-ING IN!
HA HA...
......

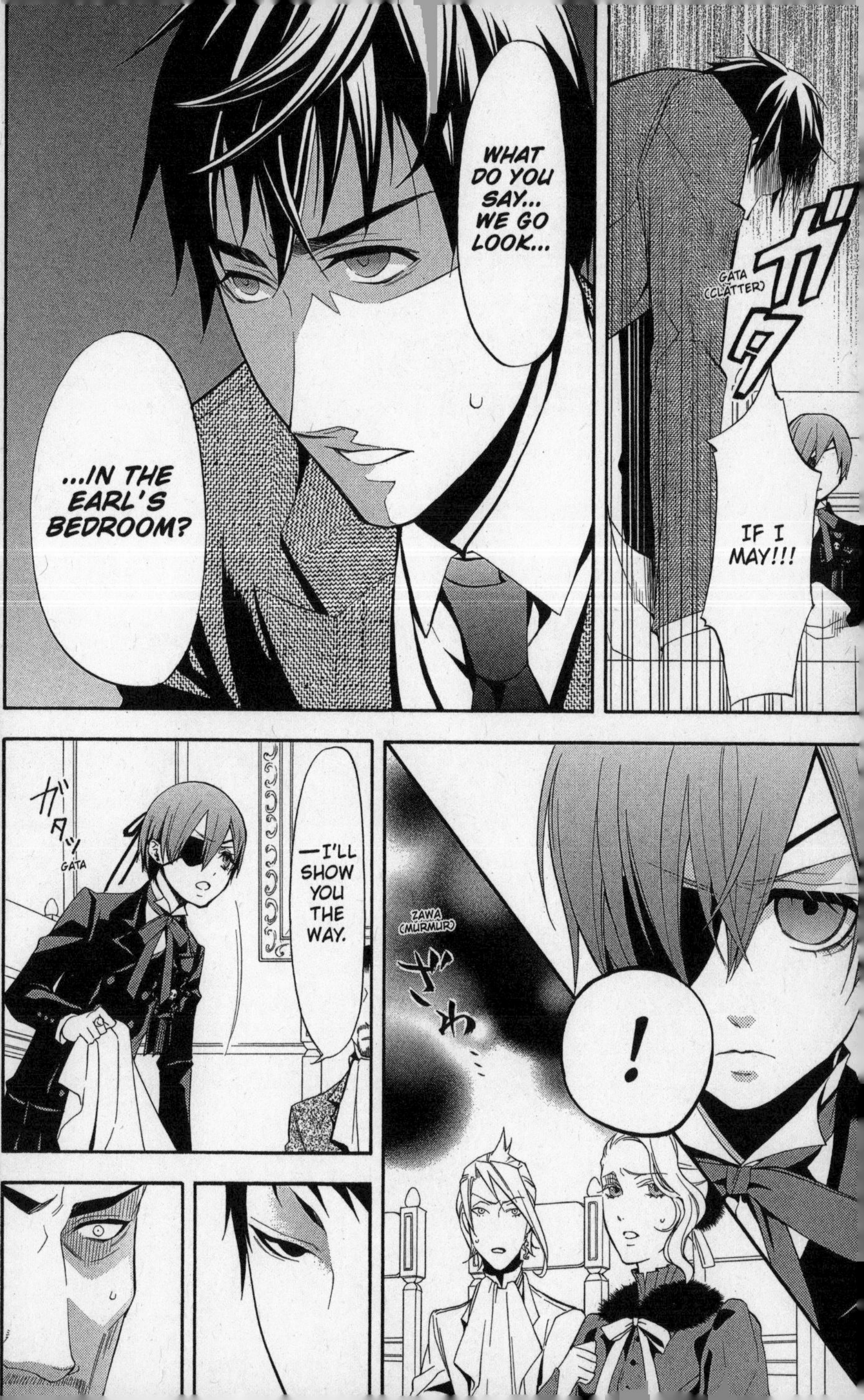
ガタ
GATA (CLATTER)
IF I MAY!!!
WHAT DO YOU SAY... WE GO LOOK...
...IN THE EARL'S BEDROOM?
ざわ
ZAWA (MURMUR)
!
ガタッ
GATA
—I'LL SHOW YOU THE WAY.

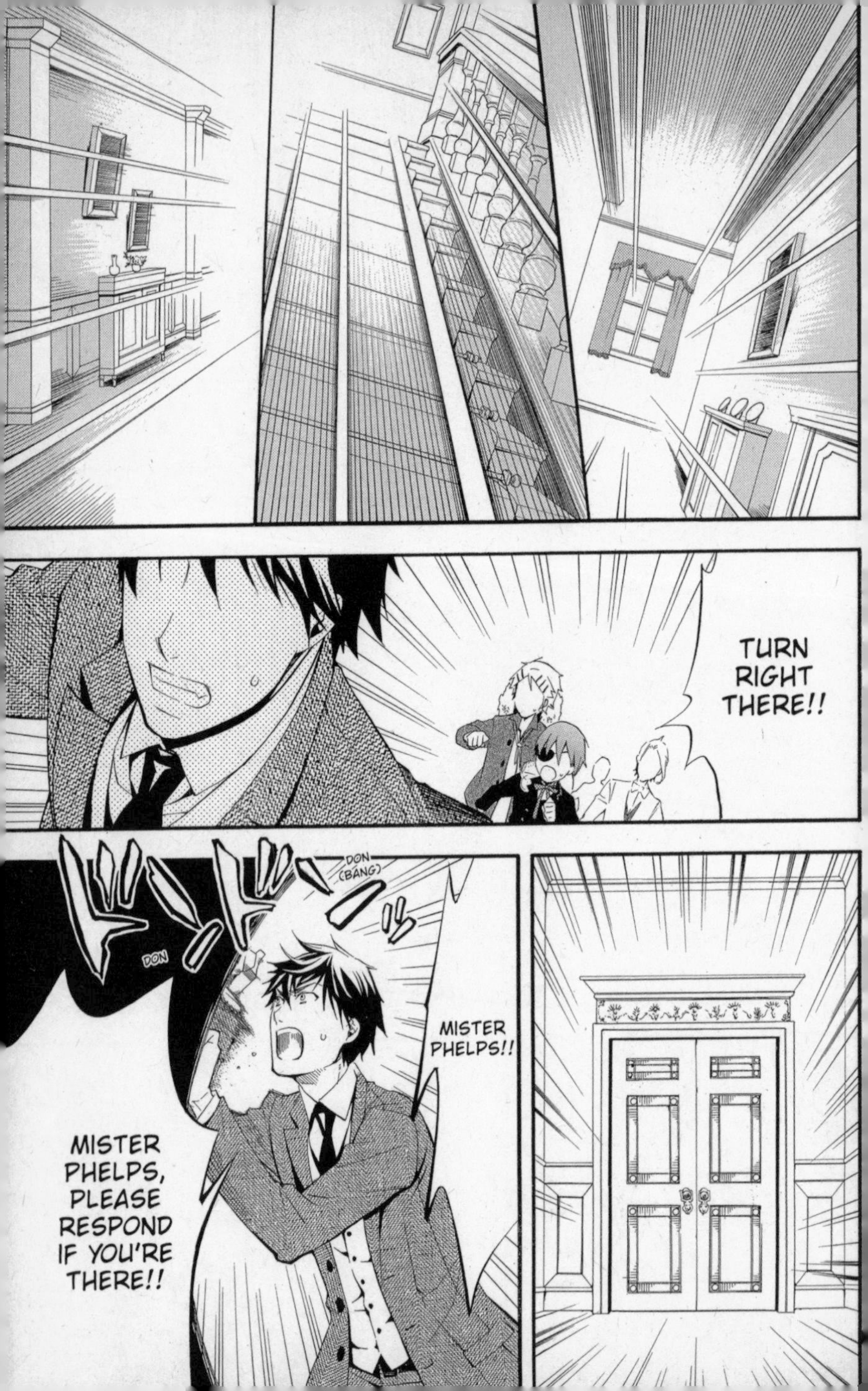
TURN RIGHT THERE!!
DON (BANG)
DON
MISTER PHELPS!!
MISTER PHELPS, PLEASE RESPOND IF YOU'RE THERE!!

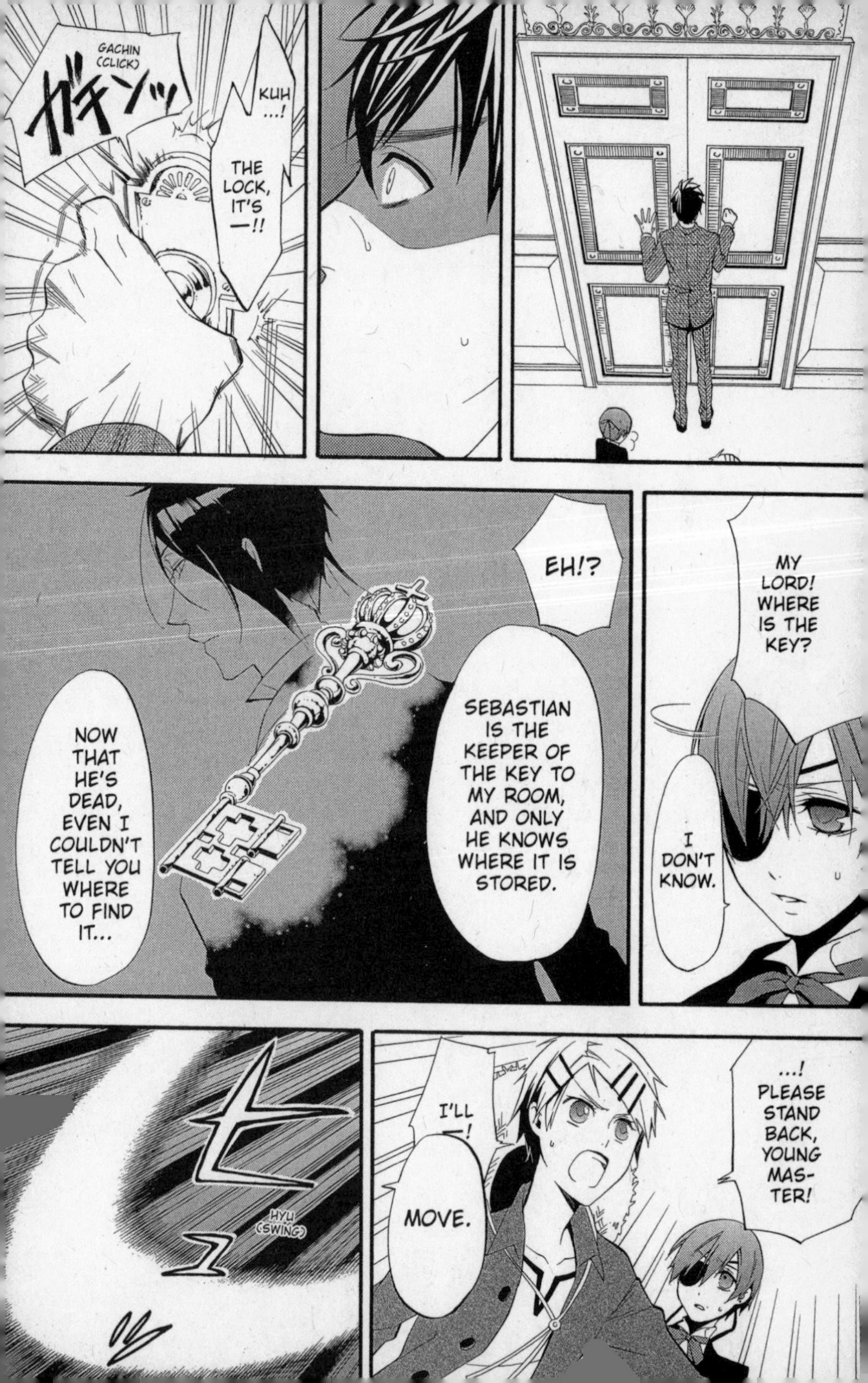
KUH ...!
THE LOCK, IT'S —!!
GACHIN (CLICK)
ガチンッ
MY LORD! WHERE IS THE KEY?
I DON'T KNOW.
EH!?
SEBASTIAN IS THE KEEPER OF THE KEY TO MY ROOM, AND ONLY HE KNOWS WHERE IT IS STORED.
NOW THAT HE'S DEAD, EVEN I COULDN'T TELL YOU WHERE TO FIND IT...
...! PLEASE STAND BACK, YOUNG MAS-TER!
I'LL —!
MOVE.
HYU (SWING)

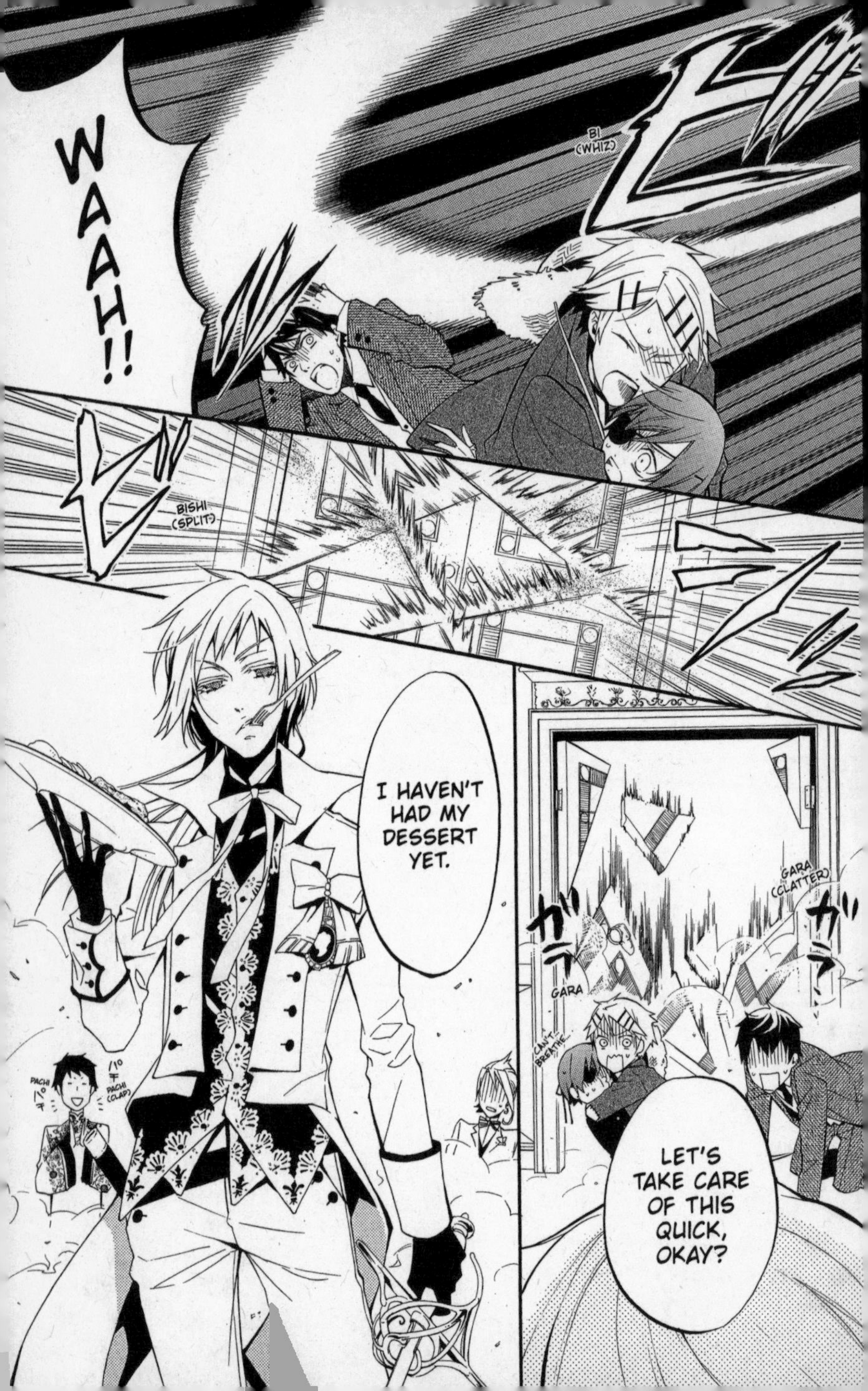
BI (WHIZ)
WAAH!!
BISHI (SPLIT)
GARA (CLATTER)
GARA
CAN'T BREATHE...
LET'S TAKE CARE OF THIS QUICK, OKAY?
I HAVEN'T HAD MY DESSERT YET.
PACHI
PACHI (CLAP)

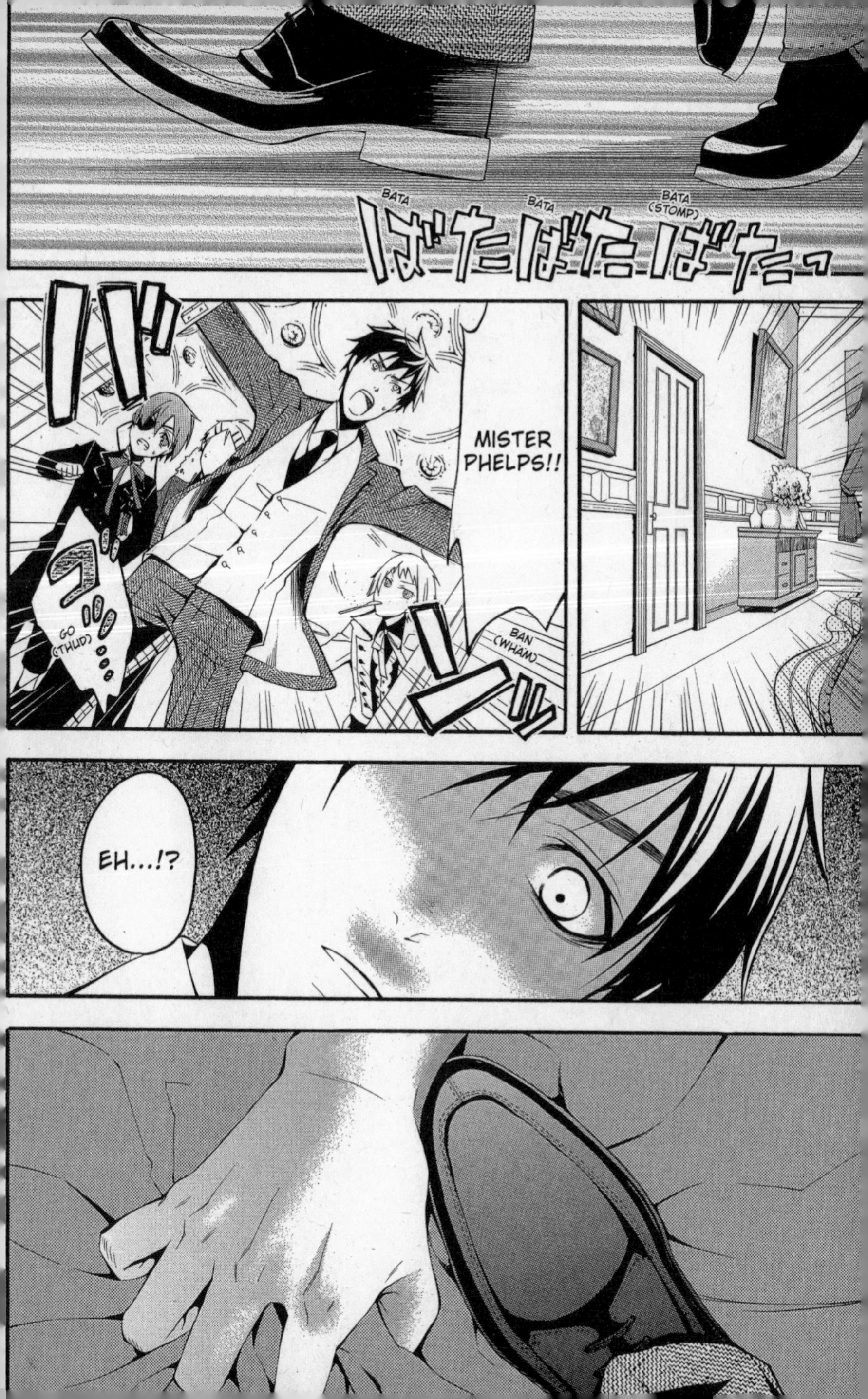
BATA BATA BATA (STOMP)
ばたばたばたっ
MISTER PHELPS!!
BAN (WHAM)
GO (THUD)
EH...!?

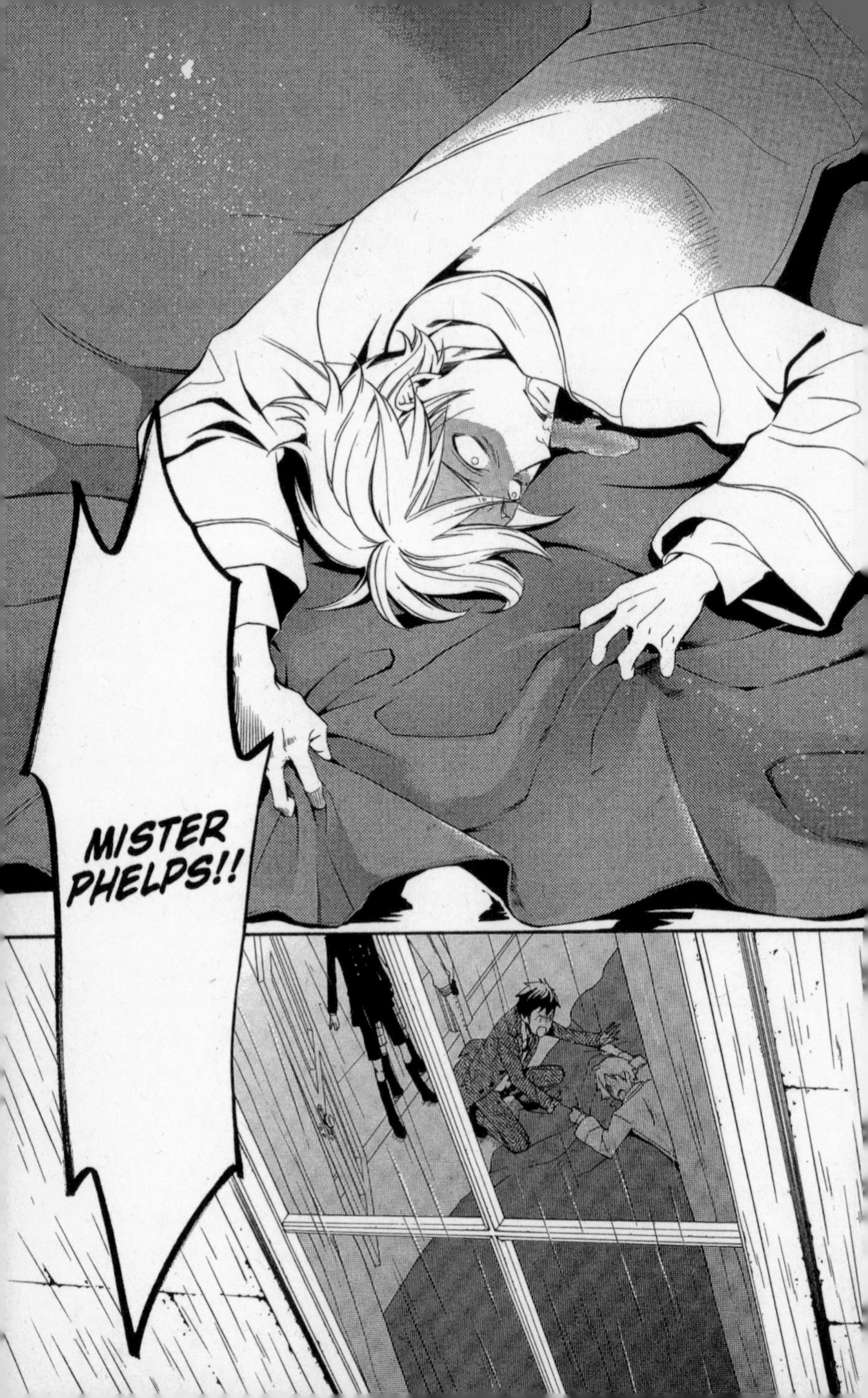
MISTER PHELPS!!

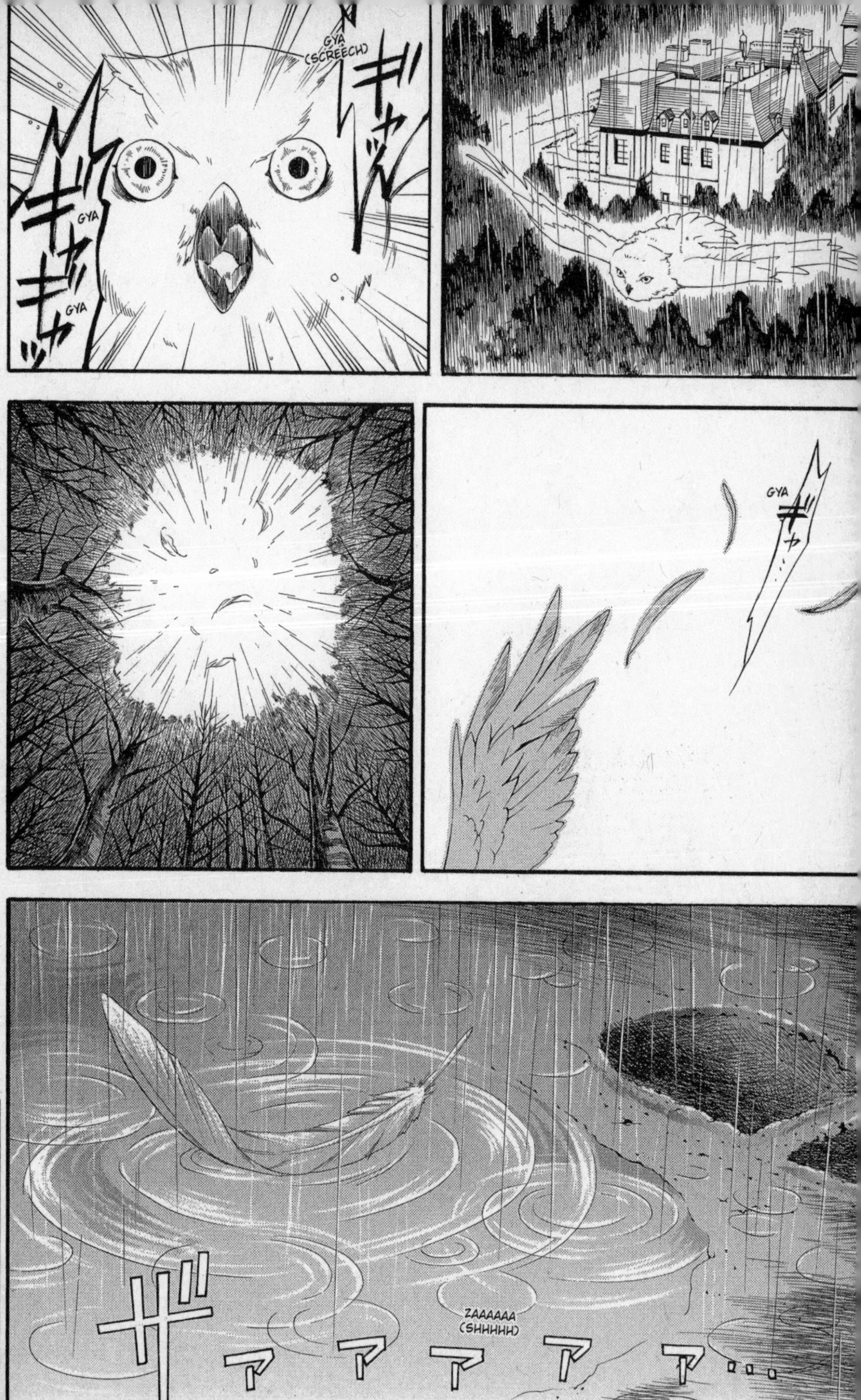
GYA (SCREECH)
ギャん
GYA
ギャ
GYA
ギャッ
GYA
ギャ…
ZAAAAAA (SHHHHH)
ザァァァァァ…

To be continued in

➤ Black Butler ➤

黒執事

Downstairs

Wakana Haduki

SuKe

7

*

Takeshi Kuma

*

Yana Toboso

SpecialThanks

Yana' s Mother

Sakuya

for You!

Translation Notes

INSIDE FRONT/BACK COVER - This is a parody of the manga *Tokumei Kakaricho Tadano Hitoshi* by Kimio Yanagisawa. The TV drama/movie versions were very popular too.

PAGE 4 - **A brougham and a pair**
A mode of Victorian transportation favoured by both the middle classes and the upper crust, which consists of a closed, four-wheel carriage with an elevated, open driver's seat in the front. A "pair" refers to the number of horses pulling it.

PAGE 16 - **Cream puffs**
Often called "profiteroles" on a Victorian menu, cream puffs were commonly served as an after-dinner dessert. The phrase "cream puff" is of American origin and was recorded as first being used in Boston, MA in 1851.

PAGE 17 - **Charles Grey**
The first, second, and fifth Earls Grey were named Charles. The second Earl Grey (1764-1845), a celebrated government reformer, held the position of Prime Minister of the United Kingdom from 1830 to 1834. He is also the Earl Grey after whom the tea is named. The fifth Earl (1879-1963) was the grandson of General Sir Charles Grey (1804-1870), younger son of the second earl. An army man and politician, General Sir Charles Grey served Queen Victoria as Private Secretary to the Sovereign in the years following Prince Albert's death. The fifth earl's great-grandfather would have been the Prime Minister, the second Earl Grey.

PAGE 17 - **Charles Phipps**
The historical Charles Phipps, better known as Colonel Honourable Sir Charles Beaumont Phipps (1801-1866), was another British army man-turned-court official who was close to both Prince Albert and Queen Victoria. A colleague of General Sir Charles Grey, he handled financial matters as Keeper of the Privy Purse and assisted Grey with his secretarial duties.

PAGE 34 - **Irene Diaz**
A reference to Irene Adler, a fictional character from Sir Arthur Conan Doyle's Sherlock Holmes stories. Adler was also an opera singer and held in high regard by the master detective, whom she was said to have outsmarted. She is featured in the novel "A Scandal in Bohemia."

PAGE 36 - **...that makes you quite the professor!**
In the original, Lau is using *sensei* to refer to the young man. The title is often used to address some one who is greatly skilled in his or her trade.

Lau's cheeky form of address is thus correct twice-over (since the young man is both a doctor and a writer), making the young man seem a cut above the rest. Ciel and the others also refer to Arthur as *sensei*, here translated as "Professor."

PAGE 42 - **Georg von Siemens**
The historical Georg von Siemens (1839-1901) was a German banker and politician who was funda-mental to the founding of Deutsche Bank and was very keen on expanding trade relations between Germany and the world. He was also a proponent of railway building, notably the Baghdad Railway.

PAGE 43 - **Blue Star Line**
The historical Blue Star Line was a shipping line established in 1911 for the purpose of importing meat from South America by the Vestey fam-ily, which hailed from Liverpool and was in the butchery business.

PAGE 48 - **Arthur**
Arthur's character is based on Sir Arthur Conan Doyle, the creator of Sherlock Holmes. Doyle was born in Edinburgh, Scotland in 1859 and received his medical degree from the University of Edin-burgh. It was as a medical student that he sold his first story. Upon opening his medical practice in Southsea, Doyle began to write in earnest when his patients were few. It was during this period that the infamous Holmes was born.

PAGE 49 - *A Study in Scarlet*
The novel in which Sherlock Holmes and Dr. John Watson first appeared. It was first published in the November 1887 issue of *Beeton's Christmas Annual*, a paperback magazine of curated fiction.

PAGE 79 - **Warded locks**
One of the oldest kinds of locks, this lock has dif-ferent obstructions, or wards, inside the path of the key, which prevents it from being opened by any key other than the one that was fitted to it.

PAGE 93 - **Penny dreadful**
A publication of cheap serialised fiction that came about in Britain in the nineteenth century. The stories contained within were typically sensational and horrific, and the serials sold for one penny.

PAGE 97 - **Coke**
The residue that results when a certain type of coal is heated at high temperatures without air present and the malodorous gas by-products driven off. Burning coke produces much less gas and smoke than coal, making it ideal for use in fireplaces.

Yana Toboso

AUTHOR'S NOTE

After the first season of the television anime ended, ***Black Butler*** became a musical, and dolls were made too.

The second season of the anime will start broadcasting soon. The second season presents many new challenges. The manga is also providing new challenges as well, so as not to lose against the anime. And that's what's happening with Volume 9, which begins a new arc.

BLACK BUTLER 9

YANA TOBOSO

Translation: Tomo Kimura • Lettering: Alexis Eckerman

KUROSHITSUJI Vol. 9 © 2010 Yana Toboso / SQUARE ENIX CO., LTD. All rights reserved. First published in Japan in 2010 by SQUARE ENIX CO., LTD. English translation rights arranged with SQUARE ENIX CO., LTD. and Hachette Book Group through Tuttle-Mori Agency, Inc.

Translation © 2012 by SQUARE ENIX CO., LTD.

Yen Press
Hachette Book Group
237 Park Avenue, New York, NY 10017

www.HachetteBookGroup.com
www.YenPress.com

Yen Press is an imprint of Hachette Book Group, Inc. The Yen Press name and logo are trademarks of Hachette Book Group, Inc.

First Yen Press Edition: April 2012

ISBN: 978-0-316-18967-5

10 9 8 7 6 5 4

BVG

Printed in the United States of America